CALVIN'S DOCTRINE
OF THE CHRISTIAN LIFE

CALVIN'S DOCTRINE
OF THE CHRISTIAN LIFE

RONALD S. WALLACE

GENEVA DIVINITY SCHOOL PRESS
Tyler, TX: 708 Hamvasy Rd.

Foreword

IT will be seen that this work has involved a study of Calvin's *Sermons* and *Commentaries* as well as of his *Institutes*. It is necessary, in studying Calvin's teaching, especially on a subject such as the Christian life, to read as widely as possible throughout his writings. The background of much of our modern theological thinking is so different from Calvin's that we are apt to misinterpret his use of words and phrases unless we study their use in more varied contexts than occur in the *Institutes* alone. Then we can come back to the *Institutes* and find there a content in his teaching and language which we might otherwise miss. In going to the *Commentaries*, it seemed obvious that those on the Psalms and on the New Testament would especially repay study.

While this is not strictly a book on Calvin's ethics, it has involved some study of that subject. Calvin's judgment on the various moral problems that faced men in his time can illustrate for us his views on the nature of the Christian life, for his ethical outlook on such problems is partly determined by his doctrine of the Christian life as a whole.

It is difficult, on a first reading of Calvin, to see how some aspects of his teaching can be reconciled with other aspects. At times he seems to speak with a great breadth of outlook, at times he is more "narrow" in his pronouncements; at times he seems to advocate a way of living and an attitude very much absorbed in this present world and its problems, at other times he seems to advocate extreme "other-worldliness"; at times he writes as if he were a man full of optimism about the victory and joy of the life lived for Christ in this world, at other times he describes the Christian life as if it had little else but labour, tears, misunderstanding and disappointment to offer the follower of Christ; at times he seems to say emphatically that there is no other rule of life to be applied to the problems of living except to follow Jesus Christ, crucified and risen, as He calls us to deny ourselves and take up our cross daily, at other times he seems to depart from such a rule and to appeal for a life lived according to the natural order and general ethical principles.

It seemed at first, therefore, an impossible task to give to each aspect of Calvin's teaching its due place within a systematic treatment of the Christian life. Yet in the course of study it was found that all Calvin's decisions on widely differing aspects of the Christian life can be understood and seen in their unity as they are seen to arise from his doctrine of the person and work of Christ as involving once-for-all the sanctification and destiny of His Church. The whole of the life and death of Christ must be regarded as a process of self-sanctification in fulfilment of His royal priesthood on our behalf.

It is only against the background of such thinking that Calvin's doctrine of sanctification and his teaching on repentance can be properly understood. The sanctification of the Church is worked out and fulfilled as men participate in the once-for-all sanctification of Christ and seek to fulfil in all that they do, their calling to royal priesthood in the response of self-consecration in gratitude and fear. Since Christ in His self-sanctification fulfilled a career of death and resurrection, repentance is to be understood as the working-out, under the providence of God, of this Christological pattern in heart (self-denial) and in outward life (Cross-bearing) as the Christian participates in Christ by faith and aspires to the heavenly life.

Moreover, when Calvin appeals, as he frequently does, to his congregation to live according to the "order of nature", or true "humanity", or according to the rule of "moderation", he is not referring to a philosophical rule of life, or to a natural source of guidance which must supplement what we know in Christ. In His life, death and resurrection, Christ has brought in the Kingdom of God, fulfilled the Law, renewed the image of God, restored the true order of nature, and revealed the true nature of humanity. By participating in the death and resurrection of Christ, His people participate here and now in this mystery, and therefore they must express in their lives as individuals, and as members of society and Church, the true humanity, image and order seen in Christ. Since excess marks the life of fallen man, moderation becomes an important element in Christian morality. The natural order can, however, illustrate for us the duties in which we are called by our knowledge of the Gospel.

This work further shows that the "priesthood of all believers" in Calvin's teaching is not a doctrine which exalts the individual in his liberty before God apart from the Church. Rather it involves participating in and with the Church in the royal priesthood of the whole body. On the other hand, it is shown that Calvin, in spite of his emphasis on the Church, in no way minimises the importance of the individual, for it is within the Church that Christ confronts and addresses the individual by name through the Word, and creates and nourishes faith. It is within the Church that the individual finds himself truly sanctified and separated from the world. Loyalty to the membership and fellowship of the Church is an important part of Christian duty.

Study had also to be undertaken to show what Calvin teaches about the attitude faith should take as it is exercised in the unceasing conflict and contradiction in which a Christian is involved in daily life in the service of Christ. Under the providence of God the Christian finds himself forced to live by prayer, by the power of faith alone and by the Word alone. But in spite of such contradiction, and contrary to what is usually imagined of Calvin's outlook, it is shown that Calvin teaches that the Christian life is predominantly one of happiness, assurance and achievement. Though the Christian experiences a constant tension between faith and sight, satisfaction and hope, trembling and assurance, there is a real victory over evil, and constant progress and growth in faith towards a final and inevitable perfection.

The argument in this work involves viewing the Christian life now in one aspect and now in another very different aspect. Such a process has inevitably involved a certain amount of apparent repetition. It has necessitated a treatment that is more spiral than logically systematic, for Calvin's view of the Christian life, since it is centred on Christ's person and work, reflects the many-sidedness of the Word of God, and is bound at least to tax the patience of those who want everything to be either "simple" or at least neatly and logically defined and arranged.

No attempt has been made here to give a critical estimate of the value of the different aspects of Calvin's teaching. Time has not permitted such an effort. A book without such criticism, however, has a certain lasting value of its own.

As to the form of this book, the main text is often a careful paraphrase of Calvin's teaching with a sparing use of direct quotation

The footnotes contain citations, mainly in Latin and French, from the *Commentaries* and *Sermons*. Full references are given so that the reader can find the passages in the English translations as well as in the standard editions of Calvin's works. The slight differences in the numbering of the verses in the Latin and English editions of the Psalms should not be forgotten. I hope that the citations from the *Sermons* will give some idea of the wonderfully vivid, straight-forward and popular style of Calvin's preaching on everyday themes.

I am grateful to the Faculty of Divinity of Edinburgh University for allowing me to take this subject in my study for a doctorate of philosophy, and specially for the kindly and helpful advice I received from Principal John Baillie and Principal J. H. S. Burleigh of New College, Edinburgh. My thanks are also due to Dr John Lamb, the librarian of New College, for an unstinted use of the books I required. I must also acknowledge my debt to Professor T. F. Torrance, whose works have several times given me the clue I was looking for in order to understand Calvin.

Three of the members of my former congregation, St Kentigern's, Lanark, were of great help to me in preparing the manuscript—Mrs W. Grant, Mrs J. Follan, and Mrs J. Burdett. My wife checked the proofs and all the citations. I wish to thank them, and the publishers, Messrs Oliver & Boyd, for their constant helpfulness and courtesy.

R.S.W.

Edinburgh

Contents

PART I

THE SANCTIFICATION OF THE CHURCH IN CHRIST

PART II

DYING AND RISING WITH CHRIST

CHAPTER I. *Self-denial*

CHAPTER II. *Bearing the Cross*

PART III

THE RESTORATION OF TRUE ORDER

PART IV

NURTURE AND DISCIPLINE WITHIN THE CHURCH

PART V

THE EXERCISE OF FAITH

CHAPTER II. *The attitude of faith in conflict and suffering*

CHAPTER III. *Prayer as the principal exercise of faith*

PART VI

THE EFFECT AND FRUIT OF FAITH

CHAPTER I. *Assurance, boldness and stability*

PART ONE

THE SANCTIFICATION
OF THE CHURCH
IN CHRIST

Abbreviations

C.O.   =   *Joannis Calvini Opera*, in Corpus Reformatorum, Brunswick 1869–96

Inst.   =   Calvin, *Institutio Christianae Religionis*, Berlin 1846.

Amst. Edn.   =   *Joannis Calvini Opera Omnia*, Amsterdam 1671.

Chapter I

The vicarious self-offering and sanctification
of Jesus Christ as priest and king

1. The language of the Bible about the death of Christet

To Calvin, the New Testament interpretation of the Cross and language about the Cross are as harsh and offensive as the actual historical event of the Crucifixion itself. Therefore when he speaks about the nature and meaning of the sufferings and death of Christ, Calvin does not hesitate to use harsh and crude language. He often speaks in terms which, unless carefully interpreted, might seem to imply unworthy ideas of God.

Christ, says Calvin, paid the price of our peace and redemption,[1] and the penalty of sin.[2] His task in offering atonement was to "interpose between us and God's anger and satisfy His righteous judgment."[3] In doing this He substituted Himself in our place,[4] and transferred to Himself the guilt which made us liable to punishment.[5] In discussing the nature of Christ's sufferings Calvin can speak of Him as bearing the vengeance, anger, or hatred of God, or at least the signs of such vengeance.[6] Being accursed on the Cross,[7] He was "beaten and struck by the hand of God."[8] In this way He appeased the wrath of God, and gave God satisfaction.[9]

Such is Calvin's language when interpreting the Cross. It is his language because it is the language he finds in the Bible. To him such language is so integral an aspect of the Cross itself that

[1] Comm. on Isa. 53 : 5, C.O. 37 : 258. Inst. 2 : 16 : 7.

[2] Inst. 2 : 12 : 3.

[3] Inst. 2 : 16 : 10.

[4] Inst. 2 : 16 : 7. *Videre est, quomodo in vicem nostram ubique se supposuerit ad solvendum nostrae redemptionis pretium.*

[5] Inst. 2 : 16 : 5. *Haec nostra absolutio est, quod in caput filii Dei translatus est reatus, qui nos tenebat poenae obnoxios.*

[6] Inst. 2 : 16 : 11. *Manu Dei percussus et afflictus, omnia irati et punientis Dei signa expertus est.* Cf. Inst. 2 : 16 : 5 & 10; serm. on Deut. 21 : 22–3, C.O. 27 : 700. *Il a porté comme en nos personnes la haine de Dieu.*

[7] Comm. on Gal. 3 : 13, C.O. 50 : 209–10.

[8] Serm. on Isa. 53 : 4–6, C.O. 35 : 624.

[9] Inst. 2 : 12 : 3; comm. on Isa. 53 : 5 & 10, C.O. 37 : 258 & 263.

to allow ourselves to be taken aback by it is to take offence at the Cross itself, and to refuse to use it is to refuse to glory in the Cross.[1]

It is true that Calvin recognises that such language, like all our human language about God, is "inappropriate,"[2] and thus inclined to be misleading. In speaking of the Atonement he seeks continually to correct false impressions that might arise from the language he is using. In one sentence he can say unequivocally that Jesus bore, as if in our place, the hatred of God; yet in the next sentence he insists with equal emphasis that Jesus never was hated by God.[3] He insists that even in afflicting Jesus, God at the same time loved Him.[4] Indeed, even when He was enduring God's wrath, Jesus could be no other than the object of His love, "for how could He reconcile the Father to us if He had incurred His hatred and displeasure?[5] It must not even be imagined that God first hates us and then, being reconciled, begins to love us, for, as Augustine says, "He loved even when He hated us."[6]

But though the language which Calvin uses in speaking of the Atonement is thus inappropriate, it is nevertheless unavoidable. Even though we know it is liable to mislead there are no more suitable terms in which to speak about the Atonement than those which the Bible uses when it speaks of propitiation and appease-

[1] Cf. comm. on Gal. 3 : 13, C.O. 50 : 209–10.

[2] When we read of God as looking down on earth to search out good and evil, or of the Spirit as descending upon men, we know that God does not need to look in order to see, nor can the Spirit ever be thought of as enclosed in any place or channel. Strictly speaking, therefore, such expressions are inappropriate. Yet they stand necessarily as the only adequate expressions we have for the spiritual events and realities which they have been used to signify, even though they but dimly point beyond themselves to such. They "enable us gradually to form some apprehension" of things "which our reason cannot all at once comprehend." Cf. comm. on Ps. 14 : 2, C.O. 31 : 137; and serm. on Matt. 3 : 13–17, C.O. 46 : 585–6. It is especially in speaking about the nature of God, e.g. in attributing passions and even contrary passions and conflict of will to God, when (strictly speaking) we could say that God was not subject to such things, that Calvin notes the necessary impropriety of Scripture. Cf. serm. on Deut. 4 : 36–8, C.O. 26 : 216, *Il est vray qu'à parler proprement, Dieu n'a point des affections diverses . . . mais ie traitte ces choses selon nostre capacite*; and serm. on Eph. 4 : 29–30, C.O. 51 : 648–9 *Nous sçavons qu'en Dieu il n'y a nulle passion: c'est aux hommes de se contrister et de se fascher: Dieu est immuable. Mais pource que nous ne comprenons la hautesse qui est en luy, . . . voilà pourquoy il use de similitude: et c'est à cause de nostre rudesse.* Cf. also comm. on Matt. 23 : 37, C.O. 45 : 644; and on Matt. 21 : 37, C.O. 45 : 593–4.

[3] Serm. on Deut. 21 : 22–3, C.O. 27 : 700.

[4] Serm. on Isa. 53 : 4–6, C.O. 35 : 623.

[5] Serm. on Gal. 3 : 13, C.O. 50 : 210; cf. Inst. 2 : 16 : 11.

[6] Inst. 2 : 16 : 3–4.

ment and substitution. Only by the use of such language can the theologian hope to unfold the true meaning of the death of Christ, and the preacher to convey a true sense of the power and relevance of the Cross to those to whom he proclaims the Gospel.

2. Christ as propitiatory victim

The background of Calvin's thought in using such language to interpret the death of Christ is the sacrificial ritual of the Old Testament. That is why the term "blood" is mentioned so often in this connexion.[1] Calvin thinks in the first place of Jesus as fulfilling in His death the role of sacrificial victim offered to God as a propitiation for the sins of the people. It is only as we interpret the Atonement with such Old Testament patterns and analogies that we can find its true meaning. "That these things may take deep root and have their seat in our hearts, we must never lose sight of sacrifice and oblation."[2]

It is true that Calvin can also speak of Jesus as fulfilling the role of a legal substitute who in some fictitious legal situation steps into the place of the accused in order to hear and meet the condemnation of the judge and satisfy the law. In this connexion he regards it as significant that the Crucifixion was preceded by a legal trial in which Jesus "sustains the character of an offender and evil-doer" and is condemned by a judge to die unjustly and on the evidence of false witnesses, thus proving that He suffers for another's and not for His own crime.[3] But Jesus did not die primarily as a substitute legal victim in a court of moral law, bowing before the necessity that one worthy man should fulfil the demands of justice in order that others might go free. He died rather as a propitiatory victim fulfilling in a unique way that cannot be deduced from any general moral principles a destiny and office decreed for Him by His Father.[4] "The only end which the Scripture uniformly assigns for the Son of God voluntarily assuming our nature . . . is that He might propitiate the Father to us by becoming a victim."[5]

[1] Inst. 2 : 16 : 6. [2] Inst. 2 : 16 : 6. [3] Inst. 2 : 16 : 5.
[4] Cf. comm. on Exod. 28 : 1, C.O. 24 : 428. *Ac certe non fuit penes totum humanum genus obtrudere aliquem Deo, qui se ad veniam et pacem impetrandam ingereret, imo ne Christus quidem ad Deum placandum idoneus fuisset, nisi munus subiisset patris decreto sibi impositum.*
[5] Inst. 2 : 12 : 4.

3. The life and death of Christ as His consecration
to priesthood

But Christ in His death fulfils not only the role of propitiatory victim offered for the sins of men, but also of the priest who consecrates himself in blood to the service of the heavenly sanctuary in order that he might be fit to offer acceptable sacrifices to God. In the ritual of the Temple the blood acted not only as a seal of the propitiatory offering but also as a laver to purge the defilement of the priest,[1] who in his consecration was himself sprinkled with blood and thus cleansed[2] before he entered the Sanctuary. Moreover not only the priest but the whole Temple and all the vessels were sanctified through the sprinkling of the blood. Calvin, reasoning from such Old Testament analogies, sees in Christ's death the perfecting of His own self-sanctification to His eternal priesthood on our behalf. The crowning feature of this infinite love shown in the Incarnation lies in the fact that, through putting on our human nature, He who could not be subject to death nevertheless becomes capable of dying,[3] and of offering Himself in death. The human nature which He assumed was the temple which He Himself sanctified through His blood and in which He consecrated Himself through death in order, as eternal High Priest, to offer Himself in expiation of our sins.[4] Calvin translates τελειωθείς in Heb. 5 : 9 by "having been sanctified" and links this verse up with John 17 : 19 ("For their sakes I sanctify myself . . .") to prove that the sufferings of Christ are to be regarded as His initiation into His eternal priesthood, and His death in enduring the Cross as "a solemn kind of consecration."[5]

The self-consecration of Christ to His eternal priesthood took place not only during His death but throughout His whole life.

---

[1] Inst. 2 : 16 : 6.

[2] Comm. on Exod. 29 : 16, C.O. 24 : 438. *Ita Christi sacerdotium sanguine dicatum fuit, ut ad nos Deo reconciliandos efficax esset.*

[3] Comm. on Heb. 2 : 14, C.O. 55 : 32. *Inaestimabilis enim erga nos eius amor hic apparet. Sed cumulus exstat in eo, quod naturam nostram induit ut moriendi conditioni se subiiceret.*

[4] Comm. on Heb. 9 : 11, C.O. 55 : 110.

[5] Comm. on Heb. 5 : 9, C.O. 55 : 64. *Finis ultimus vel remotior (ut vocant) cur pati Christum necesse fuerit: nempe quod in suum sacerdotium hoc modo fuit inauguratus. Ac si deceret apostolus, crucis tolerantiam et mortem solenne fuisse consecrationis genus in Christo. . . . Sanctificatus melius quadrat contextui, quam perfectus.*

Christ effected the reconciliation between God and man not only through His death but through the "whole course of His obedience." He declared even at His baptism that righteousness was being fulfilled in His submission there and then to the will of His Father. He did not only die to redeem us from the curse of the Law but was born to do so.[1] Therefore, though it may be right to ascribe salvation "peculiarly and appropriately (*quasi peculiare ac proprium*)" to His death, He nevertheless from the moment of His birth began to pay the cost of our redemption.[2] Likewise though the "highest illustration" of the sanctification by which we are reconciled to the Father belongs to the death of Christ, nevertheless His sanctification was effected throughout His whole life.[3]

4. The consecration of Christ by the Spirit

It is when we consider the work of the Holy Spirit in the vicarious sanctification of Jesus Christ that we are able to see most clearly the significance of His earthly life in this same connexion. In the Old Testament the priest, the tabernacle and its appendages were consecrated by being anointed with oil as well as by being sprinkled with the blood of sacrifice.[4] The oil was a type of the Spirit,[5] and the unction was a sign of the sanctification of the priest by the Spirit for his office.[6] All this was in figure and type. Christ however was the true tabernacle of God whose body was the temple of Deity, and the true High Priest whose consecration in reality took place not with oil but with the Spirit. Thus Jesus was consecrated by the fullness of gifts bestowed upon Him through the Holy Spirit[7] to be the mediator between God and man.[8]

[1] Inst. 2 : 16 : 5. Calvin cites Rom. 5 : 19 and Gal. 4 : 4.   [2] Ibid.

[3] Comm. on John 17 : 19, C.O. 47 : 385. *Porro sanctificatio haec quamvis ad totam Christi vitam pertineat, in sacrificio tamen mortis eius maxime illustris fuit.*

[4] Cf. Lev. 8 : 10–30; Exod. 30 : 26–31, 40 : 9–15; Lev. 21 : 10 and comm. in loc.

[5] Comm. on Exod. 40 : 9, C.O. 25 : 124. *Spiritus figura.*

[6] Comm. on Exod. 30 : 23, C.O. 24 : 446. *Sed unctio praecipue in sacerdote consideranda fuit, qui sanctificatus est Dei spiritu ad munus obeundum.*

[7] Comm. on Dan. 9 : 25, C.O. 41 : 183. *Sed hic significat unctionem perfectam, et vere spiritualem differri usque ad Christi adventum. Christus autem ipse proprie et merito vocatur sanctus sanctorum, vel tabernaculum Dei, quia scimus corpus eius esse templum deitatis, et scimus quaerendam ab ipso esse sanctitatem.* Comm. on Exod. 28, C.O. 24 : 427. *Unctio etiam, spiritus qui in Christo residet symbolum fuit: ideoque non externo et corruptibili oleo consecratus est, sed omnium donorum plenitudine.* Cf. Inst. 2 : 15 : 6.

[8] Comm. on Exod. 30 : 23, C.O. 24 : 446. *Spiritu sancto consecratus est Christus, ut mediator esset Dei et hominum.*

It was the consecration of Jesus in His human life by the unction of the Spirit that enabled Him to offer Himself to God in sacrifice.[1] It was His consecration as priest by the Spirit that made Him acceptable to God.[2] Calvin interprets Heb. 9 : 14 as meaning that Christ "suffered by the Spirit," and that otherwise His death would not have been efficacious to appease God.[3]

5. The consecration of Christ as king

Christ in His life and death fulfilled the mediatoral office not only of priest but also of king. His consecration to His eternal priesthood was also His consecration to become the eternal King and Head of the Church His body. He assumed our flesh not only that in it He might offer Himself as a sacrifice but also that in it He might become our triumphant champion in warring to death with sin.[4] In our flesh He destroyed those things that held us in bondage and fear.[5] As our substitute and representative He engaged "at close quarters with the powers of Hell and the terrors of eternal death,[6] and having delivered Himself, as it were, into the power of those things that held us down, and yet were powerless to hold Him, He broke through their power and proved Himself victor."[7]

6. The royal priesthood of the Mediator

Calvin emphasises in many passages that in the person of Jesus Christ and in the one action of Jesus Christ both the office of priest and the office of king in the Old Testament find their fulfilment and their true meaning. Under the Law both offices were separate and distinct. When each office was worthily filled and both the kingship and the priesthood flourished, then the state of the people was happy, for these offices were like the two eyes of the body—"the priest, a mediator between God and men—and

---

[1] Comm. on Exod. 28 : 42, C.O. 24 : 435. *Quomodo haec inter se consentiunt, unctum fuisse ut per spiritum se offerret, offerri tamen ab aliis?*

[2] Cf. Inst. 2 : 15 : 2 & 6.

[3] Comm. on Exod. 30 : 23, C.O. 24 : 446. *Atqui (teste apostolo Heb.* 9, 14) *sacrificium mortis Christi non aliter efficax fuit ad placandum Deum, nisi quia per spiritum passus est.* Cf. comm. on Heb. 9 : 14, C.O. 55 : 111–12.

[4] Inst. 2 : 12 : 3.   [5] Inst. 2 : 16 : 11.

[6] Inst. 2 : 16 : 10, cf. 2 : 16 : 7.   [7] Inst. 2 : 16 : 7, cf. 2 : 16 : 10.

the king, sustaining the person of God in governing the people."[1]
But in Christ both offices are united in the same person. He is
both priest and king at once.[2] Calvin finds this fulfilment of the
two offices in one person foreshadowed in such passages as the
story of Melchidezek, who is both priest and king in a manner
quite unique in the Old Testament;[3] in Psalm 110 where the one
who has been seated in royal dignity at the right hand of God is
addressed as "priest for ever";[4] and in the vision of Joshua in the
book of Zechariah, crowned with two crowns, one a royal diadem
and the other a sacerdotal mitre indicating a union of royalty and
priesthood in the same person which could be fulfilled only in
Jesus Christ.[5]

It is in connexion with the kingly aspect of the royal priesthood
of Christ that his unction and sanctification by the Spirit finds
especial significance.[6] The "royal unction"[7] of Christ by the Spirit
consisted in His being given the Spirit "without measure," or in
unlimited abundance,[8] and thus the fullness of all gifts and virtues,
in such a way that all His people may be enriched by drawing
from His fullness of power and grace.[9]

Calvin constantly reminds us that the gifts bestowed upon
Christ in His sanctification by royal unction were spiritual, His
kingdom being not of this world.[10] This fullness of gifts consisted

[1] Comm. on Zech. 6 : 11, C.O. 44 : 210. *Erant enim haec summa decora, et
quasi duo oculi corporis, quum scilicet sacerdos esset mediator Dei et hominum: rex
etiam Dei personam sustineret in populo gubernando.*
[2] Comm. on Exod. 28, C.O. 24 : 427. Comm. on Zech. 3 : 5, C.O. 44 : 172.
Scimus enim regnum fuisse coniunctum sacerdotio in Christi persona. Cf. comm.
on Zech. 6 : 11, C.O. 44 : 210.
[3] Comm. on Gen. 14 : 18, C.O. 23 : 201.
[4] Comm. on Zech. 6 : 9–11, C.O. 44 : 211–12.
[5] Ibid.
[6] Christ was called Messiah, says Calvin, "in view of the nature of His kingly
office, still the prophetical and sacerdotal unctions have their proper place"
(Inst. 2 : 15 : 2, cf. comm. on Exod. 30 : 23, C.O. 24 : 446). Elsewhere he looks
on the office of prophet in the Old Testament as belonging properly to the
priests, who should have been ministers of the Word (comm. on Mal. 2 : 7,
C.O. 44 : 437. *A iure sacerdotii non posse divelli docendi munus*): but since they
neglected it, prophets were raised up to make good their neglect (comm. on
Micah 3 : 11–12, C.O. 43 : 334, comm. on Zech. 7 : 1–3, C.O. 44 : 220). The
prophetic office was therefore an extraordinary office, *munus quasi extraordin-
arium* (comm. on Zech. 7 : 1–3, C.O. 44 : 220).
[7] Inst. 2 : 15 : 5.
[8] Comm. on John 3 : 34, C.O. 47 : 74–5.
[9] Inst. 2 : 15 : 4; comm. on Isa. 11 : 2, C.O. 36 : 235; comm. on Luke 4 : 17–18,
C.O. 45 : 140–1; comm. on Heb. 2 : 11, C.O. 55 : 28. *Solidam plenitudinem
sanctitatis in eam effudit Deus, ut inde hauriamus omnes.*
[10] Inst. 2 : 15 : 4–5.

in all the graces that resided in His human nature—His "power, wisdom, righteousness, purity and life."[1] Calvin insists that these gifts must not be restricted to the six or seven mentioned in Isaiah 11 : 2, but should include the "meekness, chastity, sobriety, truth and holiness" and the like virtues enumerated in other parts of Holy Scripture (2 Tim. 1 : 7, Gal. 5 : 22–3) and which filled the human nature of Jesus.[2]

[1] Comm. on John 7 : 38, C.O. 47 : 181.
[2] Comm. on Isa. 11 : 2, C.O. 36 : 235.

Chapter II

The sanctification of the Church in the royal priesthood of Christ

1. The "connexion of the priest with the people"

IN several passages in the Old Testament such language and symbolism is used as indicates an exceedingly close "connexion of the priest with the people"[1] in the fulfilment of the priestly function in the Temple. When the priest entered the Sanctuary he had the names of the Twelve Tribes engraven on the two stones on the shoulders of the ephod (Exod. 28 : 9–12), and he had twelve jewels representing the Twelve Tribes on his breastplate (Exod. 28 : 15–21). All this Calvin regards as of deep significance. It indicated that the priest "was not separate for private advantage but that in his one person they were all a kingdom of priests."[2] This meant that whatever the priest did in sanctifying himself, in entering the Sanctuary, in making atonement for the sins of the people, he acted in the name of the people and represented them with such close identity that it was as if the people themselves acted in his own person. "In the person of one man all entered the Sanctuary together."[3]

It was because they were thus to be associated with their priest in his sanctification as with their king in his triumphs that Moses called Israel a *sacred* kingdom, implying that they shared not only in royal liberty but in the sanctification of the priests chosen from their body.[4]

[1] Comm. on Exod. 28 : 9, C.O. 24 : 431. *Coniunctio sacerdotis cum populo.*

[2] Comm. on Exod. 28 : 9, C.O. 24 : 431. *Hinc sublata fuit occasio invidiae, quum populus intelligeret, unum hominem non discerni ab aliis privati commodi gratia, sed in unius persona omnes esse regnum sacerdotale.*

[3] Comm. on Heb. 6 : 19, C.O. 55 : 81. *Nam pontifex non suo tantum, sed populi etiam nomine in sanctum sanctorum ingrediebatur. . . . ut in unius hominis persona omnes sanctuarium simul ingrederentur.*

[4] Comm. on 1 Pet. 2 : 9, C.O. 55 : 240.

2. The sanctification of the Church in the sanctification of Christ

This intimate connexion between the priest and people in Israel is a foreshadowing of the way in which Christ identifies His Church with Himself in His work as mediator. In everything Christ does in fulfilling the office of His own royal priesthood He acts as the Head of the Church His body. and in such close association with His body that all His members are involved in the vicarious activity of the Head. So close and real is this involvement of the whole Church, the body, in the fulfilment of the royal priesthood of Christ, the Head, that we can speak as if what has been fulfilled in the person of Christ has really and actually already been fulfilled in all His members. "Language which is exclusively appropriate to Him is transferred to us in consequence of the intimate communion existing between the Head and the members."[1]

Therefore as the Church can be regarded as having already triumphed in Christ's victory and as sharing even now in His glory and kingdom[2] so it can also be regarded as already sanctified in the once-for-all sanctification of Christ. "All the saints have a full consecration in the one offering of Christ,"[3] says Calvin, preferring to translate τετελείωκεν in Heb. 10 : 14 by "consecrated" rather than "perfected."[4] Calvin therefore frequently speaks in the past or perfect tense when he refers to the sanctification or consecration of the Church, though he varies his phraseology. "We have been consecrated to God by Christ's death."[5] Christ

---

[1] Comm. on Dan. 7 : 27, C.O. 41 : 84. *Christus . . . nihil sibi proprium usurpat, sed communicat nobiscum quidquid habet, ac in utilitatem nostram refert: ideo merito vocamur reges, quum ipse regnat: et quemadmodum iam dixi, quod non nisi in solam eius personam proprie competit, ad nos transfertur propter communicationem, quae est inter caput et membra.* Here in Calvin's mind we possibly have a relationship similar to that between the sign and the thing signified in the Sacraments—a mystery of sacramental relationship so close that the sign, though distinct from the thing signified may be spoken of as identical with it. Cf. *Calvin's Doctrine of the Word and Sacrament,* pp. 159–74.

[2] Ibid.

[3] Comm. on Heb. 10 : 14. *Plenam enim consecrationem habent sancti omnes in unica Christi oblatione.*

[4] Cf. also in comm. on Heb. 2 : 10, C.O. 55 : 28.

[5] Comm. on 1 Pet. 3 : 18, C.O. 55 : 264. *Quid hoc sibi vult, nisi nos Christi morte ita fuisse Deo consecratos, ut illi vivamus et moriamur.*

has, "so to speak, presented us to the Father in His own person,"[1] or "devoted us to the Father with Himself."[2]

Calvin, then, finds deep meaning in the text, John 17 : 19, "For their sakes I sanctify myself, that they also might be sanctified through the truth," which he seldom fails to quote whenever he speaks about sanctification.[3] It is true that Jesus' self-consecration to His royal priesthood was in a sense entirely vicarious, unique, and something done in separation from the rest of humanity. It was nevertheless in our name that Jesus stood and acted before God. In His atoning and sanctifying work He acted not only as our substitute but also as our representative in the deepest sense of this word. In His person, then, we have indeed been presented to the Father in a full and complete act of consecration to royal priesthood.[4] "Moses called your fathers a sacred kingdom," writes Calvin, paraphrasing 1 Pet. 2 : 9, "because the whole people enjoyed, as it were, royal liberty, and from their body were chosen priests, both honours therefore were at the same time joined together. But now you are royal priests indeed in a more outstanding way because you are each of you consecrated in Christ that you may be associates of His kingdom and partakers of His priesthood."[5]

The fact that we have been once-for-all consecrated as a royal priesthood in Christ can be the basis of the confidence with which we can continually approach God in worship and prayer and thus seek to live the Christian life. In making us a royal priesthood Christ has opened up for us an entrance into Heaven not only symbolically but in reality.[6] The fact that the blood of Christ is "always in a manner distilling before the presence of the Father" means a "perpetual consecration of the way" by which we can come to Him.[7] In coming to Him our status is always assured. "The whole value in which the faithful are held by God depends

[1] Comm. on John 17 : 19, C.O. 47 : 385. *Nos in sua persona quodammodo Patri obtulit.*

[2] Inst. 2 : 15 : 6. *Nos secum Patri dicavit.*

[3] Cf. e.g. comm. on Exod. 28 : 36, C.O. 24 : 433; on Exod. 29 : 16, C.O. 24 : 439; on Dan. 9 : 25, C.O. 41 : 183; on Heb. 2 : 11, C.O. 55 : 28, etc.

[4] Cf. comm. on Zech. 6 : 12–13, C.O. 44 : 214.

[5] Comm. on 1 Pet. 2 : 9, C.O. 55 : 240 . . . *quia singuli in Christo consecrati estis, ut sitis et regni socii, et sacerdotii participes.*

[6] Comm. on Heb. 10 : 19, C.O. 55 : 128. *Non enim symbolice tantum, sed re ipsa in coelum ingressus nobis patet.*

[7] Ibid. p. 129. *Haec est perpetua viae dedicatio, quod coram facie patris semper quodammodo stillat sanguis Christi ad irrigandum coelum et terram.*

upon the sanctity of the priesthood." Therefore no matter how polluted and sinful we may feel ourselves we can be assured that God accepts us and looks on us as those who have this royal and priestly dignity.[1] Christ has sanctified us in order that our faults may not be imputed to us when we come before God.[2] Christ in His priesthood is thus the pattern and mirror in which when God sees us He chooses us to be His children and the "patron" under whose protection and sponsorship we can securely shelter and act in priestly capacity.[3]

3. The sanctification of Christ imparted to the Church

But it is not enough merely to rely on the fact that we have been once and for all consecrated in Jesus Christ unless we allow that sanctification to be at the same time worked within us. Christ "has been sanctified," says Calvin, "in order that we might be truly regenerated to serve God and walk in uprightness of life."[4] While we can rest with full assurance that all that is required for our perfection has been accomplished in the death and resurrection of Christ, nevertheless by working within us through the power of His Spirit He continues to perfect what He has already fully perfected, so that the virtue of His death may produce its fruit within us.[5] The fact that once for all we have been wholly sanctified in the life, death and resurrection of Christ, unfolds its true significance not only in our justification and acceptance with God, but also in the gradual impartation to us through the Spirit of the

---

[1] Comm. on Exod. 28 : 4, C.O. 24 : 429.

[2] Serm. on Mark 1 : 23–7, C.O. 46 : 741.

[3] Serm. on Eph. 1 : 3–4, C.O. 51 : 269. *Il faut donc, devant que Dieu nous choisisse et appelle, qu'il ait là son patron et miroir, auquel il nous contemple: c'est à sçavoir nostre Seigneur Iesus Christ. Comm. on Rom. 8 : 33, C.O. 49 : 163. Magis ergo emphatice colligit filios Dei non esse obnoxios accusationi, quia Deus iustificat, quam si dixisset Christum esse patronum.*

[4] Serm. on Mark 1 : 23–7, C.O. 46 : 471. Cf. comm. on John 17 : 19, C.O. 47 : 385. *Nos . . . Patri obtulit, ut spiritu eius renovemur.*

[5] Serm. on Luke 2 : 50–2, C.O. 46 : 477. *Voyla donc nostre Seigneur Iesus Christ qu'il n'a defailli en rien, tellement que quand nous oyons qu'apres avoir este crucifié, il est ressuscité, qu'il est monté au ciel, voyla la perfection de tout ce que nous pouvons souhaiter. Et nous avons aussi de quoy pour contenter nostre foy, et où nous reposer seurement. Mais notons que nostre Seigneur Iesus Christ ne laisse pas encores auiourd'huy de besongner tellement par la vertu de son sainct Esprit, que la mort qu'il a endurée pour un coup, produit son fruict et son effect en nous: sa resurrection nous profite à vie . . . Ainsi on peut dire qu'encores auiourd'huy le Fils de Dieu continue à parfaire ce qu'il a vrayment parfait, ouy pour l'appliquer à nostre usage, afin que nous en sentions le profit.*

actual holiness which dwelt in Christ. "He consecrated Himself
to the Father that His holiness might come to us; for as the
blessing of the first-fruits is spread over the whole harvest, so the
Spirit of God sprinkles us with the holiness of Christ and makes us
partakers of it. Nor is this done by imputation only, for in that
respect He is said to have been made to us righteousness; but He
is likewise said to have been made unto us sanctification."[1]

This inward sanctifying work of the Spirit is, however, to be
regarded simply as the impartation to us of the sanctification which
has already been worked out for us completely in Christ. The
Church can receive its sanctification only by sharing in the one
royal and priestly unction that was poured out on Jesus Christ.
Calvin insists on this point in many different ways and places.
God has made the human nature of Jesus which was sanctified by
the Spirit[2] the residing-place of all the graces of the Spirit which
are required to transform men into new creatures, re-created
after the image of God revealed in Jesus.[3] Everything that Christ
possessed of spiritual wealth and power, whether as a gift from
His Father or as a result of His own self-sanctification, He possessed not for His own sake, for He had need of nothing, but "to
enrich the poor and needy."[4] He sanctified Himself not for the
sake of any personal gain that could possibly come to Himself
but in order that the whole body of the Church,[5] and indeed the
whole world, might be filled with His sanctity.[6]

[1] Comm. on John 17 : 19, C.O. 47 : 385. *Ipse Patri se consecravit, ut eius sanctitas ad nos perveniret. Sicuti enim a primitiis benedictio diffunditur in totum
proventum, ita spiritus Dei nos Christi sanctitate adspergit facitque eius participes.
Neque id imputatione solum, nam hac ratione dicitur factus nobis esse iustitia*
(1 Cor. 1. 30), *sed dicitur etiam factus esse nobis sanctificatio.*
[2] We cannot think or speak of the divine nature of Christ as being sanctified,
cf. John 17 : 19, therefore it is through the human nature of Christ alone that
divine revelation and divine life are communicated to the human race. Inst.
2 : 13 : 4, 3 : 2 : 1; Comm. on Heb. 2 : 11, C.O. 55 : 28. *Neque enim tantum
quatenus Deus est, nos sanctificat, sed humanae quoque naturae vis sanctificandi
inest.*
[3] Serm. on Matt. 2 : 23 ff., C.O. 46 : 457. *Vray est quand il a vestu nostre chair,
que rien ne luy a defailli. Car nous sçavons ce qui est dit par le Prophete Isaie, que
l'Esprit de Dieu a reposé sur luy, l'Esprit de sagesse et d'intelligence, l'Esprit de
force et de discretion, l'Esprit de crainte de Dieu. Bref, il a falu que Iesus Christ
receust en sa nature humaine, et vestist tout ce que nous pouvons desirer, et qui est
requis à nostre felicité: voire, et a falu qu'il receust tout cela en perfection.* And
comm. on John 17 : 22, C.O. 47 : 388.
[4] Inst. 3 : 1 : 1; 2 : 17 : 6; Serm. on Matt. 2 : 23, C.O. 46 : 455; Serm. on
Acts 2 : 1–4, C.O. 48 : 633.
[5] Serm on Matt. 4 : 1, C.O. 46 : 596.
[6] Serm. on Mark 1 : 23–7, C.O. 46 : 736.

Calvin finds in the Old Testament ritual of the consecration of the priest an illustration of the way in which the sanctification of Christ is imparted to us.[1] In this rite, the ointment was poured first over the head and flowed down over the whole body. So in the communication of His gifts to the Church Christ is simply causing the heavenly anointing which He has received as Head "to flow over the whole body of the Church."[2]

The human nature of Jesus Christ, then, has been made the sole channel through which salvation and life and power can flow to the Church. A Christian must seek to find his true well-being in Christ and not apart from Christ.[3] Everything that has been given to Christ in His sanctification is given for the very purpose of being communicated and imparted to the Church by the Spirit.[4] In sanctifying the Church the Holy Spirit neither brings to the Church nor creates within the Church anything that was not first in Jesus Christ, who now, seated at the right hand of God, seeks to transfer His own graces and gifts to the Church that it may be preserved and adorned and equipped for its task.[5]

---

[1] Another Old Testament analogy used by Calvin for this transference of sanctification is that of the consecration and blessing of the first-fruits of the harvest being transferred to the whole harvest. Cf. comm. on John 17 : 19, C.O. 47 : 385; on Matt. 2 : 23, C.O. 45 : 103; on 1 Cor. 15 : 20, C.O. 49 : 545.

[2] Comm. On Isa. 11 : 2, C.O. 36 : 236–7.

[3] Serm. on Acts 2 : 1–4, C.O. 48 : 633.

[4] Comm. on Heb. 7 : 25, C.O. 55 : 94. Cf. serm. on Tit. 1 : 7–9, C.O. 54 : 442. *Il faut que Dieu y besongne. Et comment? Que nous soyons des membres de nostre Seigneur Iesus Christ. Il est dit que nous devons estre iustes, saincts, sobres, attrempez. Et comment cela? Quand le Sainct Esprit dominera en nous, alors nous aurons des vertus. Il est dit que nous devons fuir yvrongnerie, intemperance, noise, debats, fierté. Et comment? Ayans l'esprit de mansuetude, l'esprit d'humilité, l'esprit de crainte de Dieu, l'esprit de prudence et de discretion. Or tout cela a esté donné à nostre Seigneur Iesus Christ, afin qu'il le communique à ses fideles.*

[5] Inst. 2 : 16 : 16. *In excelsis ergo sedet, ut transfusa inde ad nos sua virtute, in vitam spiritualem nos vivificet, ut Spiritu suo sanctificet, ut variis gratiarum dotibus ecclesiam suam exornet, ut protectione sua tutam adversus omnes noxas conservet.* Cf. comm. on Isa. 11 : 2, C.O. 235–6.

Chapter III

The participation of the Church in the sanctification of Christ

1. The mystical union between Christ and His Church

WE have seen that the power of sanctification resides in the human nature or flesh of Christ[1] which has been made the dwelling-place of all the fullness of virtue, and the channel or fountain from which we must draw, and can draw without stint, whatever we need for our salvation.[2] It follows that our participation in the sanctification of Christ depends on our union with the human nature of Christ. Christ must "present Himself to us and invite us into such a relationship that truly we are united to Him, that He dwells in us in such a way that everything that belongs to Him is ours."[3]

It would have been of no advantage to us if Christ had merely died and risen again unless He had also bestowed upon us this "second blessing" of ingrafting us into His body and thus communicating to us His benefits.[4] The unction which flows down from the head over the body is to be shared only by those who are members of the body.[5] Calvin notes that in defining the means

---

[1] See p. 15. Calvin finds that Jesus' words in the sixth chapter of John's Gospel, about the life-giving and nourishing power of His flesh and the necessity that men should eat His flesh, refer to the power that resides in His human nature or body. Therefore he does not hesitate to say that the flesh of Christ itself has been "filled with the sanctification of the Spirit (*perfusa sanctificatione spiritus*)" and that the flesh of Christ is the channel through which the power of Christ flows to His people, and the source from which we derive life. Cf. comm. on John 6 : 51, C.O. 47 : 152–3; and C.O. 9 : 30–1.

[2] See serm. on Eph. 3 : 14–19, C.O. 51 : 489. *Or notons que non seulement Iesus Christ, entant qu'il est Fils eternel de Dieu, a en soy toute perfection de biens: mais en sa nature humaine . . . il a encores receu toute plenitude. . . . C'est à fin qu'il en distribue à tous ses membres, et que nous puisions . . . de sa plenitude, ne craignans point que ceste fontaine tarisse.*

[3] Serm. on Acts 2 : 1–4, C.O. 48 : 633.

[4] Comm. on 2 Tim. 1 : 9, C.O. 52 : 352; and on 1 Cor. 1 : 5, C.O. 49 : 310.

[5] Serm. on Acts 2 : 1–4, C.O. 48 : 633. *Nous ne pouvons communiquer a nulle grace du S. Esprit qu'estans membres de nostre Seigneur Iesus Christ:* and serm. on Tit. 1 : 7–9, C.O. 54 : 442. *Il reste maintenant de sçavoir comme nous pourrons parvenir à ces vertus. . . . Il faut que Dieu y besongne. Et comment? Que nous soyons membres de nostre Seigneur Iesus Christ.*

by which we are saved it is better to use the phrase *in Christ* rather than *by Christ*,[1] for the former phrase has more expressiveness and force and denotes the union with Christ which is such a necessary part of the Gospel.[2] In uniting us to Himself and making us His members, Christ dwells in us and He "not only brings Himself close to us by an undivided bond of fellowship, but by a wondrous communion grows with us daily more and more into one body until He becomes altogether one with us."[3]

The nature and reality of this "mystical union" of the Church with Christ in human nature or flesh Calvin regards as one of the great mysteries of the Gospel.[4] It is a real and substantial union by which believers living "out of themselves" thus live in Christ.[5] By means of it Christ becomes "of one substance" with us[6] and we become "bone of His bone and flesh of His flesh."[7] Yet it is at the same time essentially a spiritual union effected by the power of the Holy Ghost in such a way that there is no "gross mixture" of Christ and ourselves.[8] Moreover this union is effected by faith alone and cannot be experienced apart from faith.[9] Yet it is effected also by the Sacraments, which are given to faith and which must be regarded as concrete and visible means whereby we are brought into this union.[10]

The Sacraments of Baptism and the Lord's Supper were instituted by Christ in order to make this union continually

[1] Comm. on Rom. 6 : 11, C.O. 49 : 110. *Retinere malui Pauli verba: in Christo Iesu, quam cum Erasmo vertere: per Christum: quia illo modo melius exprimitur insitio illa, quae nos unum cum Christo facit.* Cf. comm. on 1 Cor. 1 : 5, C.O. 49 : 310.

[2] Serm. on Titus 1 : 7–9, C.O. 442–3. *Car quand sainct Paul veut definir en brief la fin de l'Evangile, et son vray usage, il dit que nous sommes appellez pour communiquer à nostre Seigneur Iesus, pour estre unis tellement avec luy, que nous y soyons incorporez, et qu'il habite quant et quant en nous, et que nous soyons conioints ensemble d'un lien inseparable.*

[3] Inst. 3 : 2 : 24 . . . *quia Christus non extra nos est, sed in nobis habitat: nec solum individuo societatis nexu nobis adhaeret, sed mirabili quadam communione in unum corpus nobiscum coalescit in dies magis ac magis, donec unum penitus nobiscum fiat.*

[4] Inst. 3 : 11 : 10. Cf. *Calvin's Doctrine of the Word and Sacrament*, Ch. XII.

[5] Comm. on Gal. 2 : 20, C.O. 50 : 199. *Insignis sententia, fideles extra se vivere, hoc est in Christo. Quod fieri nequit quin veram cum ipso et substantialem communicationem habeant.*

[6] Inst. 4 : 17 : 3 & 5; comm. on 1 Cor. 11 : 24, C.O. 49 : 487.

[7] Inst. 3 : 1 : 3.

[8] Inst. 3 : 11 : 10; 3 : 1 : 3.

[9] Comm. on Heb. 5 : 9, C.O. 55 : 64. *Neque enim noster fit, neque eius bona, nisi quatenus haec et ipsum fide amplectimur.*

[10] Cf. *Calvin's Doctrine of the Word and Sacrament*, especially Ch. XII.

effective in the life of the Church, and to impress upon us continually that this union is the source of our justification and sanctification. Since we are creatures who must see with our eyes and handle with our hands,[1] the Lord's Table is set before us in order that we may know that the ascended Christ is not separated from us but that we are so united to Him that He has nothing of His own which He does not wish to communicate to us.[2] The visible signs, the bread and wine which we eat and drink, and which represent the body and blood of Christ, show us how real is the fact that "our souls are fed by Christ just as our corporeal life is sustained by bread and wine."[3]

As the Lord's Supper is a repeatedly-given sign to us that we live by continually drawing life from our union with the human nature of Christ, so Baptism is a visible sign that we have really been once-for-all initiated into the mystery of this union with the body of Christ.[4] As the Lord's Supper shows that God continually supplies us from Christ with the food which sustains our life,[5] so Baptism is to be thought of as the sign that we have been once-for-all ingrafted into the body of Christ or implanted into Christ.[6] Baptism is a sign of our initiation into that "secret conjunction by which we grow up together with Him."[7]

2. The Holy Spirit as the bond of this union

In discussing the mystery of how we can be so united to the human nature of Christ as to become "bone of His bone and flesh of His flesh," Calvin does not forget that in the Ascension Jesus Christ has taken His human nature beyond this earth to Heaven where it will remain until His second coming in glory.[8] It is obvious then that the nature of any union between Christ in Heaven and ourselves on the earth is such a mystery that it cannot be conceived by the human mind.[9] Moreover it cannot be effected by any

---

[1] Comm. on Ps. 51 : 9, C.O. 31 : 515–16.
[2] Serm. on Luke 2 : 1–14, C.O. 46 : 966.
[3] Inst. 4 : 17 : 1.   [4] Inst. 4 : 18 : 19.   [5] Inst. 4 : 17 : 1.
[6] Comm. on Tit. 3 : 5, C.O. 52 : 430; serm. on Matt. 3 : 13–17, C.O. 46 : 578–80.
[7] Comm. on Rom. 6 : 5, C.O. 49 : 106.
[8] C.O. 9 : 72; 9 : 221; Inst. 4 : 17 : 26; serm. on 1 Cor. 10 : 15–18, C.O. 49 : 667.
[9] Cf. comm. on Eph. 5 : 32, C.O. 51 : 226–7.

process, spiritual or moral or otherwise, which falls within the natural order of things.[1]

It is therefore the Holy Spirit alone who can effect this union, for it is the Holy Spirit alone who can so join things in Heaven and things on earth that heavenly things can be grasped by human minds and that the life and virtue of what is in Heaven can be shared by those who are yet on earth.[2] It is the Holy Spirit alone who can bring into real being that wonderful relation of mystery between Christ's heavenly body and His Church on earth which is so clearly depicted in the act of participation in the Lord's Supper and in Baptism.[3]

The Holy Spirit has already united Heaven and earth, God and man, through the conception of the God-man in the womb of the Virgin. But even this miracle by itself does not effect the final consummation of God's purpose to join mankind to Himself forever. The miracle of the Incarnation involves its complement in the miracle of the incorporation of the Church into the body which was assumed at the Incarnation. This further miracle too is an incomprehensible work of the Holy Spirit.[4] In speaking of the union between Christ and His people Calvin can speak, with reservations, of the Holy Spirit as bringing Christ down into the lives and hearts of His people. He seems to prefer to speak of the Holy Spirit as raising men up from earth to Heaven, there to dwell with Christ and there to partake of Christ.[5] He can speak of the Holy Spirit as the link which binds us to Christ and also as the

[1] Serm. on Eph. 5 : 32, C.O. 51 : 768. *Car . . . ce n'est pas que nous devions prendre ceste audace de penser d'approcher de Iesus Christ, comme si nous estions conioints à luy de nous-mesmes et de nostre nature propre: mais ceci se fait en la vertu de son S. Esprit;* and p. 769, *Voylà donc comme par la vertu de l'Esprit et non point par ordre de nature, ni d'une façon commune, nous sommes des os de nostre Seigneur Iesus Christ et de sa chair, que nous sommes membres de son corps.*

[2] Comm. on Gal. 2 : 20, C.O. 50 : 199. And serm. on Job 15 : 11–16, C.O. 33 : 720. *Il n'y a nul qui cognoisse ce qui est en l'homme, que l'esprit qui habite en lui, dit sainct Paul: mais l'Esprit qui habite en Dieu nous est donné. Voila donc comme nous sommes faits participans des choses qui estoient du tout separees de nous, et desquelles nous ne pouvions nullement approcher.*

[3] Serm. on Acts 2 : 1–4, C.O. 48 : 634. *Quand nous venons à ceste saincte table, cognoissons que c'est un secret qui surmonte tous nos sens, et pourtant qu'il faut yci donner lieu à la foy. Et que nous sçachions que ce qui ne se peut concevoir par les hommes s'accomplit neantmoins par la grace secrete et invisible du S. Esprit: car voyla comme nous sommes faits participans du corps et du sang de Iesus Christ.*

[4] Comm. on Eph. 5 : 31, C.O. 51 : 226. Cf. serm. on Eph. 5 : 28–30, C.O. 51 : 767–9.

[5] C.O. 9 : 33; Inst. 4 : 17 : 6.

channel by which everything which Christ has and is is derived to us.[1]

3. Faith as the bond of this union

From the point of view of the human subject, it is faith that is the bond of union between Christ and His people. Calvin speaks in most exalted language about what the possession of faith does for the believing man. By faith we "obtain possession of the heavenly kingdom."[2] Faith enables us to put on the righteousness of Christ so that it becomes ours.[3] Faith enables us to partake of the life made available through the death of Christ.[4] But all this is possible only because faith actually unites us to Christ and inserts us into His body,[5] creating the bond that enables us to receive, possess and enjoy Christ Himself[6]—for the blessings which are His gifts cannot be received and enjoyed by us apart from communion with Himself by faith.[7] So much, indeed, does our union with Christ depend on our faith, that its depth and power is determined by the measure of our faith.[8]

In saying all this about the power of faith, we need in no way take back anything that has already been said about the Holy Spirit as being the sole effective bond between Christ and those united to Him, for it is the "principal work" of the Holy Spirit[9] to create in the heart of man the faith which unites him to Christ, therefore it is equally true that we are united to Christ by the Holy Spirit alone and by faith alone. Calvin uses the same language in relating union with Christ to faith as he does in relating

[1] Inst. 3 : 1 : 1. *Huc summa redit, Spiritum sanctum vinculum esse, quo nos sibi efficaciter devincit Christus.* Inst. 4 : 17 : 12. *Vinculum ergo istius coniunctionis est Spiritus Christi, cuius nexu copulamur, et quidam veluti canalis per quem, quicquid Christus ipse et est et habet, ad nos derivatur.*

[2] Inst. 3 : 2 : 1.

[3] Comm. on 2 Cor. 5 : 21, C.O. 50 : 74.

[4] Comm. on John 5 : 11, C.O. 55 : 368.

[5] Inst. 3 : 2 : 30. *Quomodo autem fides salvifica nisi quatenus nos in Christi corpus inserit?* Cf. 2 : 13 : 2 and comm. on 1 John 4 : 15, C.O. 55 : 356.

[6] Comm. on 1 John 4 : 14, C.O. 55 : 355–6; on 1 John 5 : 12, C.O. 55 : 368.

[7] Comm. on Heb. 5 : 9, C.O. 55 : 64. *Neque enim noster fit, neque eius bona, nisi quatenus haec et ipsum fide amplectimur.* Cf. Inst. 3 : 3 : 1.

[8] Serm. on Eph. 1 : 17–18, C.O. 51 : 336. *Non sans cause il nous a conioints à nostre Seigneur Iesus Christ: mais que ç'a esté à fin que nous puissions maintenant posseder un chacun selon la mesure de sa foy, les biens qui luy sont propres.* Cf. comm. on John 7 : 39, C.O. 47 : 183.

[9] Inst. 3 : 1 : 4.

it to the Holy Spirit.[1] Faith, rising from the human heart, can penetrate the heavens.[2] It can root our earthly life in the heavenly Lord,[3] and convey to our souls the heavenly life of Christ [4] as the root conveys strength to the tree which it nourishes.[5] It can thus "translate into us what is proper to Christ," and give us a free participation in His benefits.[6] It can enable us while living an earthly life to enjoy also a heavenly life, and while living in this world at the same time also to live in Heaven.[7]

Faith is thus an entirely supernatural gift—a new capacity created within man whereby what is in Heaven is really possessed and enjoyed by him. It effects such a secret and wonderful communion with Christ that even though Jesus Christ remains entire in Heaven, He is nevertheless grasped so firmly and possessed so completely that He may be said actually to dwell in our hearts.[8] Therefore, even though the man of faith stands before God devoid of all purity and all good he nevertheless finds in Christ alone all the purity and life he needs, for by faith he possesses and lives by what he does not find in himself but in Christ alone.[9]

Calvin, in exalting the power of faith, does not hesitate to add that faith has the power to reach through the humanity of Jesus even God Himself. He speaks of faith as being able to rise "from the flesh of Christ to His divinity"[10] and as being able to penetrate

---

[1] Cf. e.g. serm. on Eph, 3 : 14–19, C.O. 51 : 491. *Iesus Christ habite en nous par foy . . . Il habite en nous par la vertu de son S. Esprit.*

[2] Comm. on 1 Pet. 1 : 4, C.O. 55 : 211. *Nam ut fides in coelos usque penetrat: ita et quae in coelo sunt bona, nobis applicat.* Cf. Inst. 3 : 2 : 1.

[3] Comm. on John 15 : 7, C.O. 47 : 341. *Significat nos fide in ipso radicem agere.*

[4] Comm. on Gal. 2 : 20, C.O. 50 : 200. *Unde tanta fidei virtus ut Christi vitam in nos transfundat?*

[5] Serm. on Eph. 3 : 14–19, C.O. 51 : 491. *Nous vivons de sa propre substance, tout ainsi qu'un arbre tire vigueur de sa racine.*

[6] Comm. on Acts 15 : 9, C.O. 48 : 346. *Et certe fidei officium est, quod proprium habet Christus in nos transferre, et gratuita communicatione efficere nostrum.*

[7] Comm. on Gal. 2 : 20, C.O. 50 : 199.

[8] Serm. on Eph. 3 : 14–19, C.O. 51 : 491. *Nous avons une union secrete, et qui est admirable, et par dessus tout ordre de nature, d'autant que Iesus Christ ne laisse point d'habiter en nous, combien qu'il soit au ciel . . . il habitera en nos coeurs, voire par le moyen de la foy.*

[9] Comm. on Hab. 2 : 4, C.O. 43 : 529. *Quid autem iustus? nihil coram Deo affert praeter fidem. Ergo nihil affert proprium, quia fides quasi precario mutuatur quod non est penes hominem. Qui ergo vivit fide, non habet apud se vitam: sed quia ea indiget, ad Deum unum confugit.* Comm. on Acts 15 : 9, C.O. 48 : 346–7. *Neque enim nos purificat fides, tanquam virtus aut qualitas animis infusa: sed quia munditiem in Christo oblatam percipit.* Cf. comm. on Gal. 2 : 20, C.O. 50 : 199.

[10] Comm. on John 12 : 45, C.O. 47 : 302.

"above all the heavens, even to those mysteries which the angels behold and adore."[1] Faith unites man to God and makes God to dwell in man.[2] It should be noted that the movement of faith in thus laying hold of what is in Heaven and bringing it down to earth is reciprocal, in Calvin's thought, to the movement of the Holy Spirit who brings the heavenly grace of Christ down into the human heart, and raises our hearts up into Heaven in response to His grace.[3]

4. Justification and sanctification as the twofold fruit of faith

Calvin defines what we receive from Jesus Christ by faith as a "double grace,"[4] or a twofold benefit, the whole of which can be summed up for the purpose of theological discussion under two headings: Justification and Sanctification. "The whole may be thus summed up: Christ, given to us by the kindness of God, is apprehended and possessed by faith, by means of which we obtain in particular a twofold benefit (*duplicem gratiam*); first, being reconciled by the righteousness of Christ, God becomes, instead of a judge an indulgent Father; and, secondly, being sanctified by His Spirit, we aspire (*meditemur*) to integrity and purity of life."[5] Justification and sanctification together comprise a "twofold cleansing (*double lavement*)." This twofold cleansing gives us both a purity which is imputed to us in our justification, and also an "actual purity (*pureté actuelle*)" which comes by the process of sanctification and reformation of life.[6] When Christ insisted that Peter must be "washed" if he wished to have part in Himself, He

---

[1] Comm. on John 8 : 19, C.O. 47 : 195.
[2] Comm. on 1 John 4 : 15, C.O. 55 : 356.
[3] Comm. on Acts 15 : 9, C.O. 48 : 346. *Inter fidem et Christi gratiam mutua est relatio.*
[4] C.O. 6 : 187. Cf. serm. on Gal. 2 : 17–18, C.O. 50 : 437–8. *Il y a deux principales graces que nous recevons par nostre Seigneur Iesus Christ.*
[5] Inst. 3 : 11 : 1; cf. 3 : 11 : 14 & 3 : 2 : 8.
[6] Serm. on Gal. 2 : 17–18, C.O. 50 : 437–8. Cf. comm. on Acts 15 : 9, C.O. 48 : 347. *Duplex autem est purgandi modus, quod Christus peccata nostra, quae semel sanguine suo expiavit, quotidie delendo, puros iustosque, in patris conspectum nos offert ac sistit: deinde, quod carnis cupiditates spiritu suo mortificans nos in sanctitatem reformat.* This "double manner of purging" corresponds to need for a "double purgation." Cf. serm. on Job 14 : 1–4, C.O. 33 : 668. *Maintenant nous avons besoin de double purgation: l'une c'est, que Dieu nous pardonne nos fautes, voila comme nos macules seront lavees: l'autre c'est que par son S. Esprit il nous renouvelle, qu'il nous purge de toutes nos mauvaises affections et cupiditez. Or a-il fait cela pour un iour? il faut qu'il continue tout le temps de nostre vie. . . .*

meant by the figure of washing to refer both to the free pardon which is bound up with justification, and the newness of life which is the effect of sanctification.[1] Expressing the same thing in another way, "Christ lives in us in two ways. The one life consists in governing us by His Spirit and directing all our actions; the other in making us partakers of His righteousness, so that, while we can do nothing of ourselves, we are accepted in the sight of God."[2]

Justification is "the acceptance with which God receives us into favour as if we were righteous."[3] It is simply another word for the forgiveness of sins,[4] for our adoption into the family of God, and our coming under God's paternal favour. Justification refers to our status before God, and it involves the communication of the righteousness of Christ to us by imputation in such a way that apart from any inward change of heart and mind that may have taken place within us, and in spite of the fact that within us there may be nothing but unrighteousness, we nevertheless really possess by faith once-for-all and at the same time the perfect righteousness of Christ as our own.[5] Justification is thought of by Calvin as the completed step out of alienation to God into His divine favour and into His kingdom. This takes place at the moment when faith is created in the heart of man. Our confidence in our salvation and our final acceptance at the judgment-seat of God must rest on the fact of this once-for-all justification which gives us the right to claim as our own the full perfect righteousness of Christ.[6]

Calvin thinks of sanctification rather as the gradual process of man's becoming more and more in the course of time conformed

---

[1] Comm. on John 13 : 8, C.O. 47 : 307.

[2] Comm. on Gal. 2 : 20, C.O. 50 : 199. *Porro vivit Christus in nobis dupliciter. Una vita est, quum nos spiritu suo gubernat atque actiones nostras omnes dirigit. Altera quod participatione suae iustitae nos donat: ut quando in nobis non possumus, in ipso acceptis simus Deo.*

[3] Inst. 3 : 11 : 12.

[4] Inst. 3 : 11 : 21. "Justification may be termed in one word the remission of sins."

[5] Inst. 3 : 11 : 24. *Hinc et illud conficitur, sola intercessione iustitiae Christi nos obtinere, ut coram Deo iustificemur. Quod perinde valet acsi diceretur, hominem non in se ipso iustum esse, sed quia Christi iustitia imputatione cum illo communicatur, quod accurata animadversione dignum est. Siquidem evanescit nugamentum illud ideo iustificari hominem fide, quonian illa Spiritum Dei participat quo iustus redditur.*

[6] Inst. 3 : 11 : 11.

to Christ in heart and outward life and devoted to God.[1] Sanctification is the consecration and dedication of both body and soul to God.[2] As Christ sanctified Himself in consecrating Himself to the will of the Father in the sacrifice of the Cross, so our sanctification consists in offering ourselves to God as a sacrifice through which His will can be accomplished. Our sanctification is thus the fulfilment of Christ's presenting us in His own person to the Father in His sacrifice.[3] Since such sanctification demands the offering of what is pure and holy, and since God's will leads us against the will of this world, our sanctification implies the renouncing of the world and the cleansing of ourselves from the pollution of the flesh.[4] But only God can thus cleanse. Therefore it is God who sanctifies us by regenerating our hearts, by renewing us in every part of our being, by mortifying within us the lusts of the flesh which are so contrary to His will, by framing our hearts into obedience to His Law, and by more and more making us outwardly Christian.[5] Calvin can speak of all this as a very gradual process. It takes place "little by little"[6] and sometimes only through hard discipline. Our sanctification will be completed only after death when we will be completely renewed and glorified in the likeness of the heavenly Lord. Yet even here and now the process that is to have such a glorious completion has begun through the inward work of the sanctifying Spirit of Christ. Calvin, when he wishes to vary his language, can use many other terms such as repentance, mortification, new life, conversion, regeneration, to denote exactly the same as he means by the word sanctification.

Calvin distinguishes clearly between justification and sanctification.[7] It must not be imagined, however, that these could ever be separated in reality. They are distinct, but they can be separated

[1] Comm. on John 17 : 17, C.O. 47 : 385.
[2] Comm. on 2 Cor. 7 : 1, C.O. 50 : 84. *Ergo ut te rite sanctifices Deo, et corpus et animam illi in solidum dicare oportet.*
[3] Comm. on John 17 : 19, C.O. 47 : 385. *Dicitur etiam factus esse nobis sanctificatio, quia nos in sua persona quodammodo patri obtulit, ut spiritu eius renovemur in veram sanctitatem.*
[4] Comm. on 1 Thess. 4 : 3, C O. 52 : 161.
[5] Comm. on 1 Thess. 5 : 23, C.O. 52 : 176; comm. on John 17 : 17, C.O. 47 : 384; comm. on Rom. 3 : 31, C.O. 49 : 67. *Sanctificatio, qua formantur corda nostra ad legis observationem.* And on Rom. 6 : 14, C.O. 49 : 113. . . . *sanctificationem spiritus, per quam ad bona opera nos refingit.*
[6] Cf. comm. on Rom. 8 : 11, C.O. 49 : 146.
[7] Inst. 3 : 11 : 6. "To be justified is something else than to be made new creatures."

the one from the other only in thought, but never in experience.[1] They are to be seen in their indivisible unity with each other in the person of Christ in relation to whom no one could possibly experience one without the other. To try to separate the one from the other would be like trying to tear Christ in pieces. "As Christ cannot be divided into parts, so the two things, justification and sanctification, which we perceive to be united together in Him, are inseparable. Whomsoever, therefore, God receives into His favour, He presents with the Spirit of adoption, whose agency forms them anew into His image."[2] No more than the light of the sun can be separated from the heat which is given along with that light can we separate between justification and sanctification.[3] As Kolfhaus points out, they are together the one and the same act of God towards us and the one can be made neither the cause nor the consequence of the other.[4]

Yet in actual practice the one always involves the other. The one act of union with Christ which enables us to lay hold of the gift of forgiveness puts us also into such a relation to the living Lord that we become involved in an inevitable process of sanctification[5] and ultimate redemption from all evil. The gift of faith from Christ is always accompanied by the gift of repentance. Faith, if it is true faith, will grasp in Christ not only justification but also sanctification. "Let the faithful . . . learn to embrace Christ, not only unto righteousness, but also unto sanctification, as He was given us for both these ends, lest through their lame faith they rend Christ in pieces."[6] Faith hears in the Word of

---

[1] Comm. on Isa. 59:20, C.O. 37:351. *Ita partem iustitiae nostrae in remissione peccatorum, partem in poenitentia constituunt. . . . Sic igitur haec distinguenda sunt ut ne separentur nec misceantur: atque ita solidum nostrae salutis fundamentum retineamus.*

[2] Inst. 3 : 11 : 6. Cf. comm. on Rom. 8 : 9, C.O. 49 : 144. *Ac semper tenendum est illud apostoli consilium, gratuitam peccatorum remissionem a spiritu regenerationis non posse disiungi: quia hoc esset quasi Christum discerpere.*

[3] Serm. on Gal. 2 : 17–18, C.O. 50 : 438. *Ce sont deux choses coniointes comme d'un lien inseparable, comme la clarté du soleil ne peut point estre separee de sa chaleur. Ainsi ces deux graces (c'est à sçavoir nostre iustice et la remission de nos pechez) sont inviolablement coniointes avec ce renouvellement qui est fait par l'esprit de sanctification.*

[4] W. Kolfhaus. *Christusgemeinschaft bei Johannes Calvin*, pp. 60–1.

[5] Comm. on Ps. 32 : 11, C.O. 31 : 323.

[6] Comm. on Rom. 8 : 13, C.O. 49 : 147. *Discant ergo fideles non in iustitiam modo, sed in sanctificationem quoque amplecti, sicuti in utrumque finem nobis datus est, ne mutila sua fide eum lacerent.* Cf. serm. on Matt. 3 : 1–2, etc., C.O. 46 : 495. *Il y a deux choses qui sont requises à nostre salut: L'une, que nous cognoissions que Dieu veut ensevelir nos fautes, etc. Or la foy apprehende encore une autre chose en Iesus Christ: c'est qu'il nous apporte l'Esprit de renouvellement.*

God not only the promises which engender trust, but also the commands which compel obedience. It apprehends not only that God wills to receive us in His mercy, but also that He wills to govern and direct all our ways and to reform our whole being.[1]

Therefore though the act of faith which incorporates us in Christ is to be thought of as having a justifying virtue independent of any accompanying repentance or sanctification, it must not be imagined that such faith can exist apart from works.[2] Though we have here to distinguish justification from sanctification without confusion, we must understand the practical implications of the fact that each is merely one aspect of a twofold grace. We are justified for this very end—that afterwards we might worship God in holiness of life.[3] Typical of Calvin's insistence on sanctification as the inevitable accompaniment of justifying faith is his interpretation of the meaning of the wedding garment in the parable of the King's wedding feast—a passage which could lend itself to an extremely one-sided emphasis on justification alone. "As to the wedding garment, is it faith, or is it a holy life? This is a useless controversy, for faith cannot be separated from good works, nor do good works proceed from any other source than from faith. But Christ intended only to state that the Lord calls us on the express condition of our being renewed by the Spirit after His image, and that, in order to remain permanently in His house, we must "put off the old man with his pollutions" (Col. 3 : 9, Eph. 4 : 22) and lead a new life, that the garment may correspond to so honourable a calling."[4]

---

[1] Serm. on Matt. 3 : 1–2, etc., C.O. 46 : 496–7. *Iesus Christ nous est donné . . . pour iustice, et sanctification. . . . Ainsi donc non sans cause i'ay dit que la foy non seulement apprehende que Dieu nous est pitoyable, et qu'il nous veut recevoir à merci, mais quant et quant qu'il nous veut gouverner, et qu'il veut tellement reformer la corruption de nostre nature, que son Esprit nous gouverne en toute iustice.*

[2] Comm. on Ps. 103 : 3, C.O. 32 : 75. *Nam hi sunt gratuitae veniae effectus, quod Deus nos spiritu suo gubernans, concupiscentias carnis mortificat, et nos purgat a vitiis, veramque piae et rectae vitae sanitatem restituit.*

[3] Comm. on Rom. 6 : 2, C.O. 49 : 104. Cf. serm. on Gal. 5 : 22–6, C.O. 51 : 50. *Nous disons que Iesus Christ ne nous est pas seulement donné à fin que par son moyen nous obtenions remission de nos pechez devant Dieu: mais c'est à ce qu'estans regenerez par son sainct Esprit nous cheminions en nouveauté de vie.*

[4] Comm. on Matt. 22 : 11, C.O. 45 : 401.

Chapter IV

The self-offering of the Church in thankful response

1. The sanctification of the Church involves the priestly self-offering of the Church

THOUGH the Church has been once-for-all consecrated in Christ to participate in His royal priesthood, Calvin frequently appeals to men to consecrate themselves, echoing in various ways the Apostolic appeal to "present your bodies a living sacrifice holy and acceptable to God, which is your reasonable service."[1] Sanctification is not only a gift to be received, but is also a demand laid upon us.[2] It involves not only participating by faith in all the power and grace which have their source in Christ, but also dedicating ourselves entirely to God in body and soul,[3] offering ourselves to God in a true sacrifice of thanksgiving, yielding up ourselves to be conformed to Jesus Christ in His death and resurrection, renouncing the world and all our sins.[4]

The sanctification of the Church in Christ therefore involves the self-offering of the Church to God through Christ. All this is beautifully and fully expressed in the prayer with which Calvin closes one of his lectures on Malachi 2 : 9. "Grant, Almighty God, that since Thou hast deigned to take us as a priesthood to Thyself, and hast chosen us when we were not only in the lowest condition, but even profane and alien to all holiness, and hast consecrated us to thyself by Thy Holy Spirit, that we may offer ourselves as holy

---

[1] Rom. 12 : 1.

[2] Comm. on Rom. 12 : 1, C.O. 49 : 234. *Hoc ergo principium recti ad bona opera cursus est, si intelligamus nos esse Domino consecratos. . . . Itaque duo sunt hic consideranda. . . . Primum nos esse Domini: deinde eo ipso sacros esse oportere, quia hoc Dei sanctitate indignum est, ut illi quidpiam offeratur non prius consecratum.*

[3] Comm. on 2 Cor. 7 : 1, C.O. 50 : 84. *Ergo ut te rite sanctifices Deo, et corpus et animam illi in solidum dicare oportet.*

[4] Comm. on 1 Thess. 4 : 3, C.O. 52 : 161. *Quid valeat nomen sanctificationis, iam alibi saepius dictum est, nempe ut renuntiantes mundo, et carnis inquinamentis exuti, nos Deo velut in sacrificium offeramus: nihil enim illi offerri decet, nisi purum ac sanctum.*

victims to Thee; O grant that we may bear in mind our office and our calling, and sincerely devote ourselves to Thy service, and so present to Thee our efforts and our labours, that Thy name may be truly glorified in us, and that it may really appear that we have been ingrafted into the body of Thy only-begotten Son; and as He is the chief and the only true and perpetual priest, may we become partakers of that priesthood with which Thou hast been pleased to honour Him, so that He may take us as associates to Himself; and thus may Thy name be perpetually glorified by the whole body as well as by the Head.—Amen."[1]

The Christian man, then, in all that he does, should regard himself as acting in the capacity of a priest, offering both himself and all his works and possessions in a sacrificial act of thanksgiving at the altar of God's grace. Frequently Calvin's phraseology in his prayers implies that the Christian man must strive to devote himself or "deliver up" himself wholly to God and to consecrate himself and all his members to the service of the Word of God.[2] "Grant, Almighty God, that as Thou hast made us a royal priesthood in Thy Son, that we may daily offer to Thee spiritual sacrifices (*spirituales hostias*), and be devoted (*sacri*) to Thee both in body and soul."[3]

2. Our self-offering involves wholehearted self-immolation

In making this priestly offering of our service to God we must remember that the acceptability of the sacrifice depends upon the consecration of the priest. Therefore no sacrifice that we can offer, even in the name of Christ, is pleasing to God unless it be given from a heart devoted to the praise and glory of God. Therefore Calvin as a first condition of living the Christian life constantly appeals for the wholehearted devotion of the self to God without dissimulation. In the story of Cain and Abel, the verse about Abel's sacrifice reads, "The Lord was pleased with Abel and his gifts." "He begins with the person," Calvin comments, and then adds: "We offer first ourselves, and then all that we have."[4]

[1] Comm. in loc. Amst. Edn. Vol. 5, p. 42.
[2] Cf. e.g. comm. on Zech. 8 : 13, 7 : 4–9; on Micah 5 : 10–15. Amst. Ed. Vol. 5, pp. 510, 500, 325.
[3] Comm. on Zech. 3 : 4, Amst. Edn. Vol. 5, p. 478.
[4] Comm. on Hag. 2 : 11–15, C.O. 44 : 114–15.

The basis of the Christian life is the willing sacrifice of the heart, apart from which all our good works and virtue are in vain. "For the virtue of the virtues, the source and fountain of all holiness, justice and upright dealing, is that our aim is towards God, that we seek His honour, that we belong to Him, and that it is He who governs us."[1]

No one has emphasised more than Calvin our duty to serve God in daily life and in outward conduct. We must let God control not only the affections of our hearts but also our feet and our hands and our substance. We must love our neighbour as well as our Lord. Yet at the same time no one could insist more than Calvin that unless at the same time our hearts are so reformed that we can serve God with a true inward motive proceeding from an unfeigned love of God, and with a pure affection, then any measure of outward reformation of life to which we may have attained even with the greatest effort is worthy only of being called a vain hypocrisy displeasing in the sight of God.[2] It is not enough to abstain in outward conduct from lending our hands to evil doings and our feet to evil ways unless we at the same time purify our hearts from evil affections. In this matter of reforming the life in order to obey the will of God the heart must step out well in front of the feet and the hands, and must keep going on ahead.[3]

Calvin uses the adjective "*rond*" to describe the heart which is thus devoted wholly to the service of God with no reserve of any kind. To serve God with all our heart and all our soul is to serve God with "*rondeur*" and "*integrité*," a quality of heart which Calvin frequently refers to as if it were the one virtue to be aimed at by those who would serve God well. To have *rondeur* of heart means freedom from all hypocrisy or doubleness. It means that there is no sphere of inward affection that is given over to the

---

[1] Serm. on Deut. 8 : 3–9, C.O. 26 : 609.

[2] Serm. on Deut. 5 : 17, C.O. 26 : 333. *Nous aurons mal profité en l'eschole de Dieu, si nous gardons seulement nos mains de mal faire, et que nos coeurs cependant ne soyent point reformez.*

[3] Serm. on Deut. 5 : 8–10, C.O. 26 : 268. *Nous sommes aussi admonnestez de venir à Dieu avec une affection pure et droite. Car ce n'est point assez que nous ayons retenu nos pieds, et nos mains, et nos yeux de mal faire: mais il faut que le coeur marche devant, et que Dieu soit servi de nous en vraye affection: et ceste affection-la ne doit point estre contrainte: mais doit proceder d'une vraye amour de Dieu.* Cf. serm. on Deut. 26 : 16–19, C.O. 28 : 283. *Ce n'est point donc assez d'appliquer nos mains et nos pieds à bien faire: mais il faut que nostre coeur marche en premier degré. Car si nous servons à Dieu par force, tout cela ne sera rien.*

devotion of anything other than God, not the least secret regret at being committed wholly to God, and no hidden reserve of possible energy that could be put into any channel other than the service of God. It means, to use Calvin's own illustration, that there is no little hidden "back shop" in which a side line of business is carried on with secret customers—or to use a more modern expression, that there is nothing "under the counter" to save it from being thrown into this wholehearted sacrifice of heart and life to God. When the Scripture describes Job as a "sound" man (Fr. *entier*) Calvin interprets this adjective as denoting this quality of *rondeur*.[1]

This integrity of heart is a gift of God. It comes when Jesus Christ is allowed to reign without resistance or reserve or dispute, for the Lord Himself seeks to possess our affections at their deepest level.[2] Calvin notes that Job had not only "soundness (*rondeur et integrité*)" in heart, but also "uprightness (*droiteur*)" in outward conduct, and from this combination of "sound and upright" he draws the lesson that wherever there is this true integrity of heart it is bound to produce the fruits of godly and upright conduct.[3] The service rendered to God which arises from such integrity of heart Calvin calls a "spiritual service such as is commanded in Holy Scripture."[4] Only such service is acceptable to God.[5] Realising therefore that our outward members act only as they are moved by the heart,[6] and that God judges our actions

[1] Cf. e.g. the following: serm. on Deut. 26 : 16–19, C.O. 28 : 284. *Moyse ne parle simplement de l'affection: mais il veut que le coeur soit rond et pur. "Tu me servira donc de tout ton coeur et de toute ton ame," c'est à dire, en integrité: que nous ne soyons point doubles, comme on en verra d'aucuns qui auront quelque belle monstre, mais cela s'escoule tantost: et puis il y a quelque arriere boutique, qu'ils ne serviront à Dieu qu'à regret. Il faut donc que le coeur se desploye devant Dieu, et que nous luy presentions nos pensees, et nos desirs, et que nous tendions à nous assuiettir du tout à luy. Voilà comme il sera servi et honoré: voire, non pas à nostre guise, mais selon sa Loy.* And serm. on Job 1 : 1, C.O. 33 : 27.

[2] Serm. on 1 Tim. 4 : 1–3, C.O. 53 : 345. *Que nous cognoissions qu'en premier lieu nostre Seigneur veut posseder nos affections et comme nos entrailles, qu'il veut là regner et avoir son siege. Et ainsi mettons peine et efforçons-nous de nous nettoyer de tout feintise.*

[3] Serm. on Job 1 : 1, C.O. 33 : 29. Cf. serm. on Deut. 26 : 16–19, C.O. 28 : 284. *Si nostre coeur estoit du tout adonné à Dieu, l'execution suyvroit quant et quant.*

[4] As opposed to a *service desguisé et bastard.* Serm. on 1 Tim. 4 : 1–3, C.O. 53 : 345.

[5] Comm. on Ps. 119 : 80, C.O. 32 : 249. *Hic autem pronuntiat spiritus Dei nullum placere Deo obsequium, nisi quod ex cordis integritate profectum sit.*

[6] Comm. on Matt. 5 : 29, C.O. 45 : 180. *Si purus esset animus, oculos quoque et manus haberet sibi obsequentes, quibus certum est nullum inesse proprium motum.*

according to the disposition of the heart, we must begin all our efforts at reformation of life by making it our first aim to attain by the grace of God this inward integrity.[1]

This self-offering implies a readiness to go to extreme lengths in sacrifice, in conformity with the death of Christ. Christ, in consecrating Himself to His royal priesthood, offered Himself in death upon the Cross. In the same way our consecration of ourselves as royal priests should mean not simply a superficial dedication of everything we do to God, but rather the complete offering of our lives in face of the possibility that God's will for us might also be excruciating sacrifice.[2] In this self-offering we are not only priests but victims. "Grant," says Calvin in the prayer already quoted, "that we may offer ourselves as holy victims to Thee."[3] Since it is by Christ's death that we are consecrated to God, we must be willing to "live and die to Him."[4] We must carry on life in our hands always offering it to God as a sacrifice, ready to retain it as long as He leaves it in our hands, and ready to yield it up to His disposal should He demand it at any moment.[5] To yield to God our life in this way, willing to endure whatever cross or chastisement He may bring upon us is "the sacrifice of obedience" that is acceptable to Him.[6]

3. Our self-offering can sanctify all our earthly activity as an offering to God

When the wholehearted offering of ourselves is made in a response of faith and gratitude to Christ, then the rest of life

---

[1] Serm. on Deut. 10 : 12–14, C.O. 27 : 35–6. *Il faut commencer par le coeur.* Cf. comm. on 1 Tim. 2 : 9, C.O. 52 : 275. *Quamquam ab affectu semper est incipiendum.* Also serm. on Tit. 1 : 15–16, C.O. 54 : 492.

[2] Comm. on Ps. 44 : 23, C.O. 31 : 447. *Sit haec continua nostra meditatio, bibendum esse calicem quem nobis porrigit Deus, nec posse Christianum esse, nisi qui se in sacrificium Deo offert.*

[3] Comm. on Mal. 2 : 9, Amst. Edn. Vol. 5, p. 588. Cf. serm. on 1 Cor. 10 : 15–18, C.O. 49 : 670. *Car auiourd'huy nous ne sommes point seulement comme les Levites, portans les vaisseaux du temple: mais nous sommes les vaisseaux mesmes du temple, nous sommes mesmes les temples de Dieu, nous sommes les sacrifices.*

[4] Comm. on 1 Pet. 3 : 18, C.O. 55 : 264.

[5] Comm. on John 12 : 25, C.O. 47 : 289. *Nam hic legitimus est amandae vitae modus, si in ea manemus quamdiu Domino visum fuerit, et eiusdem arbitrio subinde parati sumus ab ea migrare, vel, ut uno verbo dicam, si eam quasi manibus gestantes offerimus Deo in sacrificium.*

[6] Comm. on Phil. 2 : 27, C.O. 52 : 41; cf. comm. on Dan. 3 : 16–18, C.O. 40 : 632.

becomes sanctified as an offering also acceptable to God. When the heart is offered first to God in repentant sacrifice, then all the rest of our works can become sacred offerings.[1] Calvin argues that when our hearts are purified by faith, then "purity is diffused over our works so that they begin to be pleasing to God."[2]

There is no limit to the extent to which sanctity may be diffused throughout all our works and activities through the attitude of our hearts. Calvin finds a great deal of significance in the text in Zechariah 14 : 20: "In that day shall there be upon the bells of the horses, HOLINESS UNTO THE LORD; and the pots in the Lord's house shall be like the bowls before the altar." He reminds us that inscribed upon the tiara of the priest were the words "Holiness to Jehovah." This is the source of the holiness of everything else around him. The mention of the bowls before the altar reminds us that everything in the Temple, even the candlesticks and the incense, are sanctified through the holiness of the priesthood. The inclusion of the pots and horses in the sphere to which this holiness extends reminds us that "nothing would be so profane as not to change its nature," and that the people of God, "whatever they ate or drank . . . would still offer a pure sacrifice to God both in eating and drinking and even in warfare."[3]

This means that in living the Christian life we must never forget that we are always priests consecrated to God and bound to offer whatever we do as a sacrifice. Whether we are engaged in teaching others in the Church, or in helping the poor or our neighbours, or in prayer, we must at the same time regard ourselves as offering therein a priestly oblation to God.[4] Nothing that we do, however good in itself, is acceptable to God unless it is offered

[1] Cf. prayer in comm. on Joel 2 : 14, Amst. Edn. Vol. 5, p. 146.
[2] Comm. on Hag. 2 : 11–15, C.O. 44 : 114. *Cor purgatum est fide: et puritas illa diffunditur ad opera ut incipiant Deo placere.*
[3] Comm. on Zech. 14 : 20, C.O. 44 : 387–9.
[4] Serm. on Matt. 2 : 9–11, C.O. 46 : 351–2. *Et au reste, que tout ce que nous avons, comme nous le tenons de luy, nous luy en facions une oblation sacree. Que celuy qui aura sçavoir cognoisse, voyla mon offrande que ie doy à nostre Seigneur Iesus Christ pour edifier mes prochains. Celuy qui aura receu quelque autre grace ou don, qu'il le communique selon qu'il est enseigné par l'Evangile: ceux qui ont des biens selon le monde, qu'ils en subvienent à leurs prochains: et quand ils en useront avec sobrieté et temperance, qu'ils cognoissent dont ils procedent. Voyla donc comme les dons spirituels et ceux mesmes qui concernent ceste vie transitoire et caduque doyvent estre pleinement dediez à nostre Seigneur Iesus Christ. Et de faict tant les prieres que les ausmones et toutes choses semblables sont appelees sacrifices en l'Escriture saincte.* Cf. comm. on Matt. 26 : 11, C.O. 46 : 695–6.

in this way as a sacrifice of gratitude in response to and in union with Him who has made us a royal priesthood.[1] Nor must we ever forget when we eat and drink and clothe ourselves or even enter our homes that our use of even the mundane gifts of God must be sanctified by the Word of God and prayer, such things being witnesses of His bounty to us in order that we might render thankful homage to Him.[2]

4. Gratitude as the inspiration of our self-offering

Our self-offering must be motivated primarily by gratitude. It is not in any sense propitiatory, but is a eucharistic offering in praise and gladness.[3] In consecrating ourselves to God in all our activity we must remember that it is only through Christ's self-consecration of Himself and Christ's propitiatory offering of Himself that we have been made a royal priesthood, and are worthy to offer anything to God.[4] Therefore in making our offering of ourselves and our activity we have "no other altar but Christ."[5] In the offering which we ourselves make, relying on the sacrifice of Christ, we must have no thought of fulfilling any imperious demand or of winning anything from God in return. Our Christian life therefore must be a voluntary sacrifice offered not merely with right motive and intention but also with a real gladness which arises from the love we have for Him to whom our self-offering is made.[6]

God's glory shines forth most in His free and spontaneous grace. Therefore the response of man to such grace must be a voluntary and spontaneous response of the heart in love. It is only through such spontaneity that all the affections of the heart in true *rondeur* and integrity can be given to God. In a response

---

[1] Serm. on Deut. 8 : 3–9, C.O. 26 : 609. *Car un homme pourra estre chaste, il pourra s'abstenir de toute iniure, de toute fraude et nuisance . . . mais cependant ce ne sera rien sinon qu'il rapporte tout à ceste fin, c'est de se dedier à Dieu en sacrifice.*
[2] Serm. on Deut. 20 : 2–9, C.O. 27 : 607–8; on 1 Cor. 10 : 15–18, C.O. 49 : 664; on Deut. 8 : 10–14, C.O. 611, 617–18.
[3] Cf. Inst. 4 : 18 : 13.
[4] Cf. prayer in comm. Zech. 6 : 15, Amst. Edn. Vol. 5, p. 497.
[5] Prayer in comm. on Hag. 2 : 6–9, Amst. Edn. Vol. 5, p. 450; cf. comm. in loc.
[6] Serm. on Deut. 7 : 7–10, C.O. 26 : 525–6. *David proteste que la Loy de Dieu luy a esté plus douce et plus amiable que miel . . . qu'il s'est dedié du tout à bien faire, et à cheminer selon Dieu. Et ainsi donc pour offrir à Dieu sacrifices volontaires.* Cf. serm. on Deut. 5 : 8–10, C.O. 26 : 267. *Le voulons-nous donc aimer? Voulons-nous estre reformez à son obeissance pour prendre tout nostre plaisir à son service?*

compelled by force or fear alone something would be kept back in reserve. Therefore gratitude enables us to give everything.[1] God, therefore, seeks rather to win us by love, than compel us by threats.[2] He wills that we should come to Him with a frank and serene boldness and that we should take real pleasure in His service. Even when it is a question of conforming our ways in obedience to His Law, such love must be our inspiration and motive, for such love is the meaning of the Law, and true happiness can be found in conforming ourselves thus willingly to His will as it is revealed in the Commandments.[3]

Calvin therefore frequently seeks to incite his congregation to the Christian life by reminding them of what Christ has done for them, and shewing them how impossible it is that anyone should remain impassive to such love.[4] Woe to the man who does not allow the goodness of God to overwhelm him and to constrain him to a complete surrender of the will and heart to God, and to inflame him with a burning affection to serve his Lord![5]

[1] Comm. on Ps. 18 : 2, C.O. 31 : 170. *Notandum vero est, amorem Dei tanquam praecipuum pietatis caput hic poni: quia nulla re melius colitur Deus. Fateor quidem Reverentiae nomine magis exprimi quem illi debemus cultum, ut in suo gradu emineat eius maiestas: sed quia nihil magis requirit quam ut omnes cordis nostri affectus possideat, nullum ei praestantius sacrificium est, quam ubi liberalis et spontanei amoris vinculo nos sibi devinctos tenet: sicuti vicissim nusquam melius, quam in gratuita bonitate, eius gloria refulget.*

[2] Serm. on Deut. 5 : 8–10, C.O. 26 : 269. *Il aime mieux nous gagner par sa bonté, que de nous retenir par menaces.*

[3] Serm. on Deut. 5 : 8–10, C.O. 26 : 266–7. *Iamais (di-ie) nous ne savons que c'est d'observer la Loy de Dieu, et nous reigler selon icelle, que nous ne commencions par cest amour. Et pourquoy? Car Dieu demande des services volontaires, il ne veut pas seulement que nous le servions par une crainte servile: mais il veut que nous y venions d'un courage franc, et alegre, que mesme nous prenions plaisir à l'honorer. Or cela ne se peut faire que nous ne l'aimions. Ainsi notons que le commencement d'obeissance et comme la source, et le fondement, et la racine, c'est cest amour de Dieu, que nous ne soyons point forcez de venir à luy, mais que nous y prenions nostre plaisir singulier: cognoissans aussi que c'est nostre vraye beatitude, et que nous ne demandions sinon d'estre gouvernez selon sa volonté, et d'y estre du tout conformez.* Cf. serm. on Deut. 10 : 12–14, C.O. 27 : 37.

[4] Serm. on Isa. 53 : 9–10, C.O. 35 : 653. *Voyla Iesus Christ, le Fils unique de Dieu, qui est emprisonné, et nous sommes delivrez: il est condamné, et nous sommes absous: il est exposé à toutes vergongnes, et nous sommes establis en honneur: il est descendu aux abysmes d'enfer, et l'ouverture nous est faite au Royaume des cieux. Quand donc nous oyons toutes ces choses, est-il question de nous tenir endormis, nous plaire et nous flatter en nos vices?*

[5] Serm. on Deut. 10 : 12–14, C.O. 27 : 33. *Puis donc que nostre Dieu nous traitte si humainement, quelle ingratitude sera-ce quand nous ne viendrons nous ranger à luy en toute obeissance? . . . Malheur donc, et double malheur sur nous, quand nous ne serons point veincus d'une telle bonté, et que nos coeurs ne seront point enflammez en une droite affection de nous adonner à nostre Dieu . . . et que nous soyons prests, et appareillez de plier sous sa main par tout où il nous voudra tourner.*

5. Fear as the accompaniment of our eucharistic
self-offering

Since our self-offering involves making a solemn and total sacrifice of all that we have and are, Calvin does not forget that in the fulfilment of our royal priesthood we must be inspired by fear and trembling as well as by love and gratitude.

There is a "servile and constrained fear" of God such as the wicked have who dread and flee from the judgment of God which they cannot escape,[1] and such as those have who serve God because they fear damnation.[2] Such servile fear is cast out of the heart by faith and love. There is, however, a true fear of God which must arise and must remain in the human heart whenever God draws near to man in redeeming grace.[3] This fear Calvin also calls "reverence."[4] In contrast to the servile fear which drives us from God, this fear rather inspires us in our trembling to submit ourselves to God in subjection to His will.[5] Calvin describes it in the *Institutes* as a "voluntary fear flowing from reverence of the divine majesty,"[6] but more frequently, at least in his sermons, he insists that such reverential fear for God is inspired mainly by the mercy and fatherly love of God.[7] It is important to note that for Calvin it is the apprehension of God's goodness, and of our utter dependence on His grace that should make the Christian

---

[1] Inst. 1 : 4 : 4. *Nec tum quoque voluntario imbuuntur timore, qui ex divinae maiestatis reverentia fluat, sed tantum servili et coacto, quem illis Dei iudicium extorquet: quod quia effugere nequeunt, exhorrent, sic tamen ut etiam abominentur.* Cf. serm. on Deut. 10 : 12–14, C.O. 27 : 36–7.

[2] Serm. on Deut. 6 : 4–9, C.O. 26 : 440; and in Deut. 8 : 3–9, C.O. 26 : 609.

[3] Serm. on Luke 1 : 11–15, C.O. 46 : 29. *Ainsi quand nous avons cela, que Dieu nous aime, qu'il nous est favorable, voyla toute crainte qui est facilement deschassee de nous. Non pas que nous n'ayons quelque crainte. . . . Notons bien donc que nous ne pouvons pas estre vuides de toute crainte. Encores que Dieu nous testifie qu'il sera nostre pere, et qu'il nous propose sa grace si doucement que rien plus, encores est-il impossible que nous ne le craignions.*

[4] Serm. on Deut. 10 : 12–14, C.O. 27 : 36.

[5] Ibid.

[6] Inst. 1 : 4 : 4 (see above).

[7] Serm. on Deut. 6 : 4–9, C.O. 26 : 440. *D'autant que le Seigneur a esté pitoyable, et qu'on l'a cogneu doux et benin, voila pourquoy il a esté craint et redouté. . . . Il faut que nous ayons cogneu la misericorde de Dieu . . . ou iamais nous ne le pourrons craindre, ni approcher de luy pour le servir.* Serm. on Deut. 8 : 3–9, C.O. 26 : 609. *Il entend la reverence que nous luy portons, non seulement comme à nostre maistre mais comme à nostre pere.*

believer tremble, and yet even in and through his trembling draw him nearer to God.[1]

Fear and gratitude are thus inseparable as the motives by which we live our Christian lives.[2] Since our fear of God is inspired by God's goodness and fatherhood, it follows that it is always mixed with love towards God. Reverence for God unaccompanied by love towards Him would immediately turn into the servile fear which drives men away from God rather than towards Him, or it could turn to a hatred which desires to dethrone God.[3] It is equally true to say that there cannot be true love and service of God unless true fear of God is also present in the heart of the one who professes to love and serve.[4] Calvin underlines the plea of Moses that God desires to be served and honoured and also loved. Such reverence and love must always be joined together in service. Without the one, the other cannot be genuine.[5]

6. Gratitude and fear must be dominated by desire for the glory of God

Both the gratitude and the fear which inspire our self-offering to God must find their true fulfilment and expression in one overmastering desire—zeal for the glory of God. It was for the glory of God that man was created, and God seeks always in the

---

[1] Serm. on Matt. 3 : 9–10, etc., C.O. 46 : 543. *Et en estions nous dignes? Non: et pourtant apprenons de cheminer en crainte et solicitude, et cognoissons que tout ainsi que Dieu a desployé sur nous une telle bonté, c'est bien raison que nous cognoissons que nous tenons tout de luy: et le cognoissant, que nous tremblions sous son Empire, que nous ne levions point les cornes, et n'ayons nulle presomption.*

[2] Serm. on Deut. 8 : 3–9, C.O. 206 : 609. *Ceste crainte donc que Dieu requierte, est coniointe avec une amour cordiale.*

[3] Serm. on Deut. 10 : 12–14, C.O. 27 : 37. *Ceste reverence-la demande aussi bien l'amour. Car Dieu veut estre honoré d'une affection cordiale. Si nous adorons sa maiesté, et cependant qu'elle nous soit terrible, et que nous en soyons effrayez: nous voudrions qu'il ne fust plus Dieu, pour l'arracher de son siege s'il nous estoit possible. . . . Ainsi il est impossible que nous craignions Dieu sinon en l'aimant, ie di que nous luy portions une reverence droite, et que nous soyons affectionnez envers luy, et que nous sentions quelle est sa bonté, et que c'est là qu'il nous faut cercher tout nostre bien. Si donc nous n'avons ceste amour, la reverence aussi sera nulle, elle sera aneantie.*

[4] Serm. on Deut. 6 : 3–15, C.O. 26 : 458. *La crainte donc va en premier lieu: . . . Sachons que Dieu n'acceptera nul service de nous, sinon que devant toutes choses nous ayons apprins de le craindre, c'est à dire, de luy porter une telle reverence, que nous demandions de luy obeir.*

[5] Serm. on Deut. 10 : 12–14, C.O. 27 : 36.

heart of the redeemed an ardent zeal to minister to His glory.[1] Indeed, "there is no part of our life, and no action so minute that it ought not to be directed to the glory of God."[2] And in the more mundane actions of life such as eating and drinking it becomes all the more necessary to think of God and to relate our activity consciously to His name and His glory, that we might not sin against Him by doing anything without such an end in view.[3] If we can become consciously concerned to maintain and expand the glory and honour of earthly causes and earthly rulers when we are called upon to do so, we should be far more concerned with maintaining, even if it had to be only in language, the glory of our heavenly king, and such concern should give real meaning to the confession and praise of His name in public worship—a practice which can otherwise seem a trifling matter.[4]

This desire for the glory of God should be so intense that it should turn to anguish of heart when the honour of God is wounded.[5] It ought so to consume us that, as in the example of our Lord Himself, no amount of suffering will make us shrink from maintaining it.[6] All human relationships, however precious and near, must be renounced, if in maintaining them we are in any way allied with those who are against the Lord.[7] All our de-

---

[1] Serm. on Job 1 : 5, C.O. 33 : 56. *Or le principal est, qu'il nous faut regarder comme nous avons à glorifier Dieu en toute nostre vie: car voila aussi pourquoi nous sommes creez, et que nous vivons. Quand donc nous voudrons que nostre vie soit approuvee de Dieu, que nous tendions tousiours à ce but-la, qu'il soit benit et glorifié de nous, et que nous ayons un tele zele et une affection ardante de servir à sa gloire.*
[2] Comm. on 1 Cor. 10 : 31, C.O. 49 : 471. Cf. serm. on Acts 1 : 1–4, C.O. 48 : 590. *Car tout ce que nous avons, voire iusqu'au bout des ongles mesmes, deveroit tendre là, que la gloire de Dieu apparust et reluisist par tout.*
[3] Cf. serm. on Job 1 : 2–5, C.O. 33 : 41–2.
[4] Comm. on Matt. 10 : 32, C.O. 45 : 291. *Porro Christi confessio, etsi a maiore hominum parte, quasi res levis negligitur, hic tamen in praecipuo Dei cultu et singulari pietatis exercitio censetur, et merito. Nam si terreni reges pro gloriae suae amplitudine tuenda augendisque opibus subditos suos ad arma vocant, cur non lingua saltem asserent fideles coelestis regis sui gloriam?*
[5] Serm. on Job 2 : 7–10, C.O. 33 : 125. *Ainsi donc Iob n'a peu souffrir de tels blasphemes, comme aussi il est dit au Pseaume (69 : 10), que le zele de la maison de Dieu nous doit ronger le coeur, et nous doit consumer, et l'opprobre qu' on luy fait, doit revenir sur nous: qu'il fait que nous soyons angoissez en cela, quand nous voyons que l'honneur de Dieu est blessé.*
[6] Comm. on Ps. 69 : 10, C.O. 31 : 641–2.
[7] Serm. on Gal. 5 : 11–14, C.O. 51 : 13. *Quand les hommes bataillent contre Dieu, qu'il nous leur faut estre tellement ennemis mortels, que là nous oublions et parentage et amitié, et tout ce qu'il y a: car autrement nous ne rendons pas à Dieu nostre devoir en façon que ce soit, quand il se nomme pere, et qu'il nous fait cest honneur de nous tenir pour ses enfans, c'est pour le moins que sa gloire nous soit recommandee par dessus toutes choses.*

sires for personal ends, no matter how good and noble these ends may be, must be entirely subordinated to this desire for the glory of God. We must subordinate to this all-consuming aim not only the desire for our own safety,[1] but also the desire for our sanctification.[2] Even our concern for our own salvation must never become of such importance to us that we forget that all that matters in this world and the next is the glory of God. Why should all the world not perish, including ourselves, rather than that the name of God should be brought to dishonour?[3] It is right indeed, that a man should have an anxious concern over the salvation of his own soul, but he must never forget that his personal salvation matters only because it is bound up with the glory of God, and it tends to that end.[4] Nor must he ever forget that the cause of the glory of God is at stake while his neighbour remains unredeemed and unresponsive to God's grace. A Christian must love his neighbour, but even to love our neighbour is not to be regarded as an end in itself. Such love must find its impulse in zeal for the glory of God. Indeed, any indifference towards the salvation of our neighbour is to be regarded as indifference to God's glory, for our neighbour is His property and possession by right. Thus if we have any zeal for God's honour we will see to it that His possessions are kept intact.[5]

[1] Comm. on Ps. 109 : 26, C.O. 32 : 157. *Quod diligenter notandum est, quia etsi cupimus omnes Dei manu servari, vix tamen centesimus quisque scopum illustrandae Dei gloriae sibi proponit. Atqui eam pluris esse nobis decebat, quam propriam salutem: sicuti ordine praecellit.*

[2] Comm. on Eph. 1 : 4, C.O. 51 : 147. *Gloria Dei summus est finis, cui nostra sanctificatio subordinatur.*

[3] Serm. on Deut. 9 : 15–21, C.O. 26: 693–4. *Nous devons preferer la gloire de Dieu non seulement à tous biens corporels, mais au propre salut de nos ames . . . Moyse se contente d'estre ravi en ce zele, qu'il aime mieux que luy, et tout le monde perisse, que de voir le nom de Dieu estre mocqué.* Cf. serm. on Luke 1 : 21–30, C.O. 46 : 68. *Il n'y a ni industrie, ni sagesse, ni vertu, ni rien qui soit, qui puisse respondre devant la gloire infinie de Dieu, et qu'il faut que tout soit englouti et aneanti.*

[4] Serm. on Gal. 5 : 11–14, C.O. 51 : 13. *Et puis quand il conioint tellement sa gloire avec nostre salut, que nous ne pouvons procurer l'un sans l'autre, et mesmes nous n'apporterons ni profit ni dommage à Dieu, quand nous serons les plus grans zelateurs qu'il est possible pour maintenir sa querelle: il n'a nulle necessité de nous: il ne faut pas qu'il emprunte nostre aide: mais il nous constitue ses procureurs. Et à quelle fin? À ce que chacun de nous cerche son profit non point de ce monde, ni des choses corruptibles: mais pour le salut eternel de nos ames.*

[5] Serm. on Deut. 22 : 1–4, C.O. 28 : 8–9. Cf. p. 29. *Or maintenant ie verray un povre homme qui s'esgare, ainsi comme s'il estoit une beste perdue, et que Dieu fust frustré de son droict, que sa possession diminuast d'autant. Il est vray que nous ne le pouvons pas enrichir: mais tant y a qu'il a monstré combien nous luy sont chers, quand il nous a rachetez par le sang de nostre Seigneur Iesus Christ. Ie voy donc*

7. Our self-offering is possible only by the power of the Holy Spirit

It must be emphasised again here that this wholehearted response in priestly self-offering is possible only by the power of the Holy Spirit and indeed is the work of the Holy Spirit within us. It is by the Spirit that the blood of Christ the High Priest which was poured out in His self-consecration on the Cross is applied to cleanse His people,[1] and that thus our sense of guilt is removed and access opened up for us into the presence of God.[2] The Spirit thus "consecrates us to God."[3] It is by the Holy Spirit that God unites our heart in integrity, gathering it to Himself, and holding it together in steadfast obedience.[4] It is by the power of the Holy Spirit that our minds and hearts are drawn towards Christ,[5] and we are "formed (*formare*)" and made ready to yield ourselves to God.[6] "No one is fit to offer sacrifices to God, or to do any other service (*cultum*) but him who has been moulded (*formatus*) by the hidden operation of the Spirit. Willingly indeed we offer ourselves and our all to God, and build His Temple: but whence this voluntary action, except that the Lord subdues us and thus renders us teachable and obedient."[7]

---

la possession de Dieu qui s'en va ruiner, et ie n'en tien conte: cela est perdu quant à luy par ma faute: quelle excuse y aura-il? . . . Il faut bien que nous taschions de procurer que Dieu demeure en son estat entier, et que ce qui est de sa maison ne s'appetisse point, c'est à dire, de son Eglise: mais que le tout luy soit conservé.

[1] Serm. on Matt. 27 : 11–26, C.O. 46 : 901–2.
[2] Comm. on Ps. 51 : 9, C.O. 31 : 516.
[3] Comm. on 1 Cor. 1 : 2, C.O. 49 : 308.
[4] Comm. on Ps. 86 : 11, C.O. 31 : 795.
[5] Serm. on Acts 2 : 1–4, C.O. 48 : 634.
[6] Comm. on Rom. 7 : 18, C.O. 49 : 132.
[7] Comm. on Hag. 1 : 14, C.O. 44 : 97.

Chapter V

The pattern of sanctification in the death and resurrection of Christ

1. The life of Jesus Christ as the pattern to which we must conform

IN his introductory remarks to the section on the Christian Life in the *Institutes*, giving the Scriptural exhortations thereto and showing their superiority to any that the schools of philosophy could bring forth, Calvin writes, "Scripture . . . after showing us that we have degenerated from our true origin, viz. the law of our Creator, adds that Christ, through whom we have returned to favour with God, is set before us as a model, the image of which our lives should express."[1] Throughout his *Sermons* he frequently refers to Christ as the *"patron"* after which the children of God must be modelled (*configurez*) or to which they must be conformed (*conformez*). It is true that this word *"patron"* can in some contexts be used to signify "patron saint" or "champion,"[2] but its frequent use along with such words as *"miroir"* and *"image"* and *"exemple"* shows that Calvin more often means by the use of it to uphold Jesus Christ in His human life as the pattern of true Christian living.[3] The purpose of Christ in making us His disciples is that He might conform us to the imitation of Himself.[4]

For Calvin, the likeness of Christ to ourselves is the "main

---

[1] Inst. 3 : 6 : 3 . . . *Christum . . . nobis propositum esse exemplar, cuius formam in vita nostra exprimamus.*

[2] Cf. Latin *patronus*—a technical term for any Roman under whose name a freed slave was adopted into citizenship.

[3] Cf e.g. serm. on Deut. 8 : 10–14, C.O. 26 : 611. *Nous avons nostre patron, et image en nostre Seigneur Iesus Christ, auquel il nous faut estre conformez, si nous voulons estre enfans de Dieu.* Serm. on Deut. 8 : 1–4, C.O. 26 : 590. *Il . . . nous propose Iesus Christ pour exemple. Car combein qu'il soit le miroir, et le patron de toute iustice: si a-il fallu neantmoins qu'il passast parmi les verges de Dieu.* Serm. on Job 4 : 7–11, C.O. 33 : 196. *Nostre Seigneur Iesus Christ, qui est le Chef, et le miroir et le patron de tous les enfans de Dieu.* Cf. also serm. on Matt. 27 : 27–44, C.O. 46 : 906; on Matt. 2 : 23, C.O. 46 : 457; and on Matt. 26 : 36–9, C.O. 46 : 839. *La regle et le miroir de tout iustice sainctete et perfection.*

[4] Comm. on Matt. 11 : 29, C.O. 45 : 322. *Potius enim . . . nos ad imitationem sui format.*

support of our faith."[1] The struggle with temptation and evil in which the Son of God was involved through the Incarnation was the same struggle in which each of us is involved by reason of our humanity.[2] The circumstances of His human life were shaped to make His life so like our own that His example might be relevant for all our practical problems.[3] Therefore we can confidently look to the example of the historic Jesus for guidance in the details of such problems.[4] We can "follow His footsteps" knowing that He is our "leader and instructor" in the midst of the dangers and temptations that He had in common with us, and that His victory is the pledge to us that those who trust in God as He did will never fail.[5]

Calvin fully realises the dangers of this doctrine of the *imitatio Christi* and is constantly trying to guard against them. There are many things which Christ did in which we should not attempt to imitate Him.[6] "We ought therefore to exercise in this respect a right judgment."[7] We must remember that we have to conform to Christ not in those actions that are the outcome of His majesty and the expression of His divine nature, such as His fasting forty days, or His cleansing of the Temple, or His miracles, but rather in faith and patience and obedience[8]—the qualities that are connec-

---

[1] Comm. on 2 Cor. 13 : 4, C.O. 50 : 150, *Quod si facimus humanam Christi naturam ita nostrae dissimilem, eversum est praecipuum fidei nostrae fundamentum.*

[2] Comm. on Matt. 4 : 3–4, C.O. 45 : 131.

[3] Comm. on Heb. 12 : 3, C.O. 55 : 172. *Una enim haec cogitatio ad vincendas omnes tentationes sufficere debet, quum intelligimus nos filii Dei esse comites: et eum qui supra nos adeo eminebat, voluisse ad conditionem nostram descendere, ut suo nos exemplo animaret.*

[4] Comm. on Col. 3 : 13, C.O. 52 : 122; on 2 Cor. 10 : 1, C.O. 50 : 112–13; on Heb. 2 : 12, C.O. 55 : 29; serm. on Matt. 26 : 40 ff, C.O. 46 : 847.

[5] Comm. on Heb. 2 : 13, C.O. 55 : 30. *Porro non leviter hoc animare nos debet ad fidendum Deo, quod Christum habemus ducem et magistrum. Quis enim vereatur eius vestigia sequendo ne erret? Periculum, inquam, non est ne fides nostra sit irrita quam habemus cum Christo communem, quem scimus non posse falli.* Serm. on Matt. 2 : 23, etc., C.O. 46 : 456. *Car sans la personne de Iesus Christ, quelle addresse aurions-nous pour nous guider? Comment est-ce que nous pourrions tenir le chemin pour parvenir au Royaume des cieux?* Comm. on Matt. 4 : 4, C.O. 45 : 131.

[6] Comm. on John 13 : 15, C.O. 47 : 309. *Neque enim omnia eius facta promiscue ad imitationem trahi convenit.*

[7] Ibid. Comm. on 1 Pet. 2 : 21, C.O. 55 : 249.

[8] Ibid. "Christ's patience is what we have to imitate." Cf. serm. on Matt. 4 : 2–4, C.O. 46 : 607–8. *Or ce n'est point sans cause aussi qu'il dit qu'il nous faut estre configurez à son image, non point en tout et par tout, mais en ce qui appartient au service de Dieu, à la foy et patience, et à l'obeissance que nous devons à Dieu. En tout cela, di-ie, il nous faut bien estre configurez a nostre Seigneur Iesus Christ. Mais en ce qui est de sa maieste (comme le iusne dont il est fait yci mention)*

ted with self-denial and cross-bearing. Moreover we must remember that we are to be "imitators not apes,"[1] and true imitation will consist rather in acting according to the spirit that moved Jesus to action rather than in an exact reduplication of the details of His outward life. His washing of the disciples' feet should inspire us not to institute an annual ecclesiastical ceremony of feet-washing, but to be ready always to serve our neighbour.[2] His cleansing of the Temple should inspire us to an inward groaning zeal for the reform of the Church and to a vocal demand for it to the right authority, but should never make us go so far as to forget our place and take action into our own hands. In seeking to imitate Christ we must always remember the difference between Himself and us in calling, station, and historical circumstances.[3]

2. The Cross and Resurrection as the main features in the pattern of Christian Life

The main feature in the pattern of the life of Christ to which we are to be conformed in our own Christian life is the Cross. The life of Jesus from His infancy was marked by cross-bearing,[4] and involved Him in a straining towards His cross. It is primarily in the pattern which He worked out in submitting to His death and resurrection that Christ's sanctification is meant to be the outward pattern of our sanctification. Indeed, Calvin can say that in submitting to His cross Jesus submitted to what was simply God's ordinary way of dealing with His people in this matter of

---

ce n'est pas à dire qu'il nous fale en cela conformer à luy: car autrement il nous faudroit ressusciter les morts, guerir les malades, donner clarte aux aveugles, faire marcher les boiteux: brief, il nous faudroit changer les hommes, et muer l'eau en vin. Et où en viendrions-nous? Mais d'autant que le Fils de Dieu nous est proposé pour exemple, et miroir de foy, d'obeissance, de patience, et de choses semblables, voyla en quoy il nous faut observer qu'il a monstré le chemin à tous fideles, afin que nous puissions marcher par les traces qu'il nous a monstrees.

[1] Comm. on John 13 : 15, C.O. 47 : 309.

[2] Ibid. p. 310.

[3] Comm. on Matt. 21 : 12, C.O. 45 : 580; cf. serm. on Gal. 5 : 11–14, C.O. 51 : 13.

[4] Serm. on Matt. 2 : 23, C.O. 46 : 451-2. Dieu a voulu que des le commencement nostre Seigneur Iesus Christ pour estre redempteur du monde, fust subiet à toutes povretez, et mesme à l'opprobre du monde. Car il n'a point falu qu'il fust seulement crucifié une fois, mais qu'il commençast dés son enfance, et voyla pourquoy il a este transporté en Egypt.

sanctification.[1] It is therefore principally in His bearing His cross
and patient submission to His suffering that Christ as our Head is
to us a "mirror of sanctity" and the example we are to imitate,[2] for
God has predestined all whom He adopts as His children to be
conformed to the image of Jesus Christ, especially in this matter
of bearing their cross as Christ bore His.[3]

Since we are destined to be conformed to Christ, we must
expect to have to bear the Cross as He did. What Jesus Christ
suffered must be fulfilled in all His members.[4] It is only right that
the course which God has begun with Christ the first-born He
should continue with all His children.[5] If we expect ultimately
to share in heavenly glory with Christ we must not be surprised if
He allots us the same hard way of entering into glory as He
Himself took.[6] If our Lord's obedience had to be tested and proved
in suffering, we should expect our own obedience to be so tested.[7]
Even though we need not all expect to die as martyrs nevertheless
there is a conformity to the image of Christ in a sharing of suffering and danger that is common to all the Church through which
disciples become "configured to their Master."[8] Therefore since
we are members of Christ, the course of our sanctification in

[1] Cf. Heb. 2 : 10–11 and Calvin's comm. in loc. C.O. 55 : 27. *Nondum tamen
videtur constare quod intendit, decuisse Christum hoc modo consecrari: sed hoc
pendet ex ordinaria ratione quam Deus in tractandis suis tenet. Vult enim eos
variis aerumnis exerceri, totamque vitam sub cruce degere. Christum ergo ut est
primogenitus, opportuit cruce inaugurari in suum primatum: quando ista est communis omnium lex et conditio.*

[2] Comm. on Isa. 53 : 7, C.O. 37 : 260; serm. on Isa. 53 : 9–10, C.O. 35 : 652.

[3] Cf. Rom. 8 : 28–9, and Calvin's comm. in loc., C.O. 49 : 160. *Summa porro
est, gratuitam adoptionem, in qua salus nostra consistit, ab hoc altero decreto
inseparabilem esse, quod nos ferendae cruci addixit: quia nemo coelorum haeres esse
potest, qui non ante unigenito Dei filio fuerit conformis.* Cf. serm. on Job 2 : 7–10,
C.O. 33 : 121. *Car voila à quelle condition (i.e. bearing the Cross) Dieu nous a entez
au corps de son Fils, ainsi qu'il est le patron general de tous fideles, comme S. Paul
en traitte au huictieme des Romains.* Cf. serm. on Deut. 8 : 10–14, C.O. 26 : 611;
on 2 Tim. 2 : 8–13, C.O. 54 : 132.

[4] Serm. on 2 Tim. 1 : 8–9, C.O. 54 : 44.

[5] Inst. 3 : 8 : 1.

[6] Comm. on 1 Pet. 4 : 12, C.O. 55 : 278. *Est quidem et illa gaudii materia,
quod Deus ad fidei nostrae probationem, persequutionibus nos exercet: sed haec
altera gaudii species longe exsuperat, quod in suum ordinem nos aggregat filius Dei,
ut in beatam coelestis gloriae societatem nos secum adducat.* Comm. on Rom.
8 : 17, C.O. 49 : 151.

[7] Serm. on Deut. 8 : 1–4, C.O. 26 : 590.

[8] Comm. on Matt. 20 : 23, C.O. 45 : 554–5. *Quia discipuli erant, necesse erat
magistro configurari. . . . Nam etsi multi fideles suo fato, non violenta, nec sangu-
inaria morte intereunt, omnibus tamen commune est (sicuti Paulus ad Rom. 8 : 29
docet) conformari ad Christi imaginem. Itaque tota vita oves sunt mactationi des-
tinatae.*

living the Christian life must be the same "sort of perpetual death" that marked out the career of Jesus Christ our Head, a career in which we must never forget that in our case as in His what is sown in death will be gained in life.[1]

The pattern of our sanctification in Christ to which we are to be conformed is not one of unrelieved suffering and cross-bearing. The whole process of our conformity to Christ in His Cross moves towards the final goal of our being "sanctified with Christ in glory"[2] and of being made conformable to His immortality and glory.[3] Christ did not rise for His own sake but for ours and therefore in His resurrection the Head will not be separated from His members.[4] He "did not ascend to Heaven in a private capacity to dwell there alone, but rather that it might be the common inheritance of all the godly, and that in this way the Head might be united to His members."[5] Nor will He come again to keep His glory to Himself, but in order to pour it out over all the members of His body.[6] There is a sense in which we even now share in the pattern of Christ's glory, for Calvin at times can speak of the new life which the regenerated man lives on this earth as a life conformable to Christ's heavenly life.[7] But more frequently he reminds us that we are conformed to Christ's glory only in a very preliminary and hidden way[8] for it is only at the second coming and final resurrection that "instead of being pitifully full of infirmities as we are at present, we will have to be conformed to the heavenly life of our Lord Jesus Christ."[9]

In the resurrection and ascension of Jesus, then, we are to see unveiled the pattern of the glory which He will share with those who are united to Him. For He took our nature upon Himself in order that in it He might reveal our true destiny.[10] The Holy Spirit

[1] Comm. on John 12 : 24, C.O. 47 : 288.
[2] Comm. on Heb. 2 : 10, C.O. 55 : 27. *Haec autem est eximia consolatio ad mitigandam acerbitatem crucis, quum audiunt fideles miseriis et tribulationibus se una cum Christo sanctificari in gloriam.*
[3] Inst. 3 : 25 : 3.   [4] Comm. on 2 Tim. 2 : 8, C.O. 52 : 363.
[5] Comm. on John 14 : 2, C.O. 47 : 322.
[6] Serm. on 2 Thess. 1 : 6–10, C.O. 52 : 234.
[7] Comm. on Rom. 6 : 10, C.O. 49 : 109. *Neque enim in coelo nos dicit victuros, sicut illic Christus vivit: sed vitam novam, quam a regeneratione in terra degimus, coelesti eius vitae facit conformem.*
[8] See pp. 83–86   [9] Serm. on 2 Thess. 6–10, C.O. 52 : 234.
[10] Serm. on Matt. 2 : 23, etc., C.O. 46 : 460–1. *Ainsi nous contemplons en sa personne quelle est la gloire de Dieu. Et cela est pour nous eslever en haut, pour nous faire compagnons des Anges de paradis. Car il nous retire de la poudre de la*

who raised Jesus and thus exalted Him to glory retains always His power to do the same thing for our equally frail and perishing humanity. Therefore "in the person of Christ was exhibited a specimen of the power which belongs to the whole body of the Church."[1] Christ in His resurrection is the pledge (*pignus*)[2] or example (*exemplum*) or living image (*imago viva*)[3] of the resurrection in which His people will finally participate.

Calvin uses various terms in describing the conformity of Christ's life to the pattern of cross and resurrection, and of our life to the pattern of His cross and resurrection. He speaks most often of the conformity of the Head and the members,[4] but he can also speak in various ways of the "analogy" or "proportion" or "symmetry" between the Head and members.[5] It is possible that by his use of the word "proportion" in this context Calvin means to emphasise that we are conformed to Christ on our own level as He is conformed to us on His level. We are not made equal to Christ in being conformed to Him, but what is begun in the Head must be fulfilled in the members "according to the degree and order of each."[6] Here while there is resemblance between us and Christ, He nevertheless remains "far above us" and is the only Mediator.[7]

---

terre, mesme du bourbier de toute corruption, et des gouffres d'enfer, quand il a voulu vestir nostre nature, et qu'en icelle il est monté au ciel, pour nous attirer apres luy. Cf. serm. on Isa. 53 : 7–8, C.O. 35 : 640; Comm. on Acts 13 : 36, C.O. 48 : 303.

[1] Comm. on Rom. 8 : 11, C.O. 49 : 145. *Sumit autem pro confesso, in Christi persona editum fuisse virtutis specimen, quae ad totum ecclesiae corpus pertinet.* Cf. Inst. 3 : 25 : 3.

[2] Comm. on 2 Tim. 2 : 8, C.O. 52 : 363.

[3] Inst. 3 : 25 : 3.

[4] Cf. comm. on Heb. 2 : 10, C.O. 55 : 27; *Conformatio capitis cum membris*; on John 15 : 10, C.O. 47 : 343. *Conformitas capitis et membrorum.*

[5] Comm. on 2 Cor. 6 : 2, C.O. 50 : 75. *Verum scimus, quae sit analogia capitis ad membra* (French edn. has *Quelle similitude et proportion ou conuenance*). Comm. on Col. 1 : 24, C.O. 52 : 94. *Deinde non recusandam esse conditionem quam ecclesiae suae ordinavit Deus, ut membra Christi congruentem cum suo capite symmetriam habeant*; also comm. on Acts 13 : 36, C.O. 48: 303, *Notanda est inter membra et caput proportio.*

[6] Inst. 3 : 25 : 3 . . . *secundum cuiusque gradum et ordinem. Nam ei per omnia aequari ne rectum quidem esset.* Cf. comm. on Acts 13 : 36, C.O. 48 : 303. In the fulfilment of Old Testament prophecies which apply to both Christ and the Church what is fulfilled perfectly in Christ the Head alone takes place in the members *iuxta cuiusque modum et ordinem.*

[7] Cf. comm. on 1 John 3 : 16, C.O. 55 : 340; on Luke 6 : 40, C.O. 45 : 285; serm. on Isa. 53 : 7–8, C.O. 35 : 638.

3. Our conformity to Christ depends on union rather than on imitation

When Calvin speaks of our conformity to the pattern of Jesus Christ, it is usually in the context of union between the Head and members of the body. It is within the relationship of union with Christ that we are exhorted to imitate Christ as our example. The conformity to Christ at which we are to aim is not a mere "conformity of example,"[1] Christ being viewed "at a distance"[2] from us and we painfully seeking by ourselves and in our own strength to shape our lives after His pattern. It is a conformity that is to be sought within a close union with Him who is the pattern, and that can result only from such union.[3] "This conformity between the Head and the members ought to be always placed before our eyes, not only that believers may form themselves after the example of Christ, but that they may entertain a confident hope that His Spirit will every day form them anew to be better and better, that they may walk in newness of life."[4] It is because Christ lives and is powerful within us that we become conformed to His image.[5] He is for us not only the example of righteousness but the cause of righteousness.[6]

4. Our conformity to Christ is worked out in outward life as well as in heart

Calvin further teaches that our lives become conformed to the pattern of Christ's life not only as a result of the inward working of Christ in the heart, but also as a result of the providential ordering by God of the outward circumstances of our lives— especially of the afflictions and sufferings which are our lot. The members of the body of Christ in union with Christ are subjected to a special providence which shapes their historical career and their ultimate destiny into a pattern similar to the pattern of death

---

[1] Comm. on Rom. 6 : 5, C.O. 49 : 106. *Insitio non exempli tantum conformitatem designat, sed arcanam coniunctionem.*
[2] Inst. 3 : 1 : 3.
[3] Comm. on 1 John 2 : 6, C.O. 55 : 312; and on 1 Pet. 4 : 1, C.O. 55 : 270.
[4] Comm. on John 15 : 10, C.O. 47 : 343.
[5] Comm. on John 8 : 44, C.O. 47 : 208. *In nobis vivit ac viget Christus.*
[6] Comm. on Rom. 5 : 12, C.O. 49 : 95.

and resurrection worked out in the life of Christ. In this way, as well as through the influence of Christ in the heart, their lives become conformed to the likeness of Christ. Calvin can speak of a "twofold likeness to the death of Christ" as recommended in Scripture. We are to be conformed to Christ "in reproaches and troubles" as well as through inward renewal.[1] To this end God "trains His people in a peculiar manner that they may be conformed to the image of His Son."[2] In every age the Church of Christ enjoying its close and mystical union with Christ has had its history shaped into a pattern of death and resurrection. "The Church of Christ has been from the beginning so constituted that the Cross has been the way to victory and death, a passage to life."[3]

[1] Comm. on 1 Pet. 4 : 1, C.O. 55 : 270. Cf. on 1 Pet. 2 : 24, C.O. 55 : 252. Cf. serm. on Job 2 : 7–10, C.O. 33 : 121. *Car voila à quelle condition* (i.e. the bearing of the Cross) *Dieu nous a entez au corps de son Fils, ainsi qu'il est le patron general de tous fideles, comme S. Paul en traitte au huictieme des Romains.* Cf. also serm. on Deut. 8 : 10–14, C.O. 26 : 611; on 2 Tim. 2 : 8–13, C.O. 54 : 132.

[2] Comm. on Matt. 16 : 24, C.O. 45 : 482.

[3] Comm. on 1 Pet. 1 : 11, C.O. 55 : 217. This is a very special kind of providential ordering confined entirely to the sphere of the Church. *Cela ne peut entrer aux coeurs des hommes, qu'il faille mourir pour vivre, qu'il faille par opprobre parvenir à la gloire de Dieu: car ce sont choses contre nature. Or tant y a que c'est la condition de l'Église.* Serm. on 2 Tim. 2 : 8–13, C.O. 54 : 131. Cf. pp. 81–2.

PART TWO

DYING AND RISING
WITH CHRIST

Chapter I

Self-denial

1. Inward and outward aspects of participation in the death of Christ

IN living the Christian life the Christian man must undergo in union with Christ a process of mortification of which the death of Christ is a type and example.[1] The pattern of dying with Christ has to be worked out in our Christian life both inwardly and outwardly. There is an inward process of mortification—a dying to self—of which Jesus in His perfect surrender to God's will and His complete self-control is the perfect example.[2] But Christ not only mortified His self-will, He laid down His life on the Cross and bore excruciating physical and outward suffering in body and estate and reputation. There is therefore also for the Christian an outward process of mortification to be undergone in union with Jesus Christ. Calvin notes that though there are many parts of the New Testament such as Romans 6 and Colossians 3 : 5,[3] where our mortification is clearly spoken of as though it were equivalent simply to the inward process of self-denial and renouncing the works of the flesh, nevertheless there are other passages such as Romans 8 : 29, 2 Corinthians 4 : 10, Philippians 3 : 10, and 2 Timothy 2 : 11,[4] where Paul speaks of the Christian as undergoing not simply an inward conformity to Christ in His death but also a conformity in outward condition of life brought about through the concrete experience of suffering and consisting of such suffering. There are passages where "to die with Christ" means being actually brought down on the way to physical death, and "to be conformed to Christ" means actually to be made like Him in outward form before the eyes of the world in suffering and shame.[5]

---

[1] Comm. on 1 Pet. 4 : 1, C.O. 55 : 271. . . . *mors eius typus sit modo ac exemplar mortificationis nostrae.*

[2] See pp. 62–3.   [3] Cf. comm. in loc.   [4] Cf. comm. in loc.

[5] Comm. on 2 Tim. 2 : 11, C.O. 52: 365. *Per mortem intelligit totam illam externam mortificationem, de qua loquitur secundae ad Corinthios 4, 10.*

Our dying with Christ is therefore always twofold. Calvin emphasises this in different ways. He speaks of a "twofold mortification (*duplex mortificatio*)," one aspect of which relates to "those things which are around us," the other aspect of which is inward—the mortification of the understanding and will.[1] He speaks also of a twofold likeness of the death of Christ (*duplex mortis Christi similitudo*) and of the necessity of our being conformed to Him outwardly in reproaches and troubles, as well as inwardly in the dying of the old man and the renewal of spiritual life.[2] He speaks also of a "twofold fellowship and communication of the death of Christ (*duplex est societas et communicatio mortis Christi*)." The inward aspect of this "fellowship" is the mortification of the flesh or the crucifixion of the old man, of which Paul treats in Romans 6, its outward aspect is "bearing the cross," of which Paul treats in Romans 8.[3] It is important for Calvin that we should not confuse the mortification of the *old* man referred to in Romans 6 : 6 and Colossians 3 : 5 with the mortification of the *outward* man referred to in 2 Corinthians 4 : 16. This mortification of the *outward* man takes place through loss of health, estate, honours and friendships and the blessings of the present life; the mortification of the *old* man being the inward mortification of the self-will and the flesh.[4] Both forms of our mortification serve the same end. They make us conformed to Christ. Inward mortification, however, accomplishes this in a direct manner. Outward mortification is our indirect means to such conformity.[5]

In the words of Jesus, "If any man will come after me, let him deny himself and take up his cross, and follow me."[6] Calvin finds a call to this twofold conformity with the death of Christ and twofold participation in the death of Christ. Self-denial is the inward or direct aspect of this twofold conformity and participation, bearing one's cross is the outward or indirect aspect. Since Jesus Christ the Head has been made to trace out the way of self-denial and cross-bearing through which alone His members can enter

[1] Comm. on Col. 3 : 5, C.O. 52 : 119.
[2] Comm. on 1 Pet. 4 : 1, C.O. 55 : 270; cf. also on 1 Pet. 2 : 24, 55 : 252.
[3] Comm. on Phil. 3 : 10, C.C. 52 : 50.
[4] Comm. on 2 Cor. 4 : 16, C.O. 50 : 58.
[5] Comm. on 2 Cor. 4 : 10, C.O. 50 : 55. *Prior illa vocetur interior mortificatio: haec vero externa. Utraque nos Christo conformes reddit: illa directe, haec indirecte, ut ita loquar.*
[6] Matt. 16 : 24.

glory, it now becomes the part of the members to seek to conform themselves to the example of Jesus, especially in these two particular respects. In this call to discipleship Jesus presents Himself to men as an "example of self-denial and patience," and excludes from discipleship any who are not "true imitators (*veri imitatores*)" of Himself.[1] "He lays down a brief rule for our imitation, in order to make us acquainted with the chief points in which He wishes us to resemble Him. It consists of two parts, *self-denial* and a voluntary *bearing of the Cross*."[2]

2. Concupiscence as the total perversion of the natural self

It is only if we first understand Calvin's teaching about the concupiscence of the human mind and heart that we can fully appreciate the place which he gives to self-denial in living the Christian life.

The human heart, as a result of Adam's sin, has become not only completely disordered in all its affections and purposes and faculties, and destitute of all rectitude, but it has also become possessed by an active principle or law of sin called "concupiscence,"[3] or "perversity," which makes it, in its natural state, a positive and most productive source of evil, from which sin continually wells out even unprovoked as water from a fountain, or as flames and sparks are thrown up from a fiery and never-dying furnace.[4] It is this disease of concupiscence in the heart of man which perpetually sends forth desires and affections, each of which is an enemy of God within us.[5] These stimulate and allure man to sin, prompt and incite him to lust, avarice, ambition and other vices,[6] and throw his whole life into "violent and lawless

[1] Comm. on Matt. 16 : 24, C.O. 45 : 481. *Se abnegationis sui et patientiae exemplar cuique proponens.*

[2] Ibid. *Porro brevem imitationis regulam praescribit, ut sciamus, qua praecipue in re velit sibi nos esse similes: ea vero duobus modis constat, abnegatione nostri, et voluntaria crucis tolerantia.*

[3] Inst. 2 : 1 : 8, *Non enim natura nostra boni tantum inops et vacua est: sed malorum omnium adeo fertilis et ferax, ut otiosa esse non possit. Qui dixerunt esse concupiscentiam, non nimis alieno verbo usi sunt.*

[4] Ibid. Cf. comm. on Heb. 12 : 1, C.O. 55 : 171. *Non loquitur autem de externis vel actualibus (ut vocant) peccatis: sed de ipso fonte, hoc est concupiscentia, quae ita omnes nostri partes occupat ut undique sentiamus nos teneri eius laqueis.*

[5] Comm. on John 12 : 27, C.O. 41 : 292.

[6] Inst. 3 : 3 : 10. *Fatentur etiam, sanctos illo concupiscendi morbo adhuc ita implicitos teneri, ut obstare nequeant quin subinde vel ad libidinem, vel ad avaritiam, vel ad ambitionem, vel ad alia vitia titillentur et incitentur.*

movements which war with the order of God."[1] Because of this "natural viciousness"[2] of heart, man cannot keep himself from making a wrong and corrupted use of all the good and beautiful created things with which God has filled this world. He draws his material for pride from the gifts which ought to lead him to piety.[3] Even that which is good in man's environment can now only incite him to an evil response and is bound to become a means of temptation,[4] and even those ample tokens of God's reality and goodness which have been left even since the fall in the noble theatre of this earth which should serve to bring man to the knowledge of the true God and of himself for the fulfilment of his eternal destiny, man can now use only as the basis of idol-worship.[5]

When we seek to study the working of concupiscence in the heart, and to define it in psychological terms, we find that concupiscence works in the springs of man's being which lie deeper than the moral philosopher or the psychologist can probe and which are revealed only through the Word.[6] Concupiscence must not be identified with mere lust or evil desire or appetite. Concupiscence is what brings forth evil desire itself.[7] Calvin, approving of St James's use of the simile of bringing sin to birth in describing the working of concupiscence, finds three stages in the conception of

[1] Inst. 3 : 3 : 12.
[2] Inst. 3 : 3 : 11.
[3] Comm. on Ezek, 16 : 15, C.O. 40 : 348.
[4] Serm. on Job 31 : 1–4, C.O. 34 : 627–8. *Si le mal n'habitoit en nous . . . il est certain que nous aurions nostre veuë pure et chaste beaucoup plus qu'elle n'est: et tous nos sens, comme l'ouye, le parler, les attouchemens, tout cela seroit comme pur et net, il n'y auroit nulle infection. . . . Or est-il ainsi que nous ne saurions pas maintenant ouvrir les yeux, que ce ne soit pour concevoir quelque mauvais appetit: nous ne saurions dire, Cela est beau, cela est bon, qu'incontinent nous n'offensions nostre Dieu: ne voila pas une grande perversité? Ainsi donc cognoissons . . . que nostre nature est tellement corrompue, que nous ne saurions regarder une chose que nous puissions nommer belle et bonne que nous n'offensions Dieu, au lieu que nous devrions estre solicitez à l'aimer, et lui rendre louange de sa bonté. . . . Au lieu donc de glorifier Dieu, et d'estre incitez à l'aimer et le servir, nous ne saurions dire, cela est beau, cela est bon, que nous ne soyons chatouillez, voire poussez ou à l'avarice, ou à paillardise, ou à autres voluptez. Bref, tout ce qui est bon, . . . cela nous destourne de nostre Dieu, là où il nous devroit conduire à lui.*
[5] Cf. *Calvin's Doctrine of the Word and Sacrament*, pp. 69–70.
[6] Comm. on Rom. 7 : 7, C.O. 49 : 124. *Nunquam enim ita iudicio privantur homines, quin suum apud eos discrimen retineant externa opera. Imo coguntur etiam scelerata consilia et similes conatus damnare: quemadmodum facere nequeunt, quin rectae voluntati suam tribuant laudem. Sed vitium concupiscentiae occultius est, ac profundius reconditum: quo fit ut nunquam in rationem veniat, quamdiu iudicant ex suo sensu homines.*
[7] Comm. on James 1 : 15, C.O. 55 : 390–1. *Principio concupiscentiam hic appellat, non quemvis appetitum, sed appetituum omnium fontem.*

sin. The first stage is an airy phantasy fluttering through the mind which may or may not be stimulated by an outside object. The next stage is a feeling of being drawn by desire towards the sin suggested by this. The third stage is when the will yields to the first desire through consent. Finally, sin is brought to perfection by the execution of the external act.[1] It will be seen that concupiscence for Calvin is something deeper than an evil will,[2] something more fugitive and unformed than an evil desire,[3] and though it is as closely related to the activity of the mind as to the will and the emotions, it cannot be defined in terms of the working of the mind either.

Speaking of the extent to which man's life is vitiated by original sin, Calvin says: "Everything which is in man, from the intellect to the will, from the soul even to the flesh, is defiled and pervaded with this concupiscence, or to express it more briefly, that the whole man is in himself nothing else than concupiscence."[4] Calvin emphasises that concupiscence should not be thought of as having a closer connexion with the "inferior appetites" which induce man to sensuality than with the natural reason and will of man.[5] Calvin admits that concupiscence can be spoken of as having its residing-place particularly in the "flesh."[6] "Flesh" in the Bible

[1] Serm. on Job 31 : 1–4, C.O. 34 : 623. *Or ie di, encores qu'il n'y ait point acte exterieur, qu'il y a trois degrez en un vice. Le premier est une imagination volage qu'un homme conçoit quand il regarde quelquechose: il luy viendra en phantasie cecy ou cela: ou bien encores qu'il ne voye rien, si est-ce que son esprit est tant agile au mal, qu'il sera transporté çà et là, et luy viendra beaucoup de phantasies au cerveau. . . . Il y a le second degré maintenant, c'est qu'apres avoir conceu une phantasie, nous sommes aucunement chatouillez, et sentons que nostre volonté tire là: et encores qu'il n'y ait point de consentement ne d'accord, tant y a qu'il y a là dedans quelque pointure pour nous soliciter. . . . Il y a puis apres le consentement, quand nous avons une volonté arrestee, et qu'il ne tiendroit pas à nous que le mal ne se fist si l'occasion s'y adonnoit.* Cf. also Inst. 3 : 3 : 10.

[2] Comm. on Rom. 7 : 7, C.O. 49 : 124. *Sed Deus hoc praecepto ad concupiscentiam usque penetrat, quae voluntate occultior est.*

[3] Ibid. *Tenenda interim est illa distinctio inter pravas libidines, quae ad consensum usque perveniunt, et concupiscentiam, quae sic corda titillat et afficit, ut in medio impulsu subsistat.*

[4] Inst. 2 : 1 : 8, cf. comm. on Ps. 119 : 37, C.O. 32 : 231.

[5] Inst. 2 : 1 : 9, cf. serm. on Gal. 5 : 19–23, C.O. 51 : 39; and comm. on Ps. 119 : 80, C.O. 32 : 249. *Scimus has esse praecipuas humanae animae facultates, quarum utramque vitiatam et perversam esse clare ostendit, qui et illuminari petit a spiritu sancto mentem suam, et cor suum ad obedientiam legis formari.* And cf. comm. on Matt. 16 : 22, C.O. 45 : 480. *Quanquam enim carnis libidines, ut similes sunt feris bestiis, cohibere difficile est, nulla tamen magis furiosa bellua est, quam carnis prudentia.*

[6] Comm. on Rom. 7 : 7, C.O. 49 : 123, on Rom. 7 : 8, C.O. 49 : 125. Inst. 2 : 1 : 9.

means everything which is natural to man[1] or whatever man is born with.[2] Not only the gross bodily activities which man has in common with the animals but also all the "higher" activities of affection and mind by which nature guides and directs man's life are "of the flesh," and are thus completely perverted by concupiscence.[3] Calvin enters controversy on this matter with the doctors of the Papacy, who tended to identify the works of the flesh with sensuality, and to have some confidence in at least the partial freedom of human reason from the blight of concupiscence, and he reminds them that Paul lists "ambition" amongst the works of the flesh, and looks on false doctrine as being due to carnality.[4]

Concupiscence can work within the heart of man independently of his environment. The human heart does not need to be incited by any external temptation before the power of concupiscence stimulates it into sinful activity of thought, passion and will.[5] Concupiscence is an innate corruption which each man is born with by a hereditary law. Calvin did not fail in preaching to his own day to assert that even young infants in spite of appearance to the contrary are nevertheless "little serpents full of venom and malice and disdain."[6]

The natural tendency of human nature is, therefore, always to fight against God. So active even in the regenerate man does the "flesh" remain with its concupiscence[7] that he must never allow

---

[1] Comm. on Gen. 6 : 3, C.O. 23 : 114. *Nam quum omni ex parte vitiata sit hominis anima, nec minus caeca sit eius ratio, quam perversi affectus, merito tota vocatur carnalis. Ideo sciamus totum hominem naturaliter carnem esse, donec per gratiam regenerationis spiritualis esse incipiat.* Cf. comm. on Rom. 7 : 18, C.O. 49 : 132.

[2] Serm. on Gal. 5 : 14–18, C.O. 51 : 22. *Par le mot`de chair sainct Paul entend tout ce qui est de l'homme, tout ce que nous apportons de nostre naissance.* Cf. subsequent pp. 23–4.　　　　　[3] Comm. on 1 Pet. 2 : 11, C.O. 55 : 242.

[4] Serm. on Gal. 5 : 19–23, C.O. 51 : 39.

[5] Serm. on Deut. 4 : 32–5, C.O. 26 : 202. *De nature nous sommes enclins à errer car encores que nous n'eussions pas les occasions devant nos yeux: chacun de soy-mesme se deçoit et se trompe: et puis le diable ne cesse de nous presenter beaucoup d'illusions.* Cf. comm. on Heb. 3 : 8, C.O. 55 : 39. *Quod tamen respuimus Dei vocem, id fit spontanea contumacia, non extraneo impulsu.*

[6] Inst. 2 : 1 : 6–7 & 11. Cf. serm. on Matt. 26 : 36–9, C.O. 46 : 843. *Les petis enfans venans au monde, combien que la malice n'apparoisse point, ne laissent pas toutesfois d'estre des petis serpens pleins de venin, de malice et de desdain. Voyla ce que nous cognoissons estre en nostre nature, voire dés le commencement. Et comme nous sommes venus en aage, qu'est-ce donc de nous?*

[7] Cf. Inst. 3 : 3 : 10; and serm. on Job 31 : 1–4, C.O. 34 : 628. *Il est vrai que les fideles ne seront pas tellement pervertis, et n'auront pas leur sens tant depravez, de tousiours tirer à mal: mais tant y a qu'ils auront tousiours quelque reliqua de ceste infection qui est du ventre de la mere, c'est qu'ils auront des pointes au dedans pour estre induits à mal, voire combien qu'ils le hayssent, et le repoussent du premier coup.*

his natural tendencies to have any serious part in the decisions which he has to make in shaping his way of life.[1] Nothing could be more fatal for a Christian man than to give loose rein to any of his natural desires or thoughts or impulses. To follow nature is to go clean against God.[2] To try to satisfy our natural cravings is to proceed to drown ourselves in an insatiable gulf.[3] Man's natural tendency of mind and heart and will is to bind himself down in affection to this earth and thus to make it impossible for him to rise upwards to his true destiny in the Kingdom of God.[4] The way dictated by nature is the way to death and destruction.[5]

3. Self-denial involves the Christian in constant conflict with his own nature and reason

Self-denial for Calvin means the mortification of our natural concupiscence, and the denial of all the motions and impulses that arise from the "flesh." Through concupiscence the heart of man always tends by the bent of its own nature to shut itself up in self-love and to exclude the claims and fellowship of God and of the neighbour. The self therefore constitutes the first and most continuous and most baffling problem that every Christian has to face. The more zeal we have to bring our life under the domination of God, the more inner rebellion and contradiction to the will of God will be aroused within us by concupiscence.[6] Our own nature

[1] Serm. on Job 10 : 16–17, C.O. 33 : 497. *Les affections de nostre chair sont autant d'inimitiez contre Dieu. Suivons-nous donc nostre naturel? Nous allons tout au rebours de la volonté de Dieu, nous n'avons point une seule pensee qui ne soit meschante et à condamner.*

[2] Serm. on Deut. 5 : 12–14, C.O. 26 : 284. *Car tous nos sens et toutes nos affections, comme dit S. Paul au 8 des Romains, sont autant d'inimitiez contre Dieu: quand les hommes laschent la bride à leurs penseez, à leurs desirs et volontez, à toutes leurs cupiditez, ils combattent manifestement contre Dieu.* Serm. on Gal. 5 : 14–18, C.O. 51 : 19. *Cependant que nous suyvrons nostre train, il faudra que nous allions tout au rebours de la volonté de Dieu.* Cf. serm. on Deut. 10 : 15–17, C.O. 27 : 53; and on Deut. 6 : 20–25, C.O. 26 : 488.

[3] Comm. on Rom. 13 : 14, C.O. 49 : 256.

[4] Serm. on 1 Tim. 6 : 12–14, C.O. 53 : 595–6. *Il n'y a rien plus contraire à nostre nature que de quitter ces choses terrestres, et n'y estre point addonnez. . . . Il faut que l'homme fidele s'eleve par dessus soy, quand il est question de penser au Royaume de Dieu, et à la vie eternelle.*

[5] Comm. on Rom. 8 : 6, C.O. 49 : 142. *Notabilis autem est locus, ex quo discimus, naturae cursu nos ruere in mortem praecipites: quia nihil a nobis concipimus nisi exitiale.*

[6] Serm. on Matt. 3 : 1–3, C.O. 46 : 491–2. *Venons à nous. Combien que nous ayons quelque zele de nous assubietir à Dieu, et que nous monstrions aussi cela par effect, neantmoins si est ce que nous sentons encores tant de cupiditez qui nous*

affords us so much vexation and disappointment and such a wide
and difficult sphere of conquest that we never have any need to
seek any other sphere of moral exercise.[1] Our own hearts are the
battlefield where by far the fiercest conflicts with evil are to be
waged,[2] and if we can succeed in overcoming Satan in this sphere
we will find no difficulty in overcoming him in any other sphere
of life where we may encounter him.[3]

The fact that the self-life is so closely identified with the principle of concupiscence which is natural to our "flesh" makes
Calvin, especially in his preaching, describe the Christian life as
a constant battle, not simply with "self," but with "our own
nature," whose affections and impulses tend always to lead us
astray. To follow nature as we have it within us is therefore to
displease God.[4] We must mortify, struggle against, seek to abolish
whatever is "of our own nature" if we wish to be conformed to
God in our sanctification and to love our neighbour.[5] Only by

poussent et incitent à estre rebelles: il y a tant de contradictions, tant d'empeschemens
qui sont cause que le Royaume de Dieu n'est point paisible en nous, que nous avons
besoin de faire tous les iours ceste requeste, que son Royaume advienne: c'est à
dire que Dieu commence par nous-mesmes, qu'il abate ces affections meschantes qui
contreviennent à sa iustice, et puis qu'il range les meschans, soit qu'il les reforme,
soit qu'il les confonde et abysme du tout.

[1] Serm. on Job 4 : 7–11, C.O. 33 : 190. Car quand Dieu nous envoye des afflictions grandes, nous concevons incontinent ce qui est ici dit à Job: il ne faut point
qu'un Eliphas viene pour nous tourmenter et pour nous faire accroire que nous
sommes desesperez: il n'y a celuy qui n'ait en soy comme une semence de despit pour
se fascher et tourmenter en ses afflictions, voire pour se ietter en desespoir: nostre
nature porte cela.

[2] Comm. on Ezek. 13 : 10–11, C.O. 40 : 283. Haec igitur unica est ratio
pacificandi Dei, ubi nobis ipsi sumus hostes, ubi pugnamus strenue cum pravis et
vitiosis carnis nostrae cupiditatibus. Serm. on Job 14 : 5–12, C.O. 33 : 679. Or le
principal combat que nous ayons à faire c'est contre nous-mesmes, et contre nos
vices.

[3] Comm. on Ps. 42 : 6, C.O. 31 : 429. Quanquam autem bellum cum Satana
et mundo gerit, non tamen recte vel aperte cum illis confligit, sed se ipsum potius
deligit antagonistam. Et certe haec optima est vincendi Satanae ratio, non egredi
extra nos, sed cum propriis affectibus suscipere intrinsecum certamen.

[4] Serm. on Deut. 10 : 15–17, C.O. 27 : 53. Or par cela nous sommes admonnestez que cependant que les hommes demeureront en leur naturel, que de nature ils
sont rebelles à Dieu, ils ne feront que le despiter, qu'ils tireront tout au rebours de sa
justice, brief, ils seront ennemis de tout bien. Et qu'ainsi soit: Dieu ne demande sinon
que nous plions le col sous luy, et que nous portions son ioug paisiblement: voyla toute
la perfection de nostre vie, c'est la plus grande saincteté que Dieu commande: c'est
que les hommes mortifient toutes leurs mauvaises affections: comme il a esté dit:
qu'il faut qu'ils soyent circoncis pour obeir à Dieu: c'est à dire . . . , que Dieu purge
tout ce qui est de leur propre, s'il en veut iouir.

[5] Serm. on Deut. 5 : 12–14, C.O. 26 : 283. Il nous faut mortifier ce qui est de
nostre nature, si nous voulons estre conformes à nostre Dieu. Serm. on 1 Cor.
10 : 31–11 : 1, C.O. 49 : 707. Brief, il nous faut oublier ce qui est nostre, si nous

doing such violence to our nature and forcing ourselves and allowing ourselves to be forced against all our natural inclinations can we attain to the true simplicity and uprightness which is the mark of the true follower of Christ.[1]

The process of self-denial involves us in deliberate and continuous conscious effort to subdue and discipline the unruly thoughts and passions that arise in our hearts and minds when the Word of God lays claim upon our minds and the Spirit of God seeks to control our hearts.[2] We must not imagine that progress in the Christian life is attained through a quiet and passive yielding to the influence of the Spirit as He quietly moulds our whole being into a blessed and harmonious unity with His will and purpose. God's grace and our own nature never come together in such harmony. They are always as antagonistic one to another as fire and water. The truth is rather that the more God obtains the control of our lives the more inward opposition to His rule is aroused within us and therefore the more are we forced to deny the perverse and rebellious natural inclinations which rise up at the presence of God. Only through such self-denial can we be said to be allies of God.[3]

An essential part of self-denial is to renounce our own judgment and our natural reason.[4] Calvin calls our natural way of thinking "carnal reason," and insists that unless this is dethroned

voulons rendre à nos prochains ce qui leur est deu. Et voyla pourquoy il est dit que la charité ne cherche point ce qui luy est propre. Cela est difficile, ie le confesse: mais il faut batailler contre nostre nature, si nous en voulons venir au bout. Serm. on Deut. 5 : 12–14, C.O. 26 : 284. Ainsi donc nous voyons bien que nous ne pouvons estre sanctifiez à nostre Dieu, c'est à dire, nous ne pouvons pas le servir en pureté, qu'estans separez des pollutions qui sont contraires: que ce qui est de nostre nature ne soit aboli.

[1] Serm. on Tim. 1 : 5–7, C.O. 53 : 36. Car nous voyons comme les hommes ne sont point attirez à droiture et simplicité que par force: cela est tant contraire à leur nature, qu'il faut bien qu'ils se captivent, et qu'ils facent violence à toutes leurs affections, devant qu'estre rangez à une pure simplicité.

[2] Serm. on Matt. 2 : 9–11, C.O. 46 : 351. Voyla donc comme nous avons à faire hommage au Fils de Dieu pour declarer que nous sommes membres de son Eglise, c'est asçavoir de renoncer à toute nostre raison et prudence pour nous laisser gouverner par la parole de Dieu, d'abatre et mettre sous les pieds toutes nos affections et tous nos appetits, afin que son Esprit domine en nous. Cf. serm. on Deut. 4 : 19–24, C.O. 26 : 160.

[3] Comm. on Gal. 5 : 17, C.O. 50 : 252–3. Quum itaque tota hominis natura rebellis sit ac contumax adversus Dei spiritum, sudandum est ac serio pugnandum, visque nobis inferenda ut spiritui obsequamur. Quare incipiendum a nostri abnegatione. Hic videmus quo encomio Dominus ingenium nostrum ornet, quod scilicet nihilo melius illi cum rectitudine conveniat quam igni cum aqua.

[4] Inst. 3 : 7 : 2.

there can be no admittance for the wisdom of God.[1] A sure test as to whether a man has denied himself is whether he has renounced his own views and indeed his own doubts, and has accepted in their place the wisdom of God revealed in the Gospel. Ignorance of God is therefore due to a refusal to renounce the self-life and self-love. This is involved in Calvin's interpretation of Jesus' word, "If any man will to do his will, he shall know of the doctrine."[2] To cherish doubt is therefore to defy God, and if the mind is closed against God the heart must also be closed. Therefore an examination of the life of the man who prefers to hold on to his doubt rather than to study the truth will reveal consistent moral rebellion against God. Moreover the Christian life involves a constant refusal to allow the mind to go out of the bounds of the Word of God into speculation over useless questions.[3] The Christian must continually examine and restrain the natural activity of his mind and bring it into subjection to Christ. This is no easy thing to do, for the carnal reason always seeks to take control even of the children of God, and it can be overcome only by constant dependence on God's grace, and by stern discipline.

Self-denial involves a like discipline over the passions and affections of the heart. These must be yielded to God in order that He may subdue them.[4] They must be resisted, condemned, despised, fought against, trampled underfoot, kept within proper bounds.[5] A Christian man thus holds himself captive, according

---

[1] Inst. 3 : 7 : 1; Comm. on 1 Cor. 3 : 3, C.O. 49 : 348. *Quamdiu caro, hoc est, naturalis vitiositas, in homine dominatur, sic occupat ipsius hominis ingenium, ut non sit ingressus sapientiae Dei.* Serm. on Deut. 4 : 19–24, C.O. 26 : 160. *Nous avons ceste folle persuasion d'estre sages. Or Dieu du contraire veut que nous soyons despouillez de tout nostre sens et raison, afin que nous permettions à son Esprit le regime dessus nous.*

[2] John 7 : 17, cf. comm. in loc. C.O. 47 : 170–1. *Denique omnes isti sceptici, qui dubitationis velum obtendunt in rebus hodie controversis, manifestum Dei contemptum in rebus minime obscuris produnt. . . . Caeterum in his Christi verbis continetur vera pietatis definitio, quum scilicet ad sequendam Dei voluntatem ex animo parati sumus, quod facere nemo potest nisi qui se proprio sensu abdicaverit.*

[3] Serm. on Acts 1 : 6–8, C.O. 48 : 613–4. *Et par cela nous pouvons reprendre ces curieux qui font des questions, et leur pouvons dire. Mon ami, puis que tu fais de telles questions sans propos, tu n'a pas encores appris que c'est de ton Baptesme: car tu cognoistrois qu'il faut que tu renonces à toy-mesme.*

[4] Inst. 3 : 7 : 8.

[5] Serm. on Job 2 : 7–10, C.O. 33 : 119. *Nous voyons comme il faut que Iob combate contre toutes ses affections, qu'il en soit despouillé, qu'il se tiene là comme captif: ou autrement il se iettera hors des gonds, il s'eslevera à l'encontre de Dieu, ou pour le moins il sera despité, en sorte qu'il ne fera que se tempester là dedans, que Dieu n'aura ni credit, ni superiorité en luy. Apprenons donc à l'exemple de Iob de resister à toutes nos affections, et de les mettre bas, si nous voulons servir à Dieu.*

to Calvin.[1] To do this is to tread the narrow way that leads to life.[2] The inward act of surrendering up to God all our worldly ambition and our longing for earthly riches and favour is part of self-denial.[3] Self-denial also implies that we yield up to God in our hearts all our actual riches and possessions. God may not will to take these earthly possessions from us but we can continue to hold them only as we constantly deny them to ourselves and hold them for the Lord. A Christian must indeed thus forsake everything he possesses in order to follow Jesus Christ.[4]

4. The substitution of self-hatred for self-love

To deny ourselves means that we substitute within ourselves self-hatred in place of self-love. Concupiscence makes us "blindly rush in the direction of self-love."[5] It is the principle of self-love within us that makes it impossible for us to love our fellow men. It "leads us to despise and neglect others—produces cruelty, covetousness, violence, deceit, and all the kindred vices, and arms us with the desire of revenge."[6] It is as opposed to self-denial as fire is to water.[7] Therefore in becoming Christians we must begin to hate ourselves. We must transfer the hatred which we naturally feel for God and our fellow men back on ourselves,[8]

[1] Cf. ibid. and serm. on Deut. 4 : 19–24, C.O. 26 : 160. *Or nos affections sont vicieuses: et Dieu veut qu'apres les avoir condamnees, nous les restraignions, que nous soyons là captifs, que nous facions resistance et force à tout ce qui nous transporte à mal.*

[2] Comm. on Matt. 7 : 13, C.O. 45 : 220–1.   [3] Inst. 3 : 7 : 2.

[4] Inst. 3 : 7 : 8, Comm. on Luke 14 : 33, C.O. 45 : 296. *Atqui nemo verius renuntiat omnibus quae possidet quam qui omnia singulis momentis relinquere paratus totum se quasi liber et solutus Domino impendit, et omnibus obstaculis superior vocationem suam prosequitur. Ita vera abnegatio, quam a suis requirit Dominus, non tam in actu, ut loquuntur, quam in affectione sita est, ut quisque in diem vivens non retineat corde, quod manu gubernat.*

[5] Inst. 3 : 7 : 4.   [6] Comm. on Gal. 5 : 14, C.O. 50 : 251–2

[7] Comm. on John 13 : 35, C.O. 47 : 319.

[8] Comm. on Ps. 4 : 5, C.O. 31 : 62. *Paulus ad Ephes. cap 4 : 26, hunc locum citans . . . prudenter tamen et concinne ad suum propositum aptavit. Nam illic docet, quum vitiose iracundiam suam profundant homines contra proximos, iustam in se ipsis irae materiam habere, ut a peccato abstineant: ideoque iubet potius intus eos fremere, sibique irasci, deinde non tam succensere in personas, quam in vitia. Cf. comm. on Eph. 4 : 26, C.O. 51 : 210. Serm. on Job. 2 : 7–10, C.O. 33 : 125–6. Sur tout quand nous sommes troublez par les phantasies mauvaises de nostre chair, il faut que nous ensuyvions Iob . . . et au lieu que nous avons accoustumé de nous despiter contre ceux qui nous auront picquez, . . .: que nous regardions, Or ça i'ay un tel vice: quand i'auray bien tout regardé, ie me courrouce contre mes ennemis, . . . et quand i'ay fait bonne consideration, ie ne trouve point de pire ennemi de mon salut que moy-mesme . . .: il faut donc que ie me courrouce en moy-mesme, puis que c'est de là que procedent mes plus grands ennemis.*

and redirect our self-love outwards towards God and man.

For Calvin, then, there is an exceedingly close connexion between love for our fellow man and self-denial. Self-denial has respect to man as well as to God. It can mean not only a dethroning of self in face of the claims of God but also a dethroning of self in face of the claims of our fellow men.[1] It is when we are faced with the demands of love that we are challenged most pointedly to do violence to our own nature, for nothing is more against our nature than to become subject to others in fulfilment of the demands of love. When self is on the throne we cannot love.[2] Calvin points out that one of the best ways in which to practice such inward self-denial as is required for the Christian life is to force ourselves to perform the duties of charity.[3]

It is obvious that the phrase "self-denial" as it is used in modern speech is inadequate to describe the radical nature of the negative aspect of the Christian life which Calvin uses it to cover. As we have seen, Calvin means that the self should be really slain, done to death in violence as Christ was done to death. This means that self-denial is not for Calvin a mere hard negative discipline, but has a glorious positive aspect in relation to the self-offering of Christ in the Cross. It is through such radical self-denial in union with Jesus Christ that we are able to offer our lives as a true sacrifice slain and done to death through the Word of God and the mortifying power of the death of Christ.[4]

5. Jesus Christ as our example in self-denial

Even in the practice of self-denial Jesus is our example. He had to bring the will of His human nature into subjection to the will of God. Certainly, the experience which Jesus had of temptation was different from our own. Our own experience of tempta-

---

[1] Inst. 3 : 7 : 4. *Porro in his verbis perspicimus abnegationem nostri partim quidem in homines respicere, partim vero (idque praecipue) in Deum.* Inst. 3 : 7 : 5.

[2] Inst. 3 : 7 : 6. . . . *id, quod humanae naturae prorsus adversum est, nedum difficile, ut diligamus eos qui nos odio habent.* Com. on 1 Pet. 5 : 5, C.O. 55 : 287. *Nihil humano ingenio magis adversum est quam subiecto. Vere enim illud olim dictum est: regis animum quemque intra se habere. Donec ergo subacti fuerint alti illi spiritus, quibus turget hominum natura; nemo alteri cedere volet: quin potius singuli, aliis contemptis, omnia sibi arrogabunt.*

[3] Inst. 3 : 7 : 7. *Haec ergo mortificatio tum demum habebit in nobis locum, si caritatis numeros impleamus.*

[4] See pp. 29–32.

tion is always corrupted by concupiscence.[1] The desires of our corrupted nature are always so aroused in answer to the tempting outward circumstances that we have no power to keep ourselves within the limits of obedience to God.[2] Jesus, however, did not experience this concupiscence. His conflict in His temptation was with the pure "weakness of nature," but not with the "vicious weakness"[3] which is the result of the fall of man. "His will, it is true, was weak, as human nature is; but it was not vicious as in those who are corrupted in Adam."[4] Nevertheless His facing of the Cross meant for Jesus a real and agonising effort to do not His own will but that of God. Even though He could be "troubled" and "vehemently agitated" in His heart, nevertheless His affections were all orderly, obedient and submissive to reason, and He kept Himself in subjection to the will of the Father.[5]

6. Self-denial as the fruit of Christ's death

We can best understand what self-denial means in Calvin's theology when we consider the relation of the whole process of self-denial to the death of Christ. Self-denial is always to be thought of as the human accompaniment of a very real and powerful process of dying with Christ which takes place within the

[1] Serm. on Matt. 4 : 1, etc., C.O. 46 : 598. *Toutesfois et quantes que nous sommes tentez, il est certain qu'il y a du vice grand.* Cf. serm. on Matt. 4 : 8–11, etc., C.O. 46 : 634. *Quand donc nous verrons . . . belles possessions (etc.) . . . il est donc impossible que l'homme . . . ne soit touché de convoitise mauvaise, d'autant que sa nature est desia infectee du peche originel.*

[2] Comm. on Matt. 4 : 8 f., C.O. 45 : 135.

[3] Serm. on Matt. 4 : 1, etc., C.O. 46 : 598. *Il nous faut donc distinguer entre l'infirmite de nature, laquelle a tousiours este en l'homme, et les infirmitez vicieuses qui sont survenus à cause du peche originel.* Cf. ibid. *En nostre Seigneur Iesus Christ nous ne pourrons trouver aucune infirmite qui soit vicieuse.* Also comm. on Matt. 26 : 37, C.O. 45 : 720. *Separari tamen a nostra debet, quae a Christo suscepta fuit carnis infirmitas.* Cf. Inst. 2 : 16 : 12; and comm. on John 12 : 27, C.O. 47 : 292.

[4] Serm. on Matt. 26 : 36–9, C.O. 46 : 842–3.

[5] Comm. on John 11 : 33, C.O. 47 : 266. It should be noted that while the ordinary human experience of temptation is always sinful, according to Calvin, Jesus could be tempted and yet remain sinless. Cf. Serm. on Matt. 4 : 1 f., C.O. 46 : 600 *Nostre Seigneur Iesus Christ . . . pouvoit estre tenté sans aucune macule.* In our temptation we cannot overcome without being wounded, but Jesus could do so. (Comm. on John 12 : 27, C.O. 47 : 292) Though the human weakness of Jesus was real weakness and He was involved in real and terrible conflict with Satan, He could not have been conquered (Serm. on Matt. 4 : 1, C.O. 46 : 598). It was impossible for Jesus to sin. In this He was different from Adam in his "intermediate condition . . . to whom it was only granted that it was possible for him not to sin" (Comm. on Matt. 4 : 1, C.O. 45 : 130–1).

Christian through living communion with the death of Christ. The death of Christ is efficacious in the life of the Christian man today not only because through it we receive by faith the forgiveness of sins but also because through it we participate by faith in the mortification of the flesh or the crucifying of the old man.[1] The death of Christ is efficacious in the life of mankind today not only as a mere historic spectacle through the remembrance and contemplation of which the evil passions of the human heart are subdued and thus mortified; it is, rather, a living force which men can encounter as a present powerful concrete factor in the shaping of their character and destiny.[2] Calvin can thus speak in terms of a living communication with the death of Christ[3] which can, by an action more direct than it is possible for any distantly contemplated event to exert, bear fruit in the life of a believer and in the life of the Church. The Christian can thus "derive a secret energy" from the death of Christ as the twig of a tree does from the root in which it grows.[4] The secret of true self-denial is thus to partake as we ought of the efficacy of the death of Christ which is thus communicated to us.[5]

It is because of this close relation between self-denial and the death of Christ that Calvin describes self-denial in terms that obviously go far beyond anything we can imagine if we think of it merely as strong self-control. It is a completely radical and major operation in which the old nature of man is not merely brought under subjection but is given a real death-blow in order that an entirely new creation may take its place. Only by an operation of such a nature can a real cure be given for the concupis-

---

[1] Comm. on Gal. 5 : 24, C.O. 50 : 256. *Verbo crucifigendi usus est ut notaret mortificationem carnis esse crucis Christi effectum.* Cf. comm. on 1 Pet. 4 : 1, C.O. 55 : 270; and on 1 Pet. 2 : 24, C.O. 55 : 252. *Hanc vim subesse morti Christi significat, ut carnem nostram mortificet.*

[2] Comm. on 1 Pet. 4 : 1, C.O. 55 : 270. *Tametsi non simpliciter considerandus est nobis Christus tanquam exemplum, ubi de carnis mortificatione agitur: sed spiritu eius vere inserimur in eius mortem, ut ipsa in nobis sit efficax ad crucifigendam carnem nostram.* Cf. Inst. 2 : 16 : 7.

[3] Comm. on Rom. 6 : 7, C.O. 49 : 108. *Sic ergo in summa habeto, si Christianus es, oportere in te signum apparere communionis cum morte Christi: cuius fructus est, ut crucifixa sit caro tua cum suis concupiscentiis omnibus.* Cf. comm. on Phil. 3 : 10, C.O. 52 : 50. *Societas et communicatio mortis Christi.*

[4] Comm. on Gal. 2 : 20, C.O. 50 : 198. *Insiti in mortem Christi, arcanam inde vim, tanquam surculus a radice, haurimus.*

[5] Comm. on 1 Pet. 4 : 1, C.O. 55 : 270. *Ideo dicit armamini, significans, vere et efficaciter nos invictis armis instrui ad subigendam carnem, si vim mortis Christi percipimus ut decet.*

cence of the human heart.[1] This concupiscence is not a mere wound or temporary disease in our nature which can be cured by wise and gentle treatment. It is, rather, a corruption that so pervades the whole of the old nature that not even its best part can be saved and used. All must be annihilated. God cannot work within us by taking hold of the corrupt affections of our hearts and modifying and transforming these according to His new purposes. His work in the heart is to subdue such corrupt affections, to annihilate them, and while holding our nature thus down in death, He gives us at the same time new affections and new powers which are His new creation within us. But in order to give the new nature scope, the old must be held down in death.[2] Such is the place and such is the force of the process of mortification in the Christian life, of which self-denial is the human sign and accompaniment.[3] Self-denial, then, must not be thought of merely as a process of imitating Christ in the example He sets of self-sacrifice. It is rather the fulfilment in inward efficacy of what is outwardly figured and indeed inwardly effected in and through Baptism, when, in union with Christ, the participant in His grace is immersed in the water as a sign that here the old man is destroyed in order that the new man may arise to newness of life.[4]

[1] Comm. on Gen. 6 : 5, C.O. 23 : 117. *Non potuit certe magis ad vivum exprimere talem fuisse pravitatem, quae nullo mediocri remedio esset sanabilis.*

[2] Serm. on Deut. 6 : 20–25, C.O. 26 : 488. *Il faut donc que nous entrions comme en une mort, et en un sepulchre pour estre renouvellez, et que nostre Seigneur nous donne un nouveau sens, un nouveau coeur, qu'il nous reforme en sorte que nous ne soyons plus ceux que nous estions auparavant: mais que nous soyons comme refondus, et nouvelles creatures, ainsi que l'Escriture use de ce langage.* Inst. 2 : 1 : 9. *Unde sequitur, partem illam, in qua maxime refulget animae praestantia et nobilitas, non modo vulneratam esse, sed ita corruptam, ut non modo sanari, sed novam prope naturam induere opus habeat.* Serm. on Deut. 5 : 12–14, C.O. 26 : 284. *Nous ne pouvons pas le servir en pureté, qu'estans separez des pollutions qui sont contraires: que ce qui est de nostre nature ne soit aboli.* Comm. on Col. 3 : 8, C.O. 52 : 120. *Nam haec mortificationis vis ac natura est, ut in nobis exstinguantur omnes corrupti affectus, ne posthac solitos fructus in nobis peccatum gignat.*

[3] Comm. on Rom. 6 : 7, C.O. 49 : 108.

[4] Inst. (1536 Edn.), C.O. 1 : 111. *Siquidem, ut ait Apostolus* (Rom. 6), *in mortem eius baptisati sumus, consepulti ipsi in mortem, ut in novitate vitae ambulemus. Quibus verbis non ad imitationem eius nos solum exhortatur, ac si diceret: admoneri nos per baptismum, ut quodam mortis Christi exemplo concupiscentiis nostris moriamur et exemplo resurrectionis, ut in iustitiam suscitemur: sed rem longe altius repetit, nempe quod per baptismum Christus nos mortis suae fecerit participes, ut in eam inseramur. Et quemadmodum surculus substantiam alimentumque ducit a radice cui insitus est, ita qui baptismum ea qua debent fide accipiunt, vere efficaciam mortis Christi sentiunt in mortificatione carnis suae; simul etiam resurrectionis, in vivificatione spiritus.*

7. Self-denial as the work of the Holy Spirit

It is through the work of the Holy Spirit that the death of Christ is made so efficacious to us that it can be spoken of as a vital factor and force in our present-day world. The Holy Spirit conveys to us the benefits of the death of Christ and makes us partakers of them. "The blood of Christ is the material cause (*materia*) of our cleansing," says Calvin. But this cleansing is of no avail unless we are made partakers of it by the Spirit.[1] It is the Spirit who sprinkles our souls with the blood of Christ as in the Old Testament dispensation the priest sprinkled the blood on that which had to be cleansed by the sacrifice.[2] "If the shedding of the sacred blood is not to be in vain, our souls must be washed in it by the secret cleansing of the Holy Spirit."[3] Calvin, in preaching, can speak of our being plunged into the blood of Christ by the Holy Spirit.[4] Writing in more theological terms he expresses the same thing when he speaks of our being "inserted into the death of Christ" by the Spirit.[5] These phrases all show how closely connected in his thought are the death of Christ and the work of the Holy Spirit.

The Holy Spirit not only makes the death of Christ efficacious for our cleansing from the guilt of sin but also for the mortification or crucifying of our flesh and self-will. It was by the power of the Holy Spirit that Jesus denied Himself, and that power was especially manifest in His death. To participate in the death of Christ by virtue of the Holy Spirit means to participate in the power of the Holy Spirit to subdue and conquer the will of the flesh. In such an effect of the Spirit, the death of Christ is producing its fruit within us.[6] Because of the connexion which the Holy Spirit

---

[1] Comm. on 1 Cor. 6 : 11, C.O. 49 : 395.

[2] Comm. on 1 Pet. 1 : 2, C.O. 55 : 209.

[3] Inst. 3 : 1 : 1. *Quibus verbis admonet, ne irrita sit sacri illius sanguinis effusio, arcana spiritus irrigatione animas nostras eo purgari.*

[4] Serm. on Isa. 53 : 9–10, C.O. 35 : 655. *Et puis son sang nous est purgation, quand nous sommes plongez la dedans, et que nous en sommes arrousez par le sainct Esprit.*

[5] Comm. on 1 Pet. 4 : 1, C.O. 55 : 270. Cf. on Gal. 2 : 20, C.O. 50 : 198.

[6] Serm. on Luke 2 : 50–2, C.O. 46 : 477. *Mais notons que nostre Seigneur Iesus Christ ne laisse pas encores auiourd'huy de besongner tellement par la vertu de son sainct Esprit, que la mort qu'il a enduree pour un coup, produit son fruict et son effect en nous: sa resurrection nous profite à vie, nous sommes maintenus et garentis sous sa protection.*

has with the death and self-denial of Christ Calvin frequently speaks of the office of the Spirit in His work in the human heart as that of restraining natural desires, subduing unruly passions, enabling men to deny themselves and the world in conformity with the death of Christ.[1]

[1] Serm. on Deut. 5 : 12–14, C.O. 26 : 284–5. *Il faut que tout cela meure* (i.e. what we inherit from Adam). *Et comment cela se fait-il Ce n'est point par nostre industrie: mais nostre Seigneur Iesus Christ mourant pour nous, et pour effacer noz pechez, à ce qu'ils ne nous soyent plus imputez, nous a aussi bien acquis ce droit-la, que par la vertu de son sainct Esprit, nous pouvons renoncer au monde, et à nous-mesmes, tellement que nos affections charnelles ne dominent plus. Et combien que nous soyons pleins de rebellion: toutes-fois l'Esprit de Dieu dominera par dessus pour les reprimer, et les tenir en bride.* Cf. comm. on Ps. 109 : 5, C.O. 32 : 148.

Chapter II

Bearing the Cross

1. The Church is conformed to Christ's death by outward affliction under the Cross

God wills that our whole life should be conformed to the death of Christ.[1] This means that we must become conformed to Christ in outward circumstances as well as in inward attitude of heart. Therefore to live the Christian life involves us not only in the necessity of inward self-denial but also in many troubles and afflictions from outside ourselves. The members of the body of Christ who are sanctified in union with Christ are subjected to a special providence which shapes their historical career into a pattern similar to the pattern of death and resurrection worked out in the sanctification of Jesus Christ Himself. The afflictions which are ordered by God for this purpose Calvin calls the Cross.

The ordinary sufferings of life are, for the Christian, to be regarded as part of the Cross,[2] for God can sanctify such suffering in the life of His people and (as we shall see) can give it a relationship to the suffering of Jesus Christ.

But those who are destined to be thus conformed to Christ are called to bear in addition to the ordinary afflictions which are the common lot of mankind also a special chastisement from the hand of God which they must suffer as the representatives of His son on earth.[3] To be a member of the Church means, for Calvin, to enter a sphere in which because we are devoted to God we are devoted also to suffering. To be one of the elect of God means to

---

[1] Comm. on Phil. 3 : 10, C.O. 52 : 50; on Rom. 6 : 11, C.O. 49 : 110.
[2] Inst. 3 : 8 : 1.
[3] Comm. on 1 Pet. 4 : 17, C.O. 55 : 281. *Nam haec, inquit, necessitas totam Dei ecclesiam manet, ut non tantum communibus hominum miseriis subiaceat, sed peculiariter et praecipue Dei manu castigetur: tanto igitur aequiore animo ferendae sunt pro Christo persequutiones. Nisi enim expungi e numero fidelium velimus, Dei ferulis nos tergum aptare convenit. Suave autem istud condimentum est, quod non ut in alios passim Deus sua in nos iudicia exercet, sed filii sui personam nobis imponit, ut non nisi eius causa et nomine laboremus.* Cf. on 1 Pet. 3 : 18, C.O. 55 : 264.

be appointed to slaughter.[1] The elect are more subject than the rest of mankind to "many and various kinds of evils."[2] It is as members of the Church and not simply as individuals that we share in those "common persecutions" which have been the lot of the people of God in every generation, not only since Christ came, but in the times of the Old Testament.[3] Whatever suffering comes to an individual on behalf of Christ comes to him as a result of his incorporation in the body of Christ, and is merely part of that conformity that all members of the body must have with the Head to whom they are united, and in whom they are united to each other.[4]

Undoubtedly a large part of the common suffering of the Church in which all Christians must share consists of suffering persecution from the enemies of Christ[5] as a result of our defence of the Gospel, or indeed as a result of the defence of righteousness in any form.[6] It also consists of the suffering of shame and indignity as a result of such a stand and such persecution.[7] Calvin urges us to regard it as a special honour when we are called upon to suffer in this way,[8] and he makes the suggestions that though all the elect are appointed to bear the Cross and to be thus conformed to Christ in His death, nevertheless, to endure persecution for the sake of the Gospel is a "special mark" which distinguishes some in the Church from others.[9]

---

[1] Comm. on Ps. 45 : 23, C.O. 31 : 447. *Quia tamen sumus Christi membra, ad societatem crucis paratos esse nos oportet. Ergo ne crucis acerbitas nos terreat: semper haec ecclesiae conditio nobis versetur ante oculos, quatenus adoptati sumus in Christo, addictos esse mactationi. . . . Ergo ne taedium vel horror crucis a pietate nos avellat, sit haec continua nostra meditatio, bibendum esse calicem quem nobis porrigit Deus, nec posse Christianum esse, nisi qui se in sacrificium Deo offert.*

[2] Inst. 3 : 8 : 1.

[3] Comm. on Heb. 11 : 37, C.O. 55 : 168–9. *Neque vero hic nobis paucorum hominum miseriae narrantur, sed communes ecclesiae persequutiones: et hae quidem non unius aut alterius anni, sed quae ab avis usque ad nepotes interdum grassatae sunt. Quare nihil mirum si iisdem hodie experimentis fidem nostram probare Deo placeat.*

[4] Cf. e.g. comm. on John 12 : 24, C.O. 47 : 288.

[5] Inst. 3 : 8 : 8, Comm. on Phil. 1 : 28, C.O. 52 : 21.

[6] Inst. 3 : 8 : 7.   [7] Inst. 3 : 8 : 8.

[8] Comm. on Phil. 1 : 7, C.O. 52 : 10. *At si vere aestimamus, honor est non vulgaris quo nos Deus dignatur, quum pro eius veritate persequutionem patimur . . . Meminerimus ergo etiam societatem crucis Christi, tanquam singularem Dei gratiam, prompto gratoque animo amplexandam nobis esse.*

[9] Comm. on Matt. 24 : 9, C.O. 45 : 653. *Sed proprie hic Christus de afflictionibus disserit, quas pro evangelio subituri erant discipuli. Etsi enim verum est illud Pauli (Rom. 8 : 29), quos Deus elegit, eos quoque destinasse ad ferendam crucem, ut conformes sint imagini filii sui: non tamen hac singulari nota omnes insignit, ut ab evangelii hostibus persequutionem sustineant.* Cf. serm. on Gal. 3 : 3–5, C.O. 50 : 474. *Car de faict ce que nous endurons pour l'Evangile nous doit servir de marque, comme si Dieu nous constituoit en office honorable.*

We must bear the Cross in an attitude of patience,[1] fortifying ourselves with the conviction that through the bearing of such a cross the process of our sanctification is being furthered[2] and we are being conformed to Christ. "We must not refuse the condition which God has ordained for His Church that the members of Christ may have congruence and symmetry with their Head."[3] We must remember that the affliction which Jesus Christ bore is the same kind of affliction which He calls on His people to bear in every age. In His sufferings He is meant to be the example and pattern of all the children of God.[4]

2. The Cross brings the Church into a sacramental relation to Christ and His death

In the process of being conformed to Christ by bearing their cross, the faithful are thereby brought into a special relation to Christ and His death. Calvin can speak in such a way of this communion with Christ and His death which is given through the Cross as to imply that the suffering of the Cross for the Christian has the value of a sacrament. "In bearing the Cross we are the companions of Christ."[5] The sufferings of the Church under the Cross have so close a relation to the death of Christ, and to His suffering, that in partaking of these sufferings both the Church and the individual within the Church may be said to "hold fellowship with the sufferings of Christ,"[6] or to experience a "communication of the death of Christ,"[7] or to participate in the "fellowship of the death of Christ."[8]

---

[1] See further, pp. 258–66.

[2] Serm. on Job 42 : 9–17, C.O. 35 : 509–10. *En cela* (i.e. Sufferings) *ils ont meilleure confirmation de la doctrine entant que nostre Seigneur Iesus Christ estant l'image vive de tous fideles et enfans de Dieu, ils sont conformez à lui: comme S. Paul en traitte au 8 chapit des Rom. (v. 28) qu'en toutes nos miseres nous sommes configurez à nostre Seigneur Iesus Christ.*

[3] Comm. on Col. 1 : 24, C.O. 52 : 94. *Deinde non recusandam esse conditionem quam ecclesiae suae ordinavit Deus, ut membra Christi congruentem cum suo capite symmetriam habeant.* Cf. comm. on John 13 : 18, C.O. 47 : 312.

[4] Serm. on Job 4 : 7–11, C.O. 33 : 196. Cf. comm. on 1 Pet. 5 : 9, C.O. 55 : 290. *E converso hic apostolus nos monet, nihil nobis accidere, quod non in reliquis ecclesiae membris cernamus. Porro minime recusanda nobis est cum sanctis omnibus societas, vel similis conditio.* And serm. on Job 2 : 7–10, C.O. 33 : 120–1.

[5] Comm. on Matt. 10 : 38, 45 : 294 . . . *nos in ferenda cruce Christi esse socios.*

[6] Inst. 3 : 8 : 1. *Unde etiam insignis consolatio ad nos redit, in rebus duris atque asperis, quae adversae malaeque existimantur, nos Christi passionibus communicare.*

[7] Comm. on Rom. 6 : 7, C.O. 49 : 108. *Mortis Christi communicatio.*

[8] Comm. on Phil. 3 : 10, C.O. 52 : 50. *Societas et communicatio mortis Christi.*

The fact that the Cross brings him into this close relationship to Christ in His death and resurrection should above all other considerations encourage the Christian to bear it with cheerfulness. "How powerfully should it soften the bitterness of the Cross, to think that the more we are afflicted with adversity, the surer we are made of our fellowship with Christ, by communion with whom our sufferings are not only blessed, but tend greatly to the further-ance of our salvation."[1] The Christian under persecution for the sake of the Gospel, then, must be ready to "embrace the fellow-ship of the Cross of Christ as a special favour from God."[2] He must be so minded as "not to decline to undertake the Cross in common with Christ"[3] knowing that Christ regards such suffer-ings as His own.[4] When he is made weak, as Paul was in his suffering, he is made "weak in Christ," and this means that he is a "partaker of Christ's weakness."[5]

Such a "sacramental" effect, however, is given to our sufferings only when God blesses them. Calvin is emphatic in teaching that viewed in itself the natural effect of suffering on the human soul is not ennobling. The natural reaction of the human heart to suffering is to harden itself against God like an anvil under the blows of a hammer, and to become more and more embittered, obstinate and incorrigible after the example of Pharaoh.[6] After surveying the teaching of James and Peter and Paul as to what suffering can do to the human soul in producing character and patience, Calvin points out that such an effect can never be regarded as the result of a general rule of life but only as the result of the supernatural inward working of the providence of God. "The minds of men are not so formed by nature that affliction of itself produces patience in them. But Paul and Peter regard not so much the nature of men, as the providence of God, through which it comes that the faithful learn patience from troubles, for the ungodly are thereby more and more provoked to madness, as

---

[1] Inst. 3 : 8 : 1.

[2] Comm. on Phil. 1 : 7, C.O. 52 : 10. *Meminerimus ergo etiam societatem crucis Christi, tanquam singularem Dei gratiam, prompto gratoque animo amplexan-dam nobis esse.*

[3] Comm. on Heb. 11 : 26, C.O. 55 : 161. *Omnes ita comparatos esse decet ut crucis societatem cum Christo subire non recusent.*

[4] Ibid.

[5] Comm. on 2 Cor. 13 : 4, C.O. 50 : 150. *Infirmum esse in Christo hic significat socium esse infirmitatis Christi.*

[6] Serm. on Job 5 : 17–18, C.O. 33 : 260–1.

the example of Pharoah proves."[1] In order, therefore, for affliction to be effective in conforming us to Christ and giving us fellowship with Christ, it is not enough for God to strike us with His
hand unless at the same time He touches us inwardly by His Holy
Spirit.[2] Only "when the favour of God breathes upon us" can
afflictions which are evil in themselves, such as exile, contempt,
imprisonment, ignominy, and even death itself, turn out to our
happiness.[3] But when God does so work within us, blessing and
sanctifying our sufferings, then, no matter how grievous or accursed in their own nature are our afflictions, they are nevertheless bound to make their contribution towards the furtherance of
our salvation and towards conforming us to the image of Jesus
Christ.[4]

Suffering can be said to have this close and living relationship
to the death and passion of Christ only in the case of those who
are united to Christ and who suffer as members of Christ through
being incorporated into His Church. "In all our miseries we are
partakers of Christ's cross if we are His members,"[5] says Calvin.
The wicked and unbelieving cannot draw any benefit or consolation from such sufferings as may come upon them, because they
themselves have no connexion with Christ and His death. The
elect participate with the Son of God in the afflictions of life, but

---

[1] Comm. on James 1 : 3, C.O. 55 : 385. *Caeterum non ita naturaliter compositi
sunt hominum animi, ut illis patientiam secum afferat afflictio. Sed Paulus et
Iacobus non tam in hominum naturam, quam in Dei providentiam respiciunt: quasi
fit ut fideles patientiam ex aerumnis discant: tametsi impii magis inde ac magis ad
insaniam provocentur: quemadmodum Pharaonis exemplum ostendit.*
[2] Serm. on Job 5 : 17–18, C.O. 33 : 260. *Ces chastiemens-là ne profitent pas à
tous, et aussi il ne fait point à tous la grace de retourner à luy. Car ce n'est point
assez que Dieu frappe de sa main, sinon qu'il nous touche là dedans par son sainct
Esprit.*
[3] Inst. 3 : 8 : 7.
[4] Serm. on Gal. 2 : 20–21, C.O. 50 : 447. *Puis qu'ainsi est donc, apprenons de
vivre par la foy de Iesus Christ, c'est à dire combien que nous soyons miserables en
ce monde, combien qu'il nous fale souffrir tant de fascheries, tant d'ennuis et d'angois-
ses, tant de troubles et difficlutez, toutesfois que nous persistions en ceste constance,
pour sentir qu'il n'y a que toute felicité en nos miseres, d'autant que Dieu les benit
et les sanctifie au nom de nostre Seigneur Iesus Christ, et que tout cela nous est con-
verti en aide à salut, comme il en est parlé au 8 chap. des Rom. e. 27.* Cf. comm. on
2 Cor. 4 : 10, C.O. 50 : 55.
[5] Comm. on Phil. 3 : 10, C.O. 52 : 50. *In omnibus miseriis sumus socii crucis
Christi, si sumus eius membra.* Cf. serm. on Gal. 6 : 12–13, C.O. 51 : 117. *Et
ainsi apprenons qu'estans appelez à nostre Seigneur Iesus Christ, il nous faut estre
participans de sa croix tant qu'il luy plaira. . . . Mais cependant si faut-il que les
passions qu'il a souffert en premier lieu s'accomplissent en nous qui sommes ses
membres.*

not the wicked.[1] The consolation that it gives to know that in bearing the Cross we are the companions of Christ is for the faithful and not for the reprobates, to whom the bearing of their Cross can only be accursed and harmful.[2] Indeed Calvin can say that even in the case of believers it is only when they endure affliction for the sake of the Gospel, and not as a result of the chastisement of their sins, that they have fellowship with the passion of Christ in their sufferings.[3] Strictly speaking, then, only true disciples of Jesus Christ can be said to "bear the Cross," although all men, even in sharing the common miseries of mankind, are faced therein with a cross that they can bear.[4] The Cross can be borne only by faith, and the benefits of bearing the Cross are given only to those who have faith.

While speaking of our sharing the sufferings of Christ, Calvin is careful to emphasise that Christ's own sufferings in His passion were and are complete in that He once suffered all that is needful for our salvation,[5] and indeed He once suffered fully and forever that which He now calls on His Church to share with Himself.[6] Therefore when the Apostle speaks of himself as daily "filling up that which is lacking in the afflictions of Christ for His body's sake," he does not mean that the sufferings of Christ require to be supplemented by the sufferings of the Church, but that the sufferings of the Church are rather the unfolding and fulfilment

---

[1] Comm. on 2 Cor. 4 : 10, C.O. 50 : 55. *Porro Christi mortificatio nonnisi in solis fidelibus vocatur: quia impii, praesentis vitae aerumnas perferendo, cum Adam communicant: electi autem participationem habent cum filio Dei.*

[2] Comm. on Matt. 10 : 38, C.O. 45 : 294. *Interea subeat etiam mentem haec consolatio, nos in ferenda cruce Christi esse socios: ita fiet ut facile mitescat omnis acerbitas. Cruci suae non minus affixi sunt reprobi, nec eam, quantumvis luctentur, excutere queunt, sed quia extra Christum crux maledicta est, manet eos infelix exitus.* Cf. on 2 Cor. 1 : 5, C.O. 50 : 11. *Miseriae quidem et aerumnae vitae praesentis malis perinde ac bonis communes sunt. Sed quum impiis accidunt, maledictionis divinae sunt signa.*

[3] Comm. on 2 Cor. 1 : 5, C.O. 50 : 11. *Non tamen proprie dicuntur socii esse passionum Christi, nisi dum eius nomine patiuntur.*

[4] Comm. on Matt. 16 : 24, C.O. 45 : 482.

[5] Serm. on Gal. 6 : 12–13, C.O. 51 : 117. *Il est vray qu'il a souffert ce qui estoit besoin pour nostre salut: mais il faut que nous soyons conformez à son image.* Cf. comm. on Eph. 1 : 23, C.O. 51 : 160. *Quod ergo vult impleri et perfectus quodammodo esse in nobis, id non accidit ex defectu vel inopia.* Cf. serm. on Eph. 1 : 23, C.O. 51 : 346.

[6] Comm. on Ps. 109 : 3, C.O. 32 : 147. *Iam sicut in Christo fuit impletum quod adumbratum fuerat in Davide: ita meminerimus impleri quotidie in fidelibus* τὰ ὑστερήματα *passionum Christi, Coloss.* 1, 24, *quia semel in se passus, illos sibi consortes ac socios accersit.*

of what Christ has already suffered.[1] As the Church through its members yields itself to bearing the sufferings to which it is pre-ordained in the divine purpose, it is thus brought more and more to perfection in becoming conformed to its Head. It is thus a gracious ordinance of Christ that the afflictions of the pious should have the effect of bringing to perfection the body of the Church, and should promote the welfare of the whole Church in conforming the Church to Christ, but this must be thought of as the sharing and unfolding of a perfection which the Church already has in its fullness in the person of Christ.[2]

3. Cross-bearing is a powerful aid to self-denial and a test of obedience

To bear the Cross with patience and faith is a powerful help to us in our efforts to deny our self-will. The process of self-denial, from the human side, is not sufficiently accomplished if it is left to our own power of inward self-discipline. Man requires also to

[1] Comm. on Col. 1 : 24, C.O. 52 : 93. *Quemadmodum ergo semel passus est in se Christus, ita quotidie patitur in membris suis: atque hoc modo implentur passiones, quas Pater illius corpori suo decreto destinavit.*

[2] Comm. on Col. 1 : 24, C.O. 52 : 94. *Nemo autem non videt Paulum ita loqui, quia oporteat per afflictiones piorum adduci corpus ecclesiae ad suam perfectionem, dum membra capiti suo configurantur.* This way of thinking is in keeping with Calvin's teaching on the relation between Christ and His Church. Christ, who fills all in all, would have all fullness in Himself even if He were separated from His Church. He no more requires to be completed by His Church than the Father requires to be completed by His creation. Therefore we cannot marvel enough at the fact that He bestows on us such honour that until He is united to us, He "reckons Himself in some measure imperfect." Comm. on Eph. 1 : 23, C.O. 51 : 159. Cf. serm. on Eph. 1 : 23, C.O. 51 : 346. *Or en ce mot d'accomplissement, il signifie que nostre Seigneur Iesus, et mesmes Dieu son Pere se tient comme imparfait, sinon que nous soyons conioints à luy. Car voilà un tesmoignage de la bonté infinie de Dieu, et de laquelle on ne se peut assez esmerveiller.* He does not wish to regard Himself, or to be regarded, as complete apart from His members in the Church which can therefore be spoken of as His completion. (Comm. on 1 Cor. 12 : 12, C.O. 49 : 501. *Hoc enim honore nos dignatur Christus, ut nolit tantum in se, sed etiam in membris suis censeri et recognosci. Ideo alibi dicit idem apostolus* (Eph. 1, 23) *ecclesiam esse illius complementum, ac si divisus a suis membris, quodammodo mutilus foret.*) He who has no need of us speaks and acts as if He found His own being imperfect and incomplete until He finds fulfilment in us. In this sense the Church is the fullness of God and of Christ. (Serm. on Eph. 1 : 23, C.O. 51 : 347. *Voilà comme Dieu parle, qu'il ne se trouve point accompli et parfait, sinon d'autant qu'il nous receuille à soy, et que nous sommes unis ensemble: il prend tout son plaisir en nous, et veut que sa gloire y reluise . . . et combien que toute gloire soit en luy, neantmoins qu'on voye qu'il veut que nous en ayons nostre part et portion. Voilà donc en somme ce que S. Paul a voulu dire, appelant l'Eglise l'accomplissement de Dieu et de Iesus Christ.*

be afflicted in order to spur him on to greater efforts of self-denial than he would otherwise make, and in order to effect a more thorough subjugation of the affections of the heart and the thoughts of the mind to the will of God.[1] The "ferocity" of the flesh is such that it requires the sternest treatment if it is to be subdued.[2] Calvin frequently likens our natural disposition to a refractory horse in its wildness, to a mule or an ass in its stubbornness, and when he wants to use stronger language he likens it to untamable wild beasts or to madmen in a frenzy.[3] Therefore God, in sending affliction to us, acts like a "rough rider to a rough horse."[4] Indeed, Calvin can go so far as to liken God's part in this ministry of affliction to that of the man with the "beetle" in his hand administering corrective blows. Thus it is that God has to "reduce us to Himself,"[5] and "soften our natural hardness by the hammer."[6] Such is the perversity of our human nature that any milder course of treatment could serve only to corrupt and spoil us.[7]

In his chapter on "Bearing the Cross" in the *Institutes*, discussing the discipline imposed upon us by the Cross, Calvin gives several closely-connected reasons why it should be necessary for the people of God to be constantly afflicted by the Cross. The experience of affliction under the Cross enables us to mortify the flesh and destroys self-confidence and self-love. No matter how

[1] Comm. on Ps. 119 : 67, C.O. 32 : 244. *Deo nunquam obsequimur nisi ferulis coacti.... Nam quum principium obedientiae sit carnis mortificatio, quam naturaliter omnes refugiunt, non mirum est si variis afflictionibus Deus in ordinem nos cogat.* Comm. on Ps. 85 : 6, C.O. 31 : 787. *Nam quia subinde relabitur caro nostra ad lasciviam, variis correctionibus penitus subigi necesse est.*

[2] Cf. comm. on Ps. 25 : 9, C.O. 31 : 255. *Carnis ferocia,* on Ps. 32 : 4, C.O. 31 : 319, and Inst. 3 : 8 : 5.

[3] Inst. 3 : 8 : 5. Comm. on John 5 : 14, C.O. 47 : 109. *Neque enim solum refractariis equis et mulis sumus similes, sed plus quam indomitae belluae.* Serm. on 2 Sam. 4 : 1, 7, 4 p. 89. *Car non seulement nous sommes lasches comme des asnes, mais nous sommes comme phrenetiques et gens insensez, transportez en noz passions pour resister a Dieu.*

[4] Cf. serm. on Job 42 : 8–17, C.O. 35 : 504. *À rude asne, rude asnier.*

[5] Ibid. Cf. serm. on Deut. 2 : 1–7, C.O. 26 : 5. *Sans que Dieu nous reduist à soy par correction: il seroit impossible que nous luy fussions tels qu'il appartient pour escouter sa voix, et pour suyvre là où il nous commande. Il faut donc que nous soyons preparez à coups de verges.*

[6] Comm. on Ps. 119 : 71, C.O. 32 : 245. Calvin recognises the moral and theological difficulties of speaking in such a way. God only adopts such a course after the gentle chastisement which would be administered by the kindest Father has failed and in adopting this course He "is constrained to assume a new character which is not natural to Him". Cf. comm. on John 5 : 14, C.O. 47 : 109. *Novam personam et quasi alienam induere cogitur.*

[7] Inst. 3 : 8 : 5. Comm. on Ps. 119 : 67, C.O. 32 : 244. *Sed tamen experientia ostendit, ubi Deus nobis indulget, semper nos ad ferociam erumpere.*

much a man has learned to trust not in himself but in God alone, nevertheless when fortune smiles too much upon him he tends (like even David), to indulge himself in his prosperity and to develop a sense of carnal security which depends more upon his inward feelings and his outward condition than on the Word of God.[1] Under such circumstances, a man seeing that his condition is better than that of many others is apt to persuade himself that his life is "privileged above the common lot of the world."[2] Thus he indulges in pride and forms an "overweening opinion of his own virtue."[3] Moreover "satiety breeds violence," says Calvin, quoting a "popular proverb" which aptly fits into his comment on the verse "When Jeshurun waxed fat he kicked."[4] To indulge in pride is, according to Calvin, to indulge in self-love, which is the very opposite of self-denial.[5] It is the experience of the Cross which destroys this "depraved confidence in the flesh." Suffering gives us as it were "an ocular demonstration of our weakness", and by humbling us tames the fierceness of our pride and destroys our self-love. In the experience of humiliation, learning to distrust ourselves, we also learn to transfer our confidence and love to His grace.[6]

But the human heart is not only purged of self-confidence through the affliction of the Cross, it is also tested to see whether it possesses obedience.[7] For it is obvious that unless God crosses our own desires by sending to us some form of affliction, it is impossible to know whether we are ready to yield to God in obedi-

---

[1] Comm. on Ps. 30 : 7, C.O. 31 : 295–7. *Fideles . . . in ea militia, ad quam se norunt destinatos, excusso torpore se exercent: trepide se conferunt in fidem Dei, nec se alibi tutos fore confidunt, quam sub eius manu. Aliter David, qui prosperi status illecebris captus, aeternam sibi quietem ex proprio sensu magis quam ex Dei verbo pollicitus est.* Cf. Inst. 3 : 8 : 2.

[2] Ibid.

[3] Inst. 3 : 8 : 3.

[4] Comm on Deut. 32 : 15, C O. 25 : 365. *Satietas quidem . . . ferociam parit.* This saying originates in the Greek Poets. Cf. comm. on Jer. 31 : 18, C.O. 38 : 670. *Et prophetae etiam hac utuntur loquendi forma, quum loquuntur de Israelitis adhuc integris, vocant boves saginatos et pingues, quia scilicet affluentia gignebat in ipsis luxuriam, et luxuria superbiam. Quum ergo ita calcitrarent adversus Deum.* Cf. serm. on Deut. 6 : 10–13, C.O. 26 : 448.

[5] Inst. 3 : 8 : 3.

[6] Inst. 3 : 8 : 2 and 3.

[7] Serm. on Job 2 : 7–10, C.O. 33 : 119. *Si Dieu en ce qu'il nous envoye se conformoit à nostre volonté, on ne pourroit pas bien discerner que c'est d'estre obeissans: mais quand il nous traitte tout au rebours de nos appetis, et que nous luy sommes alors subiets, que nous tenons sous sa bride toutes nos affections, afin de nous renger à luy. . . . En cela monstrons nous que luy sommes obeissans.* Cf. Inst. 3 : 8 : 4.

ence or not. For Calvin the first step in obedience is to mortify the flesh under the affliction of the Cross.[1] Therefore as the fire of the furnace serves not only to purify but also to bring out the true character of the gold which it refines, so also the suffering of the Cross not only purges us from self-will but brings out to the light the true quality of our obedience and of the graces which God has conferred upon us "lest they should remain within unseen and unemployed."[2]

[1] Comm. on Ps. 119 : 67, C.O. 32 : 244
[2] Inst. 3 : 8 : 4. Serm. on Job 1 : 9–12, C.O. 33 : 69–70. *Et voila pourquoy tant souvent l'Escriture nous monstre que Dieu esprouve les siens, il les examine par afflictions, il les met comme un or en la fournaise, non seulement pour estre purgez, mais aussi pour estre cognus: car les afflictions servent à ces deux usages: c'est que Dieu mortifie les vices qui sont en nous, quand il nous afflige, nous sommes domtés, il nous commande de nous retirer de ce monde, de n'estre plus adonnez à noz voluptez et delices charnelles. Mais il y a plus: c'est que tout ainsi qu'en la fournaise l'or est esprouvé, pour savoir s'il y a de l'escume, aussi Dieu monstre quels nous sommes, quand il nous afflige: car les hommes mesmes ne se cognoissent point devant qu'avoir esté ainsi esprouvez.*

Chapter III

Participation in the resurrection and glory
of Christ

1. Participation in the death of Christ is never separated
from participation in His resurrection

PARTICIPATION in the death of Christ is never experienced apart from participation in His resurrection. For the consolation of those suffering under the Cross, Calvin says, "we must always bear in mind this transition from the Cross to the Resurrection."[1] Only when our minds are "directed to the power of His resurrection" can the Cross of Christ triumph over evil in the hearts and lives of those who believe.[2] It is as important that Christians should clearly understand what they owe to and derive from the resurrection of Christ as from His death. Even though there are passages in Holy Scripture which seem to lay exclusive emphasis on the importance of the death of Christ, nevertheless even in such texts "His resurrection is included in His death."[3]

We find the commencement (*initium*) of our salvation in the death of Christ, and the "consummation (*complementum*)" in the Resurrection.[4] Calvin indicates that the more positive aspect of our Christian experience is derived from communion with the resurrection of Christ. By the death of Christ "sin was abolished and death annihilated," by His resurrection "righteousness was restored and life revived."[5] Correspondingly in our Christian life, it is by communion with His death, as we have seen, that evil is subdued and abolished within us, and it is by communion with His resurrection that we experience within us the new life of regeneration. Regeneration is, for Calvin, a sign that, even though we have to wait till the final consummation of the Kingdom for our full share in the resurrection of Christ, nevertheless this resurrection life has already begun to exert its power within us, and

---

[1] Comm. on 1 Pet. 4 : 13, C.O. 55 : 279.   [2] Inst. 3 : 9 : 6.
[3] Comm. on 1 Cor. 15 : 4, C.O. 49 : 538. Cf. Inst. 2 : 16 : 13.
[4] Ibid.   [5] Inst. 2 : 16 : 13.

here and now we participate in it. Regeneration is "the actualisation in the believer of the risen life of Christ," and "an anticipation in conditions of time of the final resurrection."[1] Calvin can actually speak of the new regenerated life which we live on earth as being already "conformed" to the celestial life of Christ and a figure (*figura*) of it.[2] When the New Testament speaks of our mortal bodies as being "quickened" by Christ it refers not simply to the last resurrection but to the "continual operation of the Spirit by which the heavenly life is gradually renewed within us while the remains of the flesh are mortified."[3]

Therefore to die with Christ is always "the cause of a better life."[4] Our experience of mortification in union with the death of Christ is always accompanied by "a corresponding effect (*fructum*) derived from His resurrection."[5] To be crucified with Christ is not a "mortal death" such as was imposed under the Law, but is the "vivifying death" which we have under the Gospel—a death which leads us to life.[6]

2. Our participation in the Kingdom of God is the fruit both of the death and resurrection of Christ

When Calvin speaks about the Kingdom of God, his teaching about the inseparable relationship between our dying and rising with Christ becomes clearer. Those who think of the Kingdom of God merely as something future, to be waited for by hope as we wait for the final resurrection, are taking an extremely superficial view of what the Kingdom is. The Kingdom is rather to be thought of as the "spiritual government," or "reformation,"[7] which

---

[1] T. F. Torrance, *Kingdom and Church*, p. 100. I am indebted to this work for one or two citations in these paragraphs.

[2] Comm. on Rom. 6 : 10, C.O. 49 : 109.

[3] Comm. on Rom. 8 : 11, C.O. 49 : 146.

[4] Comm. on Gal. 2 : 19, C.O. 50 : 198.

[5] Inst. 2 : 16 : 13. Cf. comm. on Rom. 6 : 5, C.O. 49 : 106. *Nam si insiti sumus in similitudinem mortis Christi, illa autem resurrectione non caret: ergo nec nostra sine resurrectione erit.*

[6] Serm. on Gal. 2 : 17–18, C.O. 50 : 439. *Ainsi donc en la Loy il faut qu'il y ait une mort mortelle: . . . mais en 'Evangile, la mort est vivifiante. . . . Mais ce crucifiement-là qu'emporte-il? Il est vray que c'est une espece de mort: mais tant y a que ceste mort là nous amene à la vie.*

[7] Serm. on Acts 1 : 1–4, C.O. 48 : 588. *Mais il faut scavoir que c'est que S. Luc entend par le Royaume de Dieu. Il n'entend pas par ce Royaume de Dieu la vie eternelle, comme on le prend communeement, et comme on le pourroit yci prendre de prime face, pour dire, le Royaume de Dieu est celuy que nous attendons par esperance.*

began on earth when the Gospel began with the coming of Christ,[1] and which manifests itself within us by the "inward and spiritual renewal of the soul,"[2] making constant progress towards the entire renovation of the individual and of the whole world[3] which will take place at the last coming of Christ when the Kingdom will be revealed in all its glory and majesty. All this will be the "accomplishment (*complementum*) of those things which began to take place after the resurrection of Christ."[4]

In living our Christian life the "reformation" or "spiritual government" brought about by the hidden growth of the Kingdom of God within us is, for Calvin, the fruit both of the death and the resurrection of Christ and is equally related to both. Though Calvin often emphasises the fact that the Kingdom of God within us means sharing now inwardly in the process of regeneration which began with the resurrection of Christ,[5] he can also stress the fact that to share in the Kingdom means to share in the process of mortification to the flesh which is the fruit of Christ's death on the Cross.[6] In his exposition of the clause "Thy Kingdom come" in the Lord's Prayer, almost exclusive stress is laid on the

Mais S. Luc le prend pour le gouvernement spirituel par lequel Iesus Christ nous tient en son obeissance, iusques à ce qu'il nous ait du tout reformez à son image, et que, nous ayans despouillez de ce corps mortel, il nous mette au ciel. . . . Mais pour en avoir declaration plus facile, prenons le contraire du Royaume de Dieu; c'est la vie des hommes qui sont addonnez à leur nature corrompue. . . . Car le Royaume de Dieu presuppose une reformation.

[1] Cf. Introd. Argument to comm. on Gospels C.O. 45 : 2. It should be noticed that Calvin insists that under the Old Covenant the people had not only a foreshadowing but a real experience of the effect and power of the Kingdom of God in their midst. Such events as their deliverance from Egypt and Babylon were "preludes" (*praeludium*) to what happened in Christ, and were the actual beginning of what was deferred till His coming, and made manifest at His coming. Cf. comm. on Hos. 11 : 1, C.O. 42 : 433; on Isa. 43 : 19, C.O. 37 : 94–5, 43 : 8, C.O. 37 : 86; on Ezek. 17 : 22, C.O. 40 : 417. See *Calvin's Doctrine of the Word and Sacrament*, pp. 43–6.

[2] Comm. on Luke 17 : 20, C.O. 45 : 424. Cf. Inst. 4 : 20 : 2.

[3] Comm. on Luke 17 : 20, C.O. 45 : 425. *Notandum tamen est, Christum de primordiis tantum regni Dei loqui, quia nunc spiritu reformari incipimus ad imaginem Dei, ut suo deinde tempore integra sequatur et nostri et totius mundi revocatio.*

[4] Comm. on Matt. 24 : 29, C.O. 45 : 667. Calvin sums it all up in comm. on Acts 4 : 3, C.O. 48 : 4. *Disserit de regno Dei. . . . Hoc nomine breviter indicat quorsum tendat evangelii doctrina: nempe, ut in nobis regnet Deus. Huius regni initium est regeneratio: finis ac complementum, beata immortalitas: medii progressus sunt in ampliore regenerationis profectu et augmento.* Cf. T. F. Torrance, *Kingdom and Church*, pp. 116–22.

[5] Cf. comm. on Acts 4 : 3, C.O. 48 : 4.

[6] Cf. comm. on Matt. 6 : 10, C.O. 45 : 197. *Hinc colligimus, initium regni Dei in nobis esse veteris hominis interitum et nostri abnegationem, ut renovemur in aliam vitam.*

Kingdom as involving us in denying self, subduing depraved lusts, the humbling of our pride, and contempt for this world. "This prayer, therefore, ought to withdraw us from all the corruptions of this world which separate us from God, and prevent His Kingdom from flourishing within us; secondly it ought to influence us with an ardent desire for the mortification of the flesh; and, lastly, it ought to train us to the endurance of the Cross; since this is the way in which God would have His Kingdom to be advanced."[1] Yet Calvin is careful to add that such a negative effect of communion with the death of Christ in the Kingdom of God takes place always along with the more positive effect of communion with His resurrection. "It ought not to grieve that the outward man decays, provided the inner man is renewed."[2]

It should be noted that our present participation in Christ's resurrection is not confined merely to an inward experience of regeneration. God makes His people partakers of His Kingdom and glory when by confounding the power and cunning of their enemies, He protects and guides them through every danger and enables them to persevere to the end.[3] Thus in those miraculous providential experiences of deliverance from outward evils which are at times given to us in this life and which seem to us like resurrection from death, we are not only conformed to the resurrection of Christ[4] but we are actually here and now given a real participation in it. Discussing the meaning of Isaiah 26 : 19, "Thy dead men shall live," Calvin makes the text refer not simply to the final death and resurrection of the faithful at the last day, but to the constant condition of their life on earth and to the "whole reign of Christ." The life of the faithful, as of all men, is one of such affliction that it can be described as "nothing else but mortality," the forerunner of death or the beginning of death. But whereas in the reprobate this dying condition is unrelieved because "they do not taste God's fatherly kindness," the same condition in the people of God is constantly alleviated by the providential care of God which is the fruit of their union with Christ in His resurrection. "Because, through the kindness of Christ, the curse of God is abolished equally in the beginning of death as in its end, all who are ingrafted into Christ are rightly

[1] Inst. 3 : 20 : 42. [2] Ibid.
[3] Ibid. [4] See pp. 45–6.

said to live in dying. For whatever evils come to them must work for their good. Hence it follows that they always emerge as conquerors from the abyss of death until they are wholly united to their Head."[1]

3. We already share by faith in the full glory of Christ's resurrection

In spite of all the limitations which we may experience to our enjoyment of the fruits of Christ's resurrection there is a sense in which we may be said to possess these fully here and now by faith, through communion with Christ.[2] Calvin notes that Paul in Rom. 8 : 30 uses the present tense and describes the present state of the justified as being also now a state of glorification. "The same are glorified who are now pressed with the Cross so that their miseries and reproaches do not damage them at all. Although glorification is not yet exhibited but in our Head, yet because we do in a manner see in Him now the inheritance of eternal life, His glory brings such an assurance of our glory that our hope is worthily matched or compared to present possession."[3] This pattern of glory in the life of the Christian, though it is deformed and obscure when viewed from the side of this world, is nevertheless already seen in its perfection when viewed as it appears before God and the angels.[4]

The basic principle in Calvin's thinking on this matter is that what has already happened to Christ the Head can be regarded and legitimately spoken of as having already happened to those who are the members of His body by virtue of the union effected by faith. What is possessed by Christ is also already the possession of those who are in Christ. Certainly Calvin admits that it does not look as if the children of God were already passed from death to life (1 Pet. 1 : 23), already sit in heavenly glory with Christ (Col. 3 : 3), have the Kingdom already established within them (Luke 17 : 21). But though all this is hidden, "they do not on

---

[1] Comm. on Isa. 26 : 19, C.O. 36 : 441–2.
[2] Comm. on John 14 : 2, C.O. 47 : 323. *Nam in eius persona iam spe coelum possidemus.* Cf. comm. on 2 Tim. 2 : 8, C.O. 52 : 363. *In Christi resurrectione continetur redemptionis et salutis nostrae complementum.* Cf. also Inst. 2 : 16 : 16.
[3] Comm. in loc. C.O. 49 : 161.
[4] Ibid.

that account cease to possess it by faith."[1] Calvin, while still remembering the tension and suspense of faith and hope under which the Christian life is lived, gives full emphasis to the passages of Scripture which describe the Christian's life and salvation as already fulfilled and perfected in Christ. For example, in his comment on Eph. 2 : 6, "And hath raised us up together," he writes: "The resurrection and sitting in heaven which are here mentioned are not yet seen by mortal eyes. Yet as if those blessings were in our present possession, he states that we have received them . . . and certainly although with respect to ourselves our salvation is at present hidden in hope, yet in Christ we already possess a blessed immortality and glory: and therefore he adds 'in Christ Jesus.' Hitherto it does not appear in the members but only in the Head; yet in consequence of the secret union, it belongs to the members."[2]

4. We must be content to share here and now visibly in the pattern of Christ's death rather than in the pattern of His glory

Nevertheless, as long as we live in the flesh, our participation in the resurrection of Christ is severely limited. Here we must observe God's appointed order of things, which is that we should die before we live. There are "two things in which renovation consists, the destruction of the flesh and the vivification of the Spirit. The course of good living is thus to begin with the former, but we are to advance to the latter."[3] Calvin regards it as important that if we are to make progress in the Gospel it can be made only "in a right and orderly manner." The order for such progress is to start with death before resurrection.[4] Since it was only by His ascension to Heaven that Christ's reign had its true inauguration,[5] the case cannot be otherwise with us. Moreover, the order that God has appointed is that we must wait till the coming of Christ at the

---

[1] Comm. on John 5 : 24, C.O. 47 : 116. *Nam quod abscondita est eorum vita non ideo fide eam possidere desinunt.*
[2] Comm. on Eph. 2 : 6, C.O. 51 : 164.
[3] Comm. on 1 Pet. 4 : 2, C.O.55 : 271.
[4] Comm. on 1 Cor. 15 : 14, C.O. 49 : 452. Cf. comm. on Ps. 75 : 3, C.O. 31 : 702. *Scimus in hoc regnare ut veterem hominem aboleat, et spirituale eius regnum incipere a carnis interitu: sic tamen ut deinde sequatur novi hominis instauratio*; and serm. on Gal. 2 : 20–1, C.O. 50 : 445.
[5] Inst. 2 : 16 : 14. *Sua tamen demum in coelum ascenscione regnum suum vere auspicatus est.*

last day before we can fully enjoy our inheritance of resurrection life in Him.[1]

It must be remembered, too, that no matter how much progress we make in this life, we can never progress beyond the Cross. Participation in the resurrection of Christ is never experienced apart from participation in His death. "The resurrection of Christ leads us not an inch away from the Cross," says Calvin.[2] Even though the faithful have already "passed from death to life" in that the incorruptible seed of the Word resides in them and the Kingdom is already established within them, yet "they are in life in such a manner that they always carry about with them the cause of death."[3]

In this connexion the distinction (which has already been referred to)[4] between the inward man and the outward man is of importance. The outward state of the Christian man, as far as he appears to the view of the world, is that of one who is marked out for death, subject to corruption. He is normally so ordinary and mundane in his outward behaviour that there is very little to distinguish him from the unbeliever.[5] In contrast to the frail and perishing condition of the outward man, the inward man who is hidden from the world nevertheless participates now in a real and powerful way in the renewal of creation, the promise of which is given in the Resurrection.[6]

[1] Comm. on Isa. 26 : 19, C.O. 36 : 442. *Et sane Paulus recte admonet* (Col. 3, 4), *praeposterum fore ordinem si vita fruerentur (fideles) donec Christus, qui fons est vitae eorum, apparuerit.* Cf. comm. on 1 Cor. 15 : 23, C.O. 49 : 546.

[2] Comm. on Gal. 6 : 14, C.O. 50 : 265.

[3] Comm. on John 5 : 24, C.O. 47 : 116. *Transitum autem a morte iam esse factum non inepte dicit, quia et incorruptibile est in filiis Dei vitae semen, ex quo vocati sunt et iam in coelesti gloria per spem in Christo consident, et regnum Dei intra se habent certo constitutum (Luc. 17, 21; Coloss. 3, 3). . . . Interea meminerimus fideles ita esse nunc in vita, ut mortis semper materiam circumferant.*

[4] Cf. p. 51–2.

[5] Serm. on Gal. 2 : 20–1, C.O. 50 : 444. *Car comment distinguera on entre les fideles et les incredules? ils boivent et mangent l'un comme l'autre. Il est vray que les uns boivent et mangent en sobrieté: mais on verra des incredules assez temperans, qui ne seront point adonnez à yvrongnerie ni à exces. Or quoy qu'il en soit, de prime face on iugeroit que ceste vie est commune à tous. Mais encores les fideles trainent souvent les ailes et ne font que languir en ce monde, et puis la mort est commune et égale à tous: il n'y a donc nulle diversité si on s'amuse à ce qui apparoist: bref on dira que c'est peine perdue que de croire en Iesus Christ.* Cf. comm. on John 6 : 39, C.O. 47 : 147.

[6] Comm. on Rom. 7 : 22–3, C.O. 49 : 134. *Interior autem vocatur per excellentiam, quia cor et reconditos affectus possideat. . . . Nam contemptim Paulus membrorum appellatione designat quidquid in homine apparet, ut arcanam renovationem melius ostendat sensus nostros latere ac fugere, nisi quoad fide apprehenditur.* Cf. serm. on Gal. 2 : 20–1, C.O. 50 : 445.

Calvin therefore, in view of the fact that it is the Cross rather than the Resurrection that predominates in our Christian experience here and now, often refers to the Christian life in terms of Col. 3 : 3, "Ye are dead and your life is hid with Christ in God."[1] It is not only from the eyes of the world that our new life in Christ is hidden, but also from our own eyes and senses. Even by ourselves the reality of our risen life in Christ can be apprehended and grasped only by faith.[2] In addition to his constant reference to Col. 3 : 3, Calvin never forgets that at the height of Paul's exultant description in Romans, ch. 8, of the victory he at present enjoys through the resurrection of Christ, he adds that we nevertheless are being "killed all the day long", and are like sheep destined for slaughter.[3]

We must be content, then, in this present life to share visibly rather in the pattern of Christ's death than in the pattern of His glory.[4] Indeed, our state at present, viewed outwardly, is more analogous to being buried with Christ than to having risen with Christ, and Calvin sometimes uses the analogy of burial to describe the extent of the hiddenness of our risen life in Christ.[5] The difference between Christ in His burial and ourselves is, however, that the time for His remaining buried was limited by God to last until the third day. We, however, must be willing to submit patiently to our state of burial lasting not only for a few days, but until the end of our life. We have to live in this world "like poor lost people" until the proper time assigned by God for the manifestation of our true life.[6]

---

[1] Cf. serm. on Job 14 : 5–12, C.O. 33 : 675. *Car si on regarde les enfans de Dieu, on trouvera qu'ils sont affligez, qu'il semble qu'ils doivent estre retranchez du genre humain, comme s'ils n'estoient pas dignes d'estre dessus la terre. Voila donc comme Dieu permet que les siens soyent traitez. Que faut-il donc? Que nous revenions à ce que dit sainct Paul aux Colossiens (Col. 3, 3) c'est assavoir, que nous sommes morts, mais nostre vie est cachee en nostre Seigneur Iesus Christ, et Dieu la manifestera quand il sera temps.* And serm. on Gal. 2 : 20–1, C.O. 50 : 447. In comm. on Rom. 8 : 19, C.O. 49 : 152, Calvin describes the new life as lying hid *sub deformi habitu.*

[2] Comm. on Col. 3 : 3, C.O. 52 : 119; on Rom. 7 : 23, C.O. 49 : 134.

[3] Rom. 8 : 36, cf. e.g., comm. on John 6 : 39, C.O. 47 : 147.

[4] Comm. on Phil. 3 : 21, C.O. 52 : 56–7.

[5] Comm. on 1 Pet. 1 : 7, C.O. 55 : 213. *Nunc enim abscondita est vita nostra in Christo, latebitque velut sepulta, donec e coelo Christus apparuerit.* Cf. comm. on Col. 3 : 3, C.O. 52 : 118.

[6] Serm. on Matt. 27 : 56–60, C.O. 46 : 941–2. Cf. on p. 940. *Or S. Paul nous exhorte à estre conformez à Iesus Christ, non seulement quant à sa mort mais aussi quant à sa sepulture. Car il y en a d'aucuns qui seroyent contens de mourir avec nostre Seigneur Iesus pour une minute de temps, mais à la longue ils s'ennuyent. Et pour ceste cause i'ay dit qu'il ne nous faut point seulement mourir pour un coup, mais il nous faut souffrir patiemment d'estre ensevelis iusques à la fin.*

The nature of our redemption, then, is such that we have to be content to see it fulfilled for us in Jesus Christ, to reckon it as ours because it is there for us in Jesus Christ, and to wait for the full enjoyment and effect of it at the second coming of Christ.[1] We must learn to look away from our present analysable subjective experience of Jesus Christ, and find our life in Him.[2] We must not forget that faith really possesses everything that it finds in Christ, and we are right to rejoice in what we now completely possess in this way.

Yet faith lives not merely by looking towards what is in Christ but by real present participation in Him. Faith not only looks to Christ, it also feeds on Christ. Therefore Calvin can speak of the fullness of life which at present resides only in Christ the Head as flowing to the members though merely in drops or small portions.[3] Indeed he suggests even that if we had sufficient faith such a trickle might become even a river.[4] At any rate we really now taste the first fruits of what will be ours· at the final resurrection.[5] Such first fruits are a mere foretaste (*gustus*).[6] But they are such a fore-taste as to "allure us to the desire of heavenly benefits" that in them we may find satisfaction,[7] and to be a sufficient pledge of the reality and certainty of that for which we wait.[8]

[1] Serm. on Eph. 1 : 13–14, C.O. 51 : 308. *Il est vray que nous sommes rachetez par nostre Seigneur Iesus Christ: et il nous a esté donné pour Redemption . . . : mais cependant l'effect et la iouissance n'en est pas encores. Il y a donc double redemption: il y a celle qui a este accomplie en la personne de nostre Seigneur Iesus Christ: et l'autre est celle que nous attendons, et qui se declarera en nous à sa venue.*

[2] Cf. serm. on Gal. 2 : 20–1, C.O. 50 : 447–8. *Et où est nostre vie sinon en nostre Seigneur Iesus Christ?* Cf. p. 445. *Car d'autant plus que les fideles se voyent decliner, ils sont advertis et solicitez de regarder en haut.*

[3] Comm. on Ps. 16 : 10, C.O. 31 : 157. *Unde sequitur, vitae plenitudinem quae in capite solo residet, guttatim solum vel per partes ad membra defluere.*

[4] Comm. on John 7 : 38, C.O. 47 : 182.

[5] Ibid. In his commentary on 1 Cor. 15 : 23, C.O. 49 : 546, Calvin suggests the same thought.

[6] Serm. on Gal. 2 : 20–1, C.O. 50 : 447–8. *Seulement quelque goust.*

[7] Comm. on I Tim. 4 : 8, C.O. 52 : 300. Cf. on John 7 : 38, C.O. 47 : 182.

[8] Serm. on Luke 1 : 26–30, C.O. 46 : 67. *Dieu donnera tousiours un tel goust de sa bonté à ceux qu'il aura regardez en pitie, qu'ils en auront un bon gage, pour s'asseurer en attendant la pleine possession qui leur est promise.*

Chapter IV

Meditation on the future or heavenly life

1. Our Christian life finds its focus and inspiration in the ascended Christ

Our Christian life should find its focus and inspiration not only in the death and resurrection of Christ but also in His ascension. Calvin insists that we can even now in actual practice not only rise with Christ from the death of sin into a new life, but also ascend with Christ above this world. Christ ascended in order that we might ascend with Him, not only at the last day but even now. Indeed, says Calvin, we must ascend now with Christ if we do not wish to be separated from Him, for He has entered His heavenly life in order that He might "draw believers after Him."[1] Calvin can utter a warning against a devotion that stops short with the risen Christ and does not ascend to Heaven with Him to seek happiness there. "Ascension follows resurrection: hence if we are the members of Christ we must ascend into Heaven, because He, on being raised up from the dead was *received up into Heaven* that He might draw us with Him."[2] When we ask how such an ascent of the mind and heart above this world to the ascended Christ is possible here and now, we find ourselves forced to examine what Calvin means by *meditatio coelestis vitae*, for it is by such *meditatio* that we commune with the ascended Christ, and the focal point of such *meditatio* is the ascended Christ.

2. Our Christian life strains towards the future life.

Our Christian life must, besides this focus on what is "above," also have a constant emphasis on what is held out for it in the future. *Meditatio coelestis vitae* is for Calvin the same thing as

[1] Comm. on John 20 : 18, C.O. 47 : 434–5. Cf. comm. on Matt. 6 : 21, C.O. 45 : 205.
[2] Comm. on Col. 3 : 1, C.O. 52 : 117–18.

meditatio futurae vitae. The Christian life is a life that strains
towards a completion and fulfilment that belong to it only beyond
death. It finds the present full of meaning and purpose only because it knows that the future has meaning and certainty. It is a
constant and bold forward march through the darkness of this
world to the day of resurrection.[1]

This means that when we speak of "salvation," we must think
of it as embracing the whole course of our present life and completed only in the glory of the life to come.[2] Regeneration is thus
merely the beginning of salvation. Whatever gift God gives us
here and now can be truly appreciated only if we see it as part of
this complete plan, and as a token and pledge of an eternal glory
which cannot yet be perceived or measured.[3]

3. Our participation both in the death and resurrection of Christ should stir us up to *meditatio futurae vitae*

The fact of our present participation in the resurrection of
Christ should stir us up to such meditation on the heavenly life.
It has already been pointed out that we are to regard our present
experience of regeneration as a foretaste that should make us long
for a more full and perfect participation in Christ hereafter.[4] We
must regard the gift of "life" which we now increasingly enjoy in
Christ as but a pledge of ultimate "fullness of life."[5] In the midst
of the growing measure of freedom which we at present experience
we must groan and long after the complete freedom of the life to
come.[6] We must regard our present experiences of deliverance
by the power of Christ from sin and misery as "a sort of prepara-

---

[1] Cf. comm. on John 6 : 39, C.O. 47 : 147.
[2] Comm. on Ps. 119 : 123, C.O. 32 : 269; on 2 Tim. 2 : 10, C.O. 52 : 364.
[3] Serm. on Job 14 : 13–15, C.O. 33 : 690–1. *Il a mis maintenant sa grace en
nous : à quel propos Dieu nous auroit-il donné courage de le servir et honorer, aussi
nous auroit donné l'esprit d'adoption, sinon pour estre certifiez de l'esperance que
nous avons de la gloire immortelle? tout cela seroit inutile. Ainsi donc, ce change-
ment que nous apercevons auiourd'hui en nous, est un tesmoignage infallible de
ceste gloire celeste que nous ne voyons point encores, et laquelle nous est cachee:
mais Dieu nous en donnera une bonne arre, comme il est dit que le S. Esprit en est
l'arre et le gage.* Cf. comm. on John 6 : 27, C.O. 47 : 139. *Ideo spiritus dona
recipere nos convenit, ut tesserae sint ac pignora vitae aeternae.*
[4] See pp. 78–9.
[5] Comm. on John 10 : 10, C.O. 47 : 241.
[6] Comm. on John 8 : 32, C.O. 47 : 203.

tion for the last resurrection."[1] It is thus that the first fruits which we now taste should stir us up to press forward to the full reality of which they are the pledges.[2]

Our present participation in the death of Christ should also stir us up to meditation on the future life. We are daily exercised under the Cross by God that we may seek our true rest elsewhere than in this world.[3] "As the condition of the godly during the whole course of their life is very miserable, Christ properly calls them to the hope of the heavenly life."[4] It is indeed "the principal use of the Cross"[5] that it has this effect of detaching us from this present life and of making us aspire towards the future life.[6] Our faith could not possibly stand firm in the midst of all the afflictions with which the faithful are oppressed in this present life in which the tokens of our resurrection life are few and obscure, unless we "keep out of our view the condition of the present life, and apply our minds and our senses to the last day."[7] The Cross therefore should always be regarded as a ladder by which the minds and hearts of man might ascend to Heaven.[8] Calvin insists that just as we should never become so absorbed in contemplating the death of Christ without at the same time bringing to mind the glory of His resurrection,[9] so in our experience of the Cross we ought to remember with joy and gladness that our participation in the sufferings of Christ is bound to be accompanied at length in a full participation in the glory of His resurrection. "We must always bear in mind this transition from the Cross to the Resurrection."[10] Only when the Cross thus directs our eyes to the power of His

---

[1] Comm. on John 5 : 28, C.O. 47 : 119. *Quoddam ultimae resurrectionis praeludium.*

[2] Cf. pp. 86 and 317–8.

[3] Comm. on Ps. 147 : 6, C.O. 32 : 427. *Unde etiam colligimus, quamvis sub lege mollius fovendi essent patres, non fuisse tamen expertes eius militiae, in qua nos hodie Deus exercet, ut alibi quam in mundo veram requiem quaeramus.* Cf. comm. on 2 Cor. 4 : 16, C.O. 50 : 58; and Ibid. 10, C.O. 50 : 55.

[4] Comm. on Matt. 5 : 10, C.O. 45 : 164.

[5] Inst. 3 : 9. (Summary of Chapter).

[6] Comm. on Col. 3 : 3, C.O. 52 : 119. *Hoc verum et necessarium est spei nostrae experimentum, ut tanquam morte circumdati vitam alibi quaeramus quam in mundo.*

[7] Comm. on John 6 : 39, C.O. 47 : 147.

[8] Comm. on Matt. 26 : 29, C.O. 45 : 709. *Ita videmus, ut manu ducat suos discipulos ad crucem, et inde in spem resurrectionis eos extollat. Sicut autem illos dirigi ad mortem Christi oportuit, ut per illam scalam in coelum ascenderent: ita nunc, ex quo Christus morte defunctus est ac in coelum receptus, a crucis intuitu in coelum deduci nos convenit, ut inter se cohaereant mors et vitae reparatio.*

[9] Comm. on John 10 : 17, C.O. 47 : 245–6.

[10] Comm. on 1 Pet. 4 : 12, C.O. 55 : 279

resurrection can the Cross be said to triumph in our hearts.[1] Unless our experience of the Cross achieves this end of raising our minds to Heaven, then our situation would be deplorable indeed[2].

All our sufferings, therefore, should be regarded by us as a stage in the complete process of death and resurrection in Christ which is to lead to the consummation of the final glorification of both body and soul in Christ. The life of Christ on earth (which in the Gospels is viewed as the suffering of Christ and is closely related to His death) is, for Calvin, a prelude to His death.[3] The Christian should also regard his own suffering as a prelude to death, "for the whole course of our life leads to the destruction of the external man."[4] The people of God, therefore, throughout their earthly life continually "lie under the shadow of death on account of the various afflictions which they must continually endure."[5] The life of a Christian viewed from its outward aspect "differs nothing from death,"[6] and the Christian can be described suitably as a dead man.[7]

4. *Meditatio* involves meditating, aspiration and faith

Meditatio futurae vitae involves thinking about the nature and reality and glory of the life that is beyond and above. To concentrate our minds on such a subject is all the more necessary since the signs of corruption and decay and death in this present world tend to crowd in upon our mind to the exclusion of all other thoughts.[8] It involves "intensity of aim" and concentration of the whole mind and intellect. It is "true and holy thinking (*cogitatio*)"

[1] Inst. 3 : 9 : 6.   [2] Ibid.

[3] Comm. on Phil. 3 : 10, C.O. 52 : 50. *Huc igitur comparatos esse nos omnes convenit, ut tota vita nostra nihil quam mortis imaginem repraesentet, donec mortem ipsam pariat. Sicuti vita Christi nihil aliud fuit quam mortis praeludium. Sed hac consolatione interea fruimur, quod finis est aeterna beatitudo.*

[4] Comm. on 1 Pet. 1 : 7, C.O. 55 : 213. *Totus vitae nostrae cursus ad interitum externi hominis inclinat: et quaecunque patimur, quasi mortis sunt praeludia.* Cf. comm. on John 3 : 2, C.O. 55 : 330. *Nam quantum ad corpus spectat, pulvis et umbra sumus: mors semper ante oculos versatur: interea mille aerumnis sumus obnoxii.*

[5] Comm. on Isa. 26 : 17–19, C.O. 36 : 442.

[6] Comm. on Col. 3 : 3, C.O. 52 : 118.

[7] Cf. Col. 3 : 3; Isa. 26 : 9. Comm. on John 12 : 24, C.O. 47 : 288. *Neque enim solum in morte interire nos putamus, sed vita quoque nostra instar est perpetuae mortis.*

[8] Comm. on 2 Cor. 4 : 17, C.O. 50 : 58. *Verum quia visibilis est corruptio, renovatio autem invisibilis: Paulus, ut carnalem praesentis vitae affectum nobis excutiat, miserias praesentes cum futura felicitate componit.*

which "bears us up to Heaven" that there we may adore Christ.[1] Our model for such concentration and application should be the unjust steward (of the parable) who typifies the industry and skill of the men of this world in conducting their business.[2] Such meditation should be our unceasing care and business on this earth.[3] We must struggle to discipline ourselves against opposing temptations to become mentally absorbed in the cares and pleasures of this life.[4] When Jesus calls on His disciples to "watch", He is calling us precisely to this "uninterrupted attention which keeps our minds in full activity, and makes us pass through the world like pilgrims."[5]

An important element in the mental activity of meditating on the future life is to compare soberly the worth and glory and stability of the heavenly life with the comparative poverty and miseries and uncertainty of this present world. Calvin is confident that if we soberly and fairly make this comparison it is bound to engender within us a proper hatred and contempt for this fading life, true patience to bear its miseries and true moderation in indulging in its pleasures.[6] "If Heaven is our country, what can earth be but a place of exile? If departure from the world is entrance into life, what is the world but a sepulchre, and what is residence in it but immersion in death? . . . Thus when the earthly is compared with the heavenly life, it may undoubtedly be despised and trampled underfoot."[7] Such *meditatio* should mean the end of all the exaggerated fancies about the length of life on this earth by which men drug themselves into a false sense of security.[8]

---

[1] Comm. on Col. 3 : 1, C.O. 52 : 117–18.

[2] Comm. on Luke 16 : 8, C.O. 45 : 403–4.

[3] Comm. on Matt. 6 : 20, C.O. 45 : 205. *Thesaurum autem suum in coelo reponere dicuntur, qui expediti huius mundi laqueis curas suas et studia ad coelestis vitae meditationem conferunt.*

[4] Comm. on 1 Pet. 1 : 9, C.O. 55 : 214. *Vita haec et quaecunque ad corpus pertinent, magna sunt impedimenta, ne animus noster ad futurae et spiritualis vitae cogitationem se applicet. Hanc ergo nobis toto studio meditandam proponit apostolus.*

[5] Comm. on Matt. 24 : 42, C.O. 45 : 676. *Apud Matthaeum uno vigilantiae nomine continua illa notatur attentio, quae facit ut erectis sursum mentibus in terra peregrinemur.*

[6] Comm. on 2 Cor. 4 : 17, C.O. 50 : 58. *Haec autem sola comparatio abunde sufficit ad imbuendos aequitate et moderatione piorum animos.* Cf. comm. on John 12 : 25, C.O. 47 : 289.   [7] Inst. 3 : 9 : 4.

[8] Comm. on Ps. 90 : 3–6, C.O. 31 : 835. *Nam imaginatio longi temporis sopori similis est, in quo torpemus omnes, donec coelestis vitae meditatio inane hoc terreni status figmentum absorbeat.*

It is obvious that for Calvin *meditatio* implies also a strong element of desire and aspiration after the heavenly life.[1] We must meditate on the future life not as those who are neutrally-disposed observers, but "with our whole heart."[2] *Meditatio* is the opposite of *contemptio*, and as *contemptio* indicates a revulsion from this world, so *meditatio* equally implies movement of desire towards the life to come.[3] To meditate on the Kingdom of God is, for Calvin, the same as seeking with the Spirit that realm which is invisible to the flesh.[4] It is to lay up for ourselves treasures in Heaven instead of entangling ourselves in the snares of this world.[5] What we set before our minds in this meditation on the heavenly life is the supreme good and final goal of human life. The ascended Christ in whom we find our perfect happiness is there in Heaven where our mind is raised by *meditatio*. It is but natural that we should desire what constitutes for us the supreme good and our highest happiness.[6]

There is an extremely close connexion between faith and *meditatio futurae vitae*, for faith itself, according to Calvin,[7] has the power to raise the hearts of men up to communion with the ascended Christ, and to enable men to grasp now what is their future in Christ. Thus through *meditatio* there is the real ascent of the mind or soul or heart to the ascended Christ. We thereby raise our minds to Heaven.[8] It is a "true and holy *thinking* about Christ, which forthwith bears us up to Heaven, that we may there adore Him, and that our minds may dwell with Him."[9] Those

---

[1] Inst. 3 : 9 : 1. *Sic enim habendum est, nunquam serio ad futurae vitae desiderium ac meditationem erigi animum, nisi praesentis contemptu ante imbutus fuerit.*

[2] Inst. 3 : 9 : 2. *Toto pectore.*   [3] Inst. 3 : 9 : 1.

[4] Comm. on Heb. 12 : 1, C.O. 55 : 171. *Nempe, ut regnum Dei, quod carni est invisibile sensusque omnes nostros superat, spiritu quaeramus. Nam qui in hac meditatione occupantur, facile terrena omnia contemnunt.*

[5] Comm. on Matt. 6 : 20, C.O. 45 : 205.

[6] Comm. on Matt. 6 : 21, C.O. 45 : 205.

[7] See pp. 21–3.

[8] Inst. 3 : 9 : 6. *Deploratissimi ergo essent, nisi in coelum mente erecta, superarent quicquid in mundo est.* Cf. serm. on Job 14 : 1–4, C.O. 33 : 658. *Ce n'est point assez d'avoir cognu la brefveté de nostre vie. . . . Pourtant nous avons à faire comparaison de la vie celeste, à laquelle Dieu nous appelle tous les iours: et en ce faisant, nous pourrons mepriser les choses basses et corruptibles de ce monde . . .: et puis nous pourrons estre eslevez en haut, pour prendre là tout nostre contentement et repos.*

[9] Comm. on Col. 3 : 1, C.O. 52 : 117–18. *Meminerimus ergo hanc esse veram de Christo cogitationem et sanctam, quae nos statim in coelum rapit, ut ipsum illic adoremus, et cum eo habitent mentes nostrae.*

who meditate upon the heavenly life are "those whose minds have
been raised above the world by a taste of the heavenly life."[1] It
must be remembered, too, that such movement up to Heaven
with the mind and heart cannot take place through the unaided
efforts of man's own mind,[2] but only by means of participation in
the sacramental worship of the Church, which is, for Calvin, the
ladder by which the faithful mount up to Heaven, there to participate in Christ, or the hand of God stretched down to us in order
to lift us to Himself.[3]

---

[1] Comm. on Ps. 30 : 6, C.O. 31 : 295. . . . *qui coelestis vitae gustu supra mundum feruntur.* . . .

[2] Comm. on Ps. 84 : 2, C.O. 31 : 780. *Unde colligimus nimium esse stupidos qui ordinem a Deo mandatum, quasi possent proprio marte in coelum conscendere, secure negligunt.*

[3] Cf. Ibid. *quia scalis sibi sciebat esse opus per quas in coelum conscenderet, visibile vero sanctuarium vice scalarum esse. . . . Frustra nos ad se vocaret (Deus), nisi etiam descenderet ad nos vicissim: vel saltem interpositis mediis, manus quodammodo ad nos sursum tollendos extenderet.*

Chapter V

Repentance as dying and rising with Christ

1. Our whole Christian life is repentance

THE whole process of our dying and rising with Christ is, for Calvin, repentance or sanctification. The word "sanctification" possibly refers more properly to the process when it is viewed as a whole—in its inward and outward aspects. The word "repentance" refers chiefly to the change of heart involved, and to the effect which such a change has spontaneously on the outward behaviour. Repentance is our response to Christ. Sanctification is our whole participation in Christ. The word "repentance" is used by Calvin as almost interchangeable with "conversion" or "regeneration." Calvin describes repentance as a process of "conversion to God,"[1] and he defines this conversion of the life to consist in "the mortification of the flesh and of the old man, and the quickening of the Spirit."[2] Involved in the doctrine of repentance Calvin finds a "rule for holy living." This rule consists of three continuous exercises: self-denial, the mortification of the flesh, and meditating upon the heavenly life.[3]

Repentance is therefore not to be thought of as merely a certain kind of feeling, or as one stage in the religious life which might lead to some higher form of Christian life no longer deserving of the name "repentance." Nor is repentance to be thought of as merely an attitude. It is true that the response of man to the Gospel arises from an attitude which might be called an attitude of repentance, but strictly speaking the term "repentance" should be used to cover the whole response of the man of faith to the Gospel in outward life, in mind, heart, attitude, and will. Yet repentance is a "conversion of life" which involves a "transforma-

[1] Comm. on Acts 20 : 21, C.O. 48 : 462.
[2] Inst. 3 : 3 : 5.
[3] Comm. on Acts 20 : 21, C.O. 48 : 463. *Ergo poenitentiae doctrina pie vivendi regulam continet, nostri abnegationem, carnis nostrae mortificationem vitaeque coelestis meditationem exigit.*

tion not only in external works, but in the soul itself."[1] The whole habit of the soul has to be changed before "fruits worthy of repentance" can be brought forth in the outward life.

2. Repentance involves a change of heart

Since the Roman Church divorced the outward aspect of repentance from the inward renewal of the heart and mind, looking on repentance as an external discipline, Calvin at times emphasised the inward aspect of repentance at the expense of its external aspect.[2] He can define repentance as exclusively an affair of the heart, an inward and hidden renewal of the man. He refers to the outward amendment of life which accompanies this inward change as the fruits of inward repentance.[3] Indeed he can say that "when the name 'repentance' is applied to the external profession it is used improperly."[4] Yet inappropriate ways of speaking are often the best way of expressing the truth, therefore he can also speak as if the cleansing of the heart were but the initial stage of true repentance, which also includes in itself the resultant reformation in outward behaviour.[5] The outward change of life, however, is simply the visible aspect and proof of the inward grace of repentance, and the one cannot possibly take place without the accompaniment of the other.[6]

[1] Inst. 3 : 3 : 6. Since repentance is the turning of the whole heart, repentance as well as faith unites the heart in integrity if it is sincere and serious repentance. Cf. comm. on Joel 2 : 12–13, C.O. 42 : 542. *Ideo propheta diserte hic denuntiat simulationem hanc Deo non placere, et nihil profecturos esse qui tantum poenitentiam aliquam obtendunt externis signis, sed opus esse serio et sincero cordis affectu. Hoc intelligit per totum cor, non quod possit inveniri perfecta poenitentia in hominibus, sed cor totum vel integrum opponitur dimidio.*

[2] Inst. 3 : 4 : 1. Cf. comm. on Matt. 3 : 8, C.O. 45 : 118.

[3] Serm. on Matt. 3 : 9–10, C.O. 46 : 547. *La repentance, comme nous avons touché, est une chose cachee; elle ha son siege au coeur de l'homme, mais les fruits se declairent en toute la vie.* Comm. on Matt. 3 : 8, C.O. 45 : 118. *Notandum est, quod bona opera fructus vocantur poenitentiae: est enim poenitentia res interior, quae sedem in corde et anima habet, sed fructus deinde suos profert in vitae mutatione.*

[4] Inst. 3 : 3 : 18. *Hoc tamen adhuc inseram: quum ad hanc externam professionem transfertur nomen poenitentiae, improprie a genuino illo sensu quem posui deflecti.*

[5] Comm. on James 4 : 8, C.O. 55 : 418. *Unde colligimus, quae vera sit poenitentiae ratio ac natura: ubi scilicet non tantum corrigitur vita exterior, sed initium fit ab animi repurgatione.*

[6] Comm. on Isa. 55 : 7, C.O. 37 : 289. *Itaque poenitentia totius hominis immutationem continet. In homine enim affectus, consilia, ac deinde opera consideramus. Apparent hominibus opera: radix vero intus latet. . . . Utrumque enim requiritur: nempe conversio mentis et vitae mutatio.*

3. Repentance and faith

Repentance and faith, no less than sanctification and justification, are constantly linked together in the Scriptures.[1] The one
cannot exist without the other[2] and they cannot be separated.[3]
Yet even though they cannot be separated, they must be distinguished,[4] "for repentance is a turning to God, as when we frame
ourselves and all our life to obey Him, but faith is a receiving of
the grace offered us in Christ."[5] Calvin indulges in some rather
subtle thinking when he faces the question of which grace should
be thought of as first, with respect to time, in the heart. He says
emphatically that "repentance not only always follows faith, but
is produced by it," and he strongly condemns the error of "those
who think that repentance precedes faith instead of flowing from
or being produced by it, as the fruit by the tree.[6] It is obvious that
such an error could easily give rise to a doctrine of justification by
works. Nevertheless, Calvin can include faith as part of the work of
turning to God which is repentance,[7] and when he comes to
passages in Scripture where repentance seems to be made prior
to faith, he can argue that since faith is a work of the Holy Spirit,
it can only be begotten within us after the work of renewal has
begun. Thus faith must flow from regeneration. But this preliminary regeneration which precedes faith is a very secret and obscure
work of the Spirit. As far as human sense can investigate, faith
always precedes repentance or regeneration.[8] Arguing along another
line he can make the cautious and careful statement that "the
beginning of repentance is a preparation for faith."[9] He obviously

---

[1] Inst. 3 : 3 : 5.   [2] Ibid.
[3] Comm. on Acts 20 : 21, C.O. 48 : 463. *Videmus nunc ut individuo nexu inter
se cohaereant poenitentia et fides.*
[4] Inst. 3 : 3 : 5.   [5] Comm. on Acts 20 : 21, C.O. 48 : 462-3.
[6] Inst. 3 : 3 : 1. But there is no "period of time" in which faith gives birth to
repentance. Ibid. 3 : 3 : 2.
[7] Inst. 3 : 3 : 5. *Equidem nec me latet, sub poenitentiae nomine totam ad Deum
conversionem comprehendi, cuius pars non postrema fides est.* Cf. comm. on John
1 : 13, C.O. 47 : 13. *Ergo secundum diversos respectus fides regenerationis nostrae
pars est.*
[8] Cf. comm. on John 1 : 13, C.O. 47 : 13.
[9] Comm. on Acts 20 : 21, C.O. 48 : 463. *Poenitentiam non ideo priore loco
nominat, quod tota praecedat fidem, quum pars eius ex fide emanet, eiusque sit
effectus: sed quia poenitentiae initium praeparatio sit ad fidem. Initium voco nostri
displicentiam, quae metu irae Dei serio tactos ad quaerendum remedium nos impellit.*

wants us to think of faith and repentancé as being largely simultaneous.

As a general rule, Calvin relates faith and repentance to different aspects of the Word of God. Faith is response to the Word of God in its gracious aspect. "Faith has respect to the promises of grace."[1] Faith is the response of love and confidence to God's fatherhood as it is reflected in the promises of the Word. Faith is man arising to lay hold of what is offered in Christ for his possession and salvation. Calvin finds that the response of repentance, however, arises out of the sterner aspect of the revelation of God given in the Gospel. Repentance proceeds from a "sincere and serious fear of God,"[2] rather than out of the confident apprehension of God's fatherhood out of which faith springs and is nourished. Repentance takes its rise out of the grief occasioned by the apprehension of sin in the light of God's judgment upon it and by the consideration of God's wrath.[3] The thought that inspires repentance is "that God will one day ascend His tribunal to take an account of all words and actions."[4] It must not be thought, however, that in Calvin faith is exclusively thought of as the response of grace, and repentance exclusively attached to God's wrath and judgment. Calvin can say that "fear and faith are mutually connected".[5] He can also say that "repentance has its origin in the grace of God."[6] After all we are here dealing with a realm of personal encounter and personal response where the action of God and the response of man cannot possible be systematically analysed and neatly summarised, and Calvin is too great a thinker to attempt such exact systematisation.

[1] Inst. 3 : 2 : 7.   [2] Inst. 3 : 3 : 5.

[3] Comm. on 2 Cor. 7 : 10, C.O. 50 : 89. *Hanc tristitiam Paulus causam facit et originem poenitentiae: quod est diligenter observandum. Nisi enim sibi displiceat peccator, vitam suam oderit, ac serio doleat agnitione peccati: nunquam ad Dominum convertetur. Rursum fieri nequit ut talis in homine sit tristitia, quin novum animum pariat. Ergo a dolore incipit poenitentia.* Cf. serm. on Job 42 : 6–8, C.O. 35 : 489. *Car iamais les hommes ne detesteront et leurs œuvres et leurs propos, s'ils ne sentent Dieu pour leur Iuge.* Cf. also serm. on Job 42 : 9–17, C.O. 35 : 502. *Car combien que Dieu se monstre benin et volontaire envers nous: toutes fois nous avons besoin qu'en partie il se monstre difficile. Voire, mais c'est pour nous induire à une meilleure desplaisance de nos pechez: car il nous semble souvent qu'il suffist d'avoir eu un bon souspir, comme on parle en commun langage, et nous iouons quasi avec Dieu. La repentance nous doit rendre du tout confus, elle nous doit saisir de frayeur quand nous cognoissons l'ire de Dieu qui est pour nous accabler du tout.* Cf. serm. on Matt. 3 : 1–2, etc., C.O. 46 : 497.   [4] Inst. 3 : 3 : 7.

[5] Inst. 3 : 2 : 23, Cf. serm. on Luke 1 : 26–30, C.O. 46 : 70. *Voyla donc la crainte, qui est comme un vray preparatif de la foy.*   [6] Inst. 3 : 3 : 21.

4. The signs and accompaniments of repentance

The grief or sorrow towards God which gives rise to repentance is accompanied by other "signs and accompaniments"[1] of repentance. Calvin finds a good summary of the "affections conjoined with repentance" and of the attitude of the true penitent in St Paul's catalogue in 2 Cor. 7 : 10. He enumerates these as "carefulness, excuse, indignation, fear, desire, zeal, revenge," and in the Institutes he gives a simple exposition of the meaning of these terms as a sufficient description of repentance.[2] In his preaching his language is perhaps stronger, and he uses terms to convey the impression that true repentance should at times be accompanied by feelings of utter dismay, terror, anguish of soul and despair.[3] There are times too when repentance should be accompanied by outward signs that men can see (in accordance with the ancient custom of repenting in dust and ashes), betokening the sorrow and anguish that is felt in the heart. But such extreme emotions, and such public manifestation of repentance, are normally to be reserved for times of "special repentance,"[4] when a man has been involved in a particularly grievous fall from grace, or in cases when public scandal needs to be put right by public signs of penitence.[5]

The necessity for such special exercise of repentance at particular times must not, however, obscure the fact that we are so constantly beset by sin as to require to cultivate what Calvin calls "ordinary repentance" all the days of our life.[6] Such repentance need not be accompanied by outward signs or violent emotions.

---

[1] Comm. on 2 Cor. 7 : 11, C.O. 50 : 90.

[2] Inst. 3 : 3 : 15.

[3] Cf. serm. on Matt. 3 : 1–3, etc., C.O. 46 : 498. *Or comment est-ce que L'Escriture saincte parle de penitence? C'est que nous soyons tellement aneantis, qu'il n'y ait que frayeur en nous et desespoir, cognoissant que devant Dieu nous sommes damnez, et qu'il n'y a nul remede.* Cf. serm. on Job 42 : 6–8, C.O. 35 : 491. *Il faut sur tout que le coeur soit navré, qu'ayans horreur d'avoir provoqué l'ire de nostre Dieu contre nous, nous concevions une angoisse pour nous condamner, et que nous soyons du tout confus en nous-mesmes.*

[4] Cf. Inst. 3 : 3 : 17–18.

[5] Comm. on 2 Cor. 7 : 11, C.O. 50 : 92. *Verum interest, olam coram Deo quis peccaverit, an palam coram mundo. Cuius arcanum est peccatum, satis est si coram Deo ita sit affectus. Ubi autem manifestum est peccatum, requiritur etiam manifesta poenitentiae approbatio.* Cf. serm. on Job 42 : 6–8, C.O. 35 : 490–1; and comm. on Matt. 11 : 21, C.O. 45 : 312.

[6] Inst. 3 : 3 : 18. *Specialis ergo poenitentia . . . ordinariam non tollit, cui per totum vitae curriculum operam dare nos cogit naturae corruptio.*

Indeed, such repentance must be the daily exercise of all Christians.[1] For Calvin, the Christian life is simply the constant practice of repentance.[2] "If we would stand in Christ we must aim at repentance, cultivate it during our whole lives, and continue it to the last."[3]

Repentance is characterised by self-denial. The repentant man hates himself. He knows that his whole life and being is worthy of nothing more than total condemnation before the judgment of God. Therefore in the process of repentance he condemns himself, taking revenge upon himself for his own sins with intense self-hatred.[4] This means renouncing completely our old nature.[5] This should also involve self-punishment, for in repentance we are meant to "anticipate by repentance the judgment of God."[6] But it must not be thought that such repentant self-condemnation could ever appease the anger of God or obtain His pardon.[7] Repentance is response to God's grace and judgment, but never a means of obtaining grace or averting judgment. The penitent

---

[1] Serm. on Job. 42 : 6–8, C.O. 35 : 490. *D'avantage, que ce signe n'est pas tousiours requis, mais que c'estoit pour faire une protestation publique d'un crime exorbitant. Il faut que tous fideles tout le temps de leur vie avisent à se repentir et desplaire: car nous ne passons iamais un iour qu'il n'y ait beaucoup de povretez en nous: sans que nous pensions, nous ferons des fautes infinies. . . . Ainsi nous avons occasion de gemir: et toutes fois nous ne ferons point de protestation manifeste devant les hommes. La penitence donc pourra bien estre sans avoir les signes exterieurs conioints.*

[2] Inst. 3 : 3 : 1—2. Comm. on Matt. 11 : 21, C.O. 45 : 312. *Scimus, non exigi poenitentiam a fidelibus tantum ad paucos dies, sed ut se in ea meditanda assidue usque ad mortem exerceant.*

[3] Inst. 3 : 3 : 20. Cf. serm. on Matt. 3 : 1–3, etc., C.O. 46 : 500. *La penitence n'est pas que nous commencions seulement à croire en Iesus Christ: . . . il faut que iournellement la penitence se renouvelle, par maniere de dire, c'est à dire que cest exercice soit continuel, et que ce soit nostre estude pour toute nostre vie.*

[4] Serm. on Gal. 5 : 14–18, C.O. 51 : 29. *Que nous apprenions à nous hayr nousmesmes, et à estre fachez contre nous, à nous venger de nostre malice (comme sainct Paul aussi en parle), car la penitence emporte cela que les hommes se condamnent, qu'ils se haissent, qu'ils se vengent d'eux mesmes quand ils voyent qu'ils sont corrompus en toute leur vie.* Cf. comm. on 2 Cor. 7 : 11, C.O. 50 : 91.

[5] Serm. on Job 42 : 6–8, C.O. 35 : 489. *Notons bien donc que la vraye penitence emporte la haine du peche, voire iusques au bout: tellement que l'homme se reprouve, et se haysse d'autant qu'il ne se trouve pas tel qu'il devroit: et qu'aimant la iustice de Dieu il condamne tout ce qui est en lui, et ne cerche sinon d'estre despouille de ceste vieille peau dont il est enveloppe.* Cf. comm. on Eph, 4 : 22, C.O. 51 : 207. *Requirit in homine christiano poenitentiam et renovationem vitae. Eam constituit in abnegatione nostri, et spiritus sancti regeneratione. A priore itaque parte incipit, iubens deponere aut exuere hominem veterem. . . . Qui exuere vult hominem veterem, naturae suae renuntiet.*

[6] Comm. on 1 Cor. 11 : 31, C.O. 49 : 494. Cf. comm. on 2 Cor. 7 : 11, C.O 50 : 91. *Peccata vendicando Dei iudicium quodammodo antevertimus.*

[7] Cf. ibid.

man, seeing that God has forgiven his faults, refuses to flatter and nourish the self-centred will and wisdom whose vicious nature and fearful potentiality are so clearly revealed in the event of forgiveness. Therefore the forgiven man becomes his own judge and punisher, and God establishes His righteousness more effectively and radically than through overt and catastrophic visitations of judgment on the earth.[1]

Repentance is characterised equally by newness of life. Where there is true repentant self-denial inspired by the Spirit of God, then renovation inevitably follows and this renovation is manifested in a new life of justice, judgment, and mercy.[2] With the same zeal with which we take revenge upon ourselves, we are bound also to throw ourselves into the service of righteousness. The very force of our self-condemnation becomes the impulse which makes us henceforth "range ourselves" on the side of the Lord.[3] Expressed in the simple and homely terms of the prophets: if we "depart from evil" we are bound to "do good," if we "cleanse ourselves" from the evil of our doings before God, it must follow that we "cease to do evil," and "learn to do well."[4] All this is bound to lead to that meditation on the heavenly life for which man was made in the image of God, which image will be finally restored when that heavenly life is finally attained after death. Therefore, although through repentance we are annihilated and brought down to the dust before the judgment of God, nevertheless through the same repentance we are also raised up to heaven.[5]

---

[1] Serm. on Job. 34 : 10–15, C.O. 35 : 147. *Dieu donc a bien ceste liberté d'abolir nos offenses sans les punir: et cependant cela ne deroge en rien à sa iustice. Et pourquoi? Car quand Dieu nous veut pardonner nos fautes, comment en use-il? Ce n'est pas pour nourrir le mal qui est en nous: mais il nous en touche, et nous le remonstre, il nous fait sentir combien nous l'avons offensé, et puis il nous donne ceste affection de nous desplaire en nos pechez, et d'y gemir. Quand nous sommes touchez ainsi de repentance, nous sommes iuges de nos fautes, et les condamnons: et par ce moyen voila Dieu qui a exercé son office.*

[2] Inst. 3 : 3 : 8. *Primus ad obedientiam Legis eius ingressus est illa naturae nostrae abnegatio. Postea renovationem designant a fructibus, qui inde consequuntur, iustitia, iudicio et misericordia.*

[3] Serm. on Matt. 3 : 1–2, etc., C.O. 46 : 499. *Voyla par où la penitence commence: et puis, que non seulement nous hayssions le peche et le mal qui est en nous: mais voyans que nous sommes ennemis de Dieu, que nous ayons en detestation nostre malice. . . . Or nous sommes-nous ainsi hays et despitez contre nostre meschante nature? il faut que nous desirions de nous ranger à Dieu, et de nous y ranger en telle sorte, que toutes nos affections soyent conformes à ses saincts commandemens.*

[4] Inst. 3 : 3 : 8. Cf. Ps. 34 : 14, Isa. 1 : 16–17.

[5] Inst. 3 : 3 : 9. *Uno ergo verbo poenitentiam interpretor regenerationem, cuius non alius est scopus nisi ut imago Dei . . . in nobis reformetur.*

PART THREE

THE RESTORATION OF
TRUE ORDER

Chapter I

The true order of man's life in the restored image of God

1. The original pattern of man's life as a pattern of order

THE pattern of life which man was meant to fulfil, had he not fallen from God, was a pattern of order. In the magnificent theatre of this world which was made to provide the setting of man's life, what should chiefly strike our admiration is the fair and beautiful order and arrangement of the universe[1]—the "regular order of things" in the laws and decrees by which the universe is governed. This order gives a stability to man's environment which cannot be shaken by the most violent upheavals.[2] In this orderly environment man was placed so that he could live a life that reflected a planned order that would also be a witness to the beauty and glory of his Creator. This order was meant to be seen not only in the " organic parts " but more especially in the harmonious co-operation of his undertsanding mind and will whereby all his senses were governed in a right order.[3] "There was an attempering (*temperatura*) in the several parts of the soul,

[1] Comm. on Ps. 68 : 34, C.O. 31 : 635–6. *Hic vero clarius refulget Dei gloria, quod quum immensa sit coelorum machina, tam rapidus motus, ac tam diversae revolutiones inter se confligant, constet tamen optima symmetria et temperamentum, et hic tam concinnus et pulcer ordo tot saeculis aequabili tenore continuatus fuerit.* Cf. comm. on Ps. 8 : 4, C.O. 31 : 91. *In fine quarti versus, pro eo quod alii vertunt praeparare vel fundare, reddere visum est concinnare: videtur enim respicere propheta ad pulcherrimum ordinem quo Deus stellarum positum tam apte distinxit et cursum moderatur.* Cf. Inst. 1 : 14 : 20.

[2] Comm. on Jer. 31 : 35–6, C.O. 38 : 698–99. *Dicit in persona Dei, Ego sum qui solem creavi, lunam et stellas: non cessavit continuus ordo a creatione mundi, quin sol peragat suum cursum: deinde etiam luna. . . . Ergo in coelis consideramus ordinem ita compositum et temperatum, ut nihil illic vel in hanc vel in illam partem declinat. . . . Quam certa est ordinis naturae stabilitas . . . tam certa erit salus ecclesiae. . . . Non est igitur metuendum, ne unquam excidat, salus ecclesiae, quia nunquam cessabunt naturae leges vel decreta.*

[3] Inst. 1 : 15 : 8. *Libera tamen fuit electio boni et mali: neque id modo, sed in mente et voluntate summa rectitudo et omnes organicae partes rite in obsequium compositae.* Inst. 1 : 15 : 3. *Proinde hac voce notatur integritas, qua praeditus fuit Adam quum recta intelligentia polleret, affectus haberet compositos ad rationem, sensus omnes recto ordine temperatos, vereque eximiis dotibus opificis sui excellentiam referret.*

which correspond with their various functions. In the mind perfect intelligence flourished and reigned, uprightness attended as its companion, and all the senses were prepared and moulded for due obedience to reason; and in the body there was a suitable correspondence with this internal order."[1] This order of nature in the pattern of which man was created, and which he was meant to observe, includes an ordered social life between man and man. This finds its best pattern in the marriage relationship between man and woman.[2] The main feature in Calvin's picture of the life of man in Paradise which must strike the observer is that everything is arranged and moves in perfect order.

2. The original order of man's life in the *imago Dei* includes faith and *meditatio futurae vitae*

Part of this planned order for man's life was that he should live thankfully by the grace of God in the midst of the magnificence of his earthly environment, so full of "glorious specimens of the works of God."[3] Yet while using to the full his own many splendid endowments he was nevertheless not meant to find the true and full meaning of his creation in this present life which even for him had "no firm and settled constancy." He was meant rather to use this life with its opportunities and its glory for meditation on the better and heavenly life which was to be his final destiny.[4] He was endowed with reason, and was distinguished from the brute creation, for this very purpose.[5] The glory of this earth was meant to enable him, helped by God's Word and by God's sacramental gift in the tree of life, to raise his mind to the greater glory of his heavenly inheritance.[6] Thus the *meditatio futurae vitae*, and the

---

[1] Comm. on Gen. 1 : 26, C.O. 23 : 26–7. *Erat enim in singulis animae partibus temperatura quae suis numeris constabat: in mente lux rectae intelligentiae vigebat ac regnabat, huic comes aderat mentis rectitudo, sensus omnes ad moderatum rationis obsequium prompti et formati: in corpore aequabilis quaedam ad illum ordinem proportio.*

[2] Comm. on Gen. 2 : 18, C.O. 23 : 46–7.

[3] Inst. 1 : 14 : 20.

[4] Comm. on Gen. 2 : 7, C.O. 23 : 36. *Hoc singulare (est) beneficium Christi ut renovemur in coelestem vitam, quae etiam ante lapsum Adae nonnisi terrena fuit: quia non habebat stabilem fixamque constantiam.*

[5] Arg. in Gen. C.O. 23 : 11. Cf. Inst. 1 : 15 : 6. *Sicut autem absque controversia ad coelestis vitae meditationem conditus fuit homo, ita eius notitiam animae fuisse insculptam certum est.*

[6] Ibid. Cf. T. F. Torrance, *Calvin's Doctrine of Man*, pp. 33–4.

life of faith in dependence on the grace of God, are, for Calvin, part of the original order of nature or of creation which man was made to observe.

It was through his living such an ordered and rightly proportioned life in the will of God that man's life reflected the image of God, and it is from this point of view that man is to be understood as made in the image of God. For man to have been made in the image of God does not mean for Calvin that he had some static impress on his soul, or some inherent faculty or endowment which can be neatly defined. Man possessed the image of God by living continually by the Word of God and by constantly responding to the grace of God for which he was created. Calvin relates the image of God in man to his superiority over the rest of creation,[1] to the divine righteousness which man reflects as a mirror,[2] to the healthy condition of *every part* of man's life,[3] to the response of *meditatio futurae vitae* to the grace of God,[4] and to the ordered social and political relationships which he bears to other men and women.[5] Calvin's basic thought on this matter is that "the leading feature in the renovation of the divine image must also have held the highest place in its creation."[6] It is by contemplating what happens in our regeneration that we see what the image of God must originally have been like.[7] It is on this basis that Calvin finds that for Adam to have been made in the image of God meant that he should live in an ordered integrity and righteousness, in dependence on the grace of his Creator, rising ever into communion with God through the Word of God which his mind was made to reflect and through the glory of created things, meditating on the heavenly life, and living in a truly ordered relation to his fellow creatures and his environment.

---

[1] Inst. 2 : 12 : 6; and 1 : 15 : 3.

[2] Comm. on Eph. 4 : 24, C.O. 51 : 208–9.

[3] Inst. 1 : 15 : 4. *Unde colligimus initio in luce mentis, in cordis rectitudine, partiumque omnium sanitate conspicuam fuisse Dei imaginem.*

[4] Cf. Introd. Arg. in Gen. C.O. 23 : 11. *Tertio intelligentia et ratione fuisse praeditum, ut a brutis animalibus discretus potiorem vitam meditaretur: imo ut ad Deum recta tenderet, cuius insculptam imaginem gerebat.* The tree of life was a sacramental symbol to help him to do this. Cf. comm. on Gen. 2 : 9, C.O. 23 : 38–9.

[5] Comm. on John 17 : 11, C.O. 47 : 382. Serm. on Job 10 : 7–15, C.O. 33 : 489. *Il signifie que l'image de Dieu est imprimee en nous d'autant que nous avons intelligence et raison, que nous discernons entre le bien et le mal, que les hommes sont nais pour avoir quelque ordre, quelque police entre eux.*

[6] Inst. 1 : 15 : 4.   [7] Comm. on Eph. 4 : 24, C.O. 51 : 208–9.

3. The purpose of redemption is the restoration of the original order and *imago*

Through the fall of Adam man has not only been brought under the power of concupiscence, but in this very event has had his life thrown into complete disorder and confusion so that no clear or unambiguous trace of the original order of creation in which his life reflected the image of God has been left.[1] This fall of man into disorder is reflected in the universe around him and in his relations with his environment where the original order of nature has been corrupted.[2] Man is no longer truly lord of his environment.[3] It no longer serves him in an orderly fashion and it reflects in its corruption and decay the distortion of all man's original relations. Moreover, man no longer uses his environment as a means whereby he can rise to communion with his Maker or a witness to his heavenly destiny. He uses it only for the gross ends of his immediate existence here on earth.[4] It is, however, in man's own heart and mind and in man's relations with his fellow men that the disorder is most apparent. Man employs himself otherwise than in seeking God's glory.[5] In his heart there appears a "perpetual disorder and excess"[6] in which there is no moderation, and in which "all affections with turbulent impetuosity exceed

---

[1] Inst. 1 : 15 : 4. *Dei imago . . . quae refulsit in Adam ante defectionem, postea sic vitiata et prope deleta, ut nihil ex ruina nisi confusum, mutilum, labeque infectum supersit.*

[2] Cf. serm. on Acts. 1 : 6–8, C.O. 48 : 609. *Or il nous a declaré les choses qui sont selon l'ordre de nature et comme il doit faire froid en hyver et chaut en esté. Que si quelquesfois nous voyons de grands froids en esté, cognoissons que cela vient de nos pechez qui pervertissent l'ordre de nature, et que pour l'enormité d'iceux nous meritons bien que tout soit perverti;* and Inst. 3 : 25 : 2.

[3] Comm. on Ps. 8 : 7, C.O. 31 : 94. *Certe si quid adversum est hominibus in coelo vel in terra, iam collapsa est illa ordinis integritas, unde sequitur humanum genus, postquam defectione Adae dissipatum est, non modo hac tam praeclara et honorifica sorte privatum esse, ac priori dominio non potiri: sed captivum teneri sub deformi pudendaque servitute.* Cf. comm. on Ps. 104 : 21–2, C.O. 32 : 92–3.

[4] Serm. on Job 33 : 29–34 : 3, C.O. 35 : 126. *Ceux qui ne daignent prester l'aureille à Dieu et à sa verité pour estre enseignez, et quand ils ont desia esté instruits, ne cerchent d'estre confermez de plus en plus, pervertissent l'ordre de nature, mesmes qu'ils sont comme monstres et pires que les bestes brutes. Et pourquoy? Car une beste suivra son naturel. Or voila un homme qui se dira sage, ayant raison et discretion qu'il a esté creé à l'image de Dieu pour estre illuminé en toute verité: cependant il aura bien cest advis de boire et de manger tous les iours: mais de profiter non.*

[5] Comm. on Rom. 11 : 36, C.O. 49 : 232.

[6] Inst. 3 : 3 : 12. *Iam vero quum ob naturae pravitatem omnes facultates adeo vitiatae sint ac corruptae, ut in omnibus actionibus emineat perpetua ἀταξία et intemperies: quia ab eiusmodi incontinentia separari nequeunt appetitiones, ideo vitiosas esse contendimus.*

their due bounds."[1] So liable to this "excess" has man become that even those affections which might be regarded as good and noble in man can never be kept in their proper degree, and become corrupted by being out of proportion to the other aspects of man's life.[2]

The purpose of our redemption is the restoration of the original order of man's life. "It is the glory of our faith," says Calvin, "that God, the Creator of the world, in no way disregards the order which He Himself at first established."[3] The work of Jesus Christ is to restore to man the image of God which was lost in Adam. "Adam was first created after the image of God, and reflected as in a mirror the divine righteousness; but that image, having been defaced by sin, must now be restored in Christ. The regeneration of the godly is indeed . . . nothing else than the formation anew of the image of God in them. . . . The design contemplated by regeneration is to recall us from our wanderings to that end for which we were created."[4] The work of the Spirit in our hearts is to "begin to reform us to the image of God" with a view to the complete restoration of that image both in ourselves and in the whole world.[5]

4. This true order and *imago* is seen in the revelation of God
in the Gospel and in the humanity of Jesus Christ

That our lives should be conformed to the image of God is therefore a most important aspect of Calvin's conception of the Christian life and of his ethics. This image in the pattern of which we are to be reformed has been set before us in Jesus Christ who is the "living image of God His Father."[6] This means a real effort to conform our own lives to the example of the forgiving, gentle,

[1] Inst. 3 : 16 : 12. *Moderatio in naturae nostrae depravatione conspici non potest, ubi omnes affectus turbido impetu modum excedunt.* Cf. comm. on 1 Cor. 7 : 6, C.O. 49 : 405. *Respondeo ad prius: quum in omnibus humanis affectibus inordinatum excessum esse confitear, me non negare quin sit etiam in hac parte ἀταξία, quam vitiosam esse concedo; imo hunc affectum prae aliis impotentem esse concedo, et prope belluinum*; and on Ps. 23 : 5, C.O. 31 : 241. *Plus satis ad luxuriem proni* (*sumus*) *natura*; and on Phil. 2 : 27, C.O. 52 : 41.
[2] Serm. on Matt. 26 : 36–9, C.O. 46 : 839–40.
[3] Comm. on Ps. 11 : 4, C.O. 31 : 123.
[4] Comm. on Eph. 2 : 24, C.O. 51 : 208–9. Cf. comm. on 2 Cor. 3 : 18, C.O. 50 : 47. *Nota hunc esse finem evangelii, ut Dei imago, quae inducta fuerat per peccatum, reparetur in nobis, atque huius instaurationis progressionem tota vita esse continuam.*
[5] Comm. on Luke 17 : 20, C.O. 45 : 425.
[6] Serm. on Job 1 : 6–8, C.O. 33 : 59.

and generous love of God as we see Him reflected in Jesus Christ,[1] remembering that to be the children of God involves real likeness in behaviour and attitude to the Heavenly Father. We must never forget that there is nothing in which we more truly resemble God than in doing good to others, and in this respect we are to seek to reproduce in ourselves the Father's disposition (*ingenium*).[2] "What God is in heaven, such He bids us to be in this world," says Calvin.[3] This is a very far-reaching command. It means making our Christian love reflect God's free grace towards the helpless, His providential care for the poor, His giving of light in this world's darkness, His ready defence of the widows and orphans.[4] It also means remembering at the same time that God's gentleness is the gentleness of one who hates iniquity.[5]

To live a life conformed to the image of God also means for Calvin, however, to live an ordered life, for the pattern of the restored *imago Dei* is a pattern of order. Our transformation into the *imago Dei* consists more in a reformation or restoration of order than in an "influx of substance."[6] The end of regeneration is "that we may be made like God and that His glory may shine in us," but this "glory" and likeness to God are evidenced at present not primarily by some vague radiant splendour added to our natural personalities but rather in the "rectitude and integrity of the whole soul."[7] "Christ . . . is called the second Adam because He restores us to true and substantial integrity."[8]

---

[1] Serm. on Gal. 6 : 1–2, C.O. 51 : 63. *Il nous faut estre conformez à Dieu, puis qu'il a bien daigné nous choisir pour ses enfans comme aussi nostre Seigneur Iesus le remonstre. Soyez semblables à vostre pere celeste (dit-il) qui a pitié mesme de ceux qui n'en sont pas dignes . . . Regardons à la nature de luy qui nos appelle pour estre conformes à son exemple: c'est que nous soyons humains.*

[2] Comm. on Ps. 30 : 5, C.O. 31 : 294.

[3] Comm. on 1 John 4 : 17, C.O. 55 : 357.

[4] Serm. on Matt. 3 : 9–10, C.O. 46 : 548. *Car il veut que nous-nous employons principalement envers ceux qui n'en peuvent plus: comme c'est son office de repaistre les povres affamez: d'illuminer ceux qui sont en tenebres, et d'aider à ceux qui n'ont nul secours: et d'autant qu'il est le protecteur des vefves et des orphelins, et que brief il maintient ceux qui n'ont de quoy estre supportez selon le monde, il veut aussi que nous employons toutes nos facultez en cest endroict.*

[5] Serm. on Gal. 6 : 1–2, C.O. 51 : 63.

[6] Inst. 1 : 15 : 5. *Atque ubi de imaginis instauratione disserit Paulus (2 Cor. 3, 18), ex eius verbis elicere promptum est, non substantiae influxu, sed Spiritus gratia et virtute hominem fuisse Deo conformem.*

[7] Comm. on Col. 3 : 10, C.O. 52 : 121. *Hinc etiam discimus, tum quis finis sit regenerationis nostrae, hoc est, ut Deo reddamur similes, ac in nobis reluceat eius gloria; tum quae sit Dei imago, cuius mentio fit apud Mosem, nempe totius animae rectitudo et integritas: ita ut homo sapientiam Dei, iustitiam et bonitatem quasi speculum repraesentet.*

[8] Inst. 1 : 15 : 4.

It is to be noted that Calvin lays great stress on the fact that in the humanity of Jesus we see the banishment of all excess or ἀταξία, and a perfect pattern of order, of true moderation and harmony. It is in this respect that Jesus Christ is quite different from all other human beings. "For the reason why our feelings are sinful is that they rush on without restraint, and suffer no limit; but in Christ the feelings were adjusted (*compositi*) and regulated (*moderati*) in obedience to God and were altogether free from sin."[1] The surest sign of the universal corruption of human nature is that in all men the inward affections are constantly turbulent and uncontrollable, unbalanced, continually liable to be directed to unlawful ends and to be aroused to excess by the merest trifles. But "Christ . . . had no passion or affection . . . that ever went beyond proper bounds or was not founded on reason and sound judgment."[2] This perfect moderation of all the passions so that they never became sinful through excess[3] is shown by Jesus not only through a "sobriety (*temperantia*) truly divine" in His use and enjoyment of the ordinary things of life,[4] but also in His self-restraint from over-violent emotion even in the midst of perplexity or fear or grief.[5] As a result of this perfect self-restraint, Calvin, using a figure from music, can describe even the tension between the two wills that marked the inner life of our Lord as a tension that produces complete unity and harmony. "As musical sounds, though various and differing from each other, are so far from being discordant that they produce sweet melody and fine harmony; so in Christ there was a remarkable example of adaptation between the two wills, the will of God and the will of man, so that they differed from each other without any conflict or opposition."[6]

Therefore in living our Christian lives "we must wisely observe order" says Calvin.[7] He points out that the word "religion" means gathering up a thing within bonds, and thus true religion implies an orderliness which is lacking under superstition.[8]

[1] Comm. on John 11 : 33, C.O. 47 : 265.
[2] Ibid, C.O. 47 : 266. *In Christo nihil tale: nulla enim eius passio ultra suum modum unquam erupit, nulla nisi iusta et ex ratione rectoque iudicio suscepta.* Cf. Inst. 2 : 16 : 12, for similar thought and language.
[3] Comm. on Ps. 22 : 15, C.O. 31 : 227–8.
[4] Comm. on Luke 7 : 34, C.O. 45 : 307–8.
[5] Cf. Inst. 2 : 16 : 12, Comm. on Matt. 26 : 37, C.O. 45 : 720; on Matt. 26 : 39, C.O. 45 : 723.   [6] Comm. on Matt. 26 : 39, C.O. 45 : 723.
[7] Comm. on Luke 10 : 42, C.O. 45 : 382. *Ordinem prudenter tenendum.*
[8] Inst. 1 : 12 : 1.

5. The eschatological significance of the new life of order in Christ

The overcoming of disorder in this world is therefore for Calvin a fact of profound eschatological significance. Calvin interprets our Lord's words in John 13 : 31, "Now is the Son of man glorified and in him God is glorified," as meaning that in the Cross the whole of creation has been already restored to its original glory and order. "In the Cross of Christ, as in a most splendid theatre, the incomparable goodness of God has been displayed before the whole world. Indeed, in all creatures both high and low the glory of God shines, but nowhere has it shone more illustriously than in the Cross, in which there has taken place a wonderful change (*conversio*) of things, the condemnation of all men has been made manifest, sin has been abolished, salvation has been given back to men, and in short the whole world has been renewed and all things restored to order."[1] But the fulfilment of this renewal and restoration of order through the Cross is something that has to be manifested in the life of society as the influence of the Cross is experienced from day to day. Throughout the present world, where the devil and the flesh hold sway, there is confusion and deformity. Yet the reformation is constantly taking place, for Satan is being cast out of his dominion and the power of evil is being subdued. All this is "the remarkable effect of that death of Christ which is daily being manifested."[2] Calvin approves the interpretation of the word κρίσις in the text "Now is the judgment of this word, now shall the prince of this world be cast out," as referring not so much to the *condemnation* of this world as to its *reformation* and restoration to proper order. The death of Christ is therefore the commencement of a well-regulated condition which will find its full climax in the renovation of the world.[3]

Therefore Calvin sees signs of the re-establishment of the

---

[1] Comm. on John 13 : 31, C.O. 47 : 317.

[2] Comm. on John 12 : 31–2, C.O. 47 : 293–4.

[3] Ibid. *Nam vox hebraica mishpat, quae per iuducium redditur, rectam constitutionem significat. Scimus autem extra Christum nihil in mundo nisi confusum esse. Etsi autem iam regnum Dei erigere coeperat Christus, mors tamen eius verum demun status rite compositi exordium et plena mundi instauratio fuit. Notandum tamen simul, quod haec in mundo rectitudo constitui nequeat, quin regnum Satanae prius aboleatur, quin redigatur in nihilum caro et quidquid Dei iustitiae adversum esse. Denique necessum est, ut mundi novitatem mortificatio praecedat.*

Kingdom of God whenever in the life of the regenerate man there is true self-denial and mortification of concupiscence, effected through communion with the death of Christ, and resulting in the restoration of order where there has been ἀταξία and confusion.[1] In the new ordered existence and upright living manifested by the regenerate man, he sees true signs that the image of God is here being restored.[2] It is true that these signs only faintly reflect the image which has been lost. For the final restoration of true order both in man's heart and in the universe we have to wait for the second coming of Christ to restore all things,[3] nevertheless the whole new attitude and behaviour of the regenerate man in obedience to the Word of God is indicative of the original pattern of man's life as he was created in Adam.[4]

[1] Comm. on Matt. 6 : 10, C.O. 45 : 197. *Regno Dei opponitur omnis ἀταξία et confusio: neque enim quidquam ordinatum est in mundo, nisi quum moderatur ipse manu sua consilia et affectus. Hinc colligimus, initium regni Dei in nobis esse veteris hominis interitum et nostri abnegationem, ut renovemur in aliam vitam.*
[2] Inst. 1 : 15 : 4. *Dei imago . . . nunc aliqua ex parte conspicitur in electis, quatenus spiritu regeniti sunt.* Cf. comm. on 2 Cor. 3 : 18, C.O. 50 : 47.
[3] Comm. on James 5 : 7, C.O. 55 : 425.
[4] Comm. on Gen. 1 : 26, C.O. 23 : 26. *Quoniam deleta est imago Dei in nobis per lapsum Adae, ex reparatione iudicandum est qualis fuerit.* And on Gen. 9 : 6, C.O. 23 : 147. *Deinde ipsum coelestem fictorem, utcunque corruptus sit homo, finem tamen primae creationis habere ante oculos.* Cf. comm. on Eph. 4 : 24, C.O. 51 : 209. *Quare huc spectare docet regenerationem, ut ex errore reducamur ad eum finem ad quem sumus conditi.* It should be noted, however, that the image restored in Christ is far superior to that originally in Adam. Cf. Inst. 2 : 12 : 6 ; and 1 : 15 : 4; and comm. on Eph. 4 : 24; on 1 Cor. 15 : 45.

Chapter II

The true order of man's life reflected in the Law

1. The image of God in the Law

FOR Calvin the image of God which begins to be renewed in man throughout the course of his life on this earth consists in righteousness and true holiness.[1] The effacing of the heavenly image in man through the fall meant the withdrawal of "wisdom, virtue, justice, truth and holiness."[2] The renovation of man in the heavenly image is "manifested by the fruits produced by it, viz. justice, judgment and mercy."[3] But this life of righteousness and holiness is simply life lived according to the law of God as summed up in the two tables of the Ten Commandments which sum up the fruits of repentance and outline what the image of God consists in.[4] Therefore to live a life ordered according to the image of God is to live according to the law of God.

God "as He is in Himself" is for man in his present condition unapproachable and incomprehensible,[5] in His majesty and glory and justice. There is in God a hidden justice or righteousness which it is beyond us to conceive and which must remain concealed from us in our sinful state, or the sight of it would annihilate us. Nevertheless this righteousness is an aspect of the true image of God which we ourselves must reflect in our own lives, and even now in this life we must begin making progress towards this. God, therefore, knowing our weakness, and seeking to supply our need, accommodates Himself to our capacity and gives us in the Law an image of His incomprehensible and hidden justice,[6] so that by

---

[1] Inst. 3 : 3 : 9.   [2] Inst. 2 : 1 : 5.   [3] Inst. 3 : 3 : 8.

[4] Inst. 3 : 3 : 16. *Iam et poenitentiae fructus quales sint, intelligi potest: nempe officia pietatis erga Deum, caritatis erga homines, ad haec in tota vita sanctimonia, ac puritas. Denique quo maiore quisque studio vitam suam exigit ad normam Legis Dei, eo certiora poenitentiae suae signa edit.*

[5] Cf. Inst. 2 : 16 : 13. Comm. on Ps. 86 : 8, C.O. 31 : 749; on Ezek. 1 : 28, C.O. 40 : 60; on Exod. 33 : 20, C.O. 25 : 111; on 1 Pet. 1 : 20, C.O. 55 : 226–7.

[6] Serm. on Job 9 : 29–35, C.O. 33 : 459. *Mais tant y a qu'il y a encores une iustice plus haute en Dieu. C'est à dire une perfection, à laquelle nous ne pouvons pas attaindre, et de laquelle nous ne pouvons pas approcher, iusques à ce que nous*

following the Law we can reflect His image. Calvin sees in the Law, especially as we have it in the Ten Commandments, a pattern and image which truly reflects the perfect and yet hidden justice of God.[1] "For therein God has so delineated His own character that anyone exhibiting in action what is commanded would in some measure express in life the image of God."[2]

Expressing the matter concisely Calvin asserts that there is a "double justice" in God—there is the justice which is manifested in the Law, and the hidden justice in the eternal being of God which exceeds all the capacities of men.[3] In another passage he distinguishes between the *iustice parfaite* in the being of God and the *iustice moyenne* through which God presents Himself to man.[4] The latter is a dim reflexion, as in a mirror, of the former. But though the justice of the Law reflects only dimly the glory of the higher justice in the being of God which must remain hidden as long as men remain in the flesh, it nevertheless is a true revelation of the righteousness that dwells ineffably in the being of God.[5] Even the sinless Angels, according to Calvin, in their service and adoration of God, regulate themselves not according to the ineffable justice which is too high even for them, but according to the expression of that righteousness in the Law.[6] Moreover, when God's people give themselves to keeping by faith the Law of God they are accounted as just by God, not through any merit or dignity that they thereby acquire but because God sees in their obedience to the Law a reflexion of the image of His own righteousness and thus God "contents Himself" with it. Though compared with the intrinsic righteousness of God and the final glory to which man has to be

---

soyons faits semblables à luy, et que nous ayons contemplé ceste gloire, qui maintenant nous est cachee, et que nous ne voyons sinon comme en un miroir, et par obscurité.
[1] Serm. on Job 9 : 29–35. C.O. 33 : 458–9. *Il est vray que Dieu nous a bien baillé en sa Loy un patron et une image da sa iustice, mais c'a esté selon nostre capacité. Or savons-nous que nostre entendement est si rude, qu'il ne peut monter si haut, que de concevoir ce qui est en Dieu en perfection. Ainsi donc la iustice mesme qui est contenue en la Loy de Dieu, est une iustice qui est compassee à la mesure des hommes.* Cf. also serm. on Job 15 : 11–16, C.O. 33 : 718–30; and on Job 10 : 16–17, C.O. 33 : 496. [2] Inst. 2 : 8 : 51.
[3] Serm. on Job 10 : 16–17, C.O. 33 : 496. *Nous voyons donc maintenant comme il y a double iustice en Dieu, l'une c'est celle qui nous est manifestee en la Loy, de laquelle Dieu se contente, pource qu'il luy plaist ainsi: il y a une autre iustice cachee qui surmonte tous sens et apprehensions des creatures.*
[4] Serm. on Job 15 : 11–16, C.O. 33 : 727. *Mais encores n'allons point à ceste iustice si parfaite: venons seulement à ceste iustice moyenne que Dieu nous a declaree.*
[5] Serm. on Job 9 : 29–35, C.O. 33 : 459.
[6] Serm. on Job 10 : 16–17, C.O. 33 : 496; on Job 9 : 29–35, C.O. 33 : 459.

ultimately conformed, the justice of the Law is a faint and distorted thing, it can nevertheless, in relation to our present creaturely condition, be called, as in Scripture, a perfect righteousness.[1]

In Calvin's references to the Law as the rule of the Christian life, he appeals for an ordered and balanced observation of it which gives due weight to both tables. "There are these two chief things in our life—to serve God purely, and then to deal with our fellow men with all integrity, and uprightness, rendering to each what is his due."[2] Since the duties of life can be so summarised, the Law is divided into two tables, the first table teaching us "how to cultivate piety and the proper duties of religion in which the worship of God consists," the second table showing how, "in the fear of His name, we are to conduct ourselves towards our fellow men." Our Lord Himself divided the duties of life into two such heads when He commanded us to love the Lord our God with all our heart and with all our soul and with all our strength, and our neighbour as ourselves.[3] The true Christian therefore is concerned to live towards both God and man rather than towards himself.[4] A life that would reflect on earth the image of God's righteousness given in the Law must have both a relationship of faith and worship towards God and at the same time a relationship of love and right dealing with respect to fellow men.[5] In a well-ordered life this twofold relation will be kept in due proportion.

[1] See all above passages from sermons on Job. Even if we perfectly kept the Law of God, we would not thereby attain a true righteousness which could stand before the face of God in the presence of His perfect righteousness. Cf. serm. on Job 9 : 29–35, C.O. 33 : 460. *Iob donc entend en ce passage, que quand il n'y auroit que toute pureté en luy: ie di mesmes selon la iustice de la Loy: il n'y auroit qu'ordure et infection quand il se viendroit se presenter devant Dieu.*

[2] Serm. on Deut. 5 : 16, C.O. 26 : 309. Cf. serm. on Deut. 5 : 22, C.O. 26 : 392. *D'autant qu'il y a deux poincts principaux en nostre vie, nostre Seigneur a divisé sa Loy en deux tables: c'est assavoir, que nous sachions comment il nous faut gouverner envers luy, et puis comment nous avons à converser avec nos prochains.*

[3] Inst. 2 : 8 : 11.

[4] Serm. on Job 1 : 1, C.O. 33 : 30–1; and on 2 Sam. 3 : 28 f. pp. 76–7.

[5] Calvin can thus sum up the Christian life under two headings variously described as *holiness* (piety or godliness) and *righteousness* (justice), or as *faith* and *love*. Cf. comm. on Luke 1 : 75, C.O. 45 : 50; serm. on Eph. 4 : 23–6, C.O. 51 : 621; comm. on Luke 2 : 25, C.O. 45 : 89. *Pietas et iustitia referuntur ad duas legis tabulas : itaque duabus his partibus constat integritas vitae.* When Calvin refers to the combination of sobriety, righteousness and godliness in Titus 2 : 12, and faith, love and patience in Titus 2 : 2, he seems to make Christian duty consist of "three branches". Cf. Inst. 3 : 7 : 3 and serm. on Gal. 5 : 19–32, C.O. 51 : 33–4. But in these threefold combinations he regards patience and sobriety as not distinct from each other and as a mere seasoning for the other two distinct virtues. Cf. comm. on Titus 2 : 2 and 12, C.O. 52 : 419 and 423.

While we must neglect neither our devotion to God nor our duty to man, our devotion to God must come first. Calvin in his preaching is never weary of insisting that it is vain for us to live the most upright and honest life before men, to pride ourselves that we do not steal from or do harm to our neighbours, if at the same time we do not render to God the worship and faith and devotion due to His person. For it is a far more terrible thing to rob God of His honour, and to sin against His majesty, than to injure our fellow man.[1] Indeed, to neglect our duty of worship towards God is to seek to annihilate His majesty, and that is a far worse crime than all robbery, murder, sexual licence, poisonings and lying and such like things.[2] Therefore though we must neglect neither of the two principal aspects of our duty set forth in the Law, we must make it our first concern to pay what we owe to God, and then, after this is done, to fulfil the duties that have regard to our fellow men. "We must . . . give preference to the command, the worship, and the service of God; after which, as far as we are able, we must give to men what is their due. . . . When we have obeyed God, then is the proper time to think of our parents and wife and children; as Christ attends to His mother, but it is after He is on the Cross to which He has been called by His Father's decree."[3] The service of God must therefore be the foundation of our whole life and the inspiration of our service to our neighbour, since man's chief end is to glorify His Maker.[4]

It must, however, be emphasised, at the same time, that our love for God must find its expression in love towards our fellow men. Indeed, it cannot exist without this expression. Love towards man is therefore the only real proof that we can give of the reality of the love that we profess towards God.[5] Our neigh-

---

[1] Serm. on Deut. 7 : 22–6, C.O. 26 : 576–7.

[2] Serm. on Job 34 : 4–10, C.O. 35 : 134–5. Cf. Inst. 2 : 8 : 11.

[3] Comm. on John 19 : 26, C.O. 37 : 417. Cf. serm. on Deut. 5 : 16, C.O. 26 : 309.

[4] Serm. on Job 34 : 4–10, C.O. 35 : 135. *Dieu a distingué sa Loy en deux tables, pour nous monstrer que son service et l'honneur que luy devons, va devant: et puis, qu'il y a le devoir que nous avons envers nos freres. Il faut donc que le service de Dieu soit comme le fondement de toute nostre vie: que nous le glorifions, sachans que c'est à cela qu'il nous a creez.*

[5] Serm. on Deut. 5 : 16, C.O. 26 : 309. *Il veut esprouver nostre obeissance, et l'amour que nous luy portons, quand il nous commande de cheminer avec nos prochains en toute droiture et equité. . . . Voila (di-ie) une espreuve que Dieu a mise pour cognoistre si nous l'adorons de coeur.* Cf. serm. on 1 Cor. 10 : 15–18, C.O. 49 : 668. *La charité . . . est une approbation que nous aimons Dieu.*

bour takes the place of God in order that he might be the object of the love we bear to God.[1] Since it is towards our neighbour, rather than directly towards God, that we can most clearly express the love and devotion of our hearts, Christ in His teaching emphasises the second table of the Law rather than the first,[2] and the Apostle "makes the whole perfection of the saints consist in charity."[3] Outward zeal for religious worship is no true test of real love to God. A man can make a false profession of love towards God by being hypocritically zealous in the outward profession of godliness. But the presence of real love to man is an infallible proof that the heart is right with God. This was why John the Baptist called on his hearers to prove their repentance towards God by fulfilling the practical duties of the second table of the Law.[4] In stating all this, however, Calvin still reminds us that it must not be thought that love to man is something higher than love to God. It is seen rather in its true perspective when it is looked on as the outward sign of the love of the heart for God.[5]

2. Consecration to God as the true meaning of the Law

The Law demands of us in its first table the consecration of our whole self to God our Creator.[6] The sanctity which it teaches involves in the first place the offering of our whole life to God as a living sacrifice.[7] But this sanctity, as we have seen, must pervade and modify everything we do towards our fellow men in fulfilment

[1] Cf. serm. on Deut. 5 : 16, C.O. 26 : 313; and comm. on Gal. 5 : 14, C.O. 50 : 251. *Iam dixi Deum esse invisibilem; se autem nobis repraesentat in fratribus, et in illorum persona quod sibi debetur exigit.*

[2] Inst. 2 : 8 : 52.

[3] Inst. 2 : 8 : 53.

[4] Comm. on Luke 3 : 10, C.O. 45 : 119; and on Ps. 15 : 2, C.O. 31 : 144.

[5] Ibid. *Hoc primo habendum est, nominari caritatis officia, non quod excellant supra cultum Dei, sed quatenus testantur de hominum pietate.* Cf. comm. on Gal. 5 : 14, C.O. 50 : 251; and comm. on Matt. 25 : 35, C.O. 45 : 688.

[6] Serm. on Deut. 6 : 1–4, C.O. 26 : 422. *Il faut donc commencer par ce bout, si nous voulons observer la Loy deument . . . c'est que nous luy portions reverence . . . et que nous demandions de luy faire hommage comme à nostre souverain Roy, que nous demandions de nous dedier à luy comme à nostre createur, que nous demandions de l'honorer comme nostre Pere. . . . C'est le commencement de toute la Loy, et de toute iustice.*

[7] Serm. on Eph. 4 : 23–6, C.O. 51 : 621. *Il faut que la saincteté soit coniointe avec la iustice: car les deux tables de la Loy sont inseparables. Et sous ce mot de saincteté, sainct Paul a compris tout ce qui appartient au service de Dieu . . . c'est que nous cheminions purement devant Dieu . . . que nous soyons separez des pollutions de ce monde pour luy estre offerts en sacrifice.*

of the second table of the Law. This means that all the virtues we show in our relation to our fellow men should spring from devotion and obedience to God Himself and should in their exercise be consecrated to God—indeed should themselves be offered to God as a sacrifice.[1]

In this respect the Law is superior to all the systems of morality taught by the ancient philosophers. Heathen writers, and unbelievers in general, all speak a great deal about virtue and seek to acquire virtue, but they do not relate their lives and their virtues to God.[2] Calvin admits that amongst the heathen there have been many men who have excelled in virtue, yet such virtue was vitiated and spoilt by pride and ambition because it was not related to God.[3] "There have often appeared in renewed men remarkable instances of gentleness, integrity, temperance, and generosity, but it is certain that all were but specious disguises. Curius and Fabricius were distinguished for courage, Cato for temperance, Scipio for kindness and generosity, Fabius for patience; but it was only in the sight of men and as members of civil society that they were so distinguished. In the sight of God nothing is pure but what proceeds from the fountain of all purity."[4]

3. Integrity and self-denial as the true meaning of the Law

Through the Law God is seeking a response towards Himself not only in outward behaviour but also in heart. Since God is the God who searches the heart, His Law applies "equally to our

---

[1] Serm. on Gal. 5 : 4–6, C.O. 50 : 681. *Et pourtant regardons de servir à Dieu comme il le demande. Or en quoy est-ce qu'il nous veut exercer? . . . C'est que nous cheminions en droiture et equité avec nos prochains: qu'un chacun selon sa faculté aide à ceux où il y aura pitié: que nul ne soit addonné à soy-mesmes: que nous soyons fideles . . . quand nous en verrons quelques uns despourvues et qui auront besoin de nostre secours, que là nous offrions comme une sacrifice à Dieu, sçachant qu'il nous appelle pour monstrer l'amour que nous luy portons: Ainsi donc apprenons pour bien servir à Dieu . . . c'est de cheminer en telle rondeur et humanité.*

[2] Comm. on Ps. 49 : 2, C.O. 31 : 482. Serm. on Gal. 5 : 19–23, C.O. 51 : 41.

[3] Comm. on Ps. 86 : 2, C.O. 31 : 792, Inst. 3 : 3 : 7. Cf. Inst. 2 : 8 : 5.

[4] Comm. on Gal. 5 : 22, C.O. 50 : 255. Equally vain is the virtue that has no relation to the love of fellow men. Calvin criticises the "profane historians' " applause of Crates the Theban who threw all his wealth into the sea in order to save his soul. No matter how virtuous the act, or how much good it did to his own character "he who deprives others along with himself of the use of money deserves no praise." Calvin points out that our Lord in contrast not only enjoins the rich man to *sell* but likewise to *give to the poor*. Comm. on Matt. 10 : 20, C.O. 45 : 540.

minds and our hands."[1] Our response must be "not merely in outward honesty but in inward spiritual righteousness."[2] Certainly outward honesty is demanded in the Law but the outward behaviour must be a true expression of the heart. "There can be no true keeping of the Law but what springs from free and spontaneous love."[3] Calvin in this connexion quotes Paul: "The end of the commandment is love, out of a pure heart, and of a good conscience, and of faith unfeigned."[4] Therefore it is not merely outward order that God seeks from man in the giving of the Law, but inward spiritual order, and true integrity of heart. In the Law God is seeking to possess us entirely in the integration of body, soul and spirit.

True righteousness, then, is to respond with the whole heart to the outward commandments. To respond thus is to have a purity of heart which reflects the image of God. A perfect example of the true righteousness and integrity which comes in response to the Law Calvin finds in Zacharias and Elizabeth. "They were both righteous before God, walking in all the commandments and blameless," where the emphasis is both on the inward walk before God and on the outward conduct before men.[5] Therefore the Law must be interpreted not according to the letter but as spiritual, the true interpreter of the Law in this sense being

[1] Inst. 2 : 8 : 46; 2 : 8 : 6.
[2] Inst. 2 : 8 : 6.
[3] Comm. on Ps. 119 : 159, C.O. 32 : 286. *Interea docemur, veram legis observationem non nisi ex liberali amore nasci.*
[4] 1 Tim. 1 : 5. Cf. Inst. 2 : 8 : 51. Calvin is always ready to point out that the Scripture requires on our part not only deeds of love but a genuine feeling of sympathy with others in their evils "as though they were our own." "No act of kindness except accompanied with sympathy is pleasing to God." (Comm. on 1 John 3 : 17, C.O. 55 : 341). To wear ourselves out in helping others is no great matter "if we have not the heart to be as they be and to join ourselves with them as though we felt their grief in our own persons." If a man in adversity suspects a lack of real compassion on the part of those who are helping him, our help doubles his grief instead of being a relief. "So then when we want to fulfil our duty towards those who are in adversity: let us begin at this point, i.e. to pity their miseries and to feel part of them ourselves as closely as we can. For this is the true test of love." (Serm. on Job 2 : 11–13, C.O 33 : 133–4.)
[5] Serm. on Luke 1 : 5–9, C.O. 46 : 17. *Il monstre en premier lieu quelle est la vraye iustice, c'est asçavoir où il n'y a point de feintise: et pourtant, que nous ne cherchions point seulement de vivre sainctement, et d'estre irreprehensibles devant les hommes, mais que sur tout nous ayons les yeux et les sens eslevez à Dieu, pour luy complaire, et pour conformer nostre vie à sa volonté. Si donc il n'y a point d'integrité de coeur nous pourrons estre louez des hommes . . . mais il n'y aura que fumee. . . . Apprenons donc pour bien regler nostre vie . . . que nous ayons une affection droite et pure de nous addonner à l'obeissance de nostre Dieu*

Christ Himself in the Sermon on the Mount, where He declares that "an immodest look is adultery, and that hatred of a brother is murder."[1] Calvin's own interpretation of the meaning of the Commandments always follows the principle that "there is always more in the requirements and prohibitions of the Law than is expressed in words," and that under each of them there is set forth, "by way of example, whatever is foulest and most iniquitous in each species of transgression," and moreover that the Commandments must be interpreted positively as not only condemning certain vices but as requiring "opposite duties and positive acts."[2]

For Calvin, love to God and our neighbour can arise only in a heart that has first been purged by self-denial from self-love and opened up towards God and man in true *agape*.[3] Love towards God and man is inseparable from the humility before God and man that is the fruit of self-denial and Cross-bearing.[4] Calvin therefore finds at the heart of the Law a stern call to self-denial and Cross-bearing. When the rich young ruler came to Jesus and professed to have kept all the Commandments from his youth up Jesus reminded him that "one thing" which the Law taught, and

---

[1] Inst. 2 : 8 : 6–7. Cf. serm. on 1 Tim. 1 : 5–7, C.O. 53 : 30. *Dieu en publiant sa Loy, a regardé à une fin et à un but certain, auquel aussi il nous faut tascher: et quand nous en ferons ainsi, nous aurons la vraye ame de la Loy, ce ne sera pas une lettre morte.*

[2] Inst. 2 : 8 : 8–10. Cf. e.g., Calvin's exposition of the eighth Commandment. It "requires every man to exert himself honestly in preserving his own." It forbids misuse of God's blessings (Calvin regards all unbelievers as thieves since they have no filial right to the blessings they daily take from God's hands— Cf. p. 131). It forbids "all the acts by which we obtain possession of the goods and money of our neighbour" even though these may have a "semblance of justice" in the eyes of the Law (Inst. 2 : 8 : 45. Cf. serm. on Deut. 5 : 19, C.O. 26 : 349). *Il y beaucoup d'especes de larrecin. Car les uns usent de fraude cachee, quand ils attirent par moyens subtils, et par pratiques la substance d'autruy à eux ... il semblera qu'ils n'y touchent ... ils sont larrons devant Dieu* (serm. on Deut. 5 : 19, C.O. 26 : 347). The Commandment, on the contrary involves us in helping our neighbour to retain his property (Inst. 2 : 8 : 45). It forbids withholding the help we could give him in his need—we are thieves if we do not help him (Serm. on Deut, 22 : 1–4, C.O. 28 : 10). It forbids declining any duty we owe him as our neighbour. It involves faithfully performing whatever duties or honour we owe to each other as rulers, subjects, ministers of the Gospel, elders, congregation, parents, children. It forbids all excessive eagerness to obtain wealth in order to satisfy our avarice or prodigality (Inst. 2 : 8 : 46).

[3] Cf. pp. 61–2; and comm. on Gal. 5 : 14, C.O. 50 : 251–2.

[4] Serm. on Deut. 5 : 16, C.O. 26 : 313. *Dieu declare qu'il n'est point honoré de nous sinon que nous luy facions hommage en la personne de ceux qu'il a constituez en son lieu, et ausquels il a imprimé son image. En somme nous voyons que la charité commence par ce bout, que nous soyons humbles, et modestes, et que nul ne s'esleve en fierté et presomption, que nul se prise par trop: mais que nous soyons prests de nous humilier, pour nous ranger à tout ce qu'il plaira à Dieu.*

which he had lacked in keeping the Law, was to deny himself (in his case by selling all) and to follow Jesus, taking the Cross on his shoulders.[1] To do this was merely an essential part of the keeping of the Law. Jesus thus brought the young man face to face with the true meaning of the Commandments, for the design of the Law in expressly condemning concupiscence is "to bring men to self-denial," and it is the Law truly interpreted that "teaches us to bear the Cross."[2] In the Law, therefore, God teaches us the same reversal of self-love by self-denial which we see perfectly embodied in the pattern of Christ's own self-denial and Cross-bearing. There is not a syllable of the Law that panders in any way to the "carnal nature" of man.[3] Its first demand upon us is that we should put our minds and hearts under coercion.[4] The humility and distrust in our own ability to which we are led by the stern demands of the Law[5] can also help to bring us to such self-despair and self-denial.

4. The Holy Spirit and the Law

Since the Law, according to its true meaning, teaches a full consecration of body and soul to God, self-denial, and a way of life that is nothing short of the full Christian life, it would be hopeless even to attempt to fulfil it apart from the power of the Holy Spirit. The office of the Spirit in uniting us to Christ is not only to mortify the flesh, to consecrate us wholly to God, but also to write the Law of God on our hearts. "It would be in vain for the feet and hands and eyes to be controlled to observe the Law

---

[1] Mark 10 : 21.   [2] Comm. in loc. C.O. 45 : 539.   [3] Inst. 2 : 8 : 54.
[4] Inst. 2 : 8 : 6. *Quia animis nostris lata est Lex coelestis, eorum coercitio ad iustam eius observationem imprimis necessaria est.*
[5] Inst. 2 : 8 : 3. The meaning of the fourth Commandment (the Sabbath) under the Old Covenant was to teach man the duty of resting from his own works and looking for a true spiritual rest to come. Thus the Sabbath was an ordinance by which the Jews were taught to cease trusting in their own works and to mortify concupiscence. Self-denial is therefore in a deep sense the true meaning of the Sabbath. Since Christ came and fulfilled the Sabbath promise of rest and abrogated the Sabbath law in this sense, a Christian truly observes the Sabbath and fulfils this Commandment by the practice of daily self-denial, and is thus free from the "external observation" of the Sabbath. (Inst. 2 : 8 : 28–34, comm. on Exod. 31 : 13, C.O. 24 : 584, and serm. on Deut. 5 : 12–14, C.O. 26 : 283–8). The Sabbath, however, still remains in force for the secondary purpose of providing opportunity for rest and public worship etc. (see note on p. 244). Its transference to the Lord's day is a sign of our liberty (C.O. 26 : 294).

unless obedience begins at the heart. It is the Holy Spirit's own particular office to engrave the Law of God on our hearts."[1]

The effect of the work of the Spirit in writing the Law on our hearts is that instead of being inclined to sin we begin cordially to seek after a righteousness to which we were previously altogether averse,[2] for the phrase to "write the Law in the heart" means that the Law should rule in the heart and that there should be "no feeling of the heart not conformable to and not consenting to its doctrine."[3] The love of the Law thus created in our hearts by the Holy Spirit is a sure sign of our regeneration and adoption.[4]

5. The Law as the perfect rule of righteousness

Everything we need for our sanctification, and indeed for the full perfection of our Christian life, is contained within the Law, if we will give it its true meaning and seek to fulfil it in the power of the Spirit. When Christ said to the rich young ruler, who had affirmed that he had kept the Law from his youth up, "You lack one thing. . . . If you would be perfect, go, sell what you possess and give it to the poor,"[5] He did not mean one thing "beyond the Law" but "in the very keeping of the Law,"[6] for the Law is the "rule of perfect righteousness."[7] "It is a mistake to suppose that merely the rudiments and first principles of righteousness are delivered in the Law." If we understand it properly and interpret it properly it can lead us in the way of "complete perfection."[8]

---

[1] Comm. on Ps. 40 : 8, C.O. 31: 412. Cf. serm. on 1 Tim. 1 : 8–11, C.O. 53 : 55. *Mais quand Dieu nous instruit ainsi par son sainct Esprit, il forme quant et quant nos coeurs en son obeissance, comme il est escrit aux Prophetes, tant en Ieremie qu'en Ezechiel, où nostre Seigneur dit, que Dieu engravera sa Loy en nos entrailles, qu'elle ne sera pas seulement escrite devant nos yeux, mais nous l'aurons là dedans, en sorte que nostre vie s'y conformera, sans qu'on nous y pousse.*

[2] Comm. on Ps. 40 : 8, C.O. 31 : 412.

[3] Comm. on Jer. 31 : 33, C.O. 38 : 692. *Et scribere in cordibus tantundem valet atque corda ipsa sic formare, ut lex illic dominetur, et nullus sit affectus cordis, qui non eius doctrinae subscribat atque consentiat.*

[4] Comm. on Ps. 119 : 159, C.O. 32 : 286. *Adde quod sincerus legis Dei amor certum est adoptionis signum, quum opus sit spiritus sancti.*

[5] Mark 10 : 21; Matt. 19 : 21.

[6] Comm. on loc. C.O. 45 : 539. *Ergo Christus non unum praeter legis observationem iuveni deesse intelligit, sed in ipsa legis observatione.*

[7] Inst. 2 : 8 : 5, *perfectae iustitiae regula.*

[8] Cf. Inst. 2 : 8 : 51; and serm. on Eph. 4 : 23–6, C.O. 51 : 622. *Or il est certain que la Loy de Dieu ne nous a point enseignez à demi de ce que nous avons à faire: mais Dieu nous a là monstré une droite reigle, à laquelle on ne peut adiouster ne diminuer.*

It should be noted again that the effect of a perfect fulfilment of the Law would be the restoration of true order in the life of man —a true harmony between the outward life and the feelings of the heart, and a true relationship between the fulfilment of our duty towards God and our duty towards man—between the first table and the second table, between holiness and justice. To respond to the Law with such wholeheartedness is to show that true integrity of heart which can be called perfection,[1] and is to walk in love which is the fulfilling of the law. Perfection, for Calvin, consists not in attaining to this and that virtue in the highest possible degree, but in wholeheartedness, integrity and sincerity.[2] He sometimes mentions *symetrie* along with *rondeur* as the goal to be attained in all our striving towards the ideal Christian life, and no doubt he has the idea of wishing to set before men the ideal of a truly balanced and ordered life,[3] rather than of a life with certain outstanding features. He frequently quotes the text "Love is the bond of perfection" in such a way as to suggest that it is only where love reigns that order and balance are possible amongst the other virtues a man may have.[4] He also quotes it in contexts where he wishes to correct some one-sided and unbalanced cultivation of virtue.[5]

[1] Serm. on Eph. 4 : 23–6, C.O. 51 : 621–2.

[2] Comm. on Jer. 29 : 13, C.O. 38 : 596. *Propheta cor totum opponit duplici. Non ergo hic intelligitur perfectio, quia nulla posset reperiri in hominibus, sed duntaxat integritas vel sinceritas.* Cf. comm. on Matt. 12 : 33. C.O. 45 : 343. *Non requiri a Christo exactam perfectionem, cui nihil desit, sed duntaxat simplicem ac minime simulatum affectum.*

[3] Serm. on 2 Sam. 2 : 22–3, p. 46. *Et au reste qu'entre toutes autres vertus la rondeur et symetrie nous doit estre recommandee.* Cf. Calvin's comments on Eph. 4 : 12 (C.O. 51 : 198–9.) where Calvin identifies the "perfection" of the Church with its symmetry, balance and order. The symmetry of the Church is destroyed when anything opposes the head.

[4] Comm. on Col. 3 : 14, C.O. 52 : 123. *Vinculum perfectionis: quo significat, virtutum omnium chorum sub ea contineri. Nam haec vere regula est totius vitae et omnium actionum, ad quam quidquid non exigitur, vitiosum est, qualemcunque alioqui splendorum habeat. Haec causa est cur vocetur hic vinculum perfectionis, quia nihil est in vita nostra bene compositum quod non ad ipsam dirigatur.*

[5] Comm. on Matt. 10 : 20, C.O. 45 : 540; on Matt. 22 : 40, C.O. 45 : 614. Serm. on Matt. 3 : 9–10, C.O. 46 : 547–8.

Chapter III

The Christian attitude to this present world

1. Detachment from this world

(i) *Concupiscence as the slavish love of this present world*

WHEN Adam was set in the garden of Eden to fulfil the meaning of his being created in the image of God he was meant not to find the end of his existence in the enjoyment of the immediately surrounding environment, but rather to find in created things tokens of the grace of their Creator, and to use them as helps to himself to meditate upon and aspire to the better life for which he had been created. Therefore though he was meant to rejoice in the present life, and to use every gift of God thankfully, he was also meant to be to some extent detached from this present world.

As a result of the Fall the natural man has become completely deprived of the power to rise in heart and mind above this world and to meditate upon a future life. Concupiscence manifests itself by producing in man's heart improper and intemperate love for this present world, which brings him into such bondage to this world as prevents him from even seeking God truly.[1] "We are inclined by nature to a slavish love of this world."[2] If man truly considered the brevity and vanity of this life he would realise that it is but a shadow which must pass away soon, and his desires for the things of this life would lessen. But the concern of man's mind is continually directed to earthly objects and the affection of the heart follows the mind. His heart is an insatiable gulf which it is impossible to fill to contentment with the things of this earth. Yet he goes on vainly seeking satisfaction in this earth.[3] Men bury

[1] Inst. 3 : 9 : 1–4.
[2] Inst. 3 : 9 : 1. *In belluinum mundi huius amorem (sumus) natura inclinati.*
[3] Serm. on Job 14 : 1–4, C.O. 33 : 657. *C'est un abysme et un gouffre insatiable que l'homme, tellement qu'il n'est question de se contenter de toutes choses de la terre, il n'y a ne fin ne mesure en lui. Et qui en est cause? Or si nous pensions à la brefveté de nostre vie, il est certain que nos cupiditez seroyent attrempees, que nos appetis ne seroyent point ainsi bouillans. . . . Mais cependant nous sommes si aspres pour amasser des biens, et ceci et cela, que nous ne pensons à autre chose. Et qui en est cause? Nous pensons tousiours ici bas.*

all aspiration after the heavenly life under earthly cares so that, "while living in this world, they die to God."[1] Man deceives himself by imagining that this world is his rest forever, and that he is secure in the frail nest he has built here for himself.[2] Calvin approves of the comparison made by the Apostle James of such immoderate love of this world to adultery, for it is a violation of the marriage which God seeks to make with us when He seeks to espouse us to Himself as a chaste virgin, and a transference to a baser object of the affection which we owe to God.[3]

Calvin constantly emphasises that it is impossibly hard for a man by his own strength to rid himself of this love for the present world that can so hold down his soul in evil bondage. It was to this difficulty that Jesus referred when he spoke of how hard it is for a rich man to enter the Kingdom of Heaven.[4] Our minds are naturally so set on this earth and so much given up to its pleasures and cares that it is impossible for us even to taste the pleasures of eternity, the experience of which alone can deliver us from bondage to this earth.[5] Unless some radical conversion of attitude can take place within us by the grace of God, it is as vain to expect us to respond when called away from a vain love of this world, as it would be to expect a ball to collect the water poured over it.[6]

(ii) *A truly natural detachment from this world is given in the Christian's relationship to Christ*

It is the effect of regeneration and sanctification in Christ to restore a truly detached relationship between man and this present world, by which man becomes again able, through His participation by faith in the Resurrection and Ascension of Christ, to meditate on the future life.[7] Indeed true detachment from this present world is restored to man in the gift of faith, in the acceptance of which his heart is raised above created things to the ascended

---

[1] Comm. on Ps. 119 : 144, C.O. 32 : 280. *Quando itaque terrenis curis obruitur coelestis vitae meditatio, nihil aliud quam se in sepulcrum demergunt homines, ut mundo viventes, Deo moriantur.*
[2] Comm. on Ps. 90 : 4, C.O. 31 : 835.
[3] Comm. on Jas. 4 : 4, C.O. 55 : 415–16.
[4] Comm. on Matt. 19 : 26, C.O. 45 : 543.
[5] Comm. on Ps. 119 : 132, C.O. 32 : 274; and on Ps. 90 : 4, C.O. 31 : 835.
[6] Comm. on 1 John 2 : 15, C.O. 55 : 318.
[7] Cf. pp. 87–9.

Christ who is beyond this world.[1] The whole process of *meditatio futurae vitae* in the Christian life must be thought of as the restoration of the true order of nature.

All this has a very important practical bearing on Calvin's preaching and teaching about the attitude of the Christian to this present life with its riches and enjoyments. He appeals to his hearers and readers to work out in practice the implications of this attitude of detachment from this world, not simply from motives of pure asceticism, nor merely as a necessary and regrettable condition imposed upon man through his fall into concupiscence and through the prevalence of evil in his surroundings,[2] but mainly because such an attitude is truly natural, to adopt it is to become truly human and to find the true meaning of this present life.

The part that our sufferings in fellowship with the death of Christ play in detaching us from a vain love of this present world should again be noted.[3] It is in order to train us to despise the present world and to aspire to the future life that tribulation is sent to us by God. Such tribulations have the effect of making us sensible of the vanity of the present life,[4] and to help to break the power of its fascination by which it enslaves us.[5]

But we would not require such affliction if we would respond in a true way by faith and thanksgiving to God's grace and goodness. In all the earthly gifts which He bestows upon His children in this world God's purpose is to avouch His fatherly love so that we will be drawn to Himself.[6] Calvin can speak of God as drawing us to Himself by sweetness when He puts us at our ease in this world and gives us not only food and clothing but protection from the troubles which visit others.[7] Moreover, in the provision and care which He bestows upon our bodies, God's purpose is to give us a sign of the care which in His redeeming love He bestows upon our

---

[1] Cf. p. 22.
[2] Though this does enter largely into Calvin's preaching. (See pp. 234–6.)
[3] Cf. also pp. 89–90.
[4] Inst. 3 : 9: 1. *Quocunque autem tribulationis genere premamur, respiciendus semper est hic finis, ut assuescamus ad praesentis vitae contemptum, indeque ad futurae meditationem excitemur. . . . Huic malo ut occurrat Dominus, assiduis miseriarum documentis suos de praesentis vitae vanitate edocet.*
[5] Inst. 3 : 9 : 2.
[6] Serm. on 1 Tim. 4 : 1–5, C.O. 53 : 362–3; on 1 Cor. 10 : 25–30, C.O. 49 : 692; on Deut. 8 : 3–9, C.O. 26 : 602.
[7] Serm. on Deut. 6 : 10–13, C.O. 26 : 450.

souls, which He feeds not simply with bread and wine but with the much more precious spiritual food.[1] Furthermore, all the good things which God gives us in this life are to be regarded as preliminary tokens of the heavenly heritage which the same bountiful love has destined for us, and thus by God's blessing in this life we are to be exercised in the hope of this life to come.[2] Thus the earthly gifts of God become to us ladders by which our minds and hearts are raised up to Heaven.[3] All the tokens of God's earthly providence towards us, the rising and going-down of the sun, the fruitfulness of the earth, the changes of the skies, can be beams of light illuminating our heavenward path when otherwise we would have to walk entirely by faith in the midst of darkness. These can be as the hand of God stretched forth to prove that God is not far away from us and seeks ever to draw us to Himself in anticipation of the great day when we shall come to fullness of joy and happiness in union with Him for ever.[4]

(iii) *Both nature and the Gospel imply temperance, frugality and contemptio mundi*

Calvin frequently exhorts us to temperance and frugality in the use even of those earthly commodities and pleasures which God may have put at our disposal in abundance, by reminding us that whatever God puts in our hands here He merely lends to us. At the same time as He gives it to us He keeps it in His own hands.[5] Therefore we must use it with sobriety and share it with those in need, remembering that at any time God pleases we may have to

---

[1] Serm. on 1 Cor. 10 : 25–30, C.O. 49 : 692. *Le principal est quand nous beuvons et mangeons que nous sçachions que cela nous procede de la main de Dieu, et qu'en cela il nous declare que nous sommes ses enfans, et qu'il fait desia office de Pere, et que s'il ha le soin de nos corps, par plus forte raison nos ames luy sont recommandees.* And serm. on Deut. 8 : 3–9. C.O. 26 : 602. *Il faut monter plus haut : et cognoistre que nos ames ne sont point repeues ne de pain, ne de vin, qu'elles ont une autre viande plus precieuse.*

[2] Serm. on Job 3 : 1–10, C.O. 33 : 143–4.

[3] Serm. on Matt. 5 : 11–12, C.O. 46 : 822; on Job 1 : 2–5, C.O. 33 : 41.

[4] Serm. on Cant. Ezech. v. 9–12, C.O. 35 : 535.

[5] Serm. on Deut. 7 : 1–4, C.O. 26 : 503–4. *Et de là nous sommes admonnestez, qu'en tout ce que Dieu nous a mis entre nos mains il nous faut regarder de ne point prendre trop grand liberté, pour user des biens qu'il nous fait, à nostre poste. . . . Quand Dieu aura donné abondance des biens de ce monde à quelcun . . . s'il veut dire: Ceci est mien, i'en feray ce que bon me semblera: c'est frauder Dieu du droict qu'il s'est reservé. Il est vray que nous appellerons bien nostre ce qu'il aura donné: mais c'est à ceste condition, que tousiours cela demeure en sa main, et . . . que nous en usions en toute sobrieté et modestie.* Cf. comm. on Luke 16 : 12, C.O. 45 : 405.

part with everything.[1] The man of faith who happens to be rich
in worldly wealth today will also recognise that tomorrow he may
be poor, and therefore he will not become too much attached to
the wealth that he might have to renounce so soon.[2] "The mind
of a Christian ought not to be taken up with earthly things, or to
repose in them; for we ought to live as if we were every moment
about to depart from this life."[3]

We must be constantly watchful, especially against becoming
involved in a vain and excessive love of this earth. The danger
which besets us in the use of this world is that instead of its being
a ladder to enable our hearts and minds to rise upwards to God,
it should become rather a sepulchre in which our souls become
buried on this earth.[4] Our earthly possessions, instead of becoming blessings which lead us to God, can become like cords which
strangle us.[5] Our lordship of this world must be true lordship,
and only those master this world who can refuse to be brought
into bondage to anything,[6] and who use all things with such sobriety
and frugality that their progress towards the heavenly goal is not
hindered.[7]

We must not, then, permit ourselves to enjoy "without restraint"
the vain and perishable things of this world, and we should find
our joy in the Gospel rather than in the delights and sensualities
of this age.[8] In the twenty-third Psalm the fact that the Lord
provided a furnished table full of good things for the psalmist in
the presence of his enemies made him lift up his heart, in the final
verse, to his eternal inheritance. "He valued all the comforts of
the flesh only in proportion as they served to enable him to live
to God. . . . It is therefore certain that the mind of David, by the
aid of the temporal prosperity which he enjoyed, was elevated to

[1] Comm. on Phil. 4 : 12, C.O. 52 : 64.
[2] Serm. on Matt. 5 : 11–12, C.O. 46 : 822. Cf. comm. on Phil. 3 : 8, C.O.
52 : 47–8.
[3] Comm. on 1 Cor. 7 : 29, C.O. 49 : 420.
[4] Serm. on Matt. 5 : 11–12, C.O. 46 : 822.
[5] Serm. on 1 Cor. 10 : 19–24, C.O. 49 : 682.
[6] Comm. on 1 Cor. 6 : 12, C.O. 49 : 396.
[7] Comm. on 1 Cor. 7:31, C.O. 49 : 421.
[8] Serm. on John 1 : 1–5, C.O. 47 : 468. *Quand donc nous prononcerons ce mot
Evangile qui est à dire Bonne nouvelle, que nous apprenions de ne nous point
resiouir outre mesure és choses de ce monde, qui sont caduques et vaines. Ne nous
reiouissons point en delices, en voluptez, ni en rien qui soit; mais esiouissons nous en
ce que Iesus Christ nous a este envoyé.*

the hope of the everlasting inheritance."[1] Such is the true detachment from this world which man ought to have.

This means that the light, or the shadow, of the life that is to come must fall on everything we do in this life, and we must relate all our earthly activity to our eternal destiny beyond this world, and thus find true purpose and meaning in our daily work. Calvin quotes with approval the proverb "We ought not to live in order to eat and drink; but we must eat and drink in order to be led towards the life to come."[2] It is not only ministers of the Gospel who sow to the Spirit in order to reap eternal life. All men, no matter what is their daily work, whether they be labourers or mechanics or merchants, must relate all their activity to the higher life that is to come. If our heart is thus set on the life that is to come, all our earthly toil, even for mere food, will be a sowing which will bring its eternal harvest. To care for the needs of the present life without any regard at the same time for the future life is to "sow to the flesh" that of the flesh we may "reap corruption."[3]

Calvin, of course, uses the Biblical analogy of our being "pilgrims and strangers" in this earth to describe what should be our attitude towards it. To live as such a sojourner on earth is a sign that a man is a child of God and an heir of heaven.[4] Calvin also likens the life of the children of God in this world to that of the bird flitting from branch to branch in this world but never resting long in any nest.[5] But these analogies do not include the element of hatred and contempt for this world which is bound, according

---

[1] Comm. on Ps. 23 : 5–6, C.O. 31 : 242–3.

[2] Serm. on Gal. 6 : 6–8, C.O. 51 : 95.

[3] Cf. Ibid. pp. 94 and 95. *Les ministres donc ont bien cela de special: mais tous en commun nous devons semer à la vie eternelle, c'est à dire passans par ce monde comme estrangers, ayans nos sens eslevez à cest heritage où doit estre nostre repos, et là aussi où il nous faut appliquer toutes nos estudes. Et mesmes quand nous travaillons pour la nourriture de nos corps, que ce soit tousiours tendant à ce but-là. . . . Puis ainsi est donc, quand un homme mesme s'appliquera pour gagner sa vie, soit en labeur, soit d'un art mechanique, soit un marchant, quoy qu'il en soit, quand nous aurons le soin et de nos personnes et de nos familles, que nous tendions plus haut. Car de faict c'est une chose mauvaise si un homme s'amuse seulement à gagner sa vie, qu'il ne regarde point de servir à Dieu.* Cf. comm. on Gal. 6 : 7–8, C.O. 50 : 261–2.

[4] Comm. on Ps. 119 : 54, C.O. 32 : 237.

[5] Serm. on Deut. 9 : 20–4, C.O. 26 : 708. *Il y a premierement ce pelerinage terrestre auquel Dieu nous a tous assuiettis en ce monde: combien qu'il nos donne repos, que plusieurs ne bougent de leur maison, et de leur nid: tant y a que nous serons bien mal advisez si nous ne passons par ce monde comme oiseaux sur la branche, et que nous n'y soyons estrangers. Car autrement Dieu nous desavouë, et renonce.*

to Calvin, to enter the Christian attitude to some extent. Indeed Calvin does not hesitate to define the true attitude which we should take towards this world as *contemptio mundi*,[1] the term *contemptio* being used in contrast to the *meditatio* and *desiderium* that define our attitude to the future life. Calvin insists that it is only when we contrast the earthly with the heavenly life that we are able to despise and trample the former underfoot.[2] It is especially because an improper love of this present world tends to involve us in compromise or allegiance with the evil powers that tend to dominate this present world,[3] that we must learn to hate this world.[4] We must remember that what separates the godly from the wicked is their opposite attitudes to this present world and to that beyond.[5] Moreover, if our love for this present world makes us indulge in self-love and give way to the power of concupiscence in our heart, we are bound in learning to hate and deny ourselves also to reflect the same attitude to whatever object in the world tends to bring us under bondage. Therefore Calvin looks on contempt for this world as a correlative of self-denial.[6]

Our hatred or contempt for this life must not, however, be unqualified. We must always remember that this life is the gift of God. It is "among the divine blessings not to be despised."[7] Therefore our hatred and contempt must not be directed against this life in itself, which God made good, but only against life in so far as it keeps us subject to sin. We may legitimately long for the termination of our earthly existence, but we must nevertheless be kept from murmuring or impatience by the realisation that if it is God's will that we should remain on this earth we must thankfully and obediently accept all the implications of our

---

[1] Inst. 3 : 9 : 1. *Sic enim habendum est, nunquam serio futurae vitae desiderium ac meditationem erigi animum, nisi praesentis contemptu ante imbutus fuerit.*

[2] Inst. 3 : 9 : 4.

[3] Cf. pp. 203–4.

[4] Serm. on Deut. 9 : 20–4, C.O. 26 : 708. *Ainsi ceux qui ont honte de se nommer estrangers en ce monde, qu'ils s'en aillent cercher leur heritage avec le diable: car ils n'ont ne part ne portion avec Dieu.*

[5] Comm. on Ps. 119 : 132, C.O. 32 : 274.

[6] Comm. on 1 Pet. Arg. C.O. 55 : 205. *Consilium Petri est in hac epistola, fideles ad sui abnegationem mundique contemptum hortari, ut liberi carnis affectibus, terrenisque omnibus impedimentis soluti, ad coeleste Christi regnum toto animo adspirent.* And on Gal. 6 : 14, C.O. 50 : 265–6. *Mundus est quasi obiectum et scopus veteris hominis.*

[7] Inst. 3 : 9 : 2.

earthly existence.[1] The conditions, then, for a right use of this world are to pass through it as pilgrims should who have their minds fixed on another country to which they are travelling, to offer all that we possess and enjoy here in our open hands as a sacrifice to God to take from us whenever it pleases Him, to make such tokens of the divine love as we enjoy in the midst of this present creation whet our appetites for the fuller glory that is yet to be—in other words to use this world thankfully as a preparation for that which is to come. Under such circumstances it is right for us to indulge in a real and thankful love of this life.[2] We thus have the paradoxical truth that we are able to love this life truly only when we have truly learned first to despise this life.

2. The use and enjoyment of this world

(i) *Dominion over this world has been restored to men in Christ*

Man was made to have dominion and lordship in the midst of this created world. It was made originally for man to possess and enjoy in all its goodness and fruitfulness, and Adam, before he fell, was given the power to use and enjoy with a free conscience, and in gratitude to God, all the good things which God placed before his eyes. He was created to be master of all other creatures and of all his circumstances. "The whole of the world is arranged and established for the purpose of conducing to the comfort and happiness of men."[3]

One of the main effects of the Fall has been, however, that man, in rejecting his call to live according to the image of God and in the true order of creation, has lost his right and place as possessor and lord of the world around him. "The dominion of the world was

---

[1] Inst. 3 : 9 : 4. [*Vita*] *odio certe habenda nunquam est, nisi quatenus nos peccato tenet obnoxios: quanquam ne illud quidem odium proprie in ipsam convertendum est. Utcunque sit, nos tamen ita eius vel taedio vel odio affici decet, ut finem eius desiderantes, parati quoque simus ad arbitrium Domini in ea manere, quo scilicet taedium nostrum sit procul ab omni murmure et impatientia.*

[2] Comm. on John 12 : 25, C.O. 47 : 289. *In summa, vitam hanc amare non per se malum est, modo in ea tantum peregrinemur semper ad scopum nostrum intenti. Nam hic legitimus est amandae vitae modus, si in ea manemus quamdiu Domino visum fuerit . . . si eam quasi manibus gestantes offerimus Deo in sacrificium.* Cf. Inst. 3 : 9 : 3. *Deinde altera, quod variis beneficiis divinae benignitatis suavitatem delibare in ea incipimus: quo spes ac desiderium nostrum acuatur ad plenam eius revelationem expetendam.*

[3] Comm. on Ps. 8 : 7, C.O. 31 : 94.

taken away from us in Adam," says Calvin.[1] It is true that fallen
man has to use this world, and to live by the produce of this
world, but he has no right to do so, for it is God's world made for
God's children, and he has renounced God and the status of a
child of God. Therefore he can only live as a thief in a world to
which he has no right.[2]

As a token that all this is so, man's very environment has, as it
were, turned against him in a refusal to submit to one who has
no right to dominate within this world. "As soon, then, as Adam
alienated himself from God through sin, he was justly deprived
of the good things which he had received; not that he was denied
the use of them, but that he could have no right to them after he
had forsaken God. And in the very use of them God intended that
there should be some tokens of this loss of right such as these—
the wild beasts ferociously attack us, those who ought to be awed
by our presence are dreaded by us, some never obey us, others
can hardly be trained to submit, and they do us harm in various
ways. The earth answers not our expectations in cultivating it;[3]
the sky, the air, the sea, and other things, are often adverse to us.
But were all creatures to continue in subjection, yet whatsoever
the sons of Adam possessed would be deemed as robbery; for
what can they call their own when they themselves are not
God's."[4]

The true order in man's relationship to this world has, however,
been restored in Jesus Christ. To His Son Jesus God has given
the possession of the earth in fulfilment of the promise of the
eighth Psalm, which describes the original plan of creation and the
true status of man in this universe.[5] Through being ingrafted into

[1] Comm. on 1 Tim. 4 : 5, C.O. 52 : 297.
[2] Serm. on Titus 1 : 15–16, C.O. 54 : 484. *Nous ne pourrions pas toucher une
seule viande que nous ne fussions larrons; car nous sommes privez et bannis de tous
les biens que Dieu a creez, à cause du peché d'Adam, iusques à tant que nous en
ayons la possession en nostre Seigneur Iesus Christ.*
[3] Man's daily work, according to Cálvin, as he experiences it in this life, is not
according to the order of nature. It is true that God originally made man to
work, giving him hands and feet and putting him in the garden to cultivate it,
but work as man knows it today is, generally speaking, a curse and punishment
for sin. Cf. serm. on Deut. 5 : 13–15, C.O. 26 : 296, Comm. on Gen. 3 : 19,
C.O. 23 : 74–5. Cf. also pp. 155–6.
[4] Comm. on Heb. 2 : 5, C.O. 55 : 24.
[5] Serm. on 1 Tim. 4 : 1–5, C.O. 53 : 360. *Voilà aussi pourquoy il est dit, que
ce qui est contenu au Pseaume huitieme, est accompli en la personne de nostre Seigneur Iesus Christ, c'est asçavoir que Dieu luy a donné en possession la terre, les
bestes des champs, les oiseaux du ciel, les poissons des eaux. Et pourquoy? Car par*

Christ and re-admitted into the family of God by being adopted as His children, we too are re-admitted into the inheritance of the children of God in this world and thus to our right to share in the goodness of this creation.[1] "God . . . by ingrafting us into His Son, constitutes us anew to be lords of the world, that we may lawfully use as our own all the wealth with which He supplies us."[2] Herein, then, lies the difference between the position of the unbeliever in his ordinary life in this world and the believer. An unbeliever in his ordinary life in this world, even in eating and drinking to sustain his life, has no right to what he is taking from God. He is therefore robbing God and robbing the children of God, and is continually breaking the eighth Commandment.[3]

(ii) *The Christian's new relationship to his earthly circumstances*

The restoration of true order through Jesus Christ means that those who are united to Christ and within His Kingdom enjoy even here and now during their life on this earth a new relationship to their environment.[4] God acts towards them providentially in a special way, and throughout their life in this present world they are specially protected from evil, specially provided for and specially blessed. Even though God loves all men, and maintains all men in His love, nevertheless His main business upon which He exercises His counsel and His will is now the salvation of those

---

le peché nous sommes privez de tout bien, nous ne sommes pas dignes de toucher un morceau de pain, ni une goutte d'eau: mais nous sommes restituez par le moyen et par la grace de nostre Seigneur Iesus Christ en ceste possession-là. Cf. ibid, C.O. 53 : 364–5. *Il est appelé heritier du monde.* Serm. on Deut. 6 : 1–4, C.O. 26 : 426. *Mais quand nostre Seigneur Iesus Christ est apparu, alors il a acquis la possession de tout le monde.*

[1] Comm. on Heb. 2 : 5, C.O. 55 : 24. *Hoc est quod habuimus initio huius epistolae, Christum a patre ordinatum esse haeredem universorum. Certe totam uni haereditatum vendicando, reliquos omnes excludit tanquam alienos. Et merito . . . quae ergo suis domesticis alimenta destinavit, ad nos rapere fas non est. At Christus per quem in familiam cooptamur, simul in societatem iuris sui nos admittit, ut toto mundo cum Dei benedictione fruamur.* Cf. serm. on 1 Cor. 10 : 25–30, C.O. 49 : 686.

[2] Comm. on 1 Tim. 4 : 5, C.O. 52 : 297.

[3] Serm. on 1 Tim. 4 : 1–5, C.O. 53 : 360. *Quand les incredules boyvent et mangent ils desrobbent à Dieu ce qui leur a esté donné.* Comm. on 1 Tim. 4 : 3, C. O. 52 : 296. *Quare veluti alienum furantur aut praedantur infideles quodcunque usurpant.*

[4] Though the curse of hard labour in daily work which all men generally have to bear as a result of the fall is not removed, nevertheless "God often remits a portion of the curse to His own children, lest they should sink beneath the burden," and by making such toil a sacrifice in faith to God, and by accepting it as a cross to subdue the flesh, the Christian can triumph even in this respect. Cf. comm. on Gen. 3 : 19, C.O. 23 : 74–5.

who are united to Jesus Christ, and their preservation in the midst of all their temptations and trials and the assaults of Satan.[1] "As a provident man will regulate his liberality towards all men in such a manner as not to defraud his children or family nor impoverish his own house by spending his substance prodigally on others, so God in like manner in exercising His beneficence to aliens from His family, knows well how to reserve for His own children that which belongs to them as it were by hereditary right."[2] Calvin gives due weight to the assertion of Paul that godliness has promise not only of the life that is to come but "of the life that now is."[3] Therefore the children of God are not only destined for a heavenly inheritance and blessed here and now in spiritual things but also "as to their condition in the present life."[4] Calvin also seeks to give due weight to the many Old Testament promises that the godly shall have earthly prosperity as well as everlasting blessedness, and though at the present day earthly benefits are given "in a more sparing manner."[5] than under the old dispensation, such promises still hold and the goodness which God performs towards those who trust in Him upon this earth is sufficient to be an open and clear testimony even to the wicked men who are onlookers if they care to open their eyes to see it.[6]

That the Christian man should enjoy such tokens of the restoration of the true order of creation in the providential ordering of his life by God is a sign that the Kingdom of God has already begun to be restored in this present world. When God apparently treats men harshly under His providence, depriving them of tokens of His fatherly love, this is a sign that the true order of creation, which was meant to bear witness to His fatherhood, has

---

[1] Serm. on Luke 2 : 50–2, C.O. 46 : 478.

[2] Comm. on Ps. 31 : 19, C.O. 31 : 310. Cf. comm. on Matt. 14 : 16, C.O. 45 : 438. *Certum tamen est, nunquam passurum, ut suis desint vitae subsidia* and comm. on 1 Tim. 4 : 8, C.O. 52 : 300.

[3] 1 Tim. 4 : 8. Cf. serm. on Deut. 7 : 11–15, C.O. 26 : 542. *Et voila pourquoy sainct Paul dit: Que la crainte de Dieu n'a point seulement les promesses de la vie immortelle, mais aussi de ceste vie terrienne. Que si nous cheminons en la crainte de Dieu, non seulement nous serons asseurez qu'il nous a appresté son heritage là haut: mais cependant que nous aurons à vivre en ce monde, qu'il nous conduira, que nous serons sous sa protection, qu'il ne permettra point que rien nous deffaille, entant qu'il cognoist qu'il nous fait besoin.* Cf. also comm. on Ps. 128 : 3, C.O. 32 : 328.

[4] Comm. on Ps. 25 : 13, C.O. 31 : 258. *Summa est, veros Dei cultores non spiritualiter modo beatos esse, sed ab eo quoque benedici quod ad praesentis vitae statum.*

[5] Cf. comm. on Ps. 128 : 3, C.O. 32 : 328.

[6] Comm. on Ps. 31 : 19, C.O. 31 : 309–10.

been upset.[1] But the beginning of the renovation of the world has already taken place, and whatever a Christian enjoys of the special care and providence of the Father in this life is a privilege which derives from the fact that what was lost in Adam is now already restored in Christ, even though the full manifestation and accomplishment of His Kingdom must be awaited "in our final redemption."[2] Using other terms, Calvin can say that in the provision God makes for their sustenance and happiness in this life, the faithful "receive already some fruit of their integrity."[3]

Calvin, however, has to admit that the possession of the earth is at present realised for the Christian only in a very limited way.[4] For it is God's will that His people should not be too much at home upon this earth or allow their thoughts and affections to be so engrossed in it that they forget the hope of the life to come.[5] Therefore God, indeed justly, allows the same afflictions as visit the ungodly also to fall on His own people,[6] and instead of an overflowing abundance gives them only a taste of His fatherly love.[7] A Christian will not complain "if the happiness described in this psalm (i.e. Ps. 128) is not always the lot of the godly, but if it sometimes happens that the wife is troublesome, or proud, or of depraved morals, or that the children are dissolute or vagabonds, and even bring disgrace upon their father's house, let them know that their being deprived of God's blessing is owing to their having repulsed it by their own fault. And surely if each thinks about his own vices he will acknowledge that God's earthly benefits have been justly withheld from him."[8]

Though such afflictions come upon God's children, and their

---

[1] Serm. on Job 5 : 17–18, C.O. 33 : 259. *Il est vray que Dieu signifie bien qu'il deteste le peché; et de fait l'ordre qu'il avoit institué en la creation du monde est troublé, quand nous ne sommes point traittez de luy paternellement.*
[2] Comm. on Heb. 2 : 6, C.O. 55 : 24. *Status enim primae creationis obsolevit, et una cum homine cecidit quoad ipsum hominem. Ergo quoad nova fiat restitutio per Christum, psalmus hic locum non habebit. Nunc apparet non vocari orbem futurum duntaxat qualem e resurrectione speramus, sed qui coepit ab exordio regni Christi: complementum vero suum habebit in ultima redemptione.*
[3] Comm. on Ps. 128 : 3, C.O. 32 : 328.
[4] Comm. on Ps. 85 : 13, C.O. 31 : 790. *Sed notandum est, sic restringi caducae huius vitae commoda, ne terrenis blanditiis indormiant fideles.*
[5] Comm. on Ps. 37 : 9, C.O. 31 : 371. *Terrae possessio quam filiis Dei promittit, non semper est oculis exposita, quia et peregrinos in ea vagari oportet, nec patitur Dominus sedem usquam figere.* Comm. on Ps. 128 : 4, C.O. 32 : 328–9.
[6] Comm. on Ps. 37 : 25, C.O. 32 : 379.
[7] Comm. on Ps. 85 : 13, C.O. 31 : 790.
[8] Comm. on Ps. 128 : 3, C.O. 32 : 328.

enjoyment of this present life is thus limited, yet it must not be imagined that it is a "mere fiction or imaginary thing" to say that the people of God are the heirs of this earth.[1] For their lot in this world is always infinitely better than that of the godless. "They are truly happy because, even in their extreme poverty, they are so persuaded that God is present with them, and being sustained by the strength of this consolation they rest assured."[2] In the midst of all affliction God furnishes His children with such actual experimental evidence of His grace[3] that "they most certainly know that they are the rightful heirs of this world."[4]

(iii) *The benefits of this life are to be used, enjoyed and acknowledged with thanksgiving and faith.*

In all his use and enjoyment of this present world the believing man must have an attitude of faith. "The use of earthly blessings is connected with the pure feelings of faith (*cum puro fidei sensu*), in the exercise of which we can alone enjoy them rightly and lawfully to our own welfare."[5] We must receive what we use and enjoy of this earth's goodness as something that comes to us "not otherwise than from the hand of God."[6] We must really feel that whatever we enjoy from the hand of God is indeed our rightful heritage, not because we are worthy of it, but because God has elected us to such enjoyment.[7] What we eat and drink must be to us a token of the fatherly love and care of God.[8]

It is this attitude of faith which sanctifies our hearts in our use

---

[1] Comm. on Ps. 37 : 27, C.O. 31 : 380. Cf. comm. on Matt. 5 : 5, C.O. 45 : 162–3. *Pro Dei autem filiis respondeo, etiamsi nusquam pedem in suo figere queant, terrae domicilio quiete frui: neque imaginaria est haec possessio, quia terram inhabitant, quam sibi divinitus concessam esse norunt. Deinde adversus malorum intemperiem et furias opposita Dei manu teguntur. . . .*

[2] Comm. on Ps. 25 : 13, C.O. 31 : 258.

[3] Comm. on Ps. 89 : 47, C.O. 31 : 829. *Gratiam suam re et experientia ipsis ostendat.*

[4] Comm. on Ps. 37 : 9, C.O. 31 : 371.   [5] Comm. on Ps. 36 : 9, C.O. 31 : 363.

[6] Comm. on 1 Cor. 10 : 26, C.O. 49 : 469. Cf. on Tit. 1 : 15, C.O. 52 : 418. *Nihil pure usurpant homines, nisi quod e manu Dei fide suscipiunt.*

[7] Serm. on Deut. 4 : 19–24, C.O. 26 : 164. *Mais cependant aussi, que nous meditions ceste doctrine . . . c'est de sentir quand nous iouyssons des creatures de Dieu, que nous les tenons comme nostre heritage: non pas que nous en soyons dignes . . .: mais d'autant que nostre Dieu nous a eleus.*

[8] Serm. on 1 Cor. 10 : 25–30, C.O. 49 : 686. *Tout est licite aux fideles, pour ce qu'ils sont restablis par le moyen et par la grace de nostre Seigneur Iesus Christ, à ce qu'ils puissent boire et manger pour leur nourriture, cognoissans qu'en cela Dieu se monstre leur Pere.* Cf. comm. on Ps. 36 : 8, C.O. 31 : 363.

and enjoyment of this world and enables us to partake of God's earthly blessings without polluting them with an impure conscience[1] as the unbelievers are bound to do.[2] In sanctifying our hearts this faith also sanctifies the gifts themselves so that they become pure, and makes the use of them contribute to our salvation.[3]

Calvin asserts that the conscience of man as he uses the benefits and enjoyments of this present world cannot be purified, nor can the use of created things be sanctified to him, apart from the Word of God. For it is the Word of God alone that can teach us what is the true use of the benefits of this life. It teaches us to recognise God's favours as tokens of fatherly love. It testifies to our consciences that we are indeed heirs of this world and that therefore what we enjoy of its goodness is lawfully ours.[4] "And which of us would venture to claim for himself a single grain of wheat if he were not taught by the Word of God that he is the heir of this world?"[5] It follows from all this that the true use and acceptance in faith of the earthly gifts which God gives us will be accompanied by prayer and especially thanksgiving.[6] Calvin can speak of God's

[1] Serm. on 1 Tim. 4 : 1–5, C.O. 53 : 359. *Il est dit au 15 des Actes, que c'est la foy qui purifie nos coeurs: ceste pureté-là s'estend plus avant, c'est que quand un homme ha son coeur pur, s'il reçoit les biens que Dieu luy distribue pour son usage, qu'il ne pollue rien. Pourquoy? Car il est net.* Cf. Tit. 1 : 15.

[2] Comm. on Tit. 1 : 15, C.O. 52 : 417. *Quia enim nulla est coram Deo quam fidei puritas, sequitur infideles omnes esse immundos. . . . Quia, quum impuri sint ipsi, nihil sibi in mundo purum reperient.* Cf. comm. on 1 Tim. 4 : 3, C.O. 52 : 296; on Heb. 2 : 5, C.O. 55 : 24. Serm. on 1 Tim. 4 : 1–5, C.O. 53 : 359. *Quand i'auray bien lavé mes mains, ie peux manier les choses qui sont pures, et ie ne les noirciray pas: mais si ie manie un linge le plus blanc du monde, et que i'aye les mains souillees, voyla pour tout infecter.*

[3] Serm. on 1 Cor. 10 : 15–18, C.O. 49 : 664. *Les viandes nous sont sanctifiees quand nous cognoissons qu'elles nous procedent de la bonté de Dieu, et que là dessus nous recourons à luy, et luy demandons nostre pain quotidien, et qu'il nous gouverne. . . .* Comm. on Luke 17 : 19, C.O. 45 : 424. *Sola igitur fides dona Dei nobis sanctificat, ut pura sint, et cum legitimo usu coniuncta in salutem nobis cedant.* Serm. on 1 Tim. 4 : 1–5, C.O. 53 : 359. *L'usage des bonnes creatures ne peut appartenir à tous pour leur salut, mais seulement à ceux qui ont cognu la verité.*

[4] Serm. on 1 Tim. 4 : 1–5, C.O. 53 : 364–5. *Dieu . . . nous a donné sa parole pour dedier les viandes à nostre usage. Et comment cela? Quelle est ceste parole dont parle sainct Paul? ce sont les promesses. . . . Or si ainsi est que nous ne pouvons estre nourris quant au monde, que la parole de Dieu n'aille devant, et qu'elle ne soit comme une lampe pour monstre quel est le bon usage et licite des biens de Dieu.* Cf. comm. on Ps. 60 : 8, C.O. 31 : 577. *Nam utcunque Deus innumeris gratiae suae exemplis nos obruat, nulla tamen vigebit eorum notitia, nisi praefulgente verbo.*

[5] Comm. on 1 Tim. 4 : 5, C.O. 52 : 297.

[6] Comm. on John 6 : 11, C.O. 47 : 132. *Non semel nos monuit exemplo suo Christus, quoties cibum attingimus a precibus auspicandem esse. Nam quaecunque in usum nostrum destinavit Deus, tanquam immensae eius bonitatis et paterni in nos*

gifts as being sanctified by prayer,[1] and he refers to the cure which
was given to the nine lepers who did not return to give thanks as
"debased and contaminated by their ingratitude."[2]

It is the duty of the Christian to accept this present life and its
blessings, and to rejoice in the liberty to use them which is the
right of the children of God.[3] Calvin admits that to the believer
there are many considerations that make death better and more
desirable than life on this earth, for the life that is to come is
vastly superior to this present life. But that does not mean that the
Christian has any right to despise this life or regard it as anything
but a wonderful gift of God.[4] Nor has a Christian any right to
curse the day of his birth. The celebration of our birthday, with
solemn and heartfelt thanksgiving to God for the gift of this life,
is a Christian duty and a sign of a true Christian attitude towards
this life.[5] Therefore, though there is a place for fasting in the
Christian life, for men to fast out of some ascetic principle or
man-made law is not a sign of true devotion but, rather, base
infidelity and ingratitude. We must not reject the good gifts of
food and drink which God puts in our hands.[6] Calvin notes with
approval that the Jews in Babylon ate their food during the cap-
tivity for "it would have been an evidence of having fallen into
sinful despair had they starved themselves to death."[7]

In our acceptance of this present life we must remember that
it is given to us not only to use but also to enjoy.[8] When we look
round at the flowers and fruits and the beautiful fabrics and metals

amoris symbola ad eum celebrandum nos invitant. Et gratiarum actio, sicuti Paulus
(1 Tim. 4 : 4) docet, solennis quaedam sanctificatio est, ut eorum usus nobis purus
esse incipiat. Cf. pp. 284–6.

[1] Serm. on 1 Cor. 10 : 15–18, C.O. 49 : 664.

[2] Comm. on Luke 17 : 19, C.O. 45 : 424. Cf. comm. on John 6 : 11, C.O.
47 : 132. Unde sequitur sacrilegos esse donorum Dei profanatores qui ea neglecto
Deo ingurgitant.

[3] Serm. on 1 Cor 10 : 25–30, C.O. 49 : 692. Pourquoy est-ce que ma liberté
sera condamnee? Comme s'il disoit, Mes amis, la liberté qui m'a este donnee est une
chose precieuse, quand il nous constitue en ce monde comme ses heritiers: qu'il veut
que nous iouissions de toutes creatures: comme aussi pour conclusion il en sera parle.
C'est un benefice que nous devons bien priser. Cf. Inst. 3 : 10 : 1.

[4] Cf. comm. on Phil. 2 : 27, C.O. 52 : 40.

[5] Serm. on Job 3 : 1–10, C.O. 33 : 145.

[6] Serm. on 1 Tim. 4 : 1–5, C.O. 53 : 358–9.

[7] Comm. on Ps. 102 : 5, C.O. 32 : 63. Edebant quidem in exsilio fideles: et hoc
fuisset impiae desperationis signum, inedia se conficere.

[8] Serm. on 1 Cor. 10 : 31—11 : 1, C.O. 49 : 698. Cependant Dieu nous permet
de nous esiouir en ce monde: car il veut non seulement que nous ayons ce qui est de
necessité, mais que nous ayons de superabondant et en nostre boire, et en nostre
manger, et en tout le reste.

which God has put at our disposal we find that the earth is full of beautiful and delightful things with qualities which can bring a richness and exhilaration to our earthly life far beyond the dictates of pure necessity. It is obviously the natural order of things that we should indulge in taking pleasure from those things which God has given us liberally to enjoy.[1] Calvin (as is shown clearly elsewhere) is always calling for moderation and sobriety, in language which would satisfy those with the strictest standards of temperance, yet even while using such language he can insist that it is lawful to use wine "not only in cases of necessity, but also to make us merry."[2] "Have done, then, with that inhuman philosophy which, in allowing no use of the creatures but of necessity, not only maliciously deprives us of the lawful fruit of the divine beneficence, but cannot be realised without depriving man of all his senses, and reducing him to a block."[3]

God is therefore not angry when men enjoy themselves in a holy manner and without giving offence to others. Calvin points out that when the prophets condemned those who dwelt at their ease in great sumptuousness, and who brought in tambourines and instruments of music to their banquets, it was simply the excessive indulgence in such things that they condemned but not the practices in themselves.[4] It is a fallacy to imagine that intense spirituality must necessarily be accompanied by a narrow and impoverished cultural outlook. Calvin condemns the fanatics of a former generation and the Anabaptists of his own day, who despised all learning and liberal sciences and who had "no other pretext for boasting of their being spiritual persons but that they were grossly ignorant of all science."[5] When a Christian looks out on the world, even though he sees clearly its evanescent character and the corruption which marks all things, he must also acknowledge the steadfastness which in many respects marks the framework of the world since it has its foundation in the Word of God.[6]

---

[1] Inst. 3 : 10 : 2. Cf. comm. on 1 Tim. 6 : 17, C.O. 52 : 334.
[2] Comm. on Ps. 104 : 15, C.O. 32 : 91. *Colligimus ex eius verbis, vino licere uti, non modo ad necessitatem, sed ad laetitiam, sed haec laetita sobrie temperanda est.*
[3] Inst. 3 : 10 : 3.   [4] Serm. on 1 Cor. 10 : 31–11 : 1, C.O. 49 : 697–8.
[5] Comm. on Ps. 71 : 15, C.O. 31 : 659.
[6] Comm. on Ps. 119 : 90, C.O. 32 : 253–4. *Haec igitur duo inter se optime conveniunt, verbi Dei constantiam ex statu terreno minime aestimandam esse, quia subinde fluctuat, et instar umbrae effluit: rursum tamen ingratos esse homines, nisi hanc eandem sententiam ex parte agnoscant in mundi opificio: quia terra, quae alioqui momento uno non staret, firma tamen manet, quia fundata est verbo Dei.*

A Christian is also bound to appreciate and acknowledge the presence of human virtues and graces in others as gifts of God, even in men who otherwise are wicked and who are our enemies. Calvin is eloquent in commending for our example the generous appreciation of the greatness of Saul in David's glorious lament over his bitter enemy; for if God endows men with great qualities, even though they themselves try to bury such, we must admire and utter praise.[1] Therefore the Christian will render honour wherever honour is due and in whatever sphere of life true greatness shines. "God is despised in His gifts except we honour those on whom He has conferred any excellency."[2] We must recognise that God, in withdrawing the true knowledge of Himself from man since the Fall, has not, however, left him destitute of all praiseworthy gifts. Though in "heavenly things," such as the knowledge of the Kingdom of God and true spiritual discernment, we are "blinder than moles,"[3] yet in "earthly things" which "have some connexion with the present life," such as politics and economy and the mechanical and liberal arts, we are bound to acknowledge that men in general show an understanding of civil order and honesty,[4] and a degree of aptitude and acuteness in the manual and liberal arts which is a "special gift of God."[5] "Therefore in reading profane authors, the admirable light of truth displayed in them should remind us that the human mind, however much fallen and perverted from its original integrity, is still adorned and invested with admirable gifts from its creator. If we reflect that the Spirit of God is the only fountain of truth, we will be careful, as we would avoid offering insult to Him, not to reject or condemn truth whenever it appears. In despising the gifts, we insult the giver. . . . Shall we deem anything to be noble and praiseworthy without tracing it to the hand of God?"[6]

A Christian will therefore use and accept thankfully human help and assistance of every kind if such can apply to his need, recognising that such help can come to him as from the hand of God

---

[1] Serm. on 2 Sam. 1 : 17 ff., p. 15–16. *Car l'iniure ne se fait pas a vne creature mortelle, quand les graces de Dieu sont mises souz le pied, et qu'on n'en tient plus compte, ceste ingratitude la s'adresse a Dieu. Et au reste que nous sachions que ceux qui effacent ainsi la memoire des vertus qui sont en leurs ennemys se font grand tort. Et pourquoy? Dieu nous donne occasion de le louer et priser, quand il met ainsi ses graces aux hommes.*
[2] Comm. on 1 Pet. 3 : 7, C.O. 55 : 256.   [3] Inst. 2 : 2 : 18.
[4] Inst. 2 : 2 : 13.   [5] Inst. 2 : 2 : 14.   [6] Inst. 2 : 2 : 16.

and as the "lawful instrument of God's providence."[1] Though the
Holy Spirit does not dwell in the ungodly in the same way as in
believers, He nevertheless communicates even to ungodly men
many kinds of natural gifts for the common benefit of mankind.[2]
"If the Lord has been pleased to assist us by the work and ministry
of the ungodly in physics, dialectics, mathematics, and other
similar sciences, let us avail ourselves of it, lest by neglecting the
gifts of God spontaneously offered to us, we be justly punished for
our sloth."[3]

[1] Inst. 1 : 17 : 9.   [2] Inst. 2 : 2 : 16.   [3] Inst. 2 : 2 : 16.

Chapter IV

The order of nature and the Christian life

1. The correspondence between the second table of the Law and the order of nature

CALVIN teaches that in matters relating to the first table of the Law, fallen man by nature has no significant knowledge of what is true and right.[1] Nevertheless, in matters which come under the second table of the Law, i.e. "the method of properly regulating conduct," the knowledge which even the natural man can derive from his own conscience and tradition and environment is of real significance. Indeed "nothing is more common than for a man to be sufficiently instructed in a right course of conduct by natural law."[2] Between this "natural law" or "order of nature" and the law of God given through divine revelation there is a real correspondence. "There is a conformity

---

[1] Cf. Inst. 2 : 2 : 24 and 22. Certainly he knows that there is a God who is to be worshipped and prayed to (Comm. on Rom. 2 : 15, C.O. 49 : 38; cf. on Jonah 1 : 5 and 6, C.O. 43 : 213 and 6; serm. on Deut. 5 : 16, C.O. 26 : 3 : 2–3), but he has no idea of how such worship should be given (Inst. 2 : 2 : 24; 2 : 8 : 1). Moreover the perversity of his heart forces him to turn the truth he has into a lie by turning his conception of God into an idol. Cf., *Calvin's Doctrine of Word and Sacrament*, p. 69–70.

[2] Inst. 2 : 2 : 22. *Lex naturalis* is the phrase Calvin uses here. In his comm. on Rom. 2 : 14–15, a passage to which he gives great weight, he says that the Gentiles have *nonnullam iustitiae regulam*, and are illuminated by *naturalem iustitiae fulgorem* which takes the place of the Law of the Jews. He speaks also here of *naturalis quaedam legis intelligentia*. Cf. C.O. 49 : 37–8. He speaks in his sermons most frequently of this as the *ordre de nature*. Calvin finds the basis of all good lawmaking by the civil magistrates in what he calls "equity" as well as "justice." The judicial law of the Jews (the third branch of the Law after the moral and ceremonial) delivered to them "as a kind of polity certain forms of equity and justice," Inst. 4 : 20 : 15. (*Lex*) *iudicialis, politiae loco illis data, certas aequitatis et iustitiae formulas tradebat*). But this principle of equity which is expressed in the merciful provisions of the Jewish Law is "common to all nations and ages" (comm. on Ps. 15 : 5, C.O. 31 : 148), being a natural principle finding different legal expression under different circumstances (Inst. 4 : 20 : 16). Cf. serm. on Job 1 : 6–8, C.O. 33 : 66, where Calvin defines *equité* as doing to others as you would have them do to you (Matt. 7 : 12). These words of Christ seem for Calvin to sum up the common rule of equity (*communis aequitatis regula*) and at the same time to be the foundation of the Law and the Prophets (comm. on Exod. 22 : 25, C.O. 24 : 681).

(*conformité*) between the Law of God and the order of nature which is engraven in all men."[1] When we are faced, as Christians, with the commandments of the second table of the Law of God, we are faced with something which "adds the authority of God to what we ought already to have known beforehand."[2] Therefore the written Law can be said to "remove the obscurity of the law of nature,"[3] and to enforce with the authority of God what is already acknowledged by all nations.[4] Indeed Calvin can go the length of saying "The Law of God, which we call moral, is nothing else than the testimony of natural law, and of that conscience which God has engraven on the minds of men."[5] We must not exaggerate the extent or the importance of this natural law. Calvin's phrase "not absolutely blind" may be taken to describe the degree of moral light which it gives to the natural man.[6] Moreover, his knowledge implies neither the power nor even the will to observe that which he knows.[7] Yet it does mean, for example, the power to distinguish "between what is proper and what is unjust, between what is honest and what is base."[8] It means that the man has a "natural instinct to cherish and preserve society,"[9] and to give sympathy and care to the weak,[10] a natural abhorrence of cruelty and brutality and bloodshedding and a horror and trembling before death such as was manifested by the sailors who, against their natural instincts, threw Jonah overboard.[11] It means that heathen men of all nations understand many aspects of good behaviour which are reinforced by the precepts of Scripture such as the evil effects of bad company and evil communications,[12] the

[1] Serm. on 1 Tim. 5 : 4–5, C.O. 53 : 456–7.

[2] Serm. on Deut. 5 : 17, C.O. 26 : 324.

[3] Inst. 2 : 8 : 1. Cf. comm. on Exod. 22 : 25, C.O. 24 : 679, where Calvin points out that profane writers teach what the Law teaches but "not clearly enough."

[4] Comm. on Eph. 6 : 1, C.O. 51 : 228. *Praeter naturae legem, quae recepta est inter omnes gentes. Dei quoque auctoritate sancitam docet filiorum obedientiam.*

[5] Inst. 4 : 20 : 16. He continues: "the whole of that equity of which we now speak is prescribed in it." Cf. above, p. 141 n.

[6] Inst. 2 : 2 : 22.

[7] Comm. on Rom. 2 : 15, C.O. 49 : 38.

[8] Ibid. *Inter aequum et iniquum, honestum et turpe.*

[9] Inst. 2 : 2 : 13.

[10] Comm. on Ps. 15 : 5, C.O. 31 : 148.

[11] Comm. on Jonah 1 : 14, C.O. 43 : 227–8.

[12] Cf. serm. on Eph. 4 : 29–30, C.O. 51 : 643. *Comme aussi les Payens mesmes diront. Il fait bon à la compagnie d'un tel homme. Et pourquoy? On y oit tousiours quelque bon mot, et iamais on ne se depart d'avec luy qu'on n'en rapporte quelque bien.*

need for integrity of the heart as well as of behaviour,[1] and the duties of children towards parents.[2]

2. The order of nature as an element in the Gospel

Calvin appeals to the "order of nature" in many different ways. He, of course, admits that God never binds Himself or us to act entirely according to the law of nature.[3] But he frequently points out that God's dealings with men through the Gospel conforms to the natural order of things, and calls on men to respond to the grace of God with a like regard for the order of nature. Some examples of this may now be given. For instance, it belongs to the order of nature that the Church should have been separated and remain separate from the world. This separation is parallel to, and perhaps foreshadowed by, the separation of light from darkness in the creation.[4] It is, moreover, natural for us to separate what is clean from what is filthy. For God's people to refuse to maintain such separation is to "subvert, as it were, the whole order of nature."[5] It is like mixing up heaven and earth and introducing horrible confusion into the whole creation.[6] A further example of what is natural in the realm of faith is that the Christian should learn to trust in God alone, for to trust in two objects is to confound the order of nature and to mix up heaven and earth.[7] Calvin, indeed, sees in the prominent place given to the preaching and hearing of the Word of God within the Church a restoration of the true order of nature, for we were given the power to communicate one with another "not simply to buy boots and shoes and bonnets

---

[1] Cf. serm. on 2 Sam. 3 : 12 ff., p. 64. *Ainsi donc, puisque les payens ont bien eu cela imprimé de nature et que leur sens a la conduitz, par plus forte raison d'autant que l'Escriture nous exhorte tante de fois a simplicité et rondeur et nous declare qu'il nous faut cheminer comme devant Dieu. . . .*

[2] Comm. on Eph. 6 : 1, C.O. 51 : 228.

[3] Cf. eg. serm. on Matt. 3 : 9–10, C.O. 46 : 541. *Dieu en maintenant son Eglise, n'est pas suiet à aucun ordre naturel, mais . . . il y besongne d'une façon estrange.* Cf. also comm. on John 21 : 18, C.O. 47 : 454.

[4] Comm. on Gen. 17 : 7, C.O. 23 : 237.

[5] Comm. on Zech. 2 : 7, C.O. 44 : 157.

[6] Serm. on Deut. 7 : 5–8, C.O. 26 : 515. *Il y en a bien peu qui pensent à ceci. Car nous aurions autre horreur de nous polluer parmi les infections de la papauté, si ceste doctrine nous estoit bien imprimee, que Dieu nous ait separez, et que nous allions faire un meslinge nouveau: c'est autant comme si nous assemblions le ciel et la terre, voulans renverser tout ordre de nature, et que tout soit dissipé, qu'il y ait une confusion horrible: car il est certain qu'il y doit avoir plus de distance entre les enfans de Dieu, et les incredules, qu'entre le ciel et la terre.*

[7] Comm. on Jer. 17 : 5, C.O. 38 : 265.

and bread and wine," but to use our mouths and ears to lead each other to the faith which rises heavenward to the contemplation of God Himself.[1] Calvin can go the length of implying that the true service of God is what is natural, this being an argument against inventing quite unnatural ceremonies for men such as abstaining from meat on Friday.[2] Therefore the Christian must take with the utmost seriousness the duties which "natural sense dictates."[3] Frequently he will find that the law of God commands him simply to be human and natural.[4] Submission to the natural order of things is not for Calvin a secondary or alien aspect of our duty which must be performed merely as a supplement or addition to the truly Christian part of the life of the believer, but it is an essential part of Christian piety and an integral element in his new life in Christ. It is an expression of the restored *imago Dei* in man. There is, for Calvin, as we have already seen, the closest connexion between the order of nature, the order revealed in the law of God, and the true order of man's life which we see revealed and established in Jesus Christ, in which the Christian man already shares by faith. The Christian life is the expression of such order in the daily life of this world.

Therefore Calvin himself, as we shall see, does not hesitate to appeal to his hearers and readers to live according to the order of nature and the natural law, as well as according to the Gospel. In making such an appeal to the natural order he is not turning from Jesus Christ and the Scripture to some supposedly possible second and different source of guidance and inspiration. He is rather using

[1] Serm. on Job 33 : 29–33, C.O. 35 : 127. In serm. on 1 Tim. 2 : 12–14, C.O. 53 : 219, he ranks the preaching of the Word along with the institution of marriage and government as part of the natural order.

[2] Cf. serm. on 1 Tim. 4 : 1–3, C.O. 53 : 352. His phrase is *le vraye service de Dieu et naturel*. It is to be noted that in the next sentence he asserts that to deny ourselves (i.e. the *evil* nature within us) is a *service raisonnable*.

[3] Comm. on Exod. 20 : 12, C.O. 24 : 605. *Principibus esse obediendum sensus ipse naturae dictat.* It was the same *naturae sensus* which "impelled" the pagan sailors to cry to God in the storm (comm. on Jonah 1 : 6, C.O. 43 : 216). Such invocation came *non aliunde quam ab arcano quodam instinctu et quidem duce et magistra natura* (Ibid. 1 : 5, C.O. 43 : 213). Such natural impulse is clearly different from the "natural" impulse of the "flesh" which is always contrary to God. Cf. pp. 53–8.

[4] Cf. e.g. Serm. on Eph. 5 : 28–30, C.O. 51 : 759. *Quand l'Escriture saincte nous exhorte a estre humains, debonnaires et patiens les uns envers les autres, et qu'elle nous propose l'exemple de Dieu . . . il faut bien que nous ayons les coeurs plus durs qu'acier, s'ils ne sont amollis. Or tant y a encores que toutes ces exhortations ne nous peuvent suffire pour nostre malice et corruption. Pour ceste cause Dieu à fin de nous faire plus grand'honte, nous renvoye à l'ordre naturel.*

the natural realm to illustrate and to fill out the details of the meaning of the Law of God for the Christian man. In appealing, as he
does, to men to become truly natural and human, it can never be
far from his mind that only in Christ do we have it revealed what
is truly natural and human, and only since He has died and risen
again does nature and humanity have real significance. For the
Christian, then, the law of nature is not to be separated from the
Law of God, nor is the Law of God to be separated from the law of
nature. He should be inclined to follow both.[1]

3. Christian duty and the grace of God can be illustrated from the natural world

It will be noticed that the "order of nature" to which Calvin
appeals in illustrating our Christian duty is not only the natural
law engraven on the heart of man but includes the whole arrangement and ordering by which God governs the physical and natural
world. The realm of nature reflects an order given to it through its
response to the creative Word of God. "Experience clearly shows,
that the voice of God is heard even by dumb creatures, and that
the order of nature (*naturae ordo*) is nothing else than the obedience which is rendered to Him by every part of the world, so that
everywhere His supreme authority (*imperium*) shines forth. For
at His bidding the elements observe the law prescribed for them,
and heaven and earth discharge their office. The earth produces
her fruits, the sea does not flow beyond her settled bounds, the
sun, moon and stars go through their circuits; the heavens too
revolve at stated periods—all with wonderful accuracy, though
they are devoid of reason and intelligence."[2] Throughout the whole
natural creation, then, amongst "the oxen, asses, dogs, even the
stones and the trees," Calvin finds a "natural inclination to obey
God" which can be an example to us in living the Christian life.[3]

[1] Cf. serm. on 1 Tim. 5 : 4–5, C.O. 53 : 456. Comm. on Jonah 1 : 13–14,
C.O. 43 : 227.

[2] Comm. on Isa. 1 : 2, C.O. 36 : 29.

[3] Serm. on Deut. 10 : 12–14, C.O. 27 : 34. Cf. serm. on Job 27 : 5–8, C.O.
34 : 467. *Qui pis est, il faudra que les bestes brutes nous condamnent: car combien
qu'un boeuf ne sache pourquoi il est creé, si est-ce qu'encores il suit quelque ordre
naturel. Pourquoy est-ce qu'il baisse les cornes, et qu'il plie le col pour porter le
ioug, sinon d'autant que nostre Seigneur luy donne quelque instruction sans vouloir,
sans sentiment, tellement que les povres bestes ont une inclination à faire ce qui est
de leur office.*

It is especially in the animal kingdom that we find that the realm of
nature is to us a painting (*peinture*) or a mirror (*miroir*) "in which God
shows us our duty."[1] As we watch the care of the mother bird for its
young, God is saying to us, "Train yourselves in this way to be human
and to do no act of cruelty."[2] It is true that Calvin recognises the
distortion and chaos that has entered the natural world as a result
of the Fall.[3] But in spite of this, "the beasts frequently observe the
order of nature more correctly and display more humanity than
men themselves."[4] For example, they obey their masters, they are
not cruel to their own species, for they recognise their own likeness
(*similitudo*) in each other, in meat and drink they "do not gorge
themselves and utterly ruin their constitutions." In all this they
can be our examples.[5]

Besides finding in the order of nature a "mirror of duty" we
are also meant to see in it indications of "the spiritual grace of
God."[6] For instance, in the germination into new life of the seed
thrown into the ground as if to die Calvin sees not simply an
otherwise unrelated superficial illustration of the resurrection of
the body but a real analogy based on an exceedingly close similarity in God's purpose between the ordering of nature and His
new order in Jesus Christ.[7] The steadfastness of the order of
nature is, moreover, a sign to us of the steadfastness of the promises

[1] Serm. on Deut. 22 : 5–8, C.O. 28 : 24–5.

[2] Ibid. C.O. 28 : 22.

[3] Cf. p. 106. Calvin can liken the evil behaviour of man to that of cats and
dogs and wolves and foxes. Cf. serm. on Eph. 5 : 28–30, C.O. 51 : 760 and on
Eph. 6 : 5–9, C.O. 51 : 800.

[4] Comm. on Isa. 1 : 3, C.O. 36 : 30. *Saepe enim bestiae naturae ordinem melius
sequuntur, et plus humanitatis prae se ferunt quam homines ipsi.* Cf. serm. on Eph.
5 : 28–30, C.O. 51 : 760.

[5] Ibid. Calvin suggests that it is because of such examples in the animal world
that even the heathen know the ways of kindness. Cf. serm. on Eph. 5 : 28–30,
C.O. 51 : 759. *Comme les Payens ont bien sçeu remonstrer cela: n'ayant nulle foy
en Dieu, n'ayant nulle pieté, si est-ce qu'ils ont bien sçeu dire que les bestes sauvages
ne se font point la guerre. Car un loup ne mangera point les autres: les ours et les
lions qui sont parmi les forests, ont ie ne sçay quoy qui les tient en bride, en sorte
qu'ils ne se nuisent point les uns aux autres . . . il y a comme un mouvement naturel
qui les pousse à cela, qu'ils s'entr'aiment, en sorte que chacun se nourrit avecs son
compagnon.*

[6] Cf. comm. on Isa. 6 : 13, C.O. 36 : 142. *Nam quum cernimus gratiam Dei
spiritualem in ipso naturae ordine, non parum confirmamur.*

[7] Cf. comm. on 1 Cor. 15 : 36, C.O. 50 : 556. Serm. on Job 18 : 1–11, C.O.
34 : 68–9. *Toutes fois et quantes qu'on nous parlera de Dieu, que ses œuvres . . .
nous conduisent tousiours plus haut à lui. Exemple. . . . S'il fait que la semence qui
sera iettee en terre, germe apres qu'elle sera pourrie, et qu'elle apporte fruict de
nouveau: si nous allons en corruption, Dieu ne nous pourra-il pas restablir en une
meilleure vie, veu qu'il monstre une telle vertu en l'ordre de nature?*

which have to do with our salvation.[1] The sending of the rain and the sun to nourish the earth and make it fruitful is likewise a sign to us of God's fatherly care and of the fact that as God provides for our earthly life He will also provide for our spiritual life.[2]

[1] Serm. on Job 18 : 1–11, C.O. 34 : 68–9.
[2] Ibid and Serm. on Deut. 28 : 9–14, C.O. 28 : 375. Calvin's idea that bread and wine in themselves have no power of nourishing or refreshing men, but that by the order of nature God can use them, and normally does use them, to convey strength and nourishment to our bodies as we partake of them (cf. e.g. serm. on Deut. 8 : 1–2, C.O. 26 : 595–6), seems to suggest that the mystery of the Lord's Supper too has its parallel in the natural world, but Calvin can insist that the Sacrament has no such natural counterpart. Cf. serm. on Luke 1 : 36–8, C.O. 46 : 97–8, where Calvin scorns the suggestion that in the doctrine of the Supper *nous voulions nous gouverner selon l'ordre de nature.* Comparing the influence of the sun on the earth with that of the ascended Christ on His people, he says, *Le soleil fait son office selon l'ordre de nature: mais Iesus Christ fait miracle.*

Chapter V

Mutual communication and subjection within the order of nature

1. Mutual communication

(i) *Mutual communication in love as a natural duty based on the restored imago Dei in Christ*

It is when Calvin expounds the meaning of loving our neighbour that he, in his teaching and preaching, most frequently appeals to the order of nature as he sees it revealed and restored in Jesus Christ. For instance, in his comment on Matt. 5 : 43, Calvin asserts that there is a "sacred fellowship" (*societas sancta*) between all men, including the whole human race in a "common nature" in which every man is my neighbour. This is part of the order of nature which not even man's depravity has violated. This should express itself in a "mutual communication" (*mutua communicatio*) in brotherly love between man and man "which nature itself dictates." All this is based on the recognition that I share the same human nature as my brother. "Whenever I see a man I must of necessity behold myself as in a mirror."[1]

In all this Calvin seems to base the duty of loving our neighbour on an entirely natural foundation. But from other passages it is clear that our whole duty towards our neighbour is really based on one fact that we can know only in Christ—that all men are made in the image of God. The sailors, who, taught by nature, shrank with such humanity from killing Jonah did not know this

---

[1] Comm. on Matt. 5 : 43, C.O. 45 : 187. *Mirum est, eo absurditatis delapsos fuisse scribas, ut proximi nomen restringerent ad benevolos: quum nihil clarius sit nec certius quam Deum complecti totum humanum genus, quum de proximis nostris loquitur. Nam quia sibi quisque addictus est, quoties alios ab aliis separant privata sua commoda, deseritur mutua communicatio, quam natura ipsa dictat. Deus ergo ut nos in fraterno amoris complexu retineat, propinquos esse testatur quicunque sunt homines, quia eos nobis conciliat communis natura: quoties enim hominem adspicio, quia os meum et caro mea est, me ipsum quasi in speculo intuear necesse est. Quamvis autem maior pars ut plurimum a sancta societate dissiliat, non violatur tamen eorum pravitate naturae ordo, quia spectandus est Deus coniunctionis autor.*

truth, and therefore here we must "go far beyond them."[1] Even though, through the Fall, the image of God has become so horribly distorted as to be unrecognisable, nevertheless a Christian must regard all men as being created in and indeed as possessing the image of God. This consideration is basic in determining the attitude of the Christian to his fellow men in general. "We are not to look at what men deserve in themselves, but to attend to the image of God which exists in all, and to which we owe honour and love."[2] Since man is in the image of God, any sin against our fellow man is bound to be regarded as at the same time an act calculated to injure God.[3] The reason behind the commandments that forbid us injuring human life is that since man is in the image of God, God Himself, looking on men as formed in His own image, regards them with such love and honour that He Himself feels wounded and outraged in the persons of those who are the victims of human cruelty and wickedness.[4] In this way the Gospel gives us what seems to be a natural basis for the commandment that men should love one another, and it is from this start that Calvin works out further "natural" principles.

Seeing the image of God in all men carries along with it a realisation that we are all created with one common nature.[5] When God wants to incite us to love and help one another He reminds us that we are "of one flesh and one nature." Therefore we must not despise our own flesh. No matter what divides us from any other human being, we must remember that he is of the same origin and is made in the same likeness as ourselves.[6] In his teaching on the duty of man to man, Calvin gives full weight to his belief that

[1] Comm. on Jonah 1 : 13–14, C.O. 43 : 227.
[2] Inst. 3 : 7 : 6.
[3] Serm. on 2 Sam. 2 : 14–17, p. 42. *S'ils font ung jeu de tuer, que nous considérions tousiours que c'est vne chose detestable que de ruiner et effacer l'image de Dieu qui reluyt en ses creatures, d'autant que tous hommes sont creez a son image.* Cf. on 2 Sam. 2 : 27–31, p. 49. *Vn homme estant creé a l'image de Dieu, ne peut estre tué que l'offense ne s'adresse a Dieu mesme.*
[4] Serm. on Deut. 4 : 39 : 43, C.O. 26 : 227. *Voila donc Dieu qui nous porte une telle amour, qu'il se sent blessé et outragé en nos personnes, d'autant qu'il nous a creez à son image.*
[5] Serm. on 1 Tim. 2 : 1–2, C.O. 53 : 128. *Et pour ceste cause il nous a creez d'une nature. Quand ie regarde un homme il faut que ie contemple là mon image, et que ie me regarde en sa personne et que ie m'y cognoisse.*
[6] Serm. on Eph. 5 : 28–30, C.O. 51 : 760. Cf. serm. on Gal. 6 : 9–11, C.O. 51 : 105. *Et d'autant qu'il a imprimé son image en nous, et que nous avons une nature commune, que cela nous doit inciter à subvenir les uns les autres.* Cf. serm. on Deut. 5 : 19, C.O. 26 : 351.

all mankind issue from a common human parentage,[1] therefore all men form one body.[2] He frequently quotes the appeal of Isaiah to the people of his time not to hide themselves "from their own flesh."[3] Therefore the very fact that we are human creatures means that "we cannot but behold, as in a mirror, our own face in those who are poor and despised, who have come to an end of their own power to help themselves, and who groan under their burden, even though they are utter strangers to us. Even in dealing with a Moor or a Barbarian, from the very fact of his being a man, he carries about with him a looking-glass in which we can see that he is our brother and our neighbour."[4] This recognition that we possess a common humanity, which has its basis in our recognition of the image of God in all men, itself forms the basis of the command in the Law, and in the teaching of Jesus, to "love our neighbour as ourselves." In this world, all men, whoever they may be, are neighbours. Indeed, in the Parable of the Good Samaritan, Jesus' purpose was to teach "that the word 'neighbour' extends indiscriminately to every man, because the whole human race is united by a sacred bond of fellowship."[5]

These two basic facts—that all men are created in the image of God, and that all share in a common human nature—are the foundation of all Calvin's teaching about human relationships. They themselves define the "order of nature" according to which a Christian, as well as any other man, must live. Time and again Calvin refers to this order in defining what Christian love means. The order of nature is that God has united all men together and has set them in this world so that each can help the other;[6] unless we live in peace and concord one with another we pervert the order of nature.[7] But no matter how wicked other men are, and no matter how little they deserve to be reckoned as our brothers and neigh-

---

[1] Serm. on Job 31 : 9–15, C.O. 34 : 655.
[2] Serm. on Deut. 4 : 39–43, C.O. 26 : 229.
[3] Cf. e.g. serm. on Deut. 22 : 1–4, C.O. 28 : 16; on Gal. 6 : 9–11, C.O. 51 : 105; comm. on Gal. 5 : 14, C.O. 50 : 251; Inst. 3 : 7 : 6; serm. on Eph. 5 : 28–30, C.O. 51 : 760.
[4] Serm. on Gal. 6 : 9–11, C.O. 51 : 105.
[5] Comm. on Luke 10 : 30, C.O. 45 : 613. *Poterat simpliciter docere Christus, proximi nomen ad quemvis hominum promiscue extendi, quia totum humanum genus sancto quodam societatis vinculo coniunctum sit.* Cf. serm. on Deut. 22 : 1–4, C.O. 28 : 16.
[6] Serm. on Gal. 6 : 9–11, C.O. 51 : 100.
[7] Serm. on Deut. 2 : 1–7, C.O. 26 : 9.

bours, nevertheless nothing that they do can alter this order that
God has decreed and which we are bound to observe. The wicked
man, or the man who hates us and harms us, must still be regarded
by us as in the image of God.[1]

On this basis to act with love towards our fellow man simply
means to show ourselves as human towards him. To love another
is to act with humanity in recognition of our common humanity.[2]
All the cruelty and pride which spoil human life arise from the
fact that men forget or despise the common humanity which they
share with all men and the possession of which should "teach us
with what humility and justice we ought to conduct ourselves
towards each other."[3] This is what a master must remember in
dealing with the servants and maids in his house. Though he has
a certain superiority of rank over them, and should not defer to
them to the extent of letting them sit above him at table or giving
them his own bed to sleep in, nevertheless he must always remember that they are the children of Adam of his bone and of
his flesh made in the image of God and that therefore we owe it
to them to behave with humanity towards each other and not like
savage beasts.[4] Calvin insists that those who deny to their needy
fellow men the pity and charity which is their due from the fact
of their belonging to the human brotherhood dehumanise themselves. If we show no love towards them we break the bond that
binds us to humanity and automatically rank ourselves outside the
human race and place ourselves among the animals.[5] In this way
we disfigure ourselves by exempting ourselves from giving relief
to our neighbours.[6] We renounce the image of God and make
ourselves into an ox or a lion or a bear.[7]

The same order of nature must also decide our relationship with-

---

[1] Serm. on Gal. 5 : 14–18, C.O. 51 : 19. Cf. comm. on Gal. 5 : 14, C.O.
50 : 251. *Neque enim hominum improbitas ius naturae delere potest.*

[2] Cf. e.g. serm. on 1 Tim. 4 : 1–3, C.O. 53 : 346. *Brief, que nous soyons
humains et pitoyables, et qu'il y ait equité en nous et droiture.*

[3] Comm. on Ps. 10 : 2, C.O. 31 : 109. *Saevitiam vero non parum amplificat
haec circumstantia, quod humanitatis obliti, pauperibus et afflictis contumeliose
insultent. Superba quidem semper est crudelitas, imo superbia omnium iniuriarum
mater est.*

[4] Serm. on Deut. 5 : 13–15, C.O. 26 : 304.

[5] Serm. on Deut. 5 : 19, C.O. 26 : 351.

[6] Serm. on Gal. 6 : 9–11, C.O. 51 : 105. *Car il faut que celuy qui se voudra
exempter de subvenir à ses prochains se deffigure, et qu'il declare qu'il ne veut plus
estre homme.*

[7] Serm. on Job 31 : 9–15, C.O. 34 : 655. But cf. p. 146.

in the fellowship of the Church. Calvin, it is true, can remind us that even though we are bound so closely to our fellow man in general by the order of nature, there is nevertheless a closer bond between us and our fellow Christian in the Church however poor he may be.[1] The image of God "shines more brightly in those that have been regenerated" than in others around us, and therefore the bonds that bind the disciples of Christ one to another should be regarded as closer and more sacred within the Church than outside.[2] If to injure our fellow man is to pervert the order of nature, to injure our fellow Christian is to "tear Jesus Christ in pieces."[3]

(ii) *The law of mutual communication as the basis of earthly society*

In defining more closely what it means to fulfil the order of nature on the basis of our sharing with all men a common nature, Calvin speaks of our obligation to "mutual communication" with all who need what we can give so that the whole common life may be enriched.[4] Such mutual communication is the obvious outcome both of the fact that God in creation did not make an infinite number of private worlds, one for each individual, but gave us a common habitation in one world,[5] and also of the fact that we are all "bound and united in one body."[6] It was in order to assist such mutual communication in the order of nature that the ability to communicate by speech was given to men, and the tongue created, by which we can meet, through giving encouragement and teaching and consolation, each other's needs. Therefore all abuse of speech or language is a perversion of the order of nature.[7] It was

---

[1] Serm. on 2 Sam. 1 : 12, p. 6. *Et puis il y a vne conioinction plus prochaine de nous auec les poures fideles qui sont espars ca et la.*

[2] Comm. on John 13 : 34, C.O. 47 : 318. *In regeneratis clarius elucet Dei imago.*

[3] Serm. on Deut. 2 : 1–7, C.O. 26 : 9.

[4] Serm. on 1 Cor. 11 : 11–16, C.O. 49 : 739. *Il est impossible que nul se passe de l'aide et secours de ses prochains: mais il faut qu'il y ait communication mutuelle, et qu'un chacun serve de son costé et que le tout se rapporte aussi à la vie commune.*

[5] Serm. on 1 Tim. 2 : 1–2, C.O. 53 : 128. *Car nostre Seigneur n'a point creé de mondes infinis, afin qu'un chacun demeurast là à l'escart vivant à soy et à son profit privé: mais il nous a mis les uns avec les autres. Voulant donc que l'habitation fust commune, il nous a aussi obligez, afin qu'un chacun pense qu'il doit communiquer avec ses prochains. Et pour ceste cause il nous a creez d'une nature.*

[6] Serm. on Job 1 : 6–8, C.O. 33 : 66. *Et ceste droiture tend là, qu'un chacun ne se retire point à part, pour cercher son profit, mais que nous communiquions ensemble, comme Dieu nous a liez et unis en un corps, qu'un chacun regarde à servir à ses prochains, qu'il y ait ceste communauté fraternelle.*

[7] Serm. on Eph. 4 : 29–30, C.O. 51 : 644. *Nostre Seigneur nous a donné langue pour communiquer les uns avec les autres. . . . Nous ne pourrons point marcher un pas, que nous ne voyons que l'un a besoin d'estre picqué, l'autre reprins, l'autre*

also in order to enable us to communicate one with another that the use of money was instituted by God as part of the order of nature,[1] a wrong use of, or attitude towards, money being a corruption of the order of nature.[2] We must in our use of all the "commodities of the present life" not only magnify the goodness of God towards us but also have regard to our neighbours and to the "*communauté*" which our Lord commands.[3] "Since God has united men amongst themselves by a certain bond of fellowship, hence they must mutually communicate with each other by good offices. Here then it is required that the rich succour the poor and offer bread to the hungry."[4]

It is when he speaks about the duties of Christian love that Calvin refers frequently to this mutual communication to which we are each obliged in fulfilling our office within the order which God has established amongst us.[5] He refers to the bond which binds us one to another in this way as the "common bond of love."[6] Yet such "communication of offices" on the part of the rich towards the poor is merely a payment of what is "due by the law of nature." It is to be regarded as merely the expression of a natural feeling of humanity that all men should have towards each other. A Christian will take no special pride in discharging such a duty.[7] Even heathen writers teach that all are born for the sake of mankind and that the life of society can be properly cultivated only by the interchange of such good offices among men.[8] God has so

consolé, *l'autre enseigné. Quand nostre langue se tient quoye en tout cela, et que nous n'avons souci ni des corps ni des ames de ceux qui sont conioints avec nous, et ausquels nous devons estre unis comme deux doigts de la main: quand donc nous abastardissons ainsi l'usage naturel de nostre langue, n'est-ce point comme despiter Dieu manifestement? . . . quand donc nous profanons . . . nos langues, n'est ce point pervertir tout l'ordre de nature?*

[1] Serm. on 1 Tim. 6 : 9–11, C.O. 53 : 582. *Car voici Dieu qui a regardé aux necessitez des hommes, il ne leur a voulu defailler en rien: et comme il a creé le blé, le vin, et autres choses . . . il a adiousté l'argent, afin que les hommes peussent communiquer les uns avec les autres.*

[2] Ibid, p. 581 and 2. Cf. note on usury, p. 156 below.

[3] Serm. on Deut. 20 : 2–9, C.O. 27 : 609. *Communauté* here doubtless means common sharing of goods.

[4] Comm. on Ezek. 18 : 7, C.O. 40 : 429. *Sed quia Deus homines quodam societatis vinculo inter se coniunxit, ideo necesse est communicari inter ipsos officia. . . .*

[5] Cf. serm. on Eph. 2 : 22–6, C.O 51 : 735–6.

[6] Serm. on Eph. 5 : 18–21, C.O. 51 : 732. *Dieu . . . veut que nous soyons serviables les uns aux autres et que nous ne cerchions point tellement chacun son profit, que nous ne regardions que nous sommes conioints d'un lien mutuel de charité.*

[7] Inst. 3 : 7 : 7.

[8] Comm. on Exod. 22 : 25, C.O. 24 : 679.

ordered human life that no one can be self-sufficient. It is common
sense that no matter how clever or resourceful an individual may
be, each has need of his neighbours for the provision of even the
most mundane requirements of human life. The labourer in the
fields can, by his own hard work, produce food and drink for
himself, but he requires the skill and work of others to give him a
candle to see by at night, and decent shoes for his feet and clothes
for his back, if he wants to be better clad than in the skin of one
of his sheep or oxen. The law of nature is that each must give and
each must receive. Even the rich, who might be tempted to feel
self-sufficient, and who may be held in honour, must remember
that the important parts of the human body are the more delicate
parts like the eye, and being most delicate they have all the more
need of the help and protection of the rest of the body.[1]

(iii) *Each must share in the responsibilities of society according to
his calling*

Such mutual communication between those who fulfill different
functions in the body of human society means that each must
fulfil the occupation or calling to which he has been appointed in
an orderly manner so that thus the order of nature for society
might be fulfilled. Calvin does not go the length of teaching that if
a man is born in one station and calling in life he cannot possibly
seek to change it. "It would be a very hard thing if a tailor were
not at liberty to learn another trade, or if a merchant were not at
liberty to betake himself to farming."[2] Nevertheless each individual in society must realise that he is called by God to fulfil some
useful function in the life of the social body to which he belongs.[3]
It is therefore his duty to "keep within the limits" or "bounds"
of his lawful calling, the husbandman in the fields, each tradesman
at his special task. Only so can confusion and disorder be avoided.[4]
This ordinance that each must "mind his own business" does not,
however, mean that men must in any way live apart from each
other. There is a common life in society in which men must care

[1] Serm. on 1 Cor. 11 : 11–16, C.O. 49 : 739.
[2] Comm. on 1 Cor. 7 : 20, C.O. 49 : 415. [3] Ibid.
[4] Comm. on 1 Thess. 4 : 11, C.O. 52 : 163. *Haec igitur optima tranquillae
vitae ratio, dum unusquisque vocationis suae officiis intentus, exsequitur quae sibi a
Domino mandata sunt, et in iis se occupat: dum agricola se in operibus rusticis
exercet, opifex artem suam tractat: atque ita singuli intra proprios fines se continent.
Simulatque hinc deflectunt homines, omnia incomposita sunt ac turbulenta.*

for each other and share with each other, and isolated specialisation is not naturally a good thing.[1]

Participation in the social life of man involves taking a share in the burden of hard toil which was imposed upon mankind as a result of the fall of Adam. This burden of labour is not imposed equally on all. Some have to bear more of it, some less.[2] It must not be imagined that a life of labour is dishonourable. Those who teach the superiority of a "contemplative life" to a life of toil teach falsely.[3] Though, in the form in which we experience it, labour is often excessively hard and unrewarding,[4] nevertheless we must remember that we were created by God for the purpose of being strenuously employed in a form of labour while on this earth.[5] Therefore to labour is to fulfil the gracious order of nature, which is planned according to the image of God. Moreover, in our earthly toil not only does the call of God reach us so that toil becomes a divine vocation directed by Him, but also the hand of God is stretched out to us assuring us that our labour will bear fruit.[6] We must not believe the lie that the Devil tells us when he seeks to persuade that labouring and housework are secular affairs that do not concern God. We must not separate the present mundane life from the service of the Lord. God accepts honest upright work as a service agreeable to Himself.[7] If the chambermaid and the manservant go about their domestic tasks offering themselves in their work as a sacrifice to God, then what they do is accepted by God as a holy and pure sacrifice pleasing in His sight.[8] One of Calvin's objections against the practice of usury

[1] Ibid. [2] Comm. on Gen. 3 : 19, C.O. 23 : 75.
[3] Comm. on Luke 10 : 38, C.O. 45 : 381–2. [4] Cf. pp. 131n. and 132n.
[5] Comm. on Luke 17 : 7, C.O. 45 : 414. *Meminerit ergo unusquisque, se ideo creatum esse ut laboret, ac strenue se in ministerio suo exerceat.* Cf. comm. on Luke 10 : 38, C.O. 45 : 382. [6] Comm. on 1 Tim. 6 : 12, C.O. 52 : 329.
[7] Serm. on 1 Cor. 10 : 31–11 : 1, C.O. 49 : 695. *Le diable a tellement aveuglé les hommes qu'il leur a persuadé et fait à croire, qu'en choses petites il ne faloit point estimer que Dieu fust honoré ne servi: et ce sous ombre que cela estoit du monde. Comme quand un homme travaille en son labeur pour gaigner sa vie, qu'une femme fait son mesnage, qu'un serviteur aussi s'acquite de son devoir, on pense que Dieu n'a point esgard à tout cela, et dit on que ce sont affaires seculiers. Or il est vray que tout cela est propre pour ce qui concerne ceste vie presente et caduque: mais cependant ce n'est pas à dire qu'il nous fale separer cela du service de Dieu.*
[8] Ibid., p. 696. *Si une chambriere balie la maison, si un serviteur va à l'eau, et bien, cela ne sera rien prisé: Et toutesfois quand ils le font en s'offrant à Dieu, pour ce qu'il luy fait en s'offrant à Dieu, pour ce qu'il luy plaist les appliquer à cela, un tel labeur est accepté de luy comme une oblation saincte et pure.* Cf. comm. on Luke 10 : 38, C.O. 45 : 382. . . . . *nec ulla sacrificia magis placere Deo, quam dum in suam quisque vocationem intentus utiliter in commune bonum vivere studet.*

was that it created in society a class of people who drew to themselves the benefits of other people's labour in society without contributing by their own labour and skill to the benefit of society. Cato of old justly placed the practice of usury and the killing of men in the same rank of criminality, for the object of this class of people is to suck the blood of the other men. It is also a very strange and shameful thing that while other men obtain their means of subsistence with much toil—while husbandmen fatigue themselves by their daily occupation, artisans serve the community by the sweat of their brow, and merchants not only employ themselves in labours, but also expose themselves to many inconveniences and dangers—that moneymongers should sit at ease without doing anything and receive tribute from the labours of all other people.[1]

---

[1] Comm. on Ps. 15 : 5, C.O. 31 : 148. Calvin discusses usury at some length in his commentaries (on Ps. 15 : 5, C.O. 31 : 147–8; on Ezek 18 : 8, C.O. 40 : 430–2; on Exod. 22 : 25, C.O. 24 : 680–3), though he feels that there is much more that could be said (40 : 432). He does not agree with Aristotle that all usury is contrary to nature, since it is unnatural that money alone should beget money (24 : 682), but he does regard it as significant that even amongst the heathen usury is universally detested. He frequently quotes with approval Cato's judgment that usury was almost the same as murder (24 : 681; 31 : 147–8; 40 : 431). It is, however, the pursuit of usury as a trade or profession that is to be condemned thus outrightly, and not the occasional lending of money (24 : 683; 40 : 431). Calvin's personal view is that the professional usurer ought to be "expelled from intercourse with his fellow man," and certainly he ought not to be allowed in the Church (40 : 431). The very word usury in Hebrew means "to bite" (40 : 429–30). Professional usury invariably leads to extortion and oppression of the poor (31 : 147–8; 40 : 432). But God's law does not condemn all usury, e.g. it allowed Jews to lend money to Gentiles. We must not try to be more strict (40 : 430), lest if we condemn all usury without distinction men will plunge in despair into the worst type of usury without discrimination (31 : 147). We can lend money to the rich and take interest. Otherwise why should the rich borrower reap all the advantage (24 : 682)? We must remember that apart from usury men cannot transact their business (40 : 432). In many cases usury is no worse than purchase. "Usury is not now unlawful except in so far as it contravenes equity and brotherly union" (24 : 683). But we should not exact interest from the poor and we must always beware of practising this vice under specious names (31 : 147). "The common fellowship of the human race (*communis generis humani societas*) demands that we should not grow rich by the loss of others" (24 : 680). Cf. serm. on Deut. 23 : 18–20, C.O. 28 : 117 and 121.*La somme est telle que nous ne devons point grever nos prochains, prenant aucun profit d'eux: voire i'enten profit qui leur soit à dommage. . . . Ce n'est pas le tout aussi que la police nous excuse. Car voila la Loy qui sera de cinq pour cent . . . est-ce à dire pourtant qu'il soit tousiours licite de prendre cinq pour cent? Nenni.*

2. Mutual subjection

(i) *Our common humanity involves us in mutual subjection and servitude as part of the order of nature*

All communication one with another in love within society involves subjection one to another.[1] Indeed, Calvin can sum up the whole duty of one man towards another in the order of nature as the duty of "mutual subjection."[2] There is among men a "universal bond of subjection" (*universale subiectionis vinculum*), the yoke of which no man must try to avoid.[3] Calvin often goes farther and speaks of such subjection as involving also "servitude." "God has bound us so closely one to another that no one ought to exempt himself from subjection and wherever love reigns there is mutual servitude."[4]

Calvin recognises that within society there are certain bonds, binding individuals and groups one to another, that are closer and more exacting than the universal bond of humanity.[5] The "yoke" of marriage between husband and wife is the closest and most sacred of all human relationships.[6] Then there is the close bond between parents and children, and thirdly the "yoke which connects masters and servants."[7] Since these bonds are closer than the bond of common humanity they involve men in a particular or special form of subjection which must be submitted to in the

[1] Serm. on Eph. 5 : 22–26, C.O. 51 : 735. *Nous avons veu ci dessus, comme chacun de nous est subiet à ses prochains, et ne pouvons autrement converser les uns avec les autres qu'en rendant quelque devoir comme de subietion.*
[2] Cf. comm. on 1 Pet. 5 : 5, C.O. 55 : 287.
[3] Comm. on Eph. 5 : 22, C.O. 51 : 222.
[4] Comm. on Eph. 5 : 21, C.O. 51 : 221 . . . *Ac ubicunque regnat caritas, illic mutua est servitas.* Cf. serm. on Eph. 5 : 18–21, C.O. 51 : 733. . . . *que chacun support son prochain. Et n'est-ce pas subietion que cela? Nous ne pouvons pas vivre ensemble sans ce support. Or est-il ainsi que tout support emporte servitude.* Cf. also p. 734.
[5] Comm. on Ps. 55 : 13, C.O. 31 : 540. *Interea sciamus damnari a spiritu sancto eos omnes qui sacra naturae foedera violant quibus erant inter se devincti. Quaedam est totius humani generis societas: sed quo quisque propius ad nos accedit, eo sanctiore vinculo nobis est coniunctus. Nam principium, quod profanis hominibus incognitum fuit, nobis tenendum est, non fortuito, sed Dei providentia fieri, ut vicinitas, cognatio, vocatio communis, homines ipsos inter se consociet. Sacratissimum autem est pietatis foedus.* Cf. comm. on Eph. 5 : 22, C.O. 51 : 222.
[6] Serm. on Eph. 5 : 28–30, C.O. 51 : 761. *Or le lien le plus sacré que Dieu ait mis entre nous, est du mari avec la femme.* Cf. serm. on Deut. 5 : 18, C.O. 26 : 335.
[7] Comm. on Eph. 5 : 22, C.O. 51 : 222. *Porro oeconomia tribus quasi iugis constat, in quibus mutua est partium obligatio. Iugum primum est coniugii inter virum et uxorem. Secundem iugum conficiunt parentes et liberi. Tertium dominos et servos continet.* Cf. comm. on 1 Pet. 5 : 5, C.O. 55 : 287.

same spirit of love as inspires submission to the obligations to humanity in general.[1] If love dictates mutual subjection as our duty to men in general, it much more strongly dictates to us subjection to those with whom we hold one of these specially close relationships.[2]

The subjection of the inferior to the superior in the relationship of ruler to people, master to servant, husband to wife, child to parent is part of an inviolable order established by God the Father.[3] Unless such order is observed and those in authority maintain their proper position and those under authority submit to those over them, then human society cannot be maintained.[4] Such order in society has been established by God as the only possible way in which a full and healthy human life can be lived by all men.[5]

Calvin does not always simply accept such order as being in its entirety an order of nature or creation. He asserts that certain forms of the subjection of servants to master which have prevailed in the world are "contrary to the whole order of nature," it being due only to the fall of man that one on whom God has impressed His mark should be brought into such humiliation and servitude.[6]

[1] Serm. on Eph. 5 : 22–6, C.O. 51 : 735. *Combien qu'en general il y ait ceste reigle . . . neantmoins il y a aussi en particulier subietion plus grande du fils au pere et de la femme au mari, des subiets à leurs superieurs, qu'il n'y a pas indifferemment entre tous hommes . . . et puis il y a aussi subietion special.*

[2] Serm. on Eph. 5 : 28–30, C.O. 51 : 760. *Or si cest argument-là doit valoir en general, par plus forte raison quand les hommes sont conioints ensemble d'un lien plus estroit.*

[3] Serm. on Gal. 3 : 26–9, C.O. 50 : 567–8. *Or cependant sainct Paul n'a pas voulu dire, quant à la police de ce monde, qu'il y ait des degrés divers: car nous sçavons qu'il y a des serviteurs et maistres: il y a des magistrats, et peuples suiets: il y a au mesnage l'homme qui est le chef, et la femme qui luy doit estre suiete: nous sçavons donc que ceste ordre-là est inviolable et nostre Seigneur Iesus Christ n'est pas venu au monde pour faire une telle confusion, que ce qui est establi de Dieu son Pere soit aboli.* Calvin calls such subjection *subiectio politica.* Comm. on 1 Pet. 2 : 18, C.O. 55 : 247.

[4] Comm. on Exod. 20 : 12, C.O. 24 : 602–3. *Imo non aliter foveri et integra manere potest humana societas, quam si filii parentibus se modeste subiiciant, ac reverenter etiam colantur quicunque aliis divinitus sunt praefecti.*

[5] Serm. on Deut. 5 : 10, C.O. 26 : 310. *D'avantage puis qu'ainsi est que toute preeminence vient de Dieu, et que c'est un ordre establi par luy, sans lequel mesme le monde ne peut subsister: que seroit-ce, si Dieu n'avoit tenu conte de cela, quand il nous a donné une certaine forme de bien vivre et saincte?*

[6] Serm. on Eph. 6 : 5–9, C.O. 51 : 798. *Or si nous regardons quel estoit le droict des maistres, nous dirons tousiours que ç'a esté une chose contraire à tout ordre de nature. Car nous sommes tous formez à l'image de Dieu: et qu'une creature raisonnable en laquelle Dieu a imprimé sa marque, soit mise en telle contumelie, cela est par trop exorbitant. Mais ce sont les fruits de la desobeissance et du peché de nostre pere Adam.*

He can speak of the subjection of the woman to the man as having a severity that did not belong to the original order,[1] this being in part a punishment for the woman's part in the Fall.[2] He speaks at times as if the purpose of the establishment of such order was to subdue the pride and haughtiness of fallen man expressing itself in the insatiable desire of each individual to dominate and rule,[3] and to avoid the confusion in society that would result from such unchecked pride.[4] Since the command to submit to human authority is so "repugnant to perversity," God, in order to make it easier for us to "soften and bend our minds to habits of submission," starts training us in humiliation by giving us in childhood and youth the "amiable" yoke of obedience to father and mother. Even nature itself teaches clearly that it is abhorrent to refuse such a yoke and such a yoke is often pleasant to have to bear. "From that subjection" says Calvin, "the Lord gradually accustoms us to every kind of legitimate subjection, the same principle regulating all."[5]

Yet on the whole Calvin looks not to the fall of man[6] but to the order of nature for the origin and basis of all offices involving superiority and subordination.[7] Such order is necessary, not merely to avoid confusion, but to enable society and man to express that true integrity and humanity[8] which are part of the image of

---

[1] Comm. on 1 Tim. 2 : 14, C.O. 52 : 277. *Et deinde propter peccatum accidentalis serviendi esse coeperit, ut iam minus liberalis sit subiectio quam prius fuisset.*

[2] Ibid. and serm. on 1 Tim. 2 : 12–14, C.O. 53 : 209.

[3] "Everyone has within him the soul of a king" is a proverb in which Calvin finds perfectly expressed the attitude which can alone be curbed by such political subjection. Comm. on 1 Pet. 5 : 5, C.O. 55 : 287; and serm. on 1 Tim. 2 : 1–2, C.O. 53 : 133.

[4] Serm. on 1 Tim. 2 : 1–2, C.O. 53 : 131, on Eph. 6 : 5–9, C.O. 51 : 803.

[5] Inst. 2 : 8 : 35. Cf. comm. on Exod. 20 : 12, C.O. 24 : 606. *Si generaliter dixisset obediendum esse omnibus praefectis, ut omnibus ingenita est superbia, non facile fuisset maiorem hominum partem ad paucorum obsequium flectere. Imo ut naturaliter odiosa est subiectio, multi refragati essent. Speciem ergo subiectionis proponit Deus, quam recusare immanis esset barbaries; ita ut paulatim subacta ferocia, homines assuefaciat ad ferendum iugum.* Cf. serm. on Deut. 5 : 16, C.O. 26 : 310–11. *Nous savons qu'il y a un tel orgueil aux hommes, qu'ils ne plient pas volontiers le col pour estre sous les autres, chacun pense devoir estre maistre . . . Dieu donc voyant que c'est une chose si contraire à nostre nature, que subiection, afin de nous y attirer d'une façon plus aimable, nous a ici mis en avant le pere et la mere.*

[6] Cf. Inst. 4 : 20 : 22, where he denies that the magistrate is merely a "necessary evil."

[7] Cf. serm. on 1 Tim. 2 : 12–14, C.O. 53 : 218–20; comm. on 1 Pet. 5 : 5, C.O. 55 : 287. *Ubi eorum qui vel iure vel naturae ordine praesse debent, nulla est autoritas, statim proterve omnes lasciviunt.*

[8] Comm. on Exod. 20 : 12, C.O. 24 : 602–3; Inst. 4 : 20 : 3; serm. on 1 Tim. 2 : 1–2, C.O. 53 : 133.

God in which man was originally made.[1] It is especially, however, in the relation of woman to man that we have a subordination truly grounded on creation. Apart from the conditions brought about by man's sin, the true order of nature is that "man is created to be the head of the woman and the woman is a part of and, as it were, accessory to the man (*une partie, et comme un accessoire*).[2] Even in our fallen state, though the woman in marriage suffers much as a punishment for the Fall, and the original relation between man and woman is distorted, nevertheless "some remains of the divine blessing" are to be found in the ruins, and man has not been deprived of his original authority.[3] Just as, after the Fall, God gave a sign of the original subjection of the beasts to man in allowing Adam to clothe himself in their skins, so in the continued subjection of woman to man there is some residue of the natural order[4]. "Therefore amidst the many inconveniences of marriage, which are the fruits of a degenerate nature, some residue of the divine good remains; as in the fire apparently smothered some sparks still glitter."[5]

(ii) *Even in its vitiated form since the Fall, mutual subjection is an expression of the image of God and a means of divine blessing*

The establishment within human society of the relationships which involve superiority, on the one hand, and subjection on the other, is for Calvin much more than a mere means to maintain order among men. It is a means whereby the image of God can be reflected within human life. Calvin sees the glory of God reflected in all human pre-eminence.[6] He can quote with approval

---

[1] Cf. pp. 103–4.

[2] Serm. on 1 Tim. 2 : 13–15, C.O. 53 : 224; in serm. on 1 Tim. 2 : 12–14, C.O. 53 : 209 the woman is given to the man *pour aide inferieur*. Calvin will not admit equality of degree between man and woman even though he insists that she is his companion. Serm. on 1 Cor. 11 : 4–10, C.O. 49 : 723, and 724–5.

[3] Comm. on 1 Tim. 2 : 13, C.O. 52 : 276.

[4] Serm. on 1 Tim. 2 : 12–14, C.O. 53 : 209.

[5] Comm. on Gen. 2 : 18, C.O. 23 : 47. Calvin is emphatic that according to the order of nature women should neither rule nor teach and that by nature they are "born to obey" (Comm. on 1 Tim. 2 : 12, C.O. 52 : 276). "Wherever natural propriety has been maintained women have in all ages been excluded from the public management of affairs (Comm. on 1 Cor. 14 : 34, C.O. 49 : 533). But God Himself is not bound to observe this common order and is at liberty to work by miracle, making extraordinary exceptions, as in the case of Deborah, to despite and humiliate men (Serm. on 1 Tim. 2 : 13–15, C.O. 53 : 221–2; comm. on 1 Tim. 2 : 12, C.O. 52 : 276; on Micah 6 : 4, C.O. 43 : 388).

[6] Comm. on 1 Cor. 11 : 7, C.O. 49 : 476. *In hoc superiore dignitatis gradu conspicitur Dei gloria, sicuti relucet in omni principatu.*

poetical phrases exalting the earthly magistrate as "the father of his country, the pastor of the people, the guardian of peace, the president of justice, the vindicator of innocence,"[1] and he implies that the true function of the ruler is to reflect the appearance of the image of God.[2] God lends the reflexion of His own nature to the status of earthly parenthood, and to the dignity of earthly lordship. He lends the use of His own name and communicates His own authority. "The titles of Father, God and Lord all meet in Him alone, and hence whenever any one of them is mentioned our mind should be impressed with the same feeling of reverence. Those, therefore, to whom He imparts such titles He distinguishes by some small spark of His refulgence so as to entitle them to honour, each in his own place. In this way we must consider that our earthly father possesses something of a divine nature in him, because there is some reason for his bearing a divine title, and that he who is our prince and ruler is admitted to some communion of honour with God."[3] Calvin can indeed suggest that our experience, under subjection here and now, of the blessings of earthly rule is not only a sign of God's paternal care for us, but is a foretaste of the final glory of the Kingdom of God.[4]

But it is especially in the relationship of marriage and in "the distinction which God has conferred upon the man so as to have superiority over the woman" that the glory of God shines forth.[5] Marriage is "the bond which God has preferred to all others."[6] In the story of the creation of the woman from the side of the man there is an analogy to the atoning work of Christ, who became weak so that His Church, united to Him, might become strong

[1] Inst. 4 : 20 : 24.
[2] Ibid.
[3] Inst. 2 : 8 : 35. Cf. serm. on Deut. 5 : 16, C.O. 26 : 312. *Il est dit que nous n'avons qu'un pere au ciel, à parler proprement: et cela n'est pas seulement entendu quant aux ames, mais aussi quant aux corps. Cest honneur donc est propre à Dieu seul, d'estre nommé pere, et ne peut convenir aux hommes, sinon entant qu'il luy plaist de leur communiquer. Or maintenant puis que ce tiltre de Pere est comme une marque que Dieu a imprimee aux hommes: on voit que si les enfans ne tiennent conte de pere et de mere, qu'ils font inuire à Dieu.*
[4] Serm. on Gal. 3 : 26–9, C.O. 50 : 569–70. *Et que de nostre costé nous cheminions paisiblement en leur obeissance et suietion: que nous sentions là comme des premices de ce Royaume celeste: que nous cognoissions que nostre Seigneur par un tel signe monstre desia qu'il a le soin de nous, et qu'il preside ici, et qu'il veille sur nous, iusques à ce que nous sentions cela en perfection quand il nous aura recueillis à soy.*
[5] Comm. on 1 Cor. 11 : 4 and 7, C.O. 49 : 475 and 6.
[6] Comm. on Gen. 2 : 24, C.O. 23 : 50.

through His own life and strength.[1] It is God's purpose that in
the fulfilment of the true ideal of marriage there should be illus-
trated what it means to be truly human to one another and to love
one another with a reflection of His own love towards man. It is
true marriage that can teach us how much humanity was meant to
be one body with one common nature.[2]

In true marriage there is a similitude of the relationship and
union between Christ and His Church.[3] Christ's love for the Church
is the true example for human marriage.[4]

(iii) *Authority within mutual subjection involves humility, companionship, understanding and subjection*

Calvin frequently appeals for humility and recognition of a
common humanity in the exercise of all forms of earthly authority.
There must be nothing harsh or domineering. Rulers must remember that the reason why God instituted kingdoms and
principalities is not to elevate a handful of men above the rest of
society but to provide for the welfare of the weak.[5] They must look
on their revenues as "almost the blood of the people" which it
would be the harshest inhumanity not to spare.[6] Magistrates even
in inflicting punishment must not "burn with implacable severity"
but "even pity a common nature in him in whom they punish an
individual fault."[7] Speaking of the treatment of servants by masters,
he points out that it is often the sheer ingratitude of employers

---

[1] Inst. 4 : 19 : 35; Comm. on Gen. 2 : 21, C.O. 23 : 49.

[2] Serm. on 2 Sam. 1 : 21–7, p. 26. *Ce sera vne nation brutale et cruelle qui ne
scauront que c'est de l'amour des femmes, ou du debuoir du mariage. Car nostre
Seigneur a voulu que l'humanité se monstrast principalement en cest endroit, c'est
ascauoir en la beniuolance que se doiuent le mary et la femme. Car c'est aussi la
source du mariage qu'il nous faut aymer les vns les autres. Car comme Dieu a aymé
les siens depuis le plus grand jusques au plus petit, il veut que nous soyons membres
d'vng corps. Il y a vng priuilege que Dieu fait aux hommes en ce qu'il y a vne
nature commune, mais si nous regardons, comment la nature s'entretient, c'est par
le mariage.* The love which God has instilled between sexes is for Calvin closely
analogous to the love which men ought to bear generally in fulfilling the duties
of humanity. Calvin notes that the phrase "love of woman" is used in Scripture
as comprehending all human duty. Cf. comm. Dan. 11 : 38–9, C.O. 41 : 273 ;
and serm. on loc. C.O. 42 : 93. The love of husband for wife shows in the highest
degree what all love should be.

[3] Inst. 4 : 19 : 34.

[4] Inst. 4 : 19 : 35. Though marriage is not a sacrament, cf. Inst. 4 : 19 : 33,
"it is a good and holy ordinance of God. And agriculture, shoemaking and
sharing are lawful ordinances of God. But they are not sacraments."

[5] Serm. on 1 Tim. 2 : 12–14, C.O. 53 : 220.

[6] Inst. 4 : 20 : 13.

[7] Inst. 4 : 20 : 2, quoting Augustine.

that unsettles those under them and spoils all goodwill and possibility of mutual trust.[1] If even pagans, taught by their ideas of equity, have suggested that slaves should receive pay for their work, surely under Christianity, where there is brotherhood between great and small, masters ought to be the companions of their servants in so far as both have the same hope of eternal life.[2]

It is especially when he speaks about the relationship between husband and wife in marriage that Calvin stresses the fact that there must be companionship within mutual subjection. The woman was made to be the "companion and associate to the man to assist him to live well."[3] Therefore man must not tyrannise or domineer or trample underfoot one who was made to be his companion for this purpose.[4] In the woman he is meant to find his counterpart, one who responds to him[5] as nothing else in his environment can possibly do.[6] The image of God is printed alike in both man and woman.[7] As well as being his counterpart she is also part of him, as the story of her origin bears witness.[8] If the man is over the woman it is as the head over the body, and if these be separated both are like mutilated members of a mangled body.[9]

[1] Serm. on Eph. 5 : 5–9, C.O. 51 : 800. *Mais il y a une autre raison qui nous pourroit desbaucher ou bien refroidir à nous acquitter de nostre devoir envers les hommes, c'est l'ingratitude. Car ceux qui nous employent, le plus souvent ne nous en sçavent nul gré, mesmes il leur semble que nous soyons faits pour eux. Quand nous voyons qu'ils recognoissent si mal le service que nous leur faisons, cela nous despite, et ce seroit pour nous faire tout quitter.*

[2] Serm. on Eph. 6 : 5–9, C.O. 51 : 808.

[3] Comm. on Gen. 2 : 18, C.O. 23 : 47.

[4] Serm. on 1 Cor. 11 : 11–16, C.O. 49 : 737; on 1 Tim. 2 : 12–14, C.O. 53 : 217–18; on Job 3 : 1–10, C.O. 33 : 148.

[5] Comm. on Gen. 2 : 18, C.O. 23 : 47. *Dicitur enim mulier e regione viri esse, quia illi respondeat.*

[6] Comm. on Gen. 2 : 19, C.O. 23 : 48. Adam could not choose a companion out of any other species because there was no *aequabilis proportio* elsewhere.

[7] Serm. on Job 3 : 10, C.O. 33 : 146–7.

[8] Comm. on Gen. 2 : 21, C.O. 23 : 49; serm. on 1 Cor. 11 : 4–10, C.O. 49 : 729. *Il est vray que Dieu a fait cela, afin de nous recommander l'union que nous devons avoir ensemble: car il pouvoit bien creer Eve de la terre comme Adam: mais il a voulu prendre un coste de l'homme, afin que l'homme ne pensast point avoir rien separé d'avec la femme: mais qu'on cognust qu'il nous a unis comme en un corps.*

[9] Comm. on 1 Cor. 11 : 11, C.O. 49 : 477. In discussing divorce, it is this aspect of the indissoluble union grounded on creation that Calvin stresses. "Whoever divorces his wife tears himself in pieces because such is the force of holy marriage that the husband and wife become one man." (Comm. on Matt. 19 : 5, C.O. 45 : 529). Divorce is evil primarily because it is unnatural. "He tears from him, as it were, half of himself. But nature does not allow any man to tear in pieces his own body" (comm. on Matt. 19 : 4, C.O. 45 : 528; on Deut. 24 : 1, C.O. 24 : 658; cf. on Exod. 21 : 1, C.O. 24 : 701, where divorce is likened to the barbarity of a man disembowelling himself). Calvin's other main

Since all this is so, any authority on the part of the man must be exercised "with moderation and not insult" over the woman who has been given him as a partner.[1] Calvin tells the men of his time that they would find married life taking on a new meaning if, as well as toiling at their work for the family, they would support their wives at home and give them courage and as much help as possible in their burden of care for the infants, even when they are wakened up at nights, knowing that to bear all this is as acceptable a sacrifice to God as their daily task.[2] This relationship of "mutual benevolence" between the sexes ought to prevail not only between married partners but throughout social life.[3]

argument against divorce is that if it is unnatural for anything to break the link between parent and child, it is even much more contrary to nature and natural law to separate husband and wife, where the bond of union is even closer and more sacred (comm. on Deut. 24 : 1, C.O. 24 : 657; on 1 Cor 7 : 10, C.O. 49 : 410; on Gen. 2 : 24, C.O. 23 : 50; on Matt. 19 : 5, C.O. 45 : 528). Calvin notes, too, that in the making of the marriage contract God presides and therefore the bond created is a covenant, "superior to all human contracts," which no action from the human side alone can annul (comm. on Mal. 2 : 14, C.O. 44 : 452; on 1 Cor. 7 : 11, C.O. 49 : 410, and serm. on Deut. 5 : 18, C.O. 26 : 335). But though no amount of other human sin or hardship or infirmity can possibly justify divorce, marriage is nevertheless automatically dissolved by adultery, for the adulterous party becomes a rotten member which (naturally) would be cut off (comm. on Matt. 19 : 9, C.O. 45 : 530–2). Therefore the freed partner can remarry. The case in 1 Cor. 7 (of an unbelieving partner rejecting a Christian husband or wife) Calvin regards as exceptional. Here the divorce has been made between the unbelieving partner and God. The Christian is therefore free. Calvin doubts if this could be paralleled even in his day with those married to Papists, though he seems to have regarded Coracciolus as an exception. Comm. on 1 Cor. 7 : 11 and 15, C.O. 49 : 410 and 417.

[1] Comm. on 1 Cor. 11 : 12, C.O. 49 : 478.

[2] Serm. on 1 Tim. 2 : 13–15, C.O. 53 : 229. *Il faut aussi que les hommes de leur costé recueillent ici instruction. Car si les femmes sont sauvees quand elles allaitteront leurs enfans de leurs mammelles, quand elles les torcheront et nettoyeront, quand elles auront esté fachees à les porter: aussi les hommes quand ils prendront peine à nourrir leur mesnage. . . . et s'il y a des fascheries pour le mesnage, qu'ils supportent leurs femmes, et qu'ils leur donnent courage, qu'ils les aident tant qu'il leur sera possible, comme Dieu les a conioints d'un lien inseparable: quand ils seront resveillez pour leurs enfans, qu'ils en auront des soucis, moyennant qu'ils portent cela patiemment, qu'ils se resiouissent, voyans que Dieu les benit en leur labeur, ce luy cont autant de sacrifices. . . . Si ceci estoit bien imprimé au coeur, il est certain qu'on verroit reluire un autre ordre en mariage qu'on ne fait pas.*

[3] Comm. on 1 Cor. 11 : 11–12, C.O. 49 : 477–8. Calvin is continually warning men against despising woman in general. Man has no ground to boast on apart from woman for he cannot exist without her (serm. on Job 3 : 1–10, C.O. 33 : 148). He owes his life to his mother. In rejecting woman he therefore rejects himself. In the person of his mother he owes honour to all womanhood (serm. on 1 Tim. 2 : 12–14, C.O. 53 : 217). Though God is glorified more in the birth of a boy than of a girl we must not be too desirous of having male children and in no way reject girls. Boys can scratch our eyes out and like seagulls swallow up our living (serm. on Job 3 : 1–10, C.O. 33 : 147)! A man should not despise the whole sex by remaining unmarried even though he might find

Calvin sometimes sums up the duties of those who have superiority by referring to the law of mutual subjection, which demands that the superior must be subject to the inferior as well as *vice versa*.[1] It is true that it has to be a more *voluntary* subjection on the part of the superior member, but it *must* be a voluntary subjection if the law of love is to be fulfilled.[2] Calvin finds that Aristotle enunciated the truth on this matter in his law of analogical or distributive right, and he suggests that Paul, in his appeal to masters to render to their servants "that which is just and equal," employs the Greek word ἰσότητα in Col. 3 : 1 (and also in 2 Cor. 8 : 13) in order to refer to this law.[3] Therefore kings and governors and masters must never seek to avoid the subjection of love towards those under them.[4] If they are to govern their children in such a way as to deserve the high honour of the name of father, fathers must remember that in ruling the house they will be involved in subjection to their children.[5] And he reminds husbands that to support their wives in their very frailty involves subjection to her and a prudent use of any authority in order that she may be his companion in sickness and health and that he, too,

---

this convenient (comm. on 1 Cor. 11 : 11, C.O. 49 : 477). He must not despise the wonderful gift of marriage even though he dislikes being bound to another permanently. If, through the Fall, the sweetness of marriage has been mixed with bitterness, this is accidental, and it still can be regarded as a "heavenly calling" (comm. on Matt. 19 : 10 ff, C.O. 45 : 533–4. Cf. Inst. 2 : 8 : 43; serm. on 2 Sam. 3 : 2–5, p. 55). Only a few men have the calling and ability to remain single (Inst. 2 : 8 : 42).

[1] Comm. on 1 Pet. 5 : 5, C.O. 55 : 287. *Neque enim quum senibus defertur autoritas, ius vel licentia illis datur excutiendi fraeni; sed ipsi quoque in ordinem coguntur, ut mutua sit subiectio.*

[2] Serm. on Eph. 5 : 18–21, C.O. 51 : 733. *Que ceux qui sont eslevez en haut, regardent bien que si Dieu les a honorez ainsi, c'est à fin qu'ils se rendent plus volontairement subiets pour soustenir les peines et les charges qui sont de leur office.*

[3] Comm. on Col. 4 : 1, C.O. 52 : 127. *Non dubito quin Paulus ἰσότητα hic posuerit pro iure analogo aut distributivo: quemadmodum ad Ephesios τὰ αὐτά. Neque enim sic habent domini obnoxios sibi servos, quin vicissim aliquid ipsis debeant: quemadmodum ius analogum valere debet inter omnes ordines.* Cf. comm. on 2 Cor. 8 : 13, C.O. 50 : 101, and on Eph. 6 : 9, C.O. 51 : 231. *Eodem nunc τά αὐτά posuit. Quorsum autem illud, nisi ut servetur ius analogum quod vocant? Non est quidem aequalis domini et servi conditio: sed est tamen aliquod ius mutuum inter eos, quod sicuti servum domino obnoxium reddit, ita vicissim proportione habita dominum obstringit aliquatenus servo.* Calvin adds that this law of analogy will be misunderstood unless it is interpreted as part of the law of love which is the only true rule.

[4] Comm. on Eph. 5 : 21, C.O. 51 : 221; and serm. on Eph. 5 : 18–21, C.O. 51 : 732. Cf. Inst. 4 : 20 : 29.

[5] Serm. on Eph. 5 : 18–21, C.O. 51 : 732–3. In serm. on Eph. 6 : 5–9, C.O. 51 : 803, Calvin asserts that fathers will receive subjection from their children if they treat them gently.

may receive his share in the blessings of this mutual relationship.[1]

(iv) *The extent and limitations of our duty to submit*

The duty to render obedience to those who are over us cannot
be renounced even in extreme circumstances. We must give
honour and veneration to those who are over us, corresponding
to the dignity which ought to be reflected by their office.[2] We
must value the institution of government "so highly as to honour
even tyrants while they are in power,"[3] for if we weigh up the
alternatives, putting on one side of the balance the evils of having
a tyrant as ruler, and on the other the evils of having a people
without a ruling head, we will find the latter the greater evil.[4]
Rulers and parents and husbands should be obeyed and honoured
even though they themselves may be of bad character and may
abuse their authority, for their wickedness does not cancel their
divine status. We must learn not to consider the individuals
themselves, but hold it to be enough that by the will of God they
sustain a character on which He has impressed and engraven
inviolable majesty.[5] Just as it is the providence of God which binds
us up with our neighbour, whoever he may be, in mutual obligation, so it is the same providence which binds us in closer and
even more significant ties with father, mother, master, and those
in authority.[6] Therefore it is sacrilege for a child to despise his

---

[1] Ibid. *Autant en est-il du mari envers la femme. Car n'est ce pas subietion, que
le mari supporte la fragilité de la femme, qu'il ait ceste prudence de ne point user
de rigueur envers elle, mais qu'il la tienne comme sa compagne et qu'en santé et en
maladie il reçoive une partie des charges sur soy? Ne voilà point une subietion?*

[2] Inst. 4 : 20 : 22.

[3] Comm. on 1 Pet. 2 : 14, C.O. 55 : 245.

[4] Serm. on 1 Tim. 2 : 1–2, C.O. 53 : 131.

[5] Inst. 4 : 20 : 29, Cf. serm. on 1 Tim. 2 : 1–2, C.O. 53 : 130. *Il ne faut point
que nous regardions aux personnes si elles s'acquittent auiourd'huy de leur devoir
ou non: mais que plustost nous regardions à l'ordre que Dieu a establi, lequel ne peut
estre iamais violé par la malice des hommes, ou bien ne peut estre effacé du tout,
qu'il n'en demeure quelque residu.*

[6] Serm. on Deut. 22 : 1–4, C.O. 28 : 13. *Car quand il a institué proximité entre
nous, ça esté à ceste condition, qu'encores qu'un homme s'en rende indigne, nous ne
laissions pas de luy faire tout le bien qu'il sera possible. Et ainsi, le lien de parentage
qui a esté ainsi ordonné de Dieu, ne peut estre violé en façon que ce soit.* Serm. on
Deut. 5 : 16, C.O. 26 : 314. *Quand un enfant aura son pere et sa mere, il ne faut
point qu'il dise: O voila mon pere n'est pas tel du tout qu'il devroit, i'y trouve à
redire. Or si est-il ton pere. Il faut que ce mot-la te contente, voire si tu ne veux. . . .
abolir l'ordre de nature . . . Celuy qui t'a commandé d'honorer ton pere et ta mere,
il t'a donné un tel pere que tu l'as. Autant en est-il des maistres, des princes et
superieurs: car ils ne viennent point à l'aventure, c'est Dieu qui les envoye.*

father. Even if a father may, as an individual, be unworthy of the honour, nevertheless "the perpetual law of nature is not subverted by the sins of men; and therefore, however unworthy of honour a father may be . . . inasmuch as he is a father, he still retains a right over his children."[1] Nature itself can teach us to honour parents even when they treat us harshly.[2]

But Calvin does not fail to quote, "We ought to obey God rather than men." No matter how much honour we owe to the office of those who are over us in our temporal estate there is a limit beyond which they must not go in exacting obedience from us. We owe them not blind obedience but obedience in the Lord. Daniel is our example in his refusal to obey his King when the latter exceeded his limits (Dan. 6 : 22). The Israelites who blindly and uncritically submitted to Jeroboam when he commanded unfaithfulness to the Lord are condemned as examples to be shunned (1 Kings 12 : 28, Hosea 5 : 11): "We are redeemed by Christ at the great price which our redemption cost Him, in order that we might not yield a slavish obedience to the depraved wishes of men, far less do homage to their impiety."[3] Parents likewise govern their children only under the supreme authority of God. When Paul exhorts children to obey their parents "in the Lord" he "indicates that if a father enjoins anything unrighteous, obedience is freely to be denied him. Immoderate strictness, moroseness, and even cruelty must be borne, so long as mortal man, by wickedly demanding what is not lawful, does not rob God of His right."[4]

None of the distinctions between the superior and inferior which are so important for the maintenance of human society have any validity within the Kingdom of God. They are political and civil but not spiritual. "As regards spiritual connexion in the

---

[1] Comm. on Exod. 20 : 12, C.O. 24 : 603.
[2] Comm. on Heb. 12 : 9, C.O. 55 : 175.
[3] Inst. 4 : 20 : 32. This is the last sentence of the Institutes. Calvin does not say that it can become right to rebel actively against a wicked ruler. We have no command on this matter but to obey and suffer. He approves of the fact that at times in history popular and powerful magistrates have overthrown their rulers, and he would no doubt approve of a development in a state where powerful political parties were able to overthrow a tyrannical order. But we ourselves must not be too ready to imagine that the duty of overthrowing a tyrant has been laid on our shoulders. Inst. 4 : 20 : 31.
[4] Comm. on Exod. 20 : 12, C.O. 24 : 603–4.

sight of God and inwardly in the conscience, Christ is the head of the man and the woman without any distinction."[1] Even when he is under slavery a man's spiritual freedom remains untouched.[2] God is no respecter of persons.[3]

Moreover, all such civil distinctions are transitory and temporal. Calvin refers to this fact the promise that at the resurrection Christ is going to abolish all rule (1 Cor. 15 : 24). "Hence as the world will have an end, so also will government and magistracy and laws and distinctions of ranks, and different orders of dignities, and everything of that nature. There will be no more any distinction between servant and master, between king and peasant, between magistrate and private citizen. Nay more, there will then be an end put to angelic principalities in heaven, and to ministries and superiorities in the Church, that God may exercise His power and dominion by Himself alone, and not by the hands of men or angels."[4] This fact should prevent the exalted from giving way to pride or presumption,[5] and console all oppressed woman-hood,[6] and embolden those who are tempted to defer too much to the apparent power of those who are great in this world.[7]

Yet the fact that the Kingdom of God has already come in Jesus Christ does not mean that the present order of this world is overturned.[8] Calvin denounces, as a Satanic attempt to discredit the Gospel, the heresy of those who say that since we are spiritual we must no longer acknowledge any distinctions between superior and inferior within the order of society.[9] With this in mind he appeals "that we should show our humility towards God by bear-

---

[1] Comm. on 1 Cor. 11 : 3, C.O. 49 : 474.
[2] Comm. on Eph. 6 : 5, C.O. 51 : 230–1.
[3] Comm. on Eph. 6 : 9, C.O. 51 : 232.
[4] Comm. in loc. C.O. 49 : 547.
[5] Serm. on Eph. 6 : 5–9, C.O. 51 : 803.
[6] Serm. on 1 Cor. 11 : 4–10, C.O. 49 : 727–8.
[7] Serm. on Isa. 53 : 1–4, C.O. 35 : 615. *Il est vray que selon l'estat present, ils auront une telle maieste qu'il semblera que tout doyve trembler sous eux: mais si nous pouvons eslever nos sens à Dieu, et ietter là nostre veuë, il est certain que toutes ces fanfares du monde ne nous seront rien, non plus qu'un festu.*
[8] Serm. on Eph. 6 : 5–9, C.O. 51 : 798. *L'Evangile n'est pas pour changer les polices du monde, et pour faire des loix qui appartiennent à l'estat temporel.* Cf. serm. on Gal. 3 : 26–9, C.O. 50 : 568.
[9] Serm. on Eph. 6 : 5–9, C.O. 51 : 802–3. Calvin passes over almost in silence the phrase "There is neither male nor female" in Christ (Gal. 3 : 28); cf. comm. and serm. in loc C.O. 50 : 223 and 568. His stress is on the fact that woman must render obedience. Cf. comm. on 1 Cor 11 : 10–12, C.O. 49 : 476–8.

ing easily and with a ready will the yoke of men which He has imposed upon us with His own hands."[1]

[1] Serm. on Eph. 5 : 5–9, C.O. 51 : 800. A passage from the same sermon shows that the Genevan tradesmen were not so docile as we might imagine. *Et voilà pourquoy il met la simplicité. Car nous sommes par trop subtils à cercher nostre avantage: il n'y a celuy qui ne soit grand docteur quand il est question de son proufit.* . . . *Qu'on prenne les gens mechaniques, qui iamais n'ont veu un mot de lettres, s'il est question de les avoir à iournee et d'avoir affaire en chose que ce soit avec eux, ils sçauront si bien disputer leur cause qu'on diroit que tous sont advocats.* C.O. 51 : 799.

Chapter VI

Christian Moderation

1. Moderation and restraint an essential element in the ordered Christian life

AN essential element in the ordered Christian life is the moderation of all passion, appetite, and zeal, no matter how good and well-directed such zeal, and the passion which accompanies it, might be. Calvin finds in Holy Scripture a "rule of temperance,"[1] and he can state categorically that all intemperance of the flesh is evil.[2] In his view the Christian man is one who can so moderate all his passions and desires and ambitions that sobriety, meekness and prudence mark his behaviour. One of the main differences between the ungodly and the people of God is to be seen in the way in which the latter can restrain immoderate and irregular desires for worldly comforts and pleasures, whereas the former rush into excess in many varied ways.[3] The ideal which the Christian must seek to attain is seen in the perfect moderation in all things shown by Jesus Christ in his human nature.[4] Our Lord Himself is a "remarkable example of temperance."[5] It is true that at times Jesus allowed Himself to be lavishly entertained by the rich, but even on such occasions He would never have endured wasteful and extravagant luxuries and would no doubt exhort even his generous hosts to frugality and moderation.[6]

It is noticeable that Calvin frequently interprets the teaching of Jesus as calling for moderation of passion and avoidance of excess. For instance, the words "He who loves father or mother

---

[1] Cf. serm. on Luke 1 : 11–15, C.O. 46 : 36. *Or cependant quant à l'usage du boire et du manger, il nous faut tenir la regle qui nous est donnee en l'Escriture saincte, c'est à sçavoir d'attrempance.* Cf. comm. on Ps. 104 : 15, C.O. 32 : 90.
[2] Serm. on Deut. 5 : 18, C.O. 26 : 342. *Toute intemperance de la chair est vice.*
[3] Comm. on Ps. 36 : 5, C.O. 31 : 361; and on Ps. 4 : 7–8, C.O. 31 : 63–4.
[4] Cf. p. 109.
[5] Comm. on Luke 5 : 29, C.O. 45 : 249. *Ipse singulare erat temperantiae exemplum.*
[6] Ibid.

more than me is not worthy of me" are a call for moderation and order in all the mutual love that exists between men, for in the sphere of family affection "there is never rule or moderation such as is required."[1] In his discussion of the command in the Sermon on the Mount to "turn the other cheek," Calvin approves of Augustine's interpretation that Jesus is not here laying down a rule for outward action but is seeking "to train the minds of believers to moderation and justice, that they might not, after one or two injuries, fail or grow weary."[2] He reads the words "When they persecute you in one town, flee to the next" (again following Augustine) as teaching a lesson in moderation, that a man should be neither too cowardly in facing danger, nor yet overbold in exposing himself to it.[3]

It is obvious that in order to achieve such moderation, the Christian must seek in every way to check and restrain his desires and passions.[4] Since it is the constant tendency of the flesh to break through all bounds, the ordered Christian life cannot be lived unless the flesh is constantly mortified.[5]

2. Various forms of excess that mar human society and individual life

A tendency to excess marks the life of most of us, and tends to pollute even the good we seek to do. In all our human relationships and pleasures, no matter how innocent in themselves, there is always some disorder caused by a measure of immoderate excess. At banquets and social gatherings most people eat far more than is necessary and thus, even though they do not indulge in gluttony, they sin through this disorder.[6] Most men are hardly

---

[1] Comm. on Matt. 10 : 37, C.O. 45 : 294. *Non iubet quidem exuere humanos affectus, non vetat quin debitam quisque benevolentiam suis praestet, sed tantum in ordinem cogi vult quidquid est mutuae dilectionis inter homines, ut superemineat pietas.* Serm. on Matt. 26 : 36–9, C.O. 46 : 840. *Il n'y a iamais regle ni moderation telle qu'il seroit requis*; and serm. on Job 1 : 2–5, C.O. 33 : 39.
[2] Comm. on Matt. 5 : 39, C.O. 45 : 184.
[3] Comm. on Matt. 10 : 23, C.O. 45 : 285.
[4] Comm. on Ps. 78 : 18, C.O. 31 : 729.
[5] Inst. 3 : 10 : 3. *Sed non minus diligenter altera ex parte occurrendum est carnis libidini: quae nisi in ordinem cogitur, sine modo exundat.*
[6] Serm. on Job 1 : 2–5, C.O. 33 : 39–40. *Exemple, quand un mari aime sa femme, qu'un pere aime ses enfans, ce sont choses bonnes et sainctes et louables: et neantmoins on ne trouvera point un homme au monde qui aime sa femme en telle mesure, qu'il n'y ait que redire, qui aime ses enfans d'une amour pure et entiere. . . .*

conscious of such sin. Yet such disorder and excess contaminates our otherwise innocent pursuits as a mere grain of salt or a drop of vinegar can contaminate all the good wine.[1] Thus things that are in themselves good can be spoiled by immoderate passion.

A Christian, then, must order his life so as to seek to avoid excess. He must regard as especially dubious any undertaking or engagement which forces him or other men to violence of feeling or uncontrolled passion. It is for this reason, mainly, that Calvin expresses doubt whether it is possible for a Christian to engage either in a lawsuit or in war without becoming deeply involved in sin and guilt, for though going to law or to war may be justifiable on many grounds, and may be the lesser of two evils, nevertheless if such a course involves us in giving loose rein to tumultuous and unruly passions the grounds for its justification become less tenable.

In discussing whether it is justifiable for a Christian to engage in a lawsuit, for example, Calvin insists that it is right for a Christian to resort to the civil magistrate in order to have wrongs put right,[2] "as if a good man were not permitted to recover what is his own when a just way of doing so in divinely offered to him!"[3] Yet love must moderate his conduct in this matter,[4] as in all matters. This means that he must pursue his enemy at law with "entire friendship,"[5] without any desire for personal or private revenge whatsoever,[6] and "in a calm and sound mood."[7] We must

---

Ainsi est-il de ce que les hommes ne se peuvent tenir en mesure qu'ils n'auront point leurs affections si bien reglees, qu'il n'y ait à redire. . . . Si on s'assemble, il y aura de la superfluité quelques fois aux viandes, et ceux qui seront assemblez par compagnie mangeront et boiront outre leur portion ordinaire. . . . Vray est qu'ils ne seront point gourmans pour se farcir le ventre, et pour se saouler comme des pourceaux, tant moins encores seront-ils yvrongnes pour avoir leur esprit abruti: non mais tant y a qu'ils peuvent bien exceder mesure.

[1] Ibid, cf. comm. on Ps. 104 : 15, C.O. 32 : 90.
[2] Inst. 4 : 20 : 20.
[3] Comm. on Luke 6 : 30, C.O. 45 : 185.
[4] Comm. on 1 Cor. 6 : 7, C.O. 49 : 392. *Huius rei caritas optima erit moderatrix.*
[5] Inst. 4 : 20 : 20.
[6] Calvin is very emphatic that a Christian man is absolutely prohibited from indulging in revenge or in any desire for revenge. Inst. 4 : 20 : 19, Comm. on 1 Cor. 6 : 7, C.O. 49 : 391. *Fateor ergo, christiano homini prohibitam esse, omnem ultionem, ne vel per se, vel per magistratum eam exerceat, imo ne appetat quidem.* He utters very solemn warnings against prayers or appeals to God's justice which proceed from private desire for revenge rather than from the "pure zeal of the Spirit." To indulge in such is to "seek to make God execute the wishes of our depraved cupidity." Such conduct is inexcusable. Comm. on Rom. 12 : 19, C.O. 49 : 247; Inst. 4 : 20 : 19.
[7] Comm. on Matt. 5 : 40, C.O. 45 : 185.

always be patient and prepared to endure wrongs, waiting for and not seeking to anticipate the vengeance of the heavenly judge.[1] Such a perfect attitude is extremely rare and difficult to achieve, yet unless it is achieved and kept the whole proceedings can but be wrong. "When minds are filled with malevolence, corrupted by envy, burning with anger, or in fine so inflamed by the heat of the contest that they in some measure lay aside charity, the whole pleading even of the justest cause cannot but be impious."[2]

With regard to war, Calvin asserts that God constitutes kings and magistrates as the "instruments of His vengeance."[3] Their duty is to maintain law and order not only against the violence that can be inflicted by criminal elements within a population but against the devastation that can be wrought by those who seek to plunge a whole country into disorder. It is but "natural equity" that they should be armed to "defend the subjects committed to their guardianship."[4] But in this matter, as with all use of legal force, it is not enough merely to be sure of your cause and then to take ruthless action. Every war must be properly conducted.[5] By this, Calvin means that those engaged in war must neither give way to nor encourage anger, hatred, or passion.[6] Even the individual who kills another in self-defence may be justified in doing so according to law, but if in the course of such self-defence he loses control of himself in anger and excess of passion he is inexcusable before God.[7] God allows the use of force only with modest restraint, and all excessive cruelty must be avoided.[8] "Unless such moderation accompanies the performance of their duty, it is in vain for kings to boast that they are commissioned by God to execute vengeance."[9] No war can be justified that leads to widespread and extreme confusion.[10] Calvin laments that modern

---

[1] Comm. on 1 Cor. 6 : 7, C.O. 49 : 391–2; on Luke 6 : 30, C.O. 45 : 185–6.
[2] Inst. 4 : 20 : 18.
[3] Comm. on Ps. 18 : 48, C.O. 31 : 192. *Ultionum suarum ministros.* Cf. Inst. 4 : 20 : 11. In serm. on 2 Sam. 2 : 14 ff. p. 42. Calvin says we must avoid shedding blood *sinon pour maintenir la querelle de Dieu.*
[4] Inst. 4 : 20 : 11.
[5] Serm. on Deut. 20 : 10–18, C.O. 27 : 622. *Car ce n'est point assez que nostre cause soit bonne: mais il faut aussi qu'elle soit bien demenee.*
[6] Inst. 4 : 20 : 12.
[7] Cf. serm. on Deut. 20 : 10–18, C.O. 27 : 622.
[8] Serm. on 2 Sam. 2 : 17 ff., p. 44.
[9] Comm. on Ps. 18 : 48, C.O. 31 : 192.
[10] Serm. on Deut. 20 : 16–20, C.O. 27 : 636. *Notons donc que les guerres ne sont pas tellement licites, qu'on puise tout pervertir, et qu'il y ait une confusion extreme.*

war, as he knew it in his day, was little better than brigandage, marked by such inhumanity that all order was overthrown and men became no better than furious beasts.[1] Yet even if a war were properly conducted it would be marked by the tragedy that men made in the image of God are done to death![2] Judging by Calvin's language about war in his sermons it is possible that he might have been a pacifist in face of the possibility of modern nuclear war.

Vitiated sex-relationship is another important aspect of human life by which terrible disorder can enter the life of society, and the individual can lose control of himself in fearful excess.[3] It is in the face of this temptation that men need the fear of God which alone can hold them in check, and need to pray that God "will so control us that our evil affections may be subdued, and that this accursed lust may neither reign nor have any place nor access within us."[4] It was in order that men might be on guard against such temptations that Calvin expressed his strong disapproval both of the loose talk and songs of society in his day and of dancing.[5] A text he obviously has often in mind in this connexion is 1 Cor. 15 : 33, "Evil communications corrupt good manners." If we receive such dissolute communications they, unconsciously to ourselves, sink

---

[1] Serm. on Deut. 2 : 1–7, C.O. 26 : 14. *Ainsi voyons-nous, en somme, qu'aujourd'huy ce ne sont que brigandages de toutes les guerres qui se meinent: qu'il y a des cruautez et inhumanitez si exorbitantes, que c'est une confusion extreme, qu'il semble qu'on vueille oublier toute equité, et qu'une guerre ne se puisse faire qu'on n'oublie toute droiture: qu'il n'y ait plus de loy, que les hommes deviennent comme bestes furieuses.*

[2] Serm. on Deut. 20 : 16–20, C.O. 27 : 636.

[3] Cf. serm. on Job 31 : 9–15, C.O. 34 : 652–3. *Il n'est point dit seulement, C'est une lascheté . . . : mais c'est un feu qui consume tout, qui va iusques à la racine, c'est une perdition extreme il n'y demeurera nulle substance que tout ne soit raclé. . . . Il faudra que le feu s'allume par toute la ville et par tout le pays.*

[4] Ibid. C.O. 34 : 649. It is important to note, however, that for Calvin a sin such as fornication is of special gravity, according to the New Testament (especially 1 Cor. 6 : 18), not simply because of the disorder and excess it introduces into human life, but because it is committed on the body and it leaves a trace or mark impressed on the body as other sins do not (serm. on Deut. 5 : 18, C.O. 26 : 339. *Il y demeure quelque trace imprimee au corps*): "My hand it is true, is defiled by theft or murder, my tongue by evil speaking or perjury, and the whole body by drunkenness; but fornication leaves a stain impressed upon the body such as is not impressed upon it by other sins" (comm. on 1 Cor. 6 : 18, C.O. 49 : 18). Because of this Calvin appeals to his hearers never to imagine that such a sin can be treated lightly by God (cf. Eph. 5 : 6), especially since the body of a Christian is in a real sense a member of Christ and the temple of the Holy Ghost (serm. on Job 31 : 9–15 C.O. 34 : 651).

[5] Serm. on Deut. 22 : 5–8, C.O. 28 : 20. *Dieu non seulement veut nous tenir purs et nets de toute paillardise: mais il veut que nous prevenions les dangers.*

deep into our hearts and take control of us.[1] Moreover, when our own tongues are themselves infected by such talk that is also a sign of deep-rooted evil.[2] Calvin could go the length of warning his congregation that to teach a young girl to sing suggestive love songs was to make a wanton of her before she had any knowledge of sexual vice or choice in the matter of chastity.[3] But dancing was also for Calvin a method of "evil communication." Even though it was obviously argued against him that there was no harm at all in dancing as it was conducted in Geneva in his day, Calvin asserted that such dancing was a preamble to sexual vice, and opened the door for the entrance of Satan to create disorder in human life.[4]

Within the marriage bond itself there is need for the constant avoidance of excessive intemperance. Conjugal intercourse is a thing pure, honourable and holy because it is the pure institution of God.[5] A sense of shame is inseparable from such intercourse. This shame is due to the fact that everything which proceeds from man since the Fall is corrupted, and that intemperance and excess is bound to accompany such intercourse.[6] Marriage is, however, a veil by which the fault of such intemperance in marriage is covered over and what is shameful in it is cleansed so that neither before God nor the angels has it any

[1] Serm. on Eph. 4 : 29–30, C.O. 51 : 643.
[2] Serm. on Deut. 5 : 18, C.O. 26 : 341.
[3] Serm. on Eph. 4 : 29–30, C.O. 51 : 646.
[4] Serm. on Deut. 5 : 18, C.O. 26 : 340–1. *Et par cela voit-on combien les subterfuges sont frivoles et pueriles, quand on se veut excuser que ce n'est point malfait de ceci, ne de cela, moyennant que l'intention n'y soit point. Comme ceux qui voudroyent avoir et danses et dissolutions: O! moyennant qu'il n'y ait point de paillardise, cela est-il si mauvais? C'est comme s'ils se vouloyent mocquer pleinement de Dieu, et luy boucher les yeux pour le souffleter, et cependant qu'il devine s'il y a du mal. Or on sait bien que les danses ne peuvent estres sinon des preambules à paillardise, qu'elles sont pour ouvrir la porte notamment à Satan, et pour crier qu'il vienne, et qu'il entre hardiment. Voila qu'emporteront tousiours les danses.*
[5] Comm. on 1 Cor. 7 – 6, C.O. 49 : 406. Cf. on Gen. 2 : 22, C.O. 23 : 22.
[6] Serm. on Matt. 2 : 9–11, C.O. 46 : 357. *La generation de soy, d'autant qu'elle procede de Dieu, ne peut et ne doit estre reputee pour souilleure: mesmes quand les bestes procreent lignee, en cela il n'y a nulle pollution. Pourquoy? c'est l'ordre de Dieu. Or quand les hommes et les femmes engendrent et conçoyvent, c'est une chose detestable devant Dieu. Et dont procede ceste diversite . . . ? C'est bien pour nous monstrer que c'est des hommes et de toute la race d'Adam depuis le peche. D'autant donc qu'il ne peut rien proceder de l'homme, apres qu'il s'est corrompu par sa cheute, sinon toute malediction, voyla pourquoy il a falu que les femmes se purgeassent. Mesmes il nous faut aussi noter, que le mariage, encores qu'il y ait de l'intemperance et de l'exces aux hommes et aux femmes, neantmoins par son honnestete couvre tout cela. Voire, mais cependant si ne peut il effacer encores ceste malediction.*

unworthiness.[1] Yet marriage is such a remedy for incontinency only if it is used as such temperately.[2]

Sinful intemperance finds its expression in indulgence in luxury. One of Calvin's maxims is: "Nature is content with a little and all that goes beyond the natural use is superfluous."[3] Yet men are never content in this respect to be natural. The more bountiful God is the more men abuse his benefits by giving way to excess.[4] According to Calvin, a Christian, even though he has means to do otherwise, should live in a "sober and frugal manner."[5] Even though we have liberty to use this world freely our aim must be "to indulge as little as possible," curbing luxury and cutting out all show of superfluous abundance.[6] Yet, as it was right for David to live in his palace surrounded by delicacies, so it is right for a rich man to live on a higher standard than the poor and to enjoy something of the abundance which God has given him.[7] But the rich man may indulge in luxury only to a moderate extent. "If we do not wish to pollute God's blessings, we must use them frugally."[8]

It is thus a dangerous thing to be rich, for there is no end to our desires once we begin to indulge them.[9] The rich man is always being tested searchingly as to whether he can truly moderate his

[1] Serm. on Deut. 5 : 18, C.O. 26 : 342–3. *Ceste intemperance de la chair donc estant vicieuse en soy, estant damnable, ne nous sera point imputee devant Dieu, quand ceste couverture de Mariage y sera. . . . Mais quand un homme vivra honneste-ment avec sa femme, en la crainte de Dieu: combien que la compagnie du lict soit honteuse, si est-ce toutesfois que devant Dieu elle n'a point d'opprobre, ne devant ses Anges. Et pourquoy? La couverture du mariage est pour sanctifier ce qui est pollu et prophané.* Cf. comm. on 1 Cor. 7 : 6, C.O. 49 : 405–6.

[2] Comm. on 1 Cor. 7 : 29, C.O. 49 : 420. *Coniugium est remedium incontinen-tiae: verum est si quis temperanter utatur.* Cf. comm. on Gen. 2 : 22, C.O. 23 : 49. *Deinde obviam eundum est carnis lasciviae, ut pudice cum uxoribus habitent mariti.*

[3] Comm. on 1 Tim. 6 : 8, C.O. 52 : 326.

[4] Comm. on Ps. 104 : 15, C.O. 32 : 90. Cf. serm. on 1 Cor. 10 : 3–6, C.O. 49 : 604. *C'est à dire que nous ayons tousiours une telle attrempance en nous que si Dieu nous donne plus qu'il ne nous faut, nous ne facions des chevaux eschappez: comme on en verra à qui il semble que tout soit perdu, sinon qu'ils engouffrent tant qu'il leur sera possible, quand ils auront de quoy. Ils ne regarderont point, que me faut-il pour ma refection? mais ceci sera perdu pour moy, si ie ne boy encores ce verre, et un autre.*

[5] Comm. on Mark 10 : 21, C.O. 45 : 540. *Modo parce et frugaliter.*

[6] Inst. 3 : 10 : 4.

[7] Comm. on Ps. 23 : 5, C.O. 31 : 241; on 1 Tim. 6 : 8, C.O. 52 : 326.

[8] Comm. on Zech. 9 : 15, C.O. 44 : 280.

[9] Serm. on 1 Tim. 6 : 3–7, C.O. 53 : 575. *C'est qu'un chacun oublie ce qu'il luy faut, nous ne regardons point à nostre necessité, ni à l'usage legitime des biens de Dieu, mais nous voulons estre confits en toutes nos delices. . . . Mais cependant si nous laschons la bride à nos cupiditez, il n'y a nulle fin, nous sommes du tout perdus et abysmez.*

heart and life—and he should be conscious that he is being tested.[1] He has to learn to "use his abundance by preferring abstinence in the midst of plenty."[2] It is true that the poor man is also being tested as to whether he can be patient in the midst of his poverty. "We must learn to be no less placid and patient in enduring penury, than moderate in enjoying abundance."[3] Nevertheless, to make comparison, the poor man is as if navigating a tiny craft on a small river where there is certainly the danger of overturning or striking against some tree on the bank, but where such danger is nothing to that of navigating a small boat in the wide ocean where the waves and the winds are furious. So much more dangerous, then, it is to be rich than to be poor.[4]

Calvin can utter a special warning against intemperance in drinking wine, for this is the source of other forms of profligacy and the enemy of all moderation. "Where wine reigns, profligacy naturally follows, and consequently all who have any regard to moderation and decency ought to abhor and avoid drunkenness. The children of this world are accustomed to indulge in deep drinking as an excitement to mirth. Such carnal excitement is contrasted with that holy joy of which the spirit of God is the author."[5] In his sermons he can powerfully describe the effect of drunkenness as it turns man into an uncontrolled beast without feeling of shame, destroys the image of God, and perverts all order and decency.[6] Calvin appeals to the man whose head and brain is too weak to carry drink to admit his weakness frankly to himself and either to abstain or to be extremely moderate in his indulgence.[7]

---

[1] Serm. on 2 Sam. 1 : 21–7 (pp. 24–5). *Et apres quand vng homme est riche, qu'il aduise de se bien reigler et imposer loy. Car il est certain que Dieu nous esprouue, quand il nous donne ainsi les biens comme en superfluite, que c'est pour nous examiner, si nous serons sobres, et si nous aurons vne vraye modestie.* Cf. comm. on Zech. 9 : 15, C.O. 44 : 280. *Imo affluentia bonorum probatio est frugalitatis;* also comm. on Ps. 104 : 15, C.O. 32 : 90.

[2] Prayer to lecture on Dan. 1 : 8, Amst. Edn., Vol. 5, p. 7.

[3] Inst. 3 : 10 : 4. Cf. serm. on 1 Tim. 6 : 3–7, C.O. 53 : 576. *C'est donc une science grande et forte difficile à prattiquer, de sçavoir estre riche, c'est à dire d'user sobrement des richesses: mais il faut aussi que nous sçachions que c'est d'estre povres, et ceste science n'est pas moindre qu l'autre.*

[4] Serm. on Job 1 : 2–5, C.O. 33 : 35–6.

[5] Comm. on Eph. 5 : 18, C.O. 51 : 220.

[6] Serm. on Eph. 5 : 15–18, C.O. 51 : 718–19.

[7] Serm. on Luke 1 : 11–15, C.O. 46 : 36. *Et ceux qui ne peuvent soustenir le vin, seroyent bien sages, quand ils en prendroyent par mesure: ce leur seroit une belle vertu de cognoistre, I'ay ce vice en moy de me charger de vin: I'ay la teste et le cerveau trop debile pour le porter: ainsi il faut que ie m'en abstienne, ou que ie le modere tellement que cela ne me nuise point.*

Ambition is another aspect of man's life in which our tendency to sinful excess expresses itself. To have high rank, according to Calvin, involves us in as many and as fearful temptations as to have many possessions. The honour they receive and the rivalry of others makes it a most difficult task for those who rule to "contain themselves in modesty."[1] Rulers themselves are corrupted by envy. "Ambition almost always rules them, which is the most slavish of all dispositions."[2] Calvin indeed names ambition as the mother of all the evils that exist in society at large "and especially in the Church."[3] Therefore the man who holds high position "will look with suspicion on his rank"[4] and will pray for the gift of moderation and gentleness.[5] Calvin in this connexion quotes Augustine: "As a tree must strike deep roots downwards, that it may grow upwards, so everyone who has not his soul deep fixed in humility exalts himself to his own ruin."[6]

3. Moderation expresses itself in modesty, avoidance of display, and contentment with our lot

We have noted some of the ways in which men indulge in sinful excess. The practice of moderation in the Christian life will find expression not only in the deliberate avoidance of all such excess but in the more positive exercise, by such moderation, of what are sometimes called Christian "virtues." Though Calvin himself never attempted to classify "virtues"[7] or to set the cultivation of virtues as the aim of Christian living, it is obvious from his teaching that modesty, patience and prudence can all be discussed together as different aspects of Christian moderation.

When Calvin refers to the expression of our moderation in relation to our fellow men he speaks of it often as "modesty." It may be noted, however, that Calvin does not use the word

---

[1] Serm. on 2 Sam. 3 : 26–7 (p. 72).
[2] Comm. on John 12 : 42, C.O. 47 : 300.
[3] Comm. on Gal. 5 : 26, C.O. 50 : 256–7. *Multorum malorum quum in tota hominum societate, tum praesertim in ecclesia, mater est ambitio.*
[4] Comm. on John 12 : 42, C.O. 47 : 299.
[5] Serm. on 2 Sam. 3 : 26–7 (p. 72). *Ceux qui sont ainsi esleuez en honneur et dignite, ont occasion de prier Dieu qu'il leur face la grace de se moderer en telle sorte, que chacun cognoisse qu'ils ont vn esprit de mansuetude.*
[6] Comm. on James 4 : 10, C.O. 55 : 419.
[7] Though cf. note on p. 114.

"modesty" with the limited application which it has in modern English usage. Indeed he often uses it synonymously with the word "moderation" itself. Calvin sometimes speaks as if such modesty or moderation was the chief, and indeed the only, Christian virtue,[1] for it is the power to moderate all our antisocial passions and our proud self-will and to submit to others that is the basis of all the humility and love that make up true Christian conduct.[2] "Modesty by which each gives honour to the other is the best nurse of love," he says in one place,[3] while in another passage he can call humility the "mother of moderation, the effect of which is that yielding up our own right we give preference to others, and are not easily thrown into agitation."[4] In Calvin's thinking the basis of all love is the real inward annihilation of ourselves, the inward mortification of the heart through the grace of God. This produces an unfeigned humility in the inward heart[5] which is accompanied by an "outward and civil modesty in behaviour."[6] It is of significance to Calvin that in the Ten Commandments God teaches care and love for the neighbour through the negative commandment "Thou shalt not kill," for the basis of real love must be for each man to examine his heart and deal decisively with all the natural thoughts and tendencies that would move us to seek harm to our neighbour. If we would begin to love we must mortify and moderate the heart.[7]

Such modesty of heart will find its expression in a refusal to indulge in pomp and display before others.[8] This will become especially apparent in the manner in which a Christian dresses.

[1] Comm. on Rom. 12 : 16, C.O. 49 : 244. *Siquidem praecipua fidelium virtus moderatio est.*

[2] Comm. on Col. 3 : 13, C.O. 52 : 122. *Nemo comis erit ac tractabilis, nisi qui deposito fastu et altidudine animi, ad modestiam se submiserit, sibi nihil arrogans.*

[3] Comm. on Rom. 12 : 10, C.O. 49 : 241. *Optimum amoris fomentum est modestia.*

[4] Comm. on Phil. 2 : 3, C.O. 52 : 24.

[5] Comm. on Luke 14 : 7–11, C.O. 45 : 396. *Humilitas non fucata solum deiectio censeri debet, sed vera exinanitio, quum scilicet, infirmitatis nostrae probe nobis conscii, nihil sublime spiramus, scientes nos sola Dei gratia excellere.*

[6] Ibid, p. 397. *Externa et civili modestia.*

[7] Cf. serm. on Deut. 5 : 17, C.O. 26 : 329–30.

[8] Serm. on 1 Tim. 6 : 9–11, C.O. 53 : 583. *Et puis, cependant que Dieu leur fait la grace de iouir des richesses qu'ils possedent, qu'ils en sçachent bien user modereement, que ce ne soit pas pour gourmander à eux, et pour affamer leurs prochains, pour en faire leurs pompes, et leurs bravetez.* Cf. serm. on Deut. 8 : 14–20, C.O. 26 : 631–2. *Nous serons advertis . . . de ne point abuser de nostre largesse, comme font ceux . . . qui sont adonnez à pompes, et à vanitez pour se monstrer.*

In this matter Calvin is always very ready to underline the New Testament appeals, especially to women, for a practical application of the "rule of moderation,"[1] for an avoidance of the little frills and tresses that women are apt to like, and of the sumptuous use of gold and jewels,[2] "for excessive elegance and superfluous display, in short, all excesses, arise from a corrupted mind."[3] If he seems hard on women who overdress he is much more severe on men who do so. He laments that in his day, more than ever before, there was appearing this type of man who clothed himself like a doll or a Frenchman so sumptuously that it seemed as if he wanted to change himself into a woman, who was always looking for some new fashion in which to disguise himself and to draw attention to himself, who would starve himself of food in order to buy new clothes with which to feed his vanity.[4] Yet even in avoiding such extremes we must be careful to preserve moderation. "It would be immoderate strictness wholly to forbid neatness and elegance in clothing. If the material is said to be too sumptuous, the Lord has created it, and we know that skill in art has proceeded from Him. Then Peter did not intend to condemn every sort of ornament, but the evil of vanity to which women are subject."[5] In all this we must be careful to observe "order and proportion."[6]

An important aspect of Christian modesty is contentment with our lot. Humility and modesty will constrain us to confine our-

---

[1] Comm. on 1 Tim. 2 : 9, C.O. 52 : 275. *Regula mediocritatis.*

[2] Serm. on 1 Tim. 2 : 9–11, C.O. 53 : 197.

[3] Comm. on 1 Pet. 3 : 3, C.O. 55 : 254.

[4] Calvin suggests that the most suitable punishment for such *grans seigneurs* would be to make them serve as ladies' tailors. See vivid passage in serm. on Deut. 22 : 5–8, C.O. 28 : 20.

[5] Comm. on 1 Pet. 3 : 3, C.O. 55 : 254.

[6] Serm. on Deut. 22 : 5–8, C.O. 28 : 20, *à tenir ordre et mesure.* Calvin admits that dress is an "indifferent matter" (cf. p. 309) and that it is difficult to assign any definite limits, yet pride and love of display are not indifferent matters and too often find expression in clothing (cf. comm. on 1 Tim. 2 : 9, C.O. 52 : 275 and on 1 Pet. 3 : 3, 55 : 254). If we constantly remembered when we dressed ourselves that clothes are ordained simply in order that we may hide ourselves and our shame since the image of God in our bodies has become so disfigured, then we would not be given to superfluous pomp in clothing (serm. on Deut. 22 : 5–8, C.O. 28 : 20)! The manner of our dress should be determined by necessity (that we should be protected both from cold and heat) and decency (*honnesteté*). Moreover it is dishonest for anyone to "dress up" as if on a stage to play a part (serm. on 1 Tim. 2 : 9–11, C.O. 53 : 205; and on Deut 22 : 5–8, C.O. 28 : 19). The clothes of a Christian woman should also have *quelque marque de saincteté* (28 : 20) *qu'elles monstrent un accoustrement convenable à des femmes qui font profession de crainte de Dieu par bonnes œuvres* (53 : 197).

selves within the bounds of our own calling.[1] Calvin points out
that our Lord Himself "kept Himself, as His human nature
might have led us to expect, within the limits of that calling which
God had given Him.[2] To be contented with what God gives us is
a rule of life which can be rejected only by rejecting the order of
God Himself,[3] and apart from which man is bound to be driven
hopelessly here and there by his own covetous ambition.[4]

Contentment is however no easily-acquired virtue. For the
psalmist to hold to his own vocation in face of provocation by
tyrannous rule was a "sign of remarkable modesty."[5] Contentment
is indeed a virtue so contrary to our natural tendency to break
through the limits which God sets to us, that it can only be the fruit
of a real and complete surrender to the will of God, after which we
can accept even ill-heath, poverty, and dishonour peaceably.[6] It is
important that we should remember that in placing us where we
are in life God is testing our obedience[7] which can be proved in
reality only by such an attitude of submission and contentment.[8]
We must remember too that while we can never be sure of God's
help so long as we are pursuing any course that He has not
planned,[9] His help will, nevertheless, never fail those who confine
themselves contentedly within the bounds of God's calling.[10]

---

[1] Comm. on Ps. 91 : 11, C.O. 32 : 6. Cf. serm. on 1 Cor. 10 : 10–11, C.O. 49
: 635. *Dieu nous a advertis d'estre paisibles, et qu'un chacun se contente de sa condition . . . que nous ayons ceste mansuetude de cheminer en nostre degré.* Cf. p. 154.

[2] Comm. on Mark 7 : 24, C.O. 45 : 456.

[3] Serm. on 1 Tim. 6 : 9 11, C.O. 53 : 584.

[4] Serm. on Deut. 5 : 19, C.O. 26 : 351.

[5] Comm. on Ps. 119 : 161, C.O. 32 : 288.

[6] Serm. on Deut. 8 : 1–4, C.O. 26 : 590–1. *Quand donc nous venons là, si nous
pouvons nous retenir en la subiettion de Dieu, pour dire, Seigneur, il est vray que
ceci m'est dur à porter, il m'est contraire, ma nature tend tout à l'opposite: mais
quoy qu'il en soit ie renonce à ma volonté. Ie voudroye estre sain: mais puis qu'il te
plaist que ie soye malade, ton Nom soit benit. Ie voudroye estre riche, et avoir
toutes mes commoditez et delices, et tu veux que ie soye povre, et indigent: ie voudroye
estre en honneur et en credit, et tu veux que ie soye en opprobre, et en ignominie: et
bien, Seigneur, que nous ayons ceste humilité-la de nous assuiettir à ce qu'il te plaist
nous envoyer, et non point suyvre ce que bon nous semble.*

[7] Serm. on 1 Cor. 10 : 10–11, C.O. 49 : 637.

[8] Serm. on Deut. 8 : 1–4, C.O. 26 : 591.   [9] Comm. on Ps. 91 : 11, C.O. 32 : 6.

[10] Comm. on Ps. 18 : 21, C.O. 31 : 180. Calvin can express the certainty that
contentment will be given those who follow the Lord in the way He has appointed, and that He will always provide what is lacking. Indeed he says: *On
le voit aussi à l'oeil. Car ceux qui seront les mieux vestus, ne laissent point d'estre
morfondus: voire, et où il semble que les povres gens doyvent estre transis, et que la
glace les doit percer cent fois, Dieu les eschauffe, voire qu'ils sont restaurez comme
s'il les foumentoit, comme s'il y avoit un medecin aupres d'eux qui leur administrast
bons remedes pour subvenir à la froidure.* Serm. on Deut. 8 : 3–9, C.O. 26 : 604.

4. Moderation expresses itself in patience under affliction

Our moderation will express itself not only in contentment with our vocation in life but also in patience under affliction. If it is rebellion against God to "budge" from our place in life, without His call,[1] it is equally rebellion against Him, whether we stay or move, to allow our feelings and passions and desires under trial and affliction any loose scope or expression.[2] Calvin therefore calls for the moderation of passion and grief in the face of adversity, insult, injury and every kind of care and anxiety,[3] for it is fatally easy under such circumstances to indulge in our infirmity and allow ourselves to be carried away by our feelings and reactions beyond the bounds of all moderation.[4] Indeed, the sorrows of life can carry us away into excess even more easily than the joys of life.[5] We must "compose our mind to patience"[6] by moderating even our grief.

In speaking of patience Calvin obviously has frequently in mind the expression of the psalmist's about his "silence" before God. Since the tendency of our passion under affliction is to "raise an uproar against God," he can define patience as a "kind of silence by which the godly keep their minds in subjection to His authority."[7] He notes that David in his afflictions advanced more and more in the cultivation of "silence" and was able at times to "mortify every carnal inclination and thoroughly subject himself to the will of God."[8] In such an attitude we will let no ill feeling

---

[1] Serm. on 1 Cor. 10 : 10–11, C.O. 49 : 637.

[2] Serm. on 1 Cor. 10 : 8–9, C.O. 49 : 628. *Mais tant y a que toutesfois et quantes que nous ne pouvons souffrir que Dieu nous gouverne selon sa volonté, mais sommes bouillans en nos passions, que nous voulons prevenir, que nous voulons qu'il s'assubietisse à nos souhaits, nous le tentons, c'est à dire qu'avec une desfiance nous entrons contre luy comme luy voulans faire la guerre. Puis qu'ainsi est donc, apprenons de cheminer en plus grande humilité et modestie dores en avant, et que ce passage de nous serve de bride, toutesfois et quantes que nos appetis seront trop soudains, et que mesmes il y aura de l'impatience.*

[3] Comm. on 1 Thess. 5 : 16, C.O. 52 : 174. *Semper gaudete. Hoc ad moderationem animi refero, dum placide in rebus adversis se retinet, neque fraena dolori laxat.* Cf. comm. on Luke 12 : 29, C.O. 45 : 212.

[4] Comm. on Ps. 85 : 9, C.O. 31 : 788.

[5] Serm. on Job 1 : 20–2, C.O. 33 : 94.

[6] Comm. on Ps. 39 : 2, C.O. 31 : 396.

[7] Comm. on Ps. 85 : 9, C.O. 31 : 788. *Ita patientia species est silentii, quo se sub eius imperio continent piae mentes.* Cf. on Ps. 62 : 2, C.O. 31 : 585. *Statuit sibi tacendum esse: quo verbo intelligit patienter et sedato animo ferendam esse crucem.*

[8] Comm. on Ps. 62 : 6, C.O. 31 : 587.

against God slip from us.[1] We will refuse to pass judgment on His ways with us or others, remembering that we cannot in any way measure the depths of His judgments by the standards of our own fantasy, and that it is in vain to confess that God is just unless in practice we humiliate ourselves thus before Him.[2] We must, then, patiently await God's time, in faith that He will exercise true care over His Church and His children. If a man has this faith, he will "cherish his hope in silence and calling upon Him for help will lay a restraint upon his own passions.[3] Moreover, such faith in having been taken under God's guardianship will make us commit our cause to Him rather than give way to any impatience that would drive us to retaliate against others for the injuries they have done us.[4]

To be patient under affliction, however, means to moderate but not entirely to quench our feelings of grief or anxiety or anger. We are not meant to cultivate a completely stoical indifference to all feeling, nor to cast off our human nature and harden ourselves like stones.[5] "Patience is never free from being afflicted, and the children of God cannot help feeling their misfortunes and being sad."[6] They are bound to mourn when death comes to friends or dear ones.[7] They are bound to find their faith assailed by real fears.[8] They are bound to find themselves subject to worry—for though there is a wrong kind of worry that springs from distrust, nevertheless God does not mean men to become like wooden stumps

---

[1] Comm. on Ps. 39 : 2–3, C.O. 31 : 397.
[2] Serm. on Deut. 7 : 16–19, C.O. 26 : 545. *Ce n'est pas à nous de mesurer les iugemens de Dieu à nostre fantasie: car il nous faut confesser qu'ils sont quelques fois comme des abysmes: mais cependent ils ne laissent pas d'estre iustes. Nous ne verrons point donc tousiours la raison de ce que Dieu fait: mais si nous le faut-il approuver sans contredit. Car c'est bien raison que toutes creatures s'humilient sous luy, et qu'il ne soit point tenu à rendre conte. Et ainsi, quand il nous semblera que ce que Dieu aura commandé soit estrange: retenons nos esprits en bride, et en subiection, et faisons cest honneur à Dieu, de confesser qu'il est iuste et equitable, encores que nous n'y voyons goutte. . . . Et qui plus est, quand nous verrons qu'il desploye une rigueur qui nous semblera excessive, contre les autres, cognoissons en cela sa bonté et misericorde envers nous: car il nous pourroit faire le semblable.* Cf. serm. on Job 34 : 10–15, C.O. 35 : 143. *Ce n'est point donc assez, qu'en un mot nous protestions que Dieu est iuste: mais le principal est quand ce vient à la pratique, que nous trouvions bon tout ce qu'il fait.*
[3] Comm. on Ps. 38 : 14, C.O. 31 : 392.
[4] Comm. on Ps. 97 : 10, C.O. 32 : 46.
[5] Comm. on 1 Thess. 4 : 13, C.O. 52 : 165.
[6] Serm. on Job 1 : 20–2, C.O. 33 : 96.
[7] Comm. on 1 Thess. 4 : 13, C.O. 52 : 164.
[8] Comm. on Matt. 8 : 25, C.O. 45 : 265.

without concern for their own welfare, nor does He mean that a father should have no anxious concern for his family.[1] What matters is that we should moderate our mourning, keep our fear within proper bounds, and set a limit to our care,[2] for it is the mark of the unbeliever to give loose reins to grief in the face of death,[3] and though anxiety is not wrong in itself it becomes corrupted when it is allowed any undue excess.[4] Calvin, though so human at times, is almost stoically severe in his criticism of David's lament over Saul, in which, amidst much to admire, he nevertheless finds the expression of a grief disordered and without moderation.[5]

5. Moderation expresses itself in prudence—the Christian must avoid excessive zeal

In appealing for moderation in our behaviour Calvin often means no more than that we should be prudent in a truly Christian sense.[6] He found that the life and witness of many good men tended to be spoiled by indiscreet zeal as much as any other fault. He found frequent examples in Scripture of men moved by irreproachable motives and true zeal nevertheless allowing themselves to be carried into an excess of emotion or into some foolish course of action such as is bound to incur God's displeasure. As we have just seen, David's grief over the death of Saul had such a fault. Job's friends, when they fell weeping over him, were undoubtedly moved by genuine affection, but the very fervour of their sympathy and grief rendered them useless and unable to render true practical help to their friend.[7] Moses and Paul allowed their unbalanced zeal for the fulfilment of one aspect of God's purpose

[1] Comm. on 1 Cor. 7 : 33, C.O. 49 : 422.
[2] Comm. on Luke 12 : 29, C.O. 45 : 212.
[3] Comm. on 1 Thess. 4 : 13, C.O. 52 : 164.
[4] Comm. on 1 Cor. 7 : 33, C.O. 49 : 422.
[5] Serm. on 2 Sam. 1 : 17–20, p. 14. *Car nous voyons icy comme en vng miroir vng homme qui monstre vng dueil desordonne, et n'a point eu moderation en luy. Or par la nous sommes enseignez, encores que noz dueilz et pleurs tendent a vne bonne fin, et qu'ils procedent d'vne bonne source, neantmoins il y aura tousiours du meslinge au milieu de nostre vertu, il y aura de brouillars et vices, tellement que cela doit bien rabatre tout nostre orgueil, afin de ne nous point priser, mais que nous cognoissions que Dieu trouuera toussiours a redire en tout ce que nous ferons.*
[6] Cf. p. 188.
[7] Serm. on Job 2 : 11–13, C.O. 33 : 136. *Ce n'est pas donc le tout d'avoir quelque amour, et d'en monstrer les signes, mais il faut que ceste amour-la soit bien reglee, afin que nous puissions servir les uns aux autres, comme Dieu le commande.*

to push them so far as to utter wishes for their own personal damnation. This is a sign that if a man imprudently allows himself even for a moment to take a partial view of God's purpose, he can become foolish and blind in his prayers and desires.[1] Asahel when he killed Abner showed great boldness and the best of intention, but, comments Calvin, our boldness must be ruled by wisdom rather than inspired by rashness.[2]

All such conduct is seriously at fault, for our zeal and ardour in the service of God should be moderated and given wise direction by the gift of prudence. "Indiscreet ardour is no less an evil than inactivity and softness."[3] We must not allow the fervour of our zeal to "exceed the bounds of reason and moderation."[4] In many aspects of Christian behaviour and Church life Calvin pleads that zeal requires to be prudently moderated, from the use of elaborate ceremony, to which the mind of man is too prone,[5] to the reforming ardour of the zealot within the Church. For, "if we intend to reform affairs which are in a state of disorder, we must always exercise such prudence and moderation as will convince people that we are not opposing the eternal Word of God."[6] Moreover, we must remember that it is our Lord Himself who through His angels at the last day will "thoroughly" cleanse His thrashing-floor, and if we ourselves try to be too thorough in our cleansing of the Church we are depriving the angels of their office and usurping it ourselves.[7] Even David, in spite of the ardour of his hatred of the wickedness that prevailed in the Church of his day, "prudently moderates his zeal, and while separating himself from the ungodly, ceases not to frequent the Temple"![8]

It is noticeable, too, that Calvin appeals often for prudence even in Christian giving and in the exercise of charity towards the poor. He can appeal eloquently for people to be generous in their giving to others. One of the main reasons why we are given wealth is that we may employ ourselves in the service of God by helping

---

[1] Serm. on Job 3 : 11–19, C.O. 33 : 156–7.
[2] Serm. on 2 Sam. 2 : 22–3, p. 26. *Que nous apprenions d'estre hardiz par reigle, et non pas par temerité.*
[3] Comm. on Heb. 12 : 13, C.O. 55 : 177. *Nihilo enim minus vitiosus est inconsideratus fervor quam inertia et mollities.*
[4] Comm. on Matt. 26 : 51, C.O. 45 : 730.
[5] Comm. on John 12 : 7, C.O. 47 : 279.
[6] Comm. on Matt. 5 : 17, C.O. 45 : 171.
[7] Comm. on Matt. 13 : 40, C.O. 45 : 370.
[8] Comm. on Ps. 26 : 5, C.O. 31 : 266.

others.[1] Moreover, to give to others is the best way of checking our own tendency to use our wealth for ourselves intemperately.[2] But here there is a need for discrimination. It is the teaching of our Lord that His disciples should be "generous rather than prodigal" in their giving,[3] though they must be unwearied in their prudent generosity. It is folly rather than generosity to give money without careful regard for the worthiness and the need of those to whom it is given.[4] We must not be led astray by the fanatics "who think that you have done nothing unless you have stripped yourself of everything." Calvin approves of Paul's moderate language in his appeal to the Corinthians for Christian liberality (though he notes that most of us are in more danger of going to excess in niggardliness than in generosity). He seems to desire that even within the Church giving must be moderated according to a system of proportional right (derived evidently from Aristotle) balanced out according to the stations of individuals and other circumstances, and producing a "fitting symmetry" (*apta symmetria*).[5]

In view of Calvin's reputation for severity in the case of Servetus, it is of special interest to note his frequent appeals for prudence in moderating our zeal within the Church to correct the errors and wickedness we see in others. Calvin laments that sometimes "those who set themselves boldly for the vindication of the glory of God provoke and exasperate the wicked to a higher pitch by opposing them contemptuously and without moderation." "We must beware of pouring oil upon a fire that is already burning too fiercely." In dealing with wickedness we should remember how David and Lot expressed their zeal for God, in the midst of the

[1] Serm. on 2 Sam. 1 : 21–7, p. 24–5.

[2] Comm. on Ps. 104 : 15, C.O. 32 : 90. *Mutua etiam communicatio quam Deus praecipit, optimum est intemperantiae fraenum.*

[3] Comm. on Matt. 5 : 42, C.O. 45 : 186.

[4] Comm. on Ps. 112 : 9, C.O. 321 : 176.

[5] Cf. comm. on 2 Cor. 8 : 13, C.O. 50 : 100–1. As a result of his teaching on both spending and giving, it is obvious that Calvin has at times to recommend the saving of money. "To keep what God has put in our power, provided that, by maintaining ourselves and our family in a sober and frugal manner we bestow some portion on the poor, is a greater virtue than to squander all." Comm. on Mark 10 : 21, C.O. 45 : 450. Calvin does not tackle the problem of immoderation in the mere amassing of wealth—of how to get rid of immoderate savings under his system of restricted giving and spending. But undoubtedly under modern conditions he would have been forced by his own logic to call for moderation in bank accounts and in investments—and even perhaps in business enterprise.

wickedness they could not otherwise rebuke, by grieving and fasting. Such mildness and humility are effective ways of tempering
holy zeal.[1] Even in our prayers for vengeance upon the enemies of
God we must have the prudence to beware of the same intemperate
zeal which made the disciples sin by calling fire from heaven upon
the Samaritan village.[2] The same prudence must take control
within the Church when it comes to reproving or disciplining
an erring brother. We must remember that our aim in dealing
with those who have done wrong is to bring them back to God
and back into the fellowship as our brothers.[3] Therefore, though
there may be strictness, there must not be undue severity. Calvin
found that the old canons of the Church on this matter were so
strict that the restoration of the offender became too difficult. He
found a "lack of wisdom on the part of the ancient bishops." He
finds Paul much more ready than they were to allow the offender
to be restored to his place within the Church.[4] Moreover he urges
preachers to note Paul's mildness and paternal spirit and humility
under the Cross when he admonishes the Corinthians in his first
epistle to them. "Let teachers infer from this that in reproofs
they must always use such moderation as not to wound men's
minds with excessive severity, and that agreeably to the common
proverb they must mix honey or oil with vinegar—that they must
above all things take care not to appear to triumph over those
whom they reprove, or to take delight in their disgrace. . . . For
what good will the minister do by mere bawling if he does not
season the sharpness of his reproof with that moderation of which
I have spoken? Hence if we are desirous to do any good in correcting men's faults we must distinctly give them to know that our
reproofs proceed from a friendly disposition."[5]

Yet even in showing mildness and moderation towards the
wicked and fallen we must beware of going to such an extreme
that we ignore and nourish the vice in our fellow men instead of
correcting it. To bear the burdens of our fellow Christians does

[1] Comm. on Ps. 69 : 11, C.O. 31 : 642–3.
[2] Comm. on Ps. 28 : 4, C.O. 31 : 283.
[3] Serm. on Gal. 6 : 1–2, C.O. 51 : 63. Cf. serm. on Gal. 6 : 2–5, C.O. 51 : 71.
*Nous avons declaré quant et quant pour garder une bonne mesure a reprendre ceux
qui ont failli, qu'il est besoin qu'un chacun pense à soy.*
[4] Comm. on 2 Cor. 2 : 6, C.O. 50 : 29.
[5] Comm. on 1 Cor. 4 : 14, C.O. 49 : 371–2. Cf. comm. on Gal. 6 : 1, C.O.
50 : 257.

not mean to look with a blind eye on their faults and thus deceive them and confirm them in evil. Such an attitude will indeed send them to perdition.[1] We must beware of moral confusion or of pretending that a man who remains in his sin is justified and absolved.[2] While we ourselves might forgive and overlook a fault in another in some personal injury, nevertheless God might be much more strict and demanding in calling for true repentance and reformation if there is to be real forgiveness.[3] Calvin notes that Christ in his teaching "prescribes a middle course which does not give too great offence to the weak and yet is adapted to cure their diseases. . . . Christ enjoins his disciples to forgive one another, but to do so in such a manner as to correct their faults."[4]

Calvin recognises that there is, of course, a kind of prudence which is a natural gift bestowed on men in general.[5] This amounts simply to practical common sense. A Christian must use the helps to his well-being, the safeguards against danger, and the remedies for evils which God in His providence has provided for all men— and of which all sane men will avail themselves.[6] Calvin has little patience with those who either by sloth or folly or fatalistic conviction neglect to use prudence in the management of their affairs. "The righteous will carry out their business with care and discernment so that in their domestic affairs they will neither be too lavish nor mean. They must not be too niggardly, but they will keep everything within bounds without giving way to luxury. And in all their transactions they will be guided always by the law of equity."[7] But all this is the prudence "of the flesh," and, used from selfish motives, it can amount to nothing more than mere

---

[1] Serm. on Deut. 22 : 1–4, C.O. 28 : 12.

[2] Serm. on Deut. 7 : 1–4, C.O. 26 : 500. *Et pourtant prattiquons ceste doctrine en telle sorte que nous ne soyons point misericordieux outre ce que Dieu a voulu, et que la reigle qu'il nous donne le porte. Car il y en a qui voudroyent qu'on usast de misericorde en meslant le blanc parmi le noir, en mettant toute confusion, en pretendant que le meschant fust iustifié et absout.*

[3] Serm. on Gal. 5 : 11–14, C.O. 51 : 14. *La charité donc sera d'homme à homme: quand quelqu'un m'aura fait iniure, il faut que ie l'oublie. . . . mais quand il est question de maintenir la querelle de Dieu, là il faut que les hommes soyent estimez moins que rien.*

[4] Comm. on Matt. 18 : 5, C.O. 45 : 511–12.

[5] Comm. on Matt. 11 : 25, C.O. 45 : 318.

[6] Cf. Inst. 1 : 17 : 4.

[7] Comm. on Ps. 112 : 5, C.O. 32 : 174. *Hoc autem optime convenit, iustos sua negotia ratione et iudicio metiri, ut in re domestica neque prodigi sint, neque sordidi, vel nimium tenaces, sed sine luxuria modum teneant. Deinde ut contrahendo aequitatis regulam semper observent.*

craftiness.[1] There is another "true prudence" which "can grow out of no human brain" and which is the gift of the Holy Spirit to those who are the children of God.[2]

6. Christian moderation as a gift of the Spirit

To attain such true wisdom and prudence as we have been discussing, is beyond all human capability. There is "nothing more difficult" than to know when the limits of forbearance towards other men have been reached.[3] In the practical issues of life requiring such prudence and discretion our own affections are not sufficient to guide us. Nor is it enough to have a general knowledge of what is good when we are faced with making a decision of how to act in a particular case. It is all beyond us. Nevertheless God Himself has the Spirit of prudence and discretion and by sharing in the Spirit we are given the wisdom to discern between good and evil, to know when to act and when to refrain, and when to speak and when to be silent.[4] Calvin frequently emphasises this aspect of the Spirit's work, and refers to the Spirit as the Spirit of wisdom and prudence.[5] He insists that the Spirit is not only the Spirit of power but also of "love and soberness" by which the same powerful energy is moderated.[6] "And therefore unless our zeal be directed by the Spirit of God it will be of no avail to plead on our behalf that we undertook nothing but from proper zeal. But the Spirit Himself will guide us by wisdom and prudence that we may do nothing contrary to our duty or beyond our calling—

[1] Comm. on Ps. 26 : 4, C.O. 31 : 266. *Sua quidem etiam filiis Dei prudentia est, sed quae longe a carnis astutia differt.*

[2] Serm. on 2 Sam. 2 : 1, p. 28–9. *Car d'ou vient la prudence, sinon que Dieu la donne par son Esprit? . . . Or cela ne croist point au cerueau des hommes.*

[3] Comm. on Matt. 18 : 15, C.O. 45 : 512.

[4] Serm. on Gal. 5 : 11–14, C.O. 51 : 15. *Voilà donc nous ne nous esgarions point, voire si nous regardons simplement à Dieu, et que nous ne lascherons point la bride à nos passions: mais que nous soyons gouvernez par cest esprit de droicture et de prudence, et que Dieu nous fera discerner où il nous faut batailler, et là où il nous faut resister.* Serm. on 2 Sam. 2 : 1 f., p. 29. *D'auantage nous tomberions tous les jours en plus grand perplexité, et encores qu'en general nous sceussions ce qui est bon, tant y a que nous ne pourrions encores prendre resolution en quelque acte particulier. Il faut donc suyure ce qui nous est dit: que, Dieu ayant l'Esprit de prudence et de discretion, il nous faut venir a luy et le prier qu'il nous tende la main, et qu'il nous conduise.* Comm. on 1 Pet. 3 : 15, C.O. 55 : 262.

[5] Serm. on 1 Cor. 10 : 15–18, C.O. 49 : 662. *Ce n'est point sans cause que le sainct Esprit ha ce titre de prudence et discretion, mais c'est pour nous monstrer que nous avons besoin d'estre aidez et secourus, à cause du defaut qui est en nous.*

[6] Comm. on 2 Tim. 1 : 7, C.O. 52 : 350–1.

nothing in short but what is prudent and opportune, and by removing all the filth of the flesh He may impart to our minds proper feelings that we may desire nothing but what God shall suggest (*dictaverit*)."[1]

Not only prudence but all such moderation as has been described—modesty, contentment, patience—is the gift of the Spirit of God. Moderation comes not simply through our own attempts to discipline our outward behaviour but from the rule of God in the heart.[2] But the rule of God within the heart is the hidden work of the Holy Spirit.[3] Such moderation is brought about by the mortification or crucifixion of the flesh by the Spirit in applying the effect of the death of Christ to the hearts of His people.[4] The Holy Spirit is the "Spirit of continence (*continentiae spiritus*)" who so restrains the licentious desires of the flesh that men spontaneously bring their own lives into order.[5] It should therefore be our constant prayer in face of all temptation to give way to excess, that "the Lord will moderate us by the unerring rule of His Spirit."[6]

For Calvin, then, true meekness, contentment and patience are not virtues that can be cultivated by human resolution and discipline, but the fruit of union with Christ in bearing the Cross, the effect of the grace of God and cheerful submission and surrender to His will.[7] When a Christian shows patience in enduring the Cross he is presenting to God "a sacrifice of obedience which is acceptable to Him."[8] It is this fact which makes such a wide difference between Christian patience and "philosophical patience."[9] Whereas the Christian obeys the divine will of grace, the

---

[1] Comm. on Luke 9 : 55, C.O. 45 : 526.

[2] Comm. on Ps. 106 : 14, C.O. 32 : 121. *Haec unica est moderationis ratio, si Deus affectus nostros gubernet.*

[3] Comm. on Ps. 141 : 4, C.O. 32 : 393. *Porro David tam sermones suos quam affectus Deo regendos commendans, fatetur non aliter quam arcana spiritus moderatione et mentem et linguam in officio teneri . . . quia et linguae modestia singulare est spiritus donum.*

[4] Cf. pp. 63–7.   [5] Comm. on Ps. 23 : 5, C.O. 31 : 241.

[6] Comm. on John 12 : 42, C.O. 47 : 300. . . . *ut nos moderetur certa spiritus sui regula.*

[7] Comm. on Ps. 116 : 15, C.O. 32 : 200; on Ps. 94 : 12, C.O. 32 : 24. *Et sane haec vera est patientiae ratio, non contumaciter resistere rebus adversis (sicuti praefractam duritiem Stoici pro virtute laudarunt) sed nos libenter subiicere Deo, quia in eius gratiam recumbimus.* Serm. on Deut. 8 : 1–4, C.O. 26 : 590–1.

[8] Comm. on Phil. 2 : 27, C.O. 52 : 41.

[9] Inst. 3 : 8 : 11, and Ibid. where Calvin distinguishes on the latter side further between *contumacia philosophica* and *immani duritia Stoicorum.*

Stoic bows before blind necessity.[1] Christian patience or endurance under the Cross is rooted in the humility that prostrates itself in the dust before God, whereas the Stoic endurance is inseparable from pride and independance of heart.[2] Stoic fortitude and "patience" is, indeed, mere stubborness and obstinacy in the face of adversity rather than a yielding to what is good.[3]

The most important difference between the attitude of the Christian in moderating his life and behaviour and that of the Stoic is that the Christian man allows suffering to enter his heart. He allows his feelings to be touched and moved to real response by his surroundings and circumstances, even though he is to be watchful in moderating the extent to which, and direction in which, his feelings drive him. Stoicism, on the other hand, is the "iron philosophy" that seeks to make men like stones, apathetic and impervious to what should move human nature. Christianity indeed makes men sensitive and keen in their emotional response. Stoicism blunts feeling.[4] Calvin strongly condemns all the "mad fellows" who were introducing such Stoic ideas and ideals into the preaching and teaching of the Church about the Christian life, for in his day there was "a new kind of Stoic who holds it vicious not only to groan or weep but even to be sad and anxious."[5] He insists that the affections which God has given to man's nature are, by themselves, no more corrupt than their own author Himself," though it matters that they should be held in moderation.[6] A Christian feels, though he does not indulge in, grief and sorrow.[7] Calvin frequently points out how utterly human and natural, in contrast to Stoicism, were the men of the Bible in

---

[1] Ibid.

[2] Comm. on Ps. 34 : 19, C.O. 31 : 344. *Unde etiam colligimus, verae tolerantiae nihil esse magis adversum, quam altitudinem illam de qua garriunt Stoici: quia non prius vere humiliati censemur, quam dum cordis afflictio coram Deo nos prosternit, ut iacentes erigat.*

[3] Comm. on Ps. 94 : 12, C.O. 32 : 24; and Inst. 3 : 8 : 11. A further difference between the Stoic and Christian attitude which Calvin points out is that the Stoic has to find his happiness and satisfaction in his own mental attitude which he himself creates, whereas Christ makes the Christian find his in hope of a future reward. Comm. on Matt. 5 : 10, C.O. 45 : 164–5.

[4] Inst. 3 : 8 : 9, Comm. on Phil 2 : 27, C.O. 52 : 41.

[5] Inst. 3 : 8 : 9, Comm. on Acts 8 : 2, C.O. 48 : 175. These words of Calvin are striking in view of the constant modern tendency in some quarters to say in an unqualified way that worry is sinful.

[6] Comm. on Acts 8 : 2, C.O. 48 : 175.

[7] Cf. comm. on 1 Thess. 5 : 16, C.O. 52 : 174.

their feelings, whether it be Paul anxious about Epaphroditus,[1] or the psalmist in his mood of depression,[2] or our Lord Himself both in His teaching and His example.[3]

Here again it is to be noted that the effect of the Spirit of God is to make men again truly natural, not only in the fact that they become truly human in their feelings but also truly moderate. For all excess is dehumanising and against the order of nature.[4] "Nature is content with little."[5]

[1] Comm. on Phil. 2 : 27, C.O. 52 : 41.
[2] Comm. on Ps. 30 : 12, C.O. 31 : 299.
[3] Inst. 3 : 8 : 9.
[4] Serm. on Eph. 5 : 15–18, C.O. 51 : 718; on 1 Tim. 2 : 9–11, C.O. 50 : 206.
[5] Comm. on 1 Tim. 6 : 8, C.O. 52 : 326.

PART FOUR

NURTURE AND DISCIPLINE
WITHIN THE CHURCH

Chapter I

Sanctification and separation within the Church

1. The individual sanctified through membership of the Church

IT is obvious that for Calvin the sanctification of the individual, and the growth, nurture and discipline of his Christian life, take place within the life of the Church, and the attitude and loyalty of the individual towards the Church is an extremely important factor in this matter. Nowhere, of course, does Calvin speak so clearly and memorably about this as in his section on the Church in the *Institutes*. "As it is now our purpose to discourse of the visible Church, let us learn, from her single title Mother, how useful, nay how necessary, the knowledge of her is, since there is no other means of entering into life unless she conceive us in the womb and give us birth, unless she nourish us at her breasts, and, in short, keep us under her charge and government until, divested of mortal flesh, we become like the angels."[1] It is, however, not only the maternal function that the Church fulfils towards the individual, but also the function of the school. In the Christian life we are always learners, progressing step by step under guidance and tutelage.[2] The Church is the sphere of our gradual education towards full manhood in Christ.[3] In it we are scholars all our life.[4]

Our salvation within the Church is constantly furthered by the mutual care which the members, gathered together in one body under the same Head, have for each other.[5] "The saints are united in the fellowship of Christ on this condition, that all the blessings which God bestows upon them are mutually communicated to each other."[6] Such mutual participation in each other's gifts

---

[1] Inst. 4 : 1 : 4. Cf. also 4 : 1 : 1.
[2] Serm. on Eph. 1 : 17–18, C.O. 51 : 335.
[3] Inst. 4 : 1 : 5.   [4] Inst. 4 : 1 : 4.
[5] Comm. on Ps. 20 : 10, C.O. 31 : 212. *Eius (i.e. salutis) vero tunc demum futuri sumus participes, si omnes sub communi nostro capite in unum corpus collecti, mutuam alii pro aliis curam geramus, non autem seorsum quisque sibi consulat.*
[6] Inst. 4 : 1 : 3.

within the Church is a necessary condition for living a full Christian life, for "God does not bestow the Spirit on each apart, by himself."[1] Jesus Christ was the only one who was given the Spirit "without measure" and who thus had no need to receive through other men. We ourselves, however, receive the gifts we need by participating in our own small measure in the receiving and sharing of each other's gifts within the Church, and by cultivating our unity within the Church.[2] Calvin puts the matter succinctly in his 1537 Catechism. "Christ, in giving Himself to us exhorts us to give and spend ourselves for others. Christ, in making Himself common to all, makes us also to be one in Him."[3]

God, then, does not give us the gifts and strength we need to live the Christian life directly from His own hand. He bestows upon us what we need through the ministry of others within the life of the Church. Therefore no matter how much our natural pride. makes us desire to stand alone we are nevertheless "constrained to borrow from others."[4] Within the Church we must "cleave to each other in the mutual distribution of gifts."[5] And we must acknowledge that our gifts have been given to us by the Head in order that we may communicate them to others.[6] To neglect the saints when they stand in need of our help is "to defraud them of what is their due,"[7] and it is also to deform the body, since only through such mutual communication of what each has can each maintain his respective place within the body.[8] Thus the people of God "cannot but be united together in brotherly love and mutually impart their blessings to each other."[9] Calvin, indeed, asserts that only as we are united among ourselves as members of one body can we be reconciled to God.[10]

---

[1] Comm. on 2 Cor. 13 : 13, C.O. 50 : 156. *Deus non singulis seorsum largitur spiritum, sed pro gratiae mensura cuique distribuit, ut ecclesiae membra vicissim inter se communicando unitatem foveant.*

[2] Ibid. and comm. on John 3 : 34, C.O. 47 : 74–5. Inst. 4 : 1 : 3.

[3] C.O. 22 : 70.

[4] Comm. on Rom. 12 : 6, C.O. 49 : 238.

[5] Comm. on 1 Cor. 12 : 12, C.O. 49 : 501. *Hic vero fideles hortatur ut mutua donorum collatione inter se cohaereant.*

[6] Serm. on Eph. 4 : 15–16, C.O. 51 : 588. *Mais ce qu'il a receu sera pour en communiquer aux autres, et le tout vient du chef.*

[7] Comm. on 2 Cor. 9 : 1, C.O. 50 : 106.

[8] Comm. on Eph. 4 : 7, C.O. 51 : 192. *Certum modum singulis impertit, ut nonnisi inter se communicando habeant quantum satis est ad status sui conservationem.*

[9] Inst. 4 : 1 : 3.

[10] Comm. on Col. 3 : 15, C.O. 52 : 123–4; on 1 Cor. 1 : 13, C.O. 49 : 311.

In placing us within the Church that we might share in the mutual communication of spiritual gifts, God has assigned to each his station and function within the body.[1] The unity which we must cherish within the Church is an ordered unity in which each member is assigned his place and part in the fulfilment of which the whole body will possess symmetry and proportion (*symmetria et porportio*) and will grow towards perfection[2]—a symmetry which will be destroyed if the members refuse to fulfil their function.[3] Therefore it is important that we should observe not only the unity but also the order which God has appointed within the Church for our growth in grace.[4] To try to grow spiritually apart from the Church is impossible. But to try to grow within the Church in superiority to the other members and without taking the humble place assigned to us in the body is to produce a monstrous growth which denies the true nature of the Church.[5] This symmetry and proportion and order in growth within the Church is, of course, at least a sign of the restoration of the true order of nature among men in Jesus Christ, and of the image of God amongst humanity.[6] Church order in this way reflects the true order of nature.

2. Being gathered within the visible Church implies our sanctification

Our sanctification flows from our election and incorporation into the membership of the Church. It has already been pointed out[7] that God sanctifies His Church not simply by the inward influence of the Spirit in the heart but through the Cross which He

---

[1] Comm. on 1 Cor. 4 : 7, C.O. 49 : 367.

[2] Comm. on Eph. 4 : 12, C.O. 51 : 198–9; Cf. comm. on Rom. 12 : 6, C.O. 49 : 238.

[3] Comm. on Eph. 4 : 15, C.O. 51 : 202. *Quid est igitur papatus, nisi deformis gibbus, qui totam ecclesiae symmetriam confundit, dum unus homo capiti se opponens, e membrorum numero se eximit?*

[4] Inst. 4 : 1 : 5.

[5] Serm. on Eph. 4 : 15–16, C.O. 51 : 585. *Car si nous croissions, et cependant que les espaules montassent un demi pied par dessus la teste, que seroit-ce? Ce croissement-là seroit-il desirable? Il voudroit mieux qu'un membre fust du tout amorti, que de desfigurer ainsi le corps. D'autant donc qu'il faut que le chef soit par dessus, sainct Paul notamment declare que ce n'est pas assez de croistre, mais qu'il faut que nous tendions tousiours à ceste subiection de nostre Seigneur Iesus Christ, et qu'il preside par dessus nous, et que grans et petis se rangent là. Or nous voyons par experience que ceci n'a pas este dict sans cause.*

[6] Cf. e.g. Inst. 2 : 12 : 6.

[7] Cf. pp. 68–74.

lays upon it in the course of its earthly history. Calvin teaches that whereas in this world the wickedness of men is allowed to go on often unpunished (judgment being stored up for men in general at the last day), nevertheless within the Church such is not the case. Since the Church will not come under judgment at the last day, God is especially severe in judging its sin here and now. He therefore begins His judgment in the Church. He reforms it by chastening it severely, as it were completing His whole work of judgment.[1] Therefore if we are members of the Church we must expect to be subject to a "more rigid discipline" under the providence of God than we would otherwise experience.[2] To be elected means that God is at work upon us in this special way to change us.[3] To be sanctified therefore means to be the object of this special providence and leading of the Spirit by which He separates His own people apart to Himself as sons.[4] By virtue of election we are brought into a sphere of fellowship with God and providence under God's hand in which our afflictions, being "consecrated in the name of the Head," all serve to conform us to Christ.[5]

Sanctification is therefore a work which God accomplishes in His providential dealings with the Church, and in this respect also we participate in sanctification not as isolated individuals but especially within the fellowship of the Church and as members of the Church, for it is in such fellowship that our lives can be made outwardly conformable to the death and resurrection of Christ.

[1] Serm. on Job 42 : 6–8, C.O. 35 : 492–3. *Nous voyons tous les iours que la condition des fideles est plus miserable que celle des contempteurs de Dieu. . . . Or quand on voit ces choses, on y seroit troublé, sinon que nous eussions ceste doctrine, c'est assavoir que le iugement commence par la maison de Dieu: comme aussi il est dit au Prophet Isaie* (10, 12). *Quand Dieu aura accompli tout son ouvrage sur la montagne de Sion, alors il n'espargnera point les meschans. Or notamment le Prophete Isaie dit, qu'il faut que Dieu accomplisse toutes ses corrections en son Eglise: comme ce sont ceux qui lui sont plus recommandez que les siens. Il faut donc qu'il les visite en premier lieu, qu'il les purge de leurs fautes, qu'il les reforme pour les reduire à lui . . . qu'il accomplice toute son œuvre. Et puis, il y a une vengeance horrible apprestee sur ceux qui ont abusé de sa patience.*

[2] Serm. on Matt. 27 : 11–26, C.O. 47 : 890.

[3] Serm. on Eph. 1 : 3–4, C.O. 51 : 270. *Il faut que Dieu besongne et qu'il nous change: car tout bien procede de son election.*

[4] Comm. on Rom. 8 : 14, C.O. 49 : 147. *Caeterum observare convenit, esse multiplicem spiritus actionem. Est enim universalis, qua omnes creaturae sustinentur ac moventur: sunt et peculiares in hominibus, et illae quidem variae. Sed hic sanctificationem intelligit, qua non nisi electos suos Dominus dignatur, dum eos sibi in filios segregat.*

[5] Comm. on Heb. 11 : 26, C.O. 55 : 162. *Ergo ubi hic finis est ne discedamus a corpore ecclesiae: quidquid patimur, sciamus capitis nomine esse consecratum.*

For Calvin, the whole purpose of our election is, indeed, our sanctification. The covenant which God makes with the elect is one which involves obligation to holiness.[1] God has joined together election and sanctification, and man must not separate what God has joined together.[2] We must not separate holiness of life from the grace of election.[3] The fact that we are "called to be saints" means that our holiness flows from election and that the aim of election is holiness.[4] Therefore to be elected does not give us any excuse for licence and careless living. Calvin has no hesitation in warning the elect to walk in fear and not to imagine that God cannot cast them out of His house if they prove themselves unworthy of the grace given to them. To know ourselves elected will never make us complacent or careless in our way of life but will rather stir us up to cleave to the promises of God and to seek their fulfilment all our life.[5] It is only those who have no real ground for assuming the title of the people of God who delude themselves with the idea that they are secure whatever they do.[6] Election therefore is the root that is bound to produce the fruits of goodness.[7] If we are not reprobate, our sanctification is bound to follow from our election by God, "when, having embraced by faith the doctrine of Christ, we follow it during our life.[8]

[1] Comm. on Ps. 15 : 1, C.O. 31 : 143. *Quamvis enim gratis adoptaverit Abraham, stipulatus tamen est ut viveret integer: atque haec est generalis regula foederis quod ab initio cum tota ecclesia pepigit.*

[2] Serm. on Eph. 1 : 3–4, C.O. 51 : 270. *Car ce sont choses coniointes et inseparables, que Dieu nous ait eleus, et que maintenant il nous appelle à saincteté.* And on Eph. 1 : 4–6, C.O. 51 : 270–1.

[3] Comm. on Eph. 1 : 4, C.O. 51 : 148.

[4] Comm. on 1 Cor. 1 : 2, C.O. 49 : 308. *Potest autem bifariam accipi: vel ut Paulus causam sanctificationis dicat esse vocationem Dei, propterea quod Deus ipsos elegit.*

[5] Serm. on Deut. 7 : 7–10, C.O. 26 : 524. *Notez (dit-il) puis que Dieu a promis à vostre pere Abraham, qu'il sera le Dieu de sa semence apres luy, qu'il ne vous deffaudra point. Mais advisez cependant de cheminer en crainte: car ceste alliance est faite avec condition que vous soyez entiers, que vous ayez le coeur droit. Ne pensez pas donc que vostre Dieu ne vous puisse dechasser de sa maison, et de son Eglise, quand il vous trouvera indignes du bien qu'il vous a presenté. . . . Il est vray que desia il s'allie avec nous . . .: mais ce n'est pas à dire qu'il nous faille estre nonchallans: plustost il nous faut estre resveillez pour embrasser les promesses qu'il nous envoye, pour nous y arrester du tout, et que nous soyons constans en cela toute nostre vie.*

[6] Comm. on Ps. 15 : 1, C.O. 31 : 142. *Nihil magis tritum est in mundo quam falso obtendere Dei nomen idque sibi magna pars hominum secure indulget.*

[7] Serm. on Eph. 1 : 4–6, C.O. 51 : 270–1.

[8] Comm. on John 13 : 18, C.O. 47 : 311.

3. The assurance of being within the Church is an important element in our sanctification

It is obvious that the assurance of our being elected to sanctification is a most important element in the actual accomplishment of our sanctification and in living the Christian life. We must have a sense of God's calling if our faith is to stand.[1] Election means that God chooses men for His service within and through His Church, "not because they in themselves are fit for it, nor because they spontaneously offer their service," but simply because He chooses them and inspires them.[2] Indeed, if we are brought near to God, it is never because we anticipate His grace, but only because He stretches His hand down to Hell to reach us.[3] If we know ourselves as thus elected by God's sheer grace amongst His people, then we will know that God is bound to fulfil, in us and with us, the purpose which He has begun. Our salvation and sanctification "stand with the election of God," which "cannot change or fail and is united to the stability of Christ, who will no more allow His faithful followers to be dissevered from Him than He would allow His members to be torn in pieces."[4] Election is thus the fountain from which all other blessings flow.[5] Therefore the knowledge that he is thus elected is bound to bring to the Christian a cheerfulness and certainty in doing his God-appointed task which will keep him from succumbing under failure and defeat.[6]

But we cannot have such sanctifying assurance apart from membership of the Church. "The Lord has not promised His mercy save in the communion of saints."[7] The promises that must uphold the elect in face of their temptations and trials are promises

---

[1] Serm. on Eph. 1 : 3–4, C.O. 51 : 265. *Si donc nostre foy n'estoit fondee en l'election eternelle de Dieu, il est certain qu'elle nous pourroit estre ravie de Satan à chacune minute.*

[2] Comm. on Ps. 105 : 26, C.O. 32 : 110.

[3] Comm. on Ps. 65 : 5, C.O. 31 : 605–6.

[4] Inst. 4 : 1 : 3.

[5] Comm. on Ps. 28 : 8, C.O. 31 : 285. *Quanquam praecipue tenendum est quod alibi attigimus, ex hoc fonte fluere quaecunque in nos Deus confert beneficia, quia gratis in Christo nos elegit.*

[6] Comm. on 1 Tim. 1 : 18, C.O. 52 : 263. *Quid enim plus alacritatis addere nobis vel debet, vel potest, quam quum scimus nos divinitus ordinatos ad agendum quod agimus? Haec arma sunt nostra, haec praesidia quibus muniti nunquam deficimus.* Cf. comm. on Ps. 18 : 1, C.O. 31 : 169.

[7] Inst. 4 : 1 : 20.

made to us not simply as isolated individuals but as members of the elect community, for to be elected means to be elected with the Church. It is only "as long as we continue in the bosom of the Church" that we can be sure that the truth will remain with us and that the promises of God's faithfulness towards His people will apply to us.[1] It is when we find ourselves gathered within the Church among the flock of God that we know ourselves as indeed elected and separated from the rest of the world as the objects of the free and unsearchable love of God; and it is thus that we become assured of all the benefits that flow from such election.[2]

We can, then, constantly encourage and comfort ourselves in the fact that we belong to the Church, and are thus elected among the people of God. There can be no greater privilege, then, "than to be regarded as belonging to the flock and people of God, who will always prove the best of fathers to His own, and the faithful guardian of their welfare."[3] We must remember that the God of the Bible is one whose purpose it is not simply to choose isolated individuals here and there but to choose for His Son a people who will be destined to life and therefore kept and defended by the Son for the Father.[4] If we know ourselves as numbered among this people, then we know that our individual welfare is assured.[5] We must learn to apply to ourselves the comfort that is held out for each of us in the promises that cover the welfare of the Church. Calvin notes how, "to persuade true believers that God has a special care for each of them in particular," the psalmist "brings forward the promise which God made to the whole people and declares God to be the guardian of the Church, that from this general principle, as from a fountain, each might convey streams to himself."[6] The picture of Jerusalem surrounded securely by

[1] Inst. 4 : 1 : 3.

[2] Comm. on Ps. 44 : 4, C.O. 51 : 439. *Et certe hic fons et origo est ecclesiae, nempe gratuitus Dei amor: et quibuscunque beneficiis prosequitur Deus suam ecclesiam, ex eodem fonte manat. Ideo quod collecti sumus in ecclesiam, quod fovemur ac protegimur Dei manu: causa non alibi quam in Deo quaerenda est. Nec vero hic de communi Dei benevolentia agitur, quae se extendit ad totum humanum genus, sed distinguitur electus populus a reliquo mundo, et discriminis causa ad merum Dei beneplacitum refertur.*

[3] Comm. on Ps. 106, C.O. 32 : 117.

[4] Comm. on Heb. 2 : 13, C.O. 55 : 31; cf. on Matt. 9 : 36, C.O. 45 : 262.

[5] Comm. on Ps. 94 : 6, C.O. 32 : 20.

[6] Comm. on Ps. 121 : 4, C.O. 32 : 301. *Tenemus nunc prophetae consilium, nam ut singulis persuadeat Deum peculiarem eorum curam gerere, in medium profert quid toti populo sit pollicitus, Deumque pronuntiat ecclesiae suae esse custodem, ut ex hoc fonte singuli rivos ad se derivent.* Cf. on Ps. 119 : 26, C.O. 32 : 247-8.

mountains—a symbol of how God defends His Church—can be at the same time a sign to each of the faithful "that the safety promised in common to all people belongs to him."[1]

4. Separation from the world as an aspect of sanctification within the Church

Our election to sanctification within the Church involves at the same time separation from the world. Calvin finds that throughout the Scripture "the term sanctification denotes separation,"[2] as well as election. Calvin speaks frequently of our becoming separate, e.g. "from the world,"[3] and "from all that is contrary to His service."[4]

Such separation is an aspect of the Biblical idea of holiness.[5] This is seen in the vicarious sanctification of Jesus Christ, which involved not only His identification with us in all our human limitation and conflict and need, but also His separation from us and His assumption of a place within our human nature quite unique and solitary. In order to be sanctified as Mediator, He had to be set apart from the common rank of men.[6]

---

[1] Comm. on Ps. 125 : 1–2, C.O. 32 : 313–14.

[2] Comm. on 1 Cor. 1 : 2, C.O. 49 : 308. *Porro sanctificationis verbum segregationem significat.* Cf. on Eph. 5 : 25, C.O. 51 : 223. *Iam vero addit ut eam sanctificaret: hoc est, ut segregaret eam sibi.*

[3] Serm. on Eph. 5 : 25–7, C.O. 51 : 746; comm. on Dan. 7 : 25, C.O. 41 : 77.

[4] Serm. on Deut. 5 : 12–14, C.O. 26 : 284. *Quand l'Escriture nous parle d'estre sanctifiez à Dieu: c'est pour nous separer de tout ce qui est contraire à son service.*

[5] Cf. comm. on Exod. 15 : 11, C.O. 24 : 159. *Sanctitas pro gloria accipitur quae Deum a creaturis omnibus separat.*

[6] Serm. on Mark 1 : 23–7, C.O. 46 : 739. *Quant à ce mot de Sainct de Dieu, il emporte que nostre Seigneur Iesus Christ, comme Mediateur, devoit estre separé du rang commun des hommes.* Cf. comm. on John 10 : 36, C.O. 47 : 253. Calvin finds the solitary and separate place of Jesus in this respect amongst men foreshadowed in the Old Testament, especially in the stories of Joseph and Samson, who are both referred to as Nazirites (a Nazirite being one who is separated for sanctification; cf. e.g. comm. on Zech. 7 : 3, C.O. 44 : 221. Calvin argues that, though superficial, even the similarity between the names Nazirite and Nazareth, is of divine significance). Joseph and Samson were able to save their people simply by reason of their separation from those they saved—Joseph being sold into Egypt, and Samson being consecrated a Nazirite from his birth (cf. serm. on Matt. 2 : 23, C.O. 46 : 451 ff. In this exposition Calvin admits his debt to Bucer—see comm. on Matt. 2 : 23, C.O. 45 : 103). In all this Calvin finds an illustration of the fact that the sanctification of the people of God is to depend on one Head who is to be set apart likewise unique in his own sanctification (serm. on Matt. 2 : 23, C.O. 46 : 455. *Dieu a voulu figurer desia sous la Loy que la sainctete commune depend d'un chef, qui est seul: comme Joseph.* . . . *Samson.* Cf. for Joseph, Gen. 49 : 26 and Deut. 33 : 16; for Samson, Judges 13 : 5).

The members of the Church as well as the Head require to be separated from evil in order to be sanctified. The Church is indeed a consecrated body of Christ separated from evil for the service of God. "We cannot be united into the one body of the Church under God unless we break off all bonds with impiety, separate ourselves from idolaters, and keep ourselves pure and uncontaminated from all the pollutions which corrupt and vitiate the holy service of God."[1] We can become devoted to God only as we become separated from unrighteousness.[2] Since our fellowship with Christ in the Church thus consecrates us to God, it is therefore to commit fearful sacrilege and to "profane a sanctified thing" if we do not separate ourselves from anything that might defile us.[3] "I ask you— are not these incompatible and discordant things that Jesus Christ dwells in us and at the same time we are given to all villainy and filth? Do we imagine that He wants to dwell in a pigsty?"[4] Therefore a Christian who is really consecrated to Christ and who lives by faith will detest and abhor whatever is incompatible with such a relationship to Christ.[5]

This necessarily means separation from the world. By "the world" Calvin means the present life of this world as it is organised apart from and over against the Kingdom of God. "The world" for Calvin is the sphere of the "flesh," of self-life and Satanic power. He can speak of this world as having a corrupt mode of life which is "wholly at variance with God" and adverse to the Spirit of God.[6] The "world" is organised to cater for the self-centred nature of the unregenerate man, therefore it is in the sphere

---

[1] Comm. on Ps. 16 : 4, C.O. 31 : 151. *Neque enim aliter in unum ecclesiae corpus coalescimus sub Deo, quam dum abrumpimus omnes impios nexus, disiungimus nos ad idololatris, et ab omnibus inquinamentis, quae purum Dei cultum corrumpunt ac vitiant, integri sumus ac immunes.*

[2] Comm. on Ps. 97 : 10, C.O. 32 : 46.

[3] Comm. on Rom. 12 : 1, C.O. 49 : 234.

[4] Serm. on 2 Thess. 1 : 6–10, C.O. 52 : 236.

[5] Cf. e.g. comm. on Ps. 139 : 21, C.O. 32 : 385; on Ps. 31 : 6, C.O. 31 : 304.

[6] Comm. on 1 John 2 : 15, C.O. 55 : 318. *Mundi nomine intellige quidquid ad praesentem vitam spectat, ubi separatur a regno Dei et spe vitae aeterna. Ita in se comprehendit omne genus corruptelas, et malorum omnium abyssum. In mundo sunt voluptates, delitiae, et illecebrae omnes quibus homo capitur, ut se a Deo subducat.* Cf. p. 319. *Quae propria sunt mundi, cum Deo prorsus dissideant. Tenendum est quod iam dixi, hic notari profanum vitae institutum, quod nihil habet cum regno Dei commune.* Cf. comm. on 1 John 5 : 4, C.O. 55 : 363. *Mundi nomen hic late patet: comprehendit enim quidquid adversum est Dei spiritui: ita naturae nostrae pravitas pars mundi est, omnes concupiscentiae, omnes Satanae astus, quidquid denique nos a Deo abstrahit.*

of the "world" that self-will finds its true pleasure and is most easily exercised.[1] Moreover the world, so organised, is under the dominion of Satanic power, and it is through the fascination of the world that the Devil obtains tyrannical sway over the human heart.[2] Therefore a Christian man, in seeking to separate himself from evil, must hold himself apart from that aspect of the life of this world which seeks to involve him in the life of self-love and in the service of the flesh and the Devil.[3] We can redeem our life and our time from the power of the Devil only by paying the price of withdrawal from the allurements and cares and pleasures of the world.[4]

The fact that this present world is so much under the power of evil makes it the more serious sin when we neglect to aspire to the heavenly life for which we are created, for worldliness becomes not simply materialism or the denial of another world but an active alliance with the Devil.[5] What separates the godly from the wicked is, for Calvin, their opposite attitudes both to this world and to that which is beyond.[6]

It is only within the fellowship of the Church that we can find ourselves in the true relationship of separation from this world, for separation from the world is not something we can achieve for ourselves as isolated individuals. Separation, like sanctification, is a work which God accomplishes with His Church. It is, for Calvin, an important aspect of the Sacrament of Baptism that it is a sign

---

[1] Comm. on Gal. 6 : 14, C.O. 50 : 265–6. *Quid autem mundus significat? opponitur procul dubio novae creaturae. Quidquid ergo contrarium est spirituali Christi regno, mundus est: quia ad veterem hominem pertinet. Vel, ut uno verbo dicam, mundus est quasi obiectum et scopus veteris hominis.*

[2] Comm. on Eph. 5 : 16, C.O. 51 : 220.

[3] Comm. on 1 John 2 : 15, C.O. 55 : 318.

[4] Comm. on Eph. 5 : 16, C.O. 51 : 220. *Dies malos esse dicit, hoc est omnia scandalis et corruptelis esse plena. . . . Quum ita corruptum est saeculum, videtur diabolus tyrranidem occupasse: ut tempus non possit Deo consecrari, nisi quodammodo redemptum. Quod autem erit pretium redemptionis? Infinitis illecebris, quae facile nos perverterent, cedere: extricare nos a curis et voluptatibus mundi, omnibus denique impedimentis renuntiare.* Cf. on Matt. 19 : 26, C.O. 45 : 543.

[5] Serm. on Deut. 9 : 20–24, C.O. 26 : 708. *Nous serons bien mal advisez si nous ne passons par ce monde comme oiseaux sur la branche, et que nous n'y soyons estrangers. Car autrement Dieu nous desadvoüe, et renonce. Puis qu'ainsi est: ceux qui se veulent tellement arrester au monde, qu'il semble qu'ils n'en doivent iamais partir, ils se bannissent du royaume de Dieu, ils declairent que l'heritage des cieux ne leur appartient point. . . . Ainsi ceux qui ont honte de se nommer estrangers en ce monde, qu'ils s'en aillent cercher leur heritage avec le diable: car ils n'ont ne part ne portion avec Dieu.*

[6] Comm. on Ps. 119 : 132, C.O. 32 : 274.

of division between the Church and the world separating those within from those without, proclaiming that salvation cannot be hoped for except we be "separated from the world."[1] Not only does Baptism proclaim that such a separation is necessary, it also itself constitutes the way by which men can take the step which separates them from evil, and, along with the other ordinances of the Church, it actually effects that separation.[2]

The Church, then, is the sphere in which men are "separated from the degrading pollutions of the world that they may be the holy and peculiar people of God."[3] In the Church we become united in one body in order that we may become separated and thus sanctified.[4] We become separated only as we find ourselves elected and adopted into the Church,[5] united to Christ[6] as we adhere to the fellowship of the Church.[7]

[1] Comm. on 1 Pet. 3 : 21, C.O. 55 : 267–8. Cf. comm. on Gen. 7 : 17, C.O. 23 : 133.

[2] For Calvin the sacramental signs must be regarded by faith as accompanied by what they signify, cf. e.g. comm. on Isa. 6 : 1, C.O. 36 : 126; on Isa. 42 : 3, C.O. 37 : 61. This is why it is sacrilegious for a baptised person not to remain separate from evil. Cf. serm. on Eph. 2 : 13–15, C.O. 51 : 407–8. *Et ainsi, tous ceux qui se renomment de l'Eglise, et cependant sont gens desbauchez et dissolus, sentiront quel sacrilege c'est d'avoir ainsi profané leur Baptesme que Dieu avoit dedié pour leur salut. Mais de nostre costé, advisons de cheminer comme estans separez des pollutions de ce monde.*

[3] Comm. on Ps. 16 : 3, C.O. 31 : 151.

[4] Serm. on 1 Cor. 10 : 19–24, C.O. 49 : 675. *La religion emporte qu'ils soyent comme un corps uni pour estre separé d'avec tous incredules.*

[5] Prayer in comm. on Zeph. 3 : 1–5, Amst. Edn., Vol. 5, p. 431.

[6] Serm. on Eph. 5 : 25–7, C.O. 51 : 746. . . . *que nous soyons separez du monde, à fin d'estre conionts au Fils de Dieu.*

[7] Serm. on 1 Tim. 3 : 14–15, C.O. 53 : 314. *Dieu nous a tellement unis à nostre Seigneur Iesus Christ, qu'il ne veut point que nous soyons separez en façon que ce soit d'avec luy ni distraits. Quand donc nous avons cela, n'est-il point question d'estre ravis en cest honneur inestimable, et que nous apprenions de plus en plus de nous retirer des corruptions de ce monde.*

Chapter II

The Church sanctified by the Word and Sacraments

1. The decisive place of the Word and Sacraments in the birth, growth and discipline of the Christian life within the Church

IN the birth, growth, and nourishment of our Christian life within the Church, the decisive part is played by the Word of God—or the Gospel, as it is proclaimed and taught within the Church. Calvin uses a great variety of expressions to describe the part played by the Word of God within the fellowship of the Church. It is the "spiritual food of the soul divinely offered by the hands of the Church," which if we neglect to take we deserve to perish.[1] It is the channel through which the blessings of God's promises flow from the original fountain-head to reach us.[2] By means of the Word, immortality and the Kingdom of Heaven are offered to us, and in receiving the Word we can lay hold of these divine gifts.[3] By means of the Word, God presents to us His peace.[4] The Word is the means whereby Christ Himself comes into our midst in the Church, and whereby His blood, shed for our cleansing and redemption, is applied to our souls, for there is an inseparable connexion between the blood of Christ and the preaching of the Word.[5] Moreover, God Himself "comes to meet

---

[1] Inst. 4 : 1 : 5.   [2] Comm. on Ps. 119 : 65, C.O. 32 : 243.

[3] Serm. on 2 Tim. 1 : 8–9, C.O. 54 : 48. *Seulement ouvrons la bouche afin qu'il la remplisse, ouvrons le coeur, et donnons entree à ce tesmoignage, de l'Evangile, et l'immortalité du royaume celeste habitera en nous.*

[4] Comm. on Ps. 19 : 8, C.O. 31 : 201.

[5] Serm. on Gal. 3 : 1–3, C.O. 50 : 459. *Or cependant notons que ce n'est point assez d'avoir cognu en passant que nostre Seigneur Iesus Christ nous a si cherement rachetez: mais qu'il nous faut continuer tousiours en la doctrine de l'Evangile, iusques à tant que cela soit bien imprimé en nostre coeur, comme si son sang decouloit pour appliquer le fruict qui nous en revient à nostre usage;* and ibid. p. 462. *Car nous ne pouvons pas mespriser la doctrine de l'Evangile, que nous ne profanions le sang du Fils de Dieu, qu'il a espandu pour nostre redemption: car l'un ne se peut separer d'avec l'autre. Toutes fois et quantes que Dieu parle à nous et qu'il nous presente la remission de nos pechez, qu'il nous declare qu'il est prest de nous recevoir à merci, il y a une aspersion quant et quant du sang de nostre Seigneur Iesus Christ. Toute ceste doctrine-là ne peut avoir nul effect, sinon que nostre Seigneur Iesus Christ soit là au milieu pour nous approprier l'effusion de son sang.*

us" or "comes down to us" and addresses us by means of His Word,[1] and in thus presenting Himself He makes the Word a looking-glass in which we are able to see Him who is otherwise invisible.[2]

When Calvin speaks of the Word of God in such exalted terms, the form of the Word of which he is primarily thinking is not the Word read and meditated on in private,[3] but the preached Word mediated through the ministry of the Church. It is by the "Gospel in the Church," the "external preaching," the "ministry of men," that "the renewal of the saints is accomplished and the body of Christ is edified."[4] The Church is our school of Christ, in which our faith is nourished and grows because the Word is preached in its midst.[5] It is within the fellowship of the Church and through the gift of the ministry within the Church that the true interpretation of the Scriptures is given to the individual and that he is enabled to grow in knowledge and understanding.[6] Therefore Calvin can say that, as in the Old Testament the fathers could speak of themselves as able to see the "face of God" in the sanctuary, so under the New Testament it is through preaching that we are able to see the glory of God which shone in the face of Jesus Christ.[7] So remarkable is this office of preacher in the Church, so close the relationship between the living and powerful Word of God and what is uttered by the mouth and tongues of men, that what is affirmed about the power of the Word of God can also be affirmed about the word of the preacher in fulfilling his office in the midst of the Church.[8]

The Word within the Church is always, for Calvin, the Word

---

[1] Comm. on Ps. 18 : 31, C.O. 31 : 185; and comm. on Ps. 81 : 14, C.O. 31 : 766. *Deus enim ad nos descendens per verbum suum, et sine exceptione invitans omnes, neminem frustratur.*

[2] Comm. on 1 Cor. 13 : 12, C.O. 49 : 514–15.

[3] Inst. 4 : 1 : 5.

[4] Inst. 4 : 3 : 2; 4 : 1 : 5.

[5] Serm. on Eph. 4 : 11–14, C.O. 51 : 568. *Brief, en toute sorte, sçachons que quand Dieu a mis ce regime en son Eglise, que sa Parole se presche, c'est à fin que cependant que nous sommes en ce pelerinage terrien, tousiours nous venions à l'escole ou Dieu nous enseigne: car nous cheminons en foy. . . . Or la foy dont procede-elle? Comment est-ce qu'elle se nourrit et s'augmente? C'est par la Parole de Dieu. Quand nous avons la predication . . . voilà par où et par quel bout nostre foy commence, voilà comme elle continue et comme elle croist de iour en iour.*

[6] Cf. *Calvin's Doctrine of the Word and Sacrament*, pp. 115 ff. Inst. 4 : 1 : 5; comm. on 2 Tim. 2 : 15, C.O. 52 : 367.

[7] Inst. 4 : 1 : 5.

[8] Inst. 4 : 1 : 5 and 6; 4 : 1 : 22.

inseparably sealed by the Sacraments. God seeks to further our
Christian growth within the Church by means of the continual
use both of the Lord's Supper and Baptism, along with the Word.
Our union with Christ, which is the source of all our growth, and
of which the Sacraments are signs,[1] is something which grows as
faith grows. It is not only "figured" in the Sacraments but is
more and more effected through the use of the sacraments,[2] which
thereby affect our whole Christian life and enable us to possess
Christ more fully and enjoy Him in all His richness.[3] The Lord's
Supper "is intended to make us grow in faith and confirm therein
until His second coming."[4] According to His promise, and by the
incomprehensible virtue of His Spirit,[5] Jesus Christ Himself is
present in the celebration of this mystery, so that, "as mortal men
distribute the bread and the wine," He Himself works in our midst.[6]
Baptism, it is true, is administered only once to an individual,
but, like the Lord's Supper also, its efficacy is not necessarily tied
to the moment of its administration.[7] Baptism never "becomes
obsolete" in a believer,[8] and if what is represented and offered to
us in our Baptism remains "fixed in our mind throughout our whole
life,"[9] then the sacrament remains continually efficacious[10] along
with the Word and the Lord's Supper in effecting our Christian
growth.

2. The Word and Sacraments are the means whereby, through
the Spirit, the members of the Church are consecrated to fulfil
their royal priesthood

The Word and the Sacraments effect the sanctification of
members of the Church not only because they are the means
whereby life and power are communicated from Christ to His
people, but because they are also the means by which the members
of the Church are consecrated to offer themselves and their works
in thanksgiving as living sacrifices to God in fulfilment of their
royal priesthood.[11] For Calvin the Word of the Gospel is not only
a channel by which the life of Christ flows to men, food and medi-

---

[1] Cf. pp. 18–19.   [2] Inst. 4 : 17 : 33.   [3] Inst. 4 : 14 : 6.
[4] Serm. on 1 Cor. 10 : 14 ff., C.O. 49 : 802.   [5] Ibid.
[6] Serm. on Acts. 1 : 1–4, C.O. 48 : 634.   [7] Inst. 4 : 14 : 7, C.O. 7 : 741.
[8] Inst. 4 : 15 : 3.   [9] Comm. on Ps. 63 : 3, C.O. 31 : 594.
[10] Comm. on Titus, 3 : 5, C.O. 52 : 430–1.   [11] Cf. pp. 28–9.

cine for the soul's health, it is also the spiritual sword[1] by which
the people of God, who would offer the sacrifice of their lives, are,
as it were, immolated for the sacrifice. It is by the Word of God
that the mortification is effected whereby we are consecrated to
God, and enabled to make a true offering of ourselves in faith.[2]
It is the Word of God that purges and cleanses us in consecrating
us.[3] The faithful, then, "are sacrificed (*immolari*) to God through
the Gospel."[4] The offering of the heart and life that was meant
to be given along with the offerings of oxen and rams and lambs
in the Old Testament ritual—and that was typified outwardly in
these bleeding sacrifices—is really made possible for us under the
New Testament by the mortifying and cleansing power of the
Word of God. "The true and lawful consecration is by the Word."[5]
"Mount Zion, then, is now different from what it was formerly,
for wherever the doctrine of the Gospel is preached, there is God
really worshipped, there sacrifices are offered, there, in a word,
the spiritual Temple exists."[6] "Grant, Almighty God," Calvin
prays, "that since we cannot really profit by Thy Word in any
other way than by having all our thoughts and affections subject
to Thee and offered to Thee as a sacrifice—O, grant that we may
suffer Thee, by the sound of Thy Word, so to pierce through
everything within us that, being dead in ourselves, we may live
unto Thee."[7]

The effect of the Word in consecrating the people of God is
inseparable from the mortifying and sanctifying work of the Holy
Spirit.[8] Moreover, the Sacraments, along with the Word, assist

[1] Comm. on Phil. 2 : 17, C.O. 52 : 36. *Evangelium est spiritualis gladius ad caedendas victimas.* Cf. on Heb. 4 : 12, C.O. 55 : 49–51. In Serm. on 1 Tim. 1 : 8–11, C.O. 53 : 60, Calvin refers to preaching as *glaive spirituel.*

[2] Ibid. *Nulla enim fides sine mortificatione, per quam Deo consecramur.* Cf. comm. on Exod. 20 : 8, C.O. 24 : 577. *Videndum est quae sit huius sanctificationis summa: nempe carnis interitus.*

[3] Serm. on Deut. 7 : 5–8, C.O. 26 : 514. *Qui est cause que nous devons estre un peuple sanctifié à nostre Dieu? assavoir sa parolle: car il est dit: Vous estes nets à cause de la parolle que ie vous ay preschee. Voici donc le moyen par lequel Dieu nous sanctifie à soy, c'est à dire, il nous retire de la perdition commune de tous les enfans d'Adam, et nous prend pour estre de sa maison, assavoir quand il nous declare sa volonte. Voila donc en somme une consecration solonelle que Dieu fait d'un peuple, quand il veut que sa parolle y soit preschee.*

[4] Comm. on Heb. 4 : 12, C.O. 55 : 49.

[5] Comm. on Hosea 5 : 6, C.O. 42 : 304. *Vera enim et legitima consecratio in verbo consistit.*

[6] Comm. on Micah 4 : 7, C.O. 43 : 355.

[7] Prayer in comm. on Mic. 2 : 7–11, Amst. Edn. Vol. 5, p. 297.

[8] See pp. 40 and 66.

in enabling us to offer ourselves as a living sacrifice to God, in the fulfilment of our royal priesthood. Though Calvin insists that there can be no propitiatory effect in the celebration of the Lord's Supper, it is nevertheless the occasion for a true eucharistic sacrifice of the whole Church to God in love and service to one another.[1] It would also be in line with Calvin's whole outlook (though he does not explicitly emphasise the point) to regard Baptism as the basic act of consecration to royal priesthood, and of commitment to a life of sanctification in the pattern of Christ's death and resurrection.

3. The power of the Word to reform the heart and to
create and increase faith

The Word is not only food, it is also the medicine which we must constantly use for our spiritual health. Everything that the doctor can do to the human body in face of various diseases (by purging, blood-letting, giving medicine, dieting) the Word of God can do for our souls in face of all our evil vices.[2] The Word of God is the instrument by means of which God's vineyard (whether the Church or our own hearts) is pruned and cleansed and made fruitful.[3]

Calvin, in his commentary on the Psalms in particular, frequently speaks about the power of the Word of God, or of the Law,[4] to discipline and control the mind and heart of man. It is true that the discipline and teaching of the Word are alien to our corrupt nature.[5] Yet at the same time the Word is more powerful than the corruption of our hearts and minds. It can "bridle the

---

[1] Cf. Inst. 4 : 18 : 13, 17, 3, 42.

[2] Serm. on 1 Tim. 1 : 8–11, C.O. 53 : 61. *Car dequoy nous doit servir la parole de Dieu? c'est une pasture de nos ames: et puis c'est une medecine. Nous avons le pain et les viandes qui nous servent de nourriture pour les corps: la parole de Dieu a l'usage tel envers nos ames: mais elle emporte encores plus, c'est que quand nous sommes malades de nos vices, qu'il y a beaucoup de corruptions et cupiditez meschantes, il faut que nous en soyons purgez: et la parole de Dieu nous sert maintenant de purge, maintenant de saignee, maintenant d'un bruvage, maintenant de diette; brief, tout ce que les medecins peuvent appliquer aux corps humains, pour les guarir de leurs maladies, n'est pas une dixieme partie de ce que la parole de Dieu nous sert pour la santé spirituelle de nos ames. Pour cela sainct Paul parle ici de la saine doctrine.*

[3] Comm. on John 15 : 3, C.O. 47 : 340.

[4] The two are practically identical in Calvin's comments, for the Law of God to the Psalmist was simply the Word as he knew it.

[5] Cf. comm. on Ps. 19 : 7, C.O. 31 : 200; and on Ps. 50 : 17, C.O. 31 : 505.

wild intemperance of our flesh."[1] In those who yield to its heavenly instruction it will have the power not only to restrain the impetuosity of youth but will serve as an antidote to correct vice throughout their whole life.[2] So powerful is the effect of the Word upon our life that the "best rule of moderation" is simply to follow the example of the psalmist, "to keep our eyes concentrated upon the Word of God."[3]

In effecting the reformation of our lives the Word of God works deep within our hearts.[4] Though the Law of God is "odious to the flesh, which it subdues into order,"[5] nevertheless in subduing the flesh it, at the same time, attracts us to God by its sweetness; and though in our natural state nothing is more agreeable to us than what is sinful, nevertheless the delight which we now feel in the Law carries us in the opposite direction.[6] Thus the Word of God has, in reforming us, a twofold effect upon us. It not only "compels us to obedience" by restraint but also "allures us by its sweetness,"[7] and by the expulsive power of this new love for God's Law the allurements of the flesh are overcome.[8] Calvin notes that this holy love for the Law is the dominating passion in the life of the psalmist, replacing the unholy love of money which seems to be the dominating passion in the rest of mankind,[9] and he asserts that in us, too, the same love for the Word "will serve effectually to deliver our hearts from an immoderate desire for gold and silver."[10]

It is through the creation and growth of faith within the Church that the Word of God is primarily effective in producing the growth of the Christian life of the members of the Church, for it is in the context of man's encounter by the Word of God that faith is created, confirmed and increased. Faith is indeed man's response to the Word of God as that Word addresses man. "There is no faith without God's Word, for of His faithfulness we

[1] Comm. on Ps. 119 : 147, C.O. 32 : 281.
[2] Comm. on Ps. 119 : 9, C.O. 31 : 218.
[3] Comm. on Ps. 17 : 4, C.O. 31 : 161.
[4] Comm. on Rom. 12 : 14, C.O. 49 : 244. *Deus autem verbo suo non tantum manus coercet a maleficiis, sed amarulentos quoque affectus in animis domat.*
[5] Comm. on Ps. 119 : 29, C.O. 32 : 226.
[6] Comm. on Ps. 119 : 15, C.O. 31 : 220–1.
[7] Comm. on Ps. 19 : 10, C.O. 31 : 202.
[8] Comm. on Ps. 112 : 1, C.O. 32 : 172.
[9] Comm. on Ps. 119 : 13, C.O. 32 : 220.
[10] Comm. on Ps. 19 : 10, C.O. 31 : 202.

cannot be convinced until He has spoken . . . for we must ever hold that there is a mutual relation between God's Word and our faith."[1] But when God addresses man in His Word faith is indeed awakened in man's heart, for the confidence that lays hold of the Word of God is indeed faith itself.[2] It is especially the promises of the Word of God that tend to beget and increase the response of faith within our minds and hearts,[3] for in the promises of the Word, God confronts man primarily in His gracious aspect, and faith is founded "chiefly on the benevolence and kindness of God."[4]

4. Through the Word and Sacraments the individual within the Church finds himself singled out and called by Christ

It is through the Word and the Sacraments within the Church that the individual finds himself personally confronted and addressed by Jesus Christ and is enabled to apply to himself as an individual the virtue of the atoning work of Jesus Christ. It is not enough that Christ died for the world as a whole or that His spiritual gifts are poured out upon the Church in general. The individual within the Church must be singled out and must know himself as singled out and related personally to the death and resurrection of Christ. "The words 'for me' are very emphatic," says Calvin in his comment on Gal. 2 : 20, "It will not be enough for any man to regard Christ as having died for the salvation of the world, unless each can claim for himself as an individual the effect and possession of this grace."[5] We have already noted that

[1] Comm. on Heb. 11 : 11, C.O. 55 : 154.
[2] Comm. on John 4 : 50, C.O. 47 : 102.   [3] Inst. 3 : 2 : 7; and 3 : 2 : 29.
[4] Comm. on Heb. 11 : 11, C.O. 55 : 154. Yet it must be remembered that this response to the Word of God is no mere human response. Faith can be added to the Word only when it is at the same time "begotten within us by the inward operation of the Spirit" (comm. on 1 Pet. 1 : 2, C.O. 55 : 208), for faith (cf. p. 22) "does not arise out of the ordinary faculties of men but is an extraordinary and rare gift of God (comm. on John 12 : 37, C.O. 47 : 296). Cf. serm. on Acts 1 : 9–11, C.O. 48 : 617. *Ne sçavons-nous pas que la foy surmonte tout sens humain? Car ce n'est pas une faculté que les hommes ayent d'heritage, mais c'est une grace que Dieu leur fait en corrigeant leur nature*; and serm. on Eph. 1 : 13–14, C.O. 51 : 301. *Il faut bien que Dieu besongne par son S. Esprit et par une grace speciale, outre ce qu'il veut que l'Evangile nous soit presché.*
[5] Comm. on Gal. 2 : 20, C.O. 50 : 200; cf. serm. on Gal. 2 : 20, C.O. 50 : 450. *Or il ne se contente point de dire qu'il s'est livré pour le monde en commun: car cela seroit aussi trop maigre: mais il faut qu'un chacun applique à soy en particulier la vertu et le fruict de la mort et passion de nostre Seigneur Iesus Christ. . . . Il faut qu'un chacun en son endroit se conioigne à nostre Seigneur Iesus Christ, et qu'il conclue. C'est pour moy qu'il a souffert.*

God has His Word for and His work with the Church as a whole, and that it is a great matter for the individual to realise this.[1] But the Word in its action within the Church can never remain simply a vague word addressed to the people of God as a whole. It must become a word that reaches and singles out each individual with particular relevance to the problems and circumstances that beset each individual within the Church.[2] The word that evokes faith must be some one particular word in which God personally addresses us by name and speaks precisely to our situation.[3] As Mary heard herself personally addressed by the risen Jesus in the garden, and called by name, so the Word must become not an "ordinary voice (*non communi voce*) which sounds indiscriminately in the ears of all," but a voice by which He specially (*peculiariter*) calls His own sheep.[4]

It is noticeable that in discussing this matter Calvin can emphasise that it is not only by the Word but also by the Sacraments that the individual comes to know himself personally singled out and addressed, and is enabled to apply to himself the fruit of the passion of Christ.[5]

In the response of faith to the Word of God that can so particularise itself towards the individual, there is bound to be an

---

[1] See p. 195.

[2] Cf. serm. on 2 Sam. 2 : 1, p. 29. *Quoy qu'il en soit, David scait bien que ce n'est pas assez quil ait entendu, quelle est la volonté de Dieu quant a la reigle commune, mais il faut qu'en sa vie il sache, de quel costé il se doit tourner. . . . Car nous sommes suffisamment enseignez par sa parolle de ce qui est bon droit et juste; cependant il reste que Dieu nous donne intelligence de sa volonté, et qu'estans illuminez par son Esprit, nous comprenions ce quil nous a donné par sa parolle. Mais ce n'est pas le tout. Car nous serons en quelque differend de cecy et de cela, et apres auoir balancé long temps, encores ne pourrons nous conceuoir beaucoup de choses particulieres pour certaines. Là, comme jay desia dit, il nous faut inuoquer Dieu et recourir à luy.*

[3] Comm. on Ps. 12 : 6, C.O. 31 : 129. *Neque enim satis foret, Deum apud se statuere quid facturus sit in salutem nostram, nisi recta nos et nominatim compellet, nam inde nobis spes salutis affulget, quum Deus voce sua ostendit se nobis fore propitium.*

[4] Comm. on John 20 : 16, C.O. 47 : 432.

[5] Serm. on Deut. 4 : 27–31, C.O. 26 : 197. *Ton Dieu n'a il pas dit, qu'il aura pitié de ceux qui l'invoquent? Et voire—mais ie ne say si ie suis d'un tel rang. N'ay-ie pas este baptisé au nom de nostre Seigneur Iesus Christ? N'ay-ie pas la saincte Cene, qui m'est encores un second gage par lequel Dieu me monstre qu'il me reçoit au nombre de ses enfans?* Cf. serm. on Gal. 2 : 20–1, C.O. 50 : 450. *Quand nous sommes baptizez, ce n'est pas un seul qui le soit pour luy, on ne iettera point un asperges sur chacun: mais chacun sera baptizé en son particulier, à fin d'avoir une application speciale, . . . aussi quand nous recevons la saincte Cene, chacun vient prendre sa portion, pour nous monstrer que nostre Seigneur Iesus Christ nous est communiqué, voire à chacun de nous.*

intensely personal element in which the individual applies the Word to himself, as if addressed to himself, even when it speaks in terms that are no more than a general promise. The man of faith, like the psalmist, will always tend to find strength in calling the Lord his *own* God.[1]

When we know ourselves thus personally addressed, and thus personally responding to the Word, this is a sure sign of our election. This indeed constitutes our calling. "After electing us He testifies His love towards us by calling us."[2] Though God addresses His Word to all men and disappoints no one who will respond, nevertheless "we are to trace to the fountain of the secret electing purpose of God this difference, that the Word enters the heart of some, while others only hear the sound of it."[3] Without such a response of faith election will be imperfect.[4] But election must inevitably lead to our being called to faith in Christ, and therefore our faith is a "sufficient attestation of the eternal election of God" to make our Christian life one of assurance.[5]

[1] Comm. on Ps. 7 : 2, C.O. 31 : 80. 10th serm. on Ps. 119, C.O. 32 : 601–2. *Que nous ne facions point comme les Papistes, qui diront, O, il est vray que Dieu a promis cecy et cela, mais nous ne scavons pas s'il nous appartient . . . Or au contraire, il nous faut faire ceste conclusion que fait yci David, Seigneur, selon ta parole donnée à ton serviteur. Il ne dit point, selon ta parole donnée à ie ne scay qui, aux hommes du nombre desquels ie ne suis pas, en telle sorte que ie ne m'y puisse pas appuyer: mais il dit, Selon ta parole donnée à moy Seigneur. Apprenons donc à son exemple. . . . Quand nostre Seigneur dit, Ie reçoy tous pecheurs à mercy: que chacun dise, I'en suis un, Seigneur, ie suis une povre creature desesperée, ie vien à toy, et t'allegue la promesse que tu m'as donnée. Voyla comme il nous en faut faire: ou autrement, nous ne ferons que vaguer en l'Escriture saincte tout le temps de nostre vie.*

[2] Comm. on Ps. 65 : 5, C.O. 31 : 606.

[3] Comm. on Ps. 81 : 14, C.O. 31 : 766.

[4] Comm. on John 6 : 40, C.O. 47 : 147. *Tolle fidem, et mutila erit electio.*

[5] Ibid. Cf. serm. on Eph. 1 : 3–4, C.O. 51 : 265. *Que nous soyons tout resolus et persuadez que Dieu nous tient pour ses enfans. Et comment aurons nous cela, sinon d'autant que nous embrassons sa misericorde par foy, selon qu'il nous offre en l'Evangile, et que nous sçachions aussi que nous sommes fondez en son election eternelle? Car si nostre foy dependoit de nous, il est certain qu'elle nous eschaperoit bien tost.*

Chapter III

Discipline under the Word

1. The Christian life is lived under the influence and guidance of the Word

THE Christian life is for Calvin a life lived under the influence and guidance of the Word of God. A Christian is one who gives himself up in a spirit of utter docility to the teaching of the Word, to be ruled and disciplined by its precepts, even though its teaching and discipline is alien to our own corrupt nature.[1] Whether or not we subject ourselves thus to the Word of God is the sure test of whether or not we fear God Himself.[2] "An unfeigned love of God's Law is certain evidence of adoption, since such love is the work of the Holy Spirit."[3] The hard heart is the heart that despises the Word, in contrast to the heart that is soft and pliable to the hearing of the Word in receiving it with reverence and obedience.[4] Moreover, to despise the Word of God is to despise God Himself.

Only the life that is based upon, directed, and inspired by the Word of God can truly please God. It is true that what first matters in seeking to please God is to have our hearts right with Him, for the right heart is more important than the outward behaviour. Nevertheless, even with the right heart, it is vain for any man to imagine that by himself apart from the Word of God he can devise and conceive ways of pleasing God. "No man must frame for himself, at his own pleasure, a new form of righteousness unsupported by the Word of God, but we must allow ourselves to be governed by divine authority."[5] If our life and our service

[1] Comm. on Ps. 19 : 7, C.O. 31 : 200; on Ps. 50 : 17, C.O. 31 : 505. *Itaque ferocia nostra nos exasperat contra Dei verbum, quia correctionem non libenter suscipimus, nec fieri potest ut quis mansueto et docili animo Deum loquentem audiat, eiusque verbo obtemperet, donec se regendum et corrigendum ei tradat.*

[2] Comm. on Ps. 50 : 17, C.O. 31 : 505; on Ps. 111 : 10, C.O. 32 : 171. *Merito igitur hoc examine probari Dei timorem docet propheta, si libenter iugum eius suscipimus, nosque regi patimur eius verbo.*

[3] Comm. on Ps. 119 : 159, C.O. 32 : 286.

[4] Comm. on Ps. 95 : 8, C.O. 32 : 33.

[5] Comm. on Luke 1 : 6, C.O. 45 : 10.

of God is to be acceptable, they must be ordered and guided by faith—a faith which will learn only from the Word of God.[1] We must beware in this matter of building castles in the air by doing, even with the best intentions, merely what we think right, for God wants to guide us clearly by His Word.[2] "The first thing, then, that God requires of us is this humility to allow ourselves to be controlled by His pure Word."[3] Whatever human action or worship does not arise out of the Word of God is false and unstable and is not approved by God Himself.[4]

A Christian therefore binds himself to the Word of God, obeying it simply in faith, and believing that its teaching is "so full and complete in every respect, that whatever is defective in our faith ought rightly to be attributed to our ignorance of the Scriptures."[5] He will therefore look to the Law of God alone and will refuse to allow his eyes licence to wander here and there in search of other sources of wisdom, guidance and inspiration.[6] True humility will prevent him from asking or seeking to answer questions that seek to intrude beyond what is revealed of God's will in the Word,[7] for one of the rules of religion is the "rule of modesty and soberness" —"in obscure matters not to speak, or think, or even long to

[1] Comm. on Ps. 119 : 79, C.O. 32 : 249. *Vera igitur religio et cultus Dei ex fide oriuntur: ut nemo rite Deo serviat, nisi qui edoctus fuerit in eius schola.*

[2] Serm. on Deut. 9 : 8–12, C.O. 26 : 667. *Or en ceci voyons-nous que c'est une chose de grande consequence, que la parolle de Dieu nous soit communiquee, que nous ne doutions point qu'elle ne procede de luy, et que nous sachions qu'il nous y faut assuiettir: si nous n'avons cela, il n'y aura nulle religion entre nous. Il est vray que nous en cuiderons bien avoir: mais le principal fondement de religion, c'est à dire, de foy, de service de Dieu, c'est que la doctrine nous soit certifiee. Car si nous y allons par cuider, comme les Payens, les Turcs, et tous Idolatres: comme les Papistes aussi auront leurs bonnes intentions: tout cela est frivole, c'est bastir en l'air, et par fantasie. Notons bien donc que la premiere entree que nous devons avoir pour servir Dieu, et pour estre approuvez de luy, c'est que nous ayons une reigle toute asseuree, que nous ne disions pas: Ie pense que cela soit bon, il me le semble, on me l'ainsi dit: mais nous avons la parolle de Dieu qui nous guide . . . car nostre conducteur ne nous trompera iamais.*

[3] Serm. on 1 Tim. 4 : 1–5, C.O. 53 : 366.

[4] Comm. on Luke 1 : 6, C.O. 45 : 10; on Ps. 128 : 1, C.O. 32 : 327.

[5] Comm. on John 20 : 9, C.O. 47 : 430. Cf. serm. on Deut. 9 : 8–12, C.O. 26 : 666–7. *Nous se savons point le moyen de servir Dieu, il nous faut excuser si nous forgeons a nostre teste: mais voici Dieu qui nous a donne une declaration pleine de son vouloir, il faut qu'ils s'arrestant la, et qu'ils obeissent simplement, et sans y adiouster rien qui soit*; and serm. on Deut. 26 : 16–19, C.O. 28 : 282–3. *Moyse exprime ici les commandemens, les statuts, . . . pour monstrer que Dieu ne nous enseigne point à demi, quand nous avons sa parolle, mais que nous avons une instruction parfaicte.*

[6] Cf. comm. on Ps. 119 : 30, C.O. 32 : 227.

[7] Comm. on Ps. 81 : 14, C.O. 31 : 766.

know more, than the Word of God has delivered."[1] Moreover, he will receive what the whole Word of God says to him in all its aspects. "It rightly belongs to faith to hear God whenever He speaks, and unhesitatingly to embrace whatsoever may proceed from His sacred mouth. Thus far it has regard to commands and threatenings as well as to gratuitous promises."[2] The word of God is, for him, like purified gold, free from all defilement or spot or stain.[3]

The Christian is so bound to God's Word that he will betake himself to it even in the most severe and difficult conflicts, knowing that "should he depart from God's Word no hope would be left for him."[4] In the tension and conflict that constantly take place between his own natural unregenerate human reason and the Word of God the Christian will say goodbye to the prudence of the flesh in order to follow the guidance of the Spirit.[5] For "what sort of insanity is it to embrace nothing but what is welcome to our human reason? What authority will God's will have if it is admitted only as far as it pleases us?"[6] This applies, of course, especially to the ordinary Christian man when he is asked to judge God and his own situation solely by looking at the state of affairs before his own eyes. Calvin is constantly telling us that we must always have our eyes shut to everything that might prevent us from believing in God, in order that we may rest in His promises.[7]

---

[1] Inst. 1 : 14 : 4. Our response to the Word must always be mixed with a sobriety that refuses to speculate about the hidden mysteries of God (comm. on Matt. 20 : 23, C.O. 45 : 555). This sobriety will make us "tremblingly adore what exceeds our senses" (comm. on Matt. 23 : 34, C.O. 45 : 639) and will prevent us from attempting anything which God has not given us liberty to do (serm. on Job 3 : 11–19, C.O. 33 : 162).

[2] Comm. on Heb. 11 : 7, C.O. 55 : 151.

[3] Comm. on Ps. 119 : 140, C.O. 32 : 278.

[4] Comm. on Ps. 119 : 25, C.O. 32 : 225.

[5] Comm. on Ps. 81 : 13, C.O. 31 : 765.

[6] Comm. on Ps. 115 : 25, C.O. 32 : 109.

[7] Serm. on Luke 1 : 39–44, C.O. 46 : 101. *Il est vray qu'il nous faut avoir les yeux fermez, quant à tous obiects de ce monde qui nous pourroyent divertir de nous reposer en Dieu et en ses promesses. Car il est certain que si nous voulons entrer en conseil avec nostre sens naturel, si nous en voulons iuger selon les apparences, que tousiours nous serons en branle, et iamais Dieu n'aura son autorite envers nous telle qu'il merite. Et pourtant, que la parole de Dieu nous soit pour une verite certaine et infallible. Car les hommes opposeront tousiours, Voire ceci, Voire cela; mais de nostre costé ayons tousiours les yeux fermez à ce qui nous peut empescher de croire à Dieu. Cependant il nous les faut ouvrir à ce qui nous peut servir de bien contempler ses œuvres.* Cf. serm. on Gal. 5 : 4–6, C.O. 50 : 674. *Or Dieu veut esprouver nostre obeissance quand il nous remet à sa pure et simple parole. Et c'est aussi le vray honneur que nous luy rendons, quand nous fermons les yeux à tout cela, et qu'il nous suffit que Dieu nous ait declaré sa volonté.*

2. The place of meditation in the discipline of the Christian life

According to Calvin our response in love and gratitude to the Word of God must include in a pre-eminent place a response of the mind and thinking to the Word of God. We must love the Lord with all our heart and soul and mind and strength.

In this response of our faculties to God's grace the mind must play the leading part, and we must discipline ourselves to constant, true and deliberate thinking about God's Word.[1] A true response to the Word will mean not only obeying it with hands and feet but also giving it the chief place in the mind and affections.[2] Only if the Word of God is allowed first to dominate all our thinking is it possible for us to love God at all, or to respond to him with our heart and strength. "Do we know God with our minds as we ought? This matters much. Otherwise it is impossible to love him with all our strength and with all our feelings: for knowledge comes before love. If our knowing God is only partial, if there should be still much haziness surrounding us, our love will also be very weak."[3]

If, however, we do surrender all our mental and cognitive faculties to the Word of God, this is bound to draw the other faculties and powers also into love and obedience, and to have a profoundly sanctifying effect on our life.[4] The sanctification of the thoughts is of supreme importance, moreover, because it is by

[1] Serm. on Deut. 6 : 4–9, C.O. 26 : 434–5. *Il met donc Ame, Coeur, Pensee; comme s'il disoit, qu'il faut qu'un homme qui voudra bien observer la Loy, se dedie en tout et par tout en l'obeissance de Dieu, et en son amour. Or nous voyons qu'en nos ames il y a premierement la vertu de penser, quand nous concevons les choses pour iuger, pour discerner: voila la premiere faculté de l'ame. C'est qu'apres avoir veu les choses, nous entrons en deliberation, et iugement, nous concluons ceci ou cela: Dieu donc veut retenir à soy toutes ses pensees-la.*

[2] Comm. on Ps. 119 : 2, C.O. 32 : 216. *Non satis est pedibus et manibus obsequium praestare, nisi primum locum teneat cordis veritas.*

[3] Serm. on Deut. 6 : 4–9, C.O. 24 : 435. *Si tu fais la moindre chose du monde, et que toutes tes pensees ne tendent à aimer Dieu, que l'amour de Dieu ne te conduise: tout cela est corrompu.*

[4] Serm. on Deut. 6 : 13–15, C.O. 26 : 457–8. *Car il est impossible que nous pensions à Dieu, que nous ne soyons incitez à l'honorer, sinon que nous en facions une idole. Car quand la maiesté de Dieu nous vient en memoire, ne faut-il pas que nous soyons touchez, pour nous humilier devant icelle? Ne faut-il pas que nous sachions qu'il nous a creez à ceste condition-la, d'estre du tout à luy, et de nous dedier à son service? Notons bien donc que la memoire de Dieu emporte que nous le craignions.*

seeking to insinuate evil first into our minds that Satan seeks to enmesh us in his snares and errors, and thus by evil communications corrupt our whole lives.[1] Calvin reminds us that as the body can be weighed down by surfeiting and drunkenness, so the mind can be overpowered by the cares and lusts of this world, and that true watchfulness and victory over such temptations involves us in meditating on the things of God.[2]

Therefore we cannot be good Christians merely by going to sermons, and in that way being taught what we need for salvation, and "yet at the same time be negligent and think no more in meditation on the things we have already heard." To behave like this is to behave like a warrior who has fine armour but hangs it up and lets it rust.[3] We must meditate on and apply to ourselves the Word we hear from the pulpit.[4] The Word, then, must not be received in a superficial manner but must be allowed deeply and constantly to influence the mind and heart of the Christian. It was by "long" and "assiduous" meditation that the psalmists strengthened themselves to resist their temptations.[5] It was only by such meditation that the Word could become "imprinted on"[6] or "deeply fixed within"[7] the soul, or "deeply enclosed within the intimate recess of the heart,"[8] in order to effect its sanctifying work in the heart.

In considering the nature and place of meditation as an aspect of Christian discipline we cannot forget the place Calvin gives to "meditation on the future life" in forming the attitude of the Christians to this present world and claims and pleasure.[9] Yet the future life need not be the only focus of our meditation. "It is of great importance that we should be told what is necessary for us to know and what the Lord desires us to contemplate. . . . The

[1] Cf. comm. on 1 Cor. 15 : 33, C.O. 49 : 554; on Ps. 119 : 29, C.O. 32 : 226.
[2] Comm. on 1 Cor. 16 : 13, C.O. 49 : 570. *Haec autem vigilantia mentis est: dum soluti et expediti a curis terrenis meditamur quae sunt Dei.*
[3] Serm. on Job 3 : 11–19, C.O. 33 : 158.
[4] Serm. on Matt. 2 : 9–11, C.O. 46 : 356. *Mais il suffit de l'avoir touché en bref, afin que chacun y pense. Car les choses qui se disent en chaire, quand elle sont entendues, se doyvent puis apres mediter, et chacun y doit appliquer son estude en particulier.*
[5] Comm. on Ps. 39 : 2, C.O. 31 : 396; comm. on Ps. 38 : 16, C.O. 31 : 393.
[6] Serm. on Gal. 3 : 1–3, C.O. 50 : 459.
[7] Comm. on Ps. 19 : 11, C.O. 32 : 203.
[8] Comm. on Ps. 119 : 166, C.O. 32 : 290. . . . *penitus atque intimo cordis recessu clausam.*
[9] Cf. pp. 85–93

love of Christ is held out before us in meditation on which we
ought to exercise ourselves by day and night, and in which we
ought to be wholly plunged. He who has this one thing has
enough."[1] Calvin frequently recommends us to meditate upon the
meaning of the passion and death of Christ. If we meditate on
this we will be made strong to face and overcome our difficulties
and temptations,[2] to endure the waves of persecution,[3] and be
given courage when our hearts are tempted to waver and desert
His cause.[4] It is true, of course, that we need not confine ourselves
to meditation only on the Cross. Indeed if we begin with meditation on the Cross, we are bound to be led through this very exercise to contemplate Christ in the heavenly glory of His resurrection,[5] but it is at least safe to anchor our meditation on to His
passion and death.[6] It is true also that the glory of God which
must be the subject of our contemplation is not confined to the
events of the Gospel but "shines forth" and may be viewed as
extending to the entire structure of the world.[7] Therefore there
must be time and place in the life of the Christian who in Christ
knows the true Creator, for thankful contemplation of God's
work in creation, and for learning from its order.[8] But Calvin's
whole attitude on this matter of the place of natural theology even
in the devotional life is determined by the fact that in Jesus Christ
there are hid *all* treasures of wisdom and knowledge. "Beyond
this there is nothing solid, nothing useful—nothing, in short,
that is proper or sound. Though you survey the heaven and earth
and sea, you will never go beyond this without overstepping the
lawful boundary of wisdom."[9]

[1] Comm. on Eph. 3 : 18, C.O. 51 : 188.
[2] Serm. on Gal. 2 : 20–1, C.O. 50 : 449.
[3] Comm. on 1 Pet. 4 : 12, C.O. 55 : 278. *Ergo ut praesenti simus animo quum
excipiendi sunt persequutionum fluctus, mature assuefieri nos oportet ad meditationem assiduam crucis.*
[4] Comm. on 1 Tim. 6 : 13, C.O. 52 : 330.   [5] Cf. pp. 78–9 and 329–30.
[6] Serm. on Gal. 2 : 20–21, C.O. 50 : 449–50. *Il est certain que la victoire nous
sera bien aisee contre toutes tentations, quand nous pourrons considerer que vaut la
mort et passion de nostre Seigneur Iesus Christ, et ce qu'elle emporte.* . . . *Car il nous
faut estre arrestez à la mort et passion de nostre Seigneur Iesus Christ, cognoissans
qu'elle est suffisante pour nous retirer des abysmes de mort. Et au reste, il nous faut
contempler nostre Seigneur Iesus Christ non seulement comme mort en l'infirmité
de sa chair, mais comme estant ressuscité en sa vertu divine et celeste.* Cf. e.g. we
are to meditate on His second coming (Inst. 2 : 16 : 17).
[7] Comm. on 1 Cor. 13 : 12, C.O. 49 : 514.
[8] Cf. pp. 103–4 and 145–7, and e.g. comm. on Ps. 104 : 1, C.O. 32 : 85; on
Ps. 68 : 33, C.O. 31 : 635.   [9] Comm. on Eph. 3 : 18, C.O. 51 : 188.

3. The cultivation of fear by meditation on God's anger

We must meditate also on those aspects of God's dealings with us that help to make us fear God. When we contemplate the Cross and try to understand the meaning of the sufferings of Christ and His cry of dereliction it is impossible for us not to tremble with fear and astonishment at the revelation it gives us both of our own sins and God's wrath against us.[1] To ignore this aspect of God's grace which should make us tremble, and to take His grace for granted is to tempt God.[2] "There is nothing that more provokes God's wrath to its limit, than when He sees that we take no account of His anger."[3] It is therefore our Christian duty to have the fear of God always before our eyes, so that we may regulate our lives by it and that like a bridle it may restrain our unruly passions.[4]

To restrain ourselves by the fear of God must involve us in solemn thought about the consequences of sin.[5] Calvin, for example, in appealing to his congregation to keep watch over their hearts and minds lest they fall into sexual sin, urges them to let the fear of God restrain them and, reminding them how such sin is punished, he says, "Let us have always before our eyes the judgment that is here spoken of."[6] And in another sermon, after quoting some very severe texts from Holy Scripture in warning about the consequences of evil,[7] he says, "Hearing such texts,

---

[1] Serm. on Isa. 53 : 4–6, C.O. 35 : 625–6. *Mais quand nous voyons que Dieu n'a point espargné son Fils unique . . . et qu'en son ame mesme il a este affligé iusques au bout, iusques a s'ecrier, Mon Dieu, mon Dieu, pourquoy m'as-tu laissé? Quand nous oyons toutes ces choses, il est impossible (ou nous sommes plus endurcis que pierres) que nous ne fremissions et concevions une telle crainte et estonnement en nous, que ce soit pour nous rendre du tout confus: et que nos offenses et iniquitez ne nous soyent detestables, veu qu'elles provoquent ainsi l'ire de Dieu contre nous.*

[2] Serm. on Deut. 6 : 15–19, C.O. 26 : 474.

[3] Serm. on Job 14 : 13–15, C.O. 33 : 682.

[4] Comm. on Ps. 36 : 1, C.O. 31 : 359. *Ideo dicitur timor Dei esse ante oculos, quum vitam hominum regit, ac quaecunque se vertunt, occurrens, obiectu suo libidines refraenat.* Cf. comm. on 1 Cor. 7 : 9, C.O. 49 : 408; and on 2 Cor. 7 : 1, C.O. 50 : 84.

[5] Calvin does insist, however, that forgiveness can be followed even during our earthly life, by deliverance from the punishment due for sin. Such deliverance testifies that God is no longer displeased with us. In this Calvin argued against those who said, "God retains the punishment though he forgives the fault." Yet Calvin admits that God does not always immediately on forgiveness give men relief. He can chastise the forgiven. Yet even here he "moderates His rigour" (cf. comm. on Ps. 85 : 3, C.O. 31 : 786; on Ps. 130 : 8, C.O. 32 : 338).

[6] Serm. on Job 31 : 9–15, C.O. 34 : 652–3.

[7] Isa. 33 : 1; Ps. 17 : 16; Jas. 2 : 13.

let us tremble, and let us take heed to walk so justly and so truly uprightly with our neighbours that men will know that we are continually restrained by the fear of God." After all, it is no virtue to be stupid and to fear nothing where there is real danger, to act like a drunk man throwing himself out of the window, or like a madman casting himself into the fire.[1] A Christian tempted to inflict injury on a neighbour or commit any wickedness will do well to remember God's way of avenging things, even in this life, by which those who prepare a pit for others are cast into it themselves, and consulting his own salvation, should restrain himself from even the smallest crime.[2] It is not the wicked, but those who believe, who "contemplate with the eye of faith the judgments of God," who are thereby "quickened to the observance of the Divine Law".[3]

The thought that we live always under the eyes of One who sees and marks all that we do, and whose hand and judgment we cannot escape must continually be allowed to enter our mind.[4] This thought that God is a personal God infinitely close at hand should serve to check and restrain our conduct,[5] and to this must be added serious meditation on the fact that we must one day give account before the final judgment seat. Through this the Christian comes to "know the terror of the Lord" of which Paul spoke, and becomes so touched with fear that all careless living disappears.[6]

It will be seen that for Calvin there is an experience of the wrath or terror of God that a Christian man should have and should allow himself to live with. It is a holy awe of God "which makes us truly and seriously feel His anger."[7] No other fearful

[1] Serm. on Deut. 7 : 19–24, C.O. 26 : 562.
[2] Comm. on Ps. 7 : 17, C.O. 31 : 87.
[3] Comm. on Ps. 119 : 127, C.O. 32 : 271.
[4] Serm. on Job 34 : 4–10, C.O. 35 : 137. *Ce mot ici Cheminer avec Dieu emporte que l'homme s'addonne tellement au service de Dieu, qu'il pense tousiours à rendre conte, qu'il cognoisse, Celui qui m'a creé et formé, me conduit et gouverne, ie ne puis pas fuir sa main, ni eschapper de son iugement; et ainsi il faut que ie lui soye present devant ses yeux, il faut qu'il cognoisse non seulement toutes mes œuvres, mais aussi mes pensees.* Cf. serm. on Job 31 : 1–4, C.O. 34 : 634–5.
[5] Comm. on Ps. 94 : 7, C.O. 32 : 21.
[6] Comm. on 2 Cor. 5 : 11, C.O. 50 : 66. *Scire igitur terrorem Domini est esse participem illius cogitationis, quod semel reddenda sit ratio coram Christi tribunali. Nam qui hoc serio meditatur, necesse est ut tangatur timore et neglectum omnem excutiat.* Cf. comm. on Ps. 10:3, C.O. 32:110.
[7] Comm. on Ps. 90 : 11, C.O. 31 : 838.

experience in life can be compared to it. It is a sense of God that brings trembling and dread and "absorbs the whole man."[1] This experience can, of course, be specially acute when our conscience is specially awakened, as with David (Ps. 51), "his eyes and all his senses transfixed in God," "pressed down and even overwhelmed by the weight of God's judgments."[2] But it is not the wicked nor peculiarly great sinners who pass through such experiences; it is rather the faithful and the godly. The wicked indeed "are full of trouble and cry aloud, yet the Divine anger does not so penetrate into their souls as to abate their ferocity. The minds of the godly alone are wounded by the wrath of God, nor do they wait his thunderbolts (to which the reprobate hold out their hard and iron necks), but they tremble at the very moment when God lifts even His little finger. . . . The faithful alone are sensible of God's wrath, under which, when it subdues them, they acknowledge that they are nothing, and with true humility devote themselves wholly to Him."[3]

But the cultivation of fear has its dangers and its limits. Calvin recognises that there is a kind and degree of fear that instead of rousing us with real active concern for God's service merely serves to destroy all the confidence of our faith and to stupefy us.[4] Therefore, if fear is to have its true place in our Christian life, it must always rest on a firm basis of confidence in God's mercy, and it must thus never be separated from gratitude and love towards God. To contemplate solely the tokens of God's anger would plunge us into the dark death of despair, did we not at the same time discover anew that God is merciful, and thus become restored to life.[5] We cannot praise and serve God, as we should, with either our lives or our hearts merely by letting His power and justice provoke us to fear and obedience, but rather we must

[1] Comm. on Heb. 10 : 3, C.O. 55 : 138. *Itaque quisquis sibi cum Deo esse negotium reputabit, eum (nisi valde sit stupidus) serio trepidare et expavescere necesse est. Imo fieri nequit quin ille Dei sensus totum hominem absorbeat: ut nulli dolores vel cruciatus cum eo sint conferendi.*
[2] Comm. on Ps. 51 : 6, C.O. 31 : 511.
[3] Comm. on Ps. 90 : 11, C.O. 31 : 839. But here it must be remembered that to speak of God's anger is an inappropriate mode of speaking (Cf. p. 4 and esp. comm. on Ps. 74 : 1, C.O. 31 : 692).
[4] Comm. on Heb. 4 : 1, C.O. 55 : 45. *Caeterum hic nobis commendatur timor, non qui fidei certitudinem excutiat, sed tantam incutiat sollicitudinem ne securi torpeamus.*
[5] Comm. on Ps. 6 : 9–11, C.O. 31 : 78.

let Him win us to a prompt and hearty response by His goodness and mercy.[1]

4. The cultivation of gratitude by meditation on God's goodness

While we must fear, then, we must not allow ourselves to be beaten down by fear,[2] and we must remember that gratitude and love give us a more powerful incentive to resist our temptation and to serve God from the heart than merely an enforced fear.[3] In true godliness, then, reverence for God is inseparable from the love which comes from knowing His benefits.[4] It is gratitude, rather than fear, that can create in us an all-consuming desire to do the will of God,[5] gives us the power to be patient in the midst of tribulation,[6] and to overcome evil. "As long as this thought prevails in our minds, that God cares for us, it is the best means of resisting powerful temptations."[7]

Therefore we must meditate on every aspect of God's providential goodness towards us, so that we may "thereby stir ourselves up to trust, invocation, praise and love of Him."[8] for the purpose of our redemption and of all the gifts of God is to keep us entirely devoted to Him through remembering and meditating on His goodness.[9] In calling to remembrance the benefits God has showered upon us they become not only bridles to the wantonness of the flesh but also ladders by which we can ascend nearer to Him.[10]

But we can only fully benefit from the blessings God confers on us when we "exercise ourselves in constant meditation upon

[1] Cf. comm. on Rom. 12 : 1, C.O. 49 : 233–4; and on Ps. 118 : 1–4, C.O. 32 : 202.

[2] Serm. on Deut. 7 : 19–24, C.O. 26 : 562.

[3] Serm. on Job 31 : 9–15, C.O. 34 : 654. *Et au reste, que nous avisions de n'estre point seulement retenus d'une crainte forcee, pour ne point commettre l'acte de paillardise; mais voyons que Dieu nous a fait ceste grace de nous choisir pour estre temples de son sainct Esprit, et qu'il nous a attirez à soy. . . . Et d'autant que nous sommes entez au corps de nostre Seigneur Iesus Christ . . . regardons de ne luy faire point cest approbre que de nous aller ainsi polluer en telle turpitude. Voila donc comme les fideles se doivent induire à chasteté. non point d'une crainte forcee seulement, mais en cognoissant la grace et l'honneur que Dieu leur a fait.*

[4] Inst. 1 : 2 : 1.   [5] Comm. on Phil. 4 : 6, C.O. 52 : 61.

[6] Comm. on Rom. 8 : 33, C.O. 49 : 163.

[7] Comm. on Ps. 25 : 4, C.O. 31 : 252.

[8] Inst. 1 : 14 : 22.   [9] Comm. on John 5 : 14, C.O. 47 : 109.

[10] Comm. on Ps. 23 : 1, C.O. 31 : 238.

them."[1] If we keep it in remembrance, as we ought, each experience of God's goodness in stirring us up to gratitude should strengthen our hope for the future.[2] It is because we fail to consider and meditate on the experiences we have of the grace of God that we do not grow in our faith.[3] Therefore, especially when we are in trouble, our meditation should be to collect together every evidence we can of the goodness of God and remember His former loving kindnesses, both to ourselves from our very childhood, and to His people throughout history. In this way our faith will be strengthened and sustained.[4] Moreover, in the midst of adversity "it behoves us to consider that He has created us and put us in this world, imprinting His own image upon us, and giving us many tokens by which we can know that we are His children. This ought to make us lift our minds aloft to yield Him His worthy praise, and, moreover, it must serve as a spur to make us trust Him."[5] Even our food and drink and clothes, and the gifts of sight and hearing, are meant to be to our minds tokens of His goodness that can rouse us to magnify His name for His liberality.[6]

5. The place of self-examination under the Word in the discipline of the Christian life

Our meditation on the Word should be accompanied by constant self-examination. "The only way of pleasing God is for us to be severe critics of ourselves."[7] In Scripture we are taught that in order to be absolved it is not enough merely to make a confession of our guilt in words but that we must "make a rigid and formidable examination of our sins."[8] Nor is it enough to be

[1] Comm. on Phil. 1 : 6, C.O. 52 : 9. *Ergo assidua beneficiorum Dei meditatione se exerceant fideles, quo spem futuri temporis foveant et confirment.*

[2] Comm. on Ps. 63 : 5, C.O. 31 : 596; cf. serm. on Deut. 7 : 19–24, C.O. 26 : 558. *Car quand Dieu nous fait du bien, ce n'est pas seulement pour l'heure: mais il veut que cela nous serve en toute nostre vie, et que nous concluyons hardiment, que s'il a bien commencé, il poursuyvra.*

[3] Comm. on Ps. 77 : 13, C.O. 31 : 717.

[4] Comm. on Ps. 4 : 1, C.O. 31 : 59; on Ps. 22 : 10, C.O. 31 : 226; on Ps. 143 : 4, C.O. 32 : 402; and serm. on Job 3 : 20–6, C.O. 26 : 165.

[5] Serm. on Job 3 : 11–19, C.O. 33 : 153–4.

[6] Serm. on Deut. 4 : 19–24, C.O. 26 : 163.

[7] Comm. on Ps. 106 : 6, C.O. 32 : 118.

[8] Comm. on Ps. 51 : 5, C.O. 31 : 510. *Ideo discamus, non modo ore nos damnare, sed rigidum et formidable examen habere de peccatis nostris, si cupimus a Deo absolvi.*

content with formally acknowledging our share in the common sins of mankind, but "each must privately examine himself so that each can make his particular confession of his own guilt."[1] This self-examination must not be a spasmodic and momentary feature of our Christian experience but should be a duty which we perform diligently each morning and evening.[2] And when our sins are brought to our mind we must think about them and "let the bitterness of them dwell within us" in order that we may be driven not to despair but to increased watchfulness over our lives.[3] In the midst of such self-examination, to be reminded of one sin "should be the means of recalling others to our recollection until we are brought to prostrate ourselves before God in deep self-abasement."[4] And, further, we must be led to think about the sins of the fathers in which we too are involved and which are visited upon their children unto the fourth generation.[5]

But in this matter of self-examination we have no natural ability nor willingness to come to true self-knowledge. We may be infected before God and stinking like lepers, but we do not know it. We can throw our anchor to the bottom of the sea, but God alone can sound our hearts.[6] We cannot trust our own conscience in this matter, for even the saints are so entangled in the snares of Satan that they are unconscious even of their grosser sins, quite apart from the hundred lesser sins of ignorance and inadventure.[7] Left to our conscience alone we are full of guile and we cover over our nakedness with leaves.[8]

Therefore if we would truly know ourselves we must present

---

[1] Comm. on Ps. 65 : 4, C.O. 31 : 604.

[2] Serm. on Deut. 9 : 6–7, C.O. 26 : 657. *Il nous faut entrer en cognoissance de nos pechez; et non pas seulement pour un coup, mais qu'un chacun s'appareille a un tel examen, et soir et matin, et quand nous aurons cogneu une faute, que nous entrions en cognoissance de l'autre.* Cf. serm. on Deut. 9 : 20–4, C.O. 26 : 706.

[3] Serm. on Deut. 6 : 15–19, C.O. 26 : 476–7.

[4] Comm. on Ps. 51 : 8, C.O. 31 : 515.

[5] Serm. on Deut. 9 : 6–7, C.O. 26 : 662–3. *Et voila comme il nous est expedient de penser aux pechez qui ont esté commis devant que nous fussions nais: que nous regardions: Helas! il est vray que i'estoye à naistre de ce temps-la: mais que sera-ce si nos peres ont failli, et que de nostre part nous soyons mis avec eux? Car il est dit que Dieu recueille l'iniquité des peres iusques en la quatriesme generation.*

[6] Serm. on Acts 1 : 4–5, C.O. 49 : 603.

[7] Comm. on Ps. 19 : 12, C.O. 31 : 204.

[8] Comm. on Ps. 32 : 2, C.O. 31 : 317. *Quisquis ergo se non examinat coram Deo quin potius Dei iudicium fugitans, vel se abdit in tenebras, vel foliis obtegit: secum dolose agit, et cum ipso Deo.*

ourselves before God, praying to Him to sound our hearts.[1] It is only when we are conscious of ourselves as in the presence of God, whom nothing escapes, and who sees close at hand with intimate detail all our ways, and counts all our steps, overlooking none of our deeds or thoughts, that we begin to form a true estimate of our sins.[2] Moreover, in the presence of God we must examine ourselves not according to our own standards but according to the teaching of the Word as to what is sin in the sight of God.[3]

Self-examination is a necessary discipline in the Christian life. It should destroy our peaceful self-confidence, and make us groan within ourselves at our imperfections,[4] for in the process we denude ourselves of every drop of pride or presumption and of anything in which we can glory.[5] Only through self-knowledge can we become truly humbled. Calvin quotes Augustine's saying that "the whole humility of man consists in the knowledge of himself."[6] He also suggests that the popular proverb "He who knows himself much, praises himself little," would be better amended to ". . . praises himself not at all, but is rather annihilated in the

---

[1] Serm. on 2 Sam. 3 : 28 f. p. 76. *Presentons nous a Dieu, afin qu'il nous sonde, comme il est dit au Pseaume: "Seigneur, que tu examines mes reins."*

[2] Serm. on Job 31 : 1–4, C.O. 34 : 634–5. Calvin, noting especially how the Psalmists communed with themselves at night upon their bed when they were apart from other men, recommends solitude for self-examination, for in solitude our thoughts are not distracted or deceived through intercourse with men, and there is less to hinder our thinking without disguise about our faults (comm. on Ps. 4 : 5, C.O. 31 : 61–2). "Solitude enables men to collect themselves together, thoroughly to examine themselves and to speak to themselves seriously without any others looking on." (Comm. on Ps. 77 : 6, C.O. 31 : 713. Cf. also on Ps. 66 : 3, C.O. 31 : 611).

[3] Serm. on Luke 2 : 25–8, C.O. 46 : 372. *Apprenons donc, de tout ce que Dieu nous aura enseigné par sa parole, de le recevoir en toute humilité, et que nous ne facions point comme ces gaudisseurs qui diront. He, c'est un peche veniel, il n'y a pas là si grande importance. Dieu a ouvert sa bouche sacree pour declarer, Voyla qui me plaist, voyla que ie condamne: et cependant les hommes viendront ietter de leur gosier puant ces blasphemes. Ho cela ne vaut pas le parler, cela n'est pas de grande consequence, cela est bien petit. Est-ce ainsi que nous prisons la maiesté de Dieu?*

[4] Serm. on Luke 1 : 5–9, C.O. 46 : 18. *Quand donc nous voudrons nous conformer à la volonte de nostre Dieu, il est certain que nous sonderons toutes nos pensees les plus profondes, et toutes nos affections: et quand nous aurons trouvé quelque chose à redire là dedans, nous gemirons, voyans que nous sommes encores bien eslongnez de la perfection, à laquelle il nous faut tendre.*

[5] Serm. on Deut. 7 : 5–8, C.O. 26 : 519.

[6] Comm. on Ps. 9 : 20–1, C.O. 31 : 108. Self-knowledge comes not only through the discipline of self-examination but also through the chastisements with which God visits us and others in this life. Cf. ibid. and serm. on Deut. 9 : 1–9, C.O. 26 : 644. *Ainsi donc voulons-nous estre despouillez de toute vaine gloire? Advisons de nous mirer en ceux que Dieu punit, et contre lesquels il use de sa rigueur extreme. Valons-nous mieux qu'eux?*

confusion of his shame."[1] But far from making us fall into care-lessness or despair, such inward "groaning" over our past life should stimulate us to repentance and to new thankful effort in gratitude to God.[2]

The benefits of self-examination is a theme to which Calvin often returns. Self-examination should prepare us better to re-ceive the grace of God.[3] If it leads to our finding anything good within us, it should lead to our celebrating the free and undeserved goodness of God for such a wonderful gift.[4] It should make us realise that we ourselves are very near to the evils we sometimes have to condemn and rebuke in others, and therefore while hating evil the more, it can make us far more mild and gentle in our judgment if we examine ourselves before we judge other men.[5] It should help to prepare us for the final judgment, for it is better to face our sins now than to wait till God opens the books, when it will be too late for us to condemn ourselves.[6] It should enable us to prevent ourselves from being overwhelmed by our tempta-tions, for it will give us a better knowledge of where we are weak and of how weak we are, and it will enable us to eradicate those evil affections through which Satan is able to gain possession of our lives.[7]

[1] Serm. on Deut. 9 : 1–6, C.O. 26 : 645.

[2] Comm. on 1 Pet. 4 : 3, C.O. 55 : 271; serm. on Deut. 10 : 15–17, C.O. 27 : 55. *Et toutesfois nous devrions estre attentifs, et de soir, et de matin de penser à nos fautes passees: non point pour estre nonchallons, ou pour en tomber en desespoir: mais afin de gemir, afin d'estre plus soigneux de cheminer autrement que nous n'avons point fait, afin de remercier Dieu de sa bonté, d'autant qu'il luy a pleu de nous corriger.*

[3] Serm. on Deut. 7 : 5–8, C.O. 26 : 519. *Quand donc un tel examen sera fait: voila les hommes qui seront disposez à recevoir la grace de Dieu, et de l'en glorifier, quand ils l'auront receuĕ.*

[4] Comm. on Ps. 8 : 4–5, C.O. 31 : 91.

[5] Serm. on Gal. 6 : 1–2, C.O. 51 : 66; and on Gal. 6 : 2–5, C.O. 51 : 77.

[6] Serm. on Deut. 9 : 20–4, C.O. 26 : 706. *Qu'un chacun regarde à ses pechez et n'attendons pas que Dieu œuvre ses registres, comme il fera au dernier iour, et ce sera trop tard de passer alors condamnation: mais auiourd'huy qu'il nous adiourne par sa parolle, qu'il nous advertit, qu'il nous faut penser à nos fautes, qu'un chacun se vienne rendre comme un povre malfaicteur devant son iuge.*

[7] Serm. on Deut. 7 : 5–8, C.O. 26 : 510. *Ainsi il n'y a rien meilleur, que de cognoistre nostre infirmité, et en la cognoissant user du remede que Dieu nous donne. Si un homme sent son cerveau debile, et qu'il ne puisse porter trois verres de vin qu'il ne soit surprins: s'il boit sans discretion, n'est-il pas comme un porceau? . . . Ne doit-il pas penser au vice qui est en luy pour le prevenir?* Cf. serm. on 2 Sam. 3 : 26–7, pp. 72–3.

6. Self-discipline and fasting

We have seen that for Calvin "self-denial" primarily means communion by faith with the death of Christ through the Holy Spirit, for it is through such communion that we are given the power to die inwardly with Christ and to mortify concupiscence. As this communion with the death of Christ is nurtured within the life of the Church, there is, however, also a place for responding, by the deliberate discipline of the "flesh," to the grace that God is seeking to work within us. We must not only hate ourselves, we must also discipline ourselves. Even though a Christian is regenerated and has a new nature, he dare not imagine that he may now follow his "natural" impulses, for the old nature is always too ready to assert itself. He must continue always to keep "nature" under strict and deliberate control. "Our nature drags everything back, and we will never love goodness unless we are made to do so by force or violence. Therefore men must enforce and constrain themselves to do violence against a mortal enemy when they want to progress in goodness. And who are our enemies? Truly the Devil is the chief . . . but at the same time all our own thoughts, all our own affections, all our desires are all deadly enemies that labour to bring us to destruction."[1] We have, then, a duty to "force and constrain ourselves." We must "struggle with" ourselves and "do violence to opposing desires,"[2] suppress our natural feelings,[3] and sedulously keep ourselves from our iniquity.[4]

All this involves the deliberate practice of self-discipline. We should wish to be angels so that our energies need not be directed from the service of God to such self-centred effort, but since we are not so, we must "learn to force ourselves and to hold ourselves as prisoners, even though it goes entirely against the grain to do so. Let us indeed go even further, that God may win the upper hand of us."[5] One aspect of the yoke which Christ invited His

[1] Serm. on Gal. 5 : 14–18, C.O. 51 : 28. Cf. on pp. 57–61.
[2] Comm. on Phil. 2 : 21, C.O. 52 : 38; cf. on Rom. 12 : 14, C.O. 49 : 243; on 1 Thess. 4 : 5, C.O. 52 : 161; on 1 Tim. 6 : 7, C.O. 52 : 326.
[3] Inst. 3 : 7 : 4.
[4] Comm. on Ps. 18 : 24–5, C.O. 31 : 182.
[5] Serm. on Gal. 5 : 14–18, C.O. 51 : 29. Calvin also speaks of our need to "hold ourselves in" (*se retenir*). Serm. on Job 2 : 11–13, C.O. 33 : 130; cf. serm. on 2 Sam. 1 : 17 ff., pp. 10–11. *Ne laissons pas de nous tenir en bride courte.*

disciples to bear was "to train them under the burden of discipline (*exercere sub disciplinae onere*)" with a view to enabling them to engage in the warfare of the flesh.[1] Christians therefore must "diligently labour in training and mortifying the flesh, so that it may appear that they are controlled by the study of piety."[2] Certainly Calvin would agree that Christian virtues are the fruit of the indwelling of the Spirit of Christ in the heart and that to acquire them we must yield our hearts to the influence of the Spirit yet this is not the only aspect of the matter. Since a virtue such as meekness is so difficult to attain we must labour for it with "the more intense application (*intentiore studio*)."[3]

This habitual process of holding ourselves in check and curbing our desires is true fasting. "That sobriety and temperance which ought to be habitual (*perpetua*) in Christians is a kind of fasting."[4] Calvin recommends the deliberate cultivation of temperance by such voluntary fasting.[5] But besides this constant process of fasting there is occasionally place for a more definite exercise of fasting after the example of the men of the Old Testament who fasted with sackcloth and ashes when they were visited by calamities and signs of God's displeasure. We do not need to copy them in sackcloth and ashes, "yet the exercise of fasting remains in force amongst us at this day."[6] Such fasting is a "solemn expression of penitence with a view to deprecating God's anger."[7] But, on the whole, fasting is a secondary activity[8] and can be dangerous. Where austerity of life is practised, men always tend to delude themselves and to think it achieves more than it does, for after all "Christ did not lead so austere a life as John the Baptist—was He therefore any whit inferior?"[9] We must keep fasting in its proper

[1] Comm. on Matt. 11 : 29, C.O. 45 : 322.
[2] Comm. on Rom. 8 : 1, C.O. 49 : 136.
[3] Comm. on Rom. 12 : 14, C.O. 49 : 243.
[4] Comm. on 1 Cor. 7 : 5, C.O. 49 : 404.
[5] Serm. on Deut. 9 : 8–12, C.O. 26 : 672. *Car quand nous ne ferons point de Karesme, il y a les iusnes qui nous sont commandez par l'Escriture saincte: c'est assavoir en premier lieu attrempance, et sobrieté en toute nostre vie, que nous ne gourmandions point un iour pour estre sobres l'autre: mais que nous usions moderement des biens que Dieu nous donne. Que ceux qui en ont à largesse n'abusent point de cela à superfluité: mais que nous iusnions, voire nous constraignant d'une bride volontaire tant au boire et au manger, qu'aux autres choses où nous pourrions commettre exces, et intemperance, que nous ayons tousiours une abstinence volontaire.*
[6] Comm. on Ps. 35 : 14, C.O. 31 : 352.
[7] Comm. on 1 Cor. 7 : 5, C.O. 49 : 404; cf. on Ps. 102 : 4–5, C.O. 32 : 63.
[8] Comm. on Luke 2 : 37, C.O. 45 : 96
[9] Comm. on 1 Tim. 4 : 8, C.O. 52 : 299.

place. It is a subordinate aid to prayer. It is good if it helps us to pray better. Fasting must not be indulged in merely for the sake of being austere. "It is pleasing to God only in so far as it is directed to another end, that is, to train us to abstinence, to subdue the lust of the flesh, to excite us to earnestness in prayer and to testify our repentance."[1]

[1] Comm. on Matt. 6 : 16, C.O. 45 : 204; cf. comm. on Luke 2 : 37, C.O. 45 : 96; serm. on Deut. 9 : 8–12, C.O. 26 : 672. *Quand nostre Seigneur nous afflige, ou que nous sommes en quelque difficulté, que nous recourions aux iusnes, voire pour nous picquer à prieres, et oraisons; et que cela soit pour mieux eslever nos coeurs en haut, et pour nous humilier, rendons tesmoignage de nos fautes devant Dieu.*

Chapter IV

Adherence and loyalty to the visible Church

1. We must adhere loyally to the visible Church in spite of its defects

SINCE the individual is dependent on the Church for his sanctification, it becomes his duty to adhere loyally to the visible Church. He may assume that there is an "invisible Church which is manifest to the eye of God only." Calvin himself finds that Scripture in referring to the Church sometimes speaks of this Church "as it really is before God—the Church into which none are admitted but those who by the gift of adoption are sons of God, and by sanctification of the Spirit true members of Christ."[1] But this invisible Church cannot be thought of as something in anyway divorced from the "whole body of mankind scattered throughout the world who profess to worship one God and Christ, who by Baptism are initiated into the faith, by partaking the Lord's Supper profess unity in true doctrine and charity, agree to hold the Word of the Lord, and observe the ministry which Christ has appointed for preaching of it."[2] For all practical purposes membership of the invisible Church is inseparable from membership of the visible Church which Calvin thus carefully defines. To believe in the Holy Catholic Church "relates in some measure to the external Church," involves cultivating its communion, submitting duly to its authority and conducting ourselves as sheep of the flock.[3]

We must adhere loyally to such a Church in spite of all its defects. Even although the Church includes in its membership those whose sincerity and the reality of whose faith we may have good reason to doubt, we must accept them as brethren if the Church accepts them,[4] and if they perform outwardly the duties expected of Church members.[5] Calvin has much to say in warn-

---

[1] Inst. 4 : 1 : 7. [2] Ibid. [3] Inst. 4 : 1 : 3 and 7.
[4] Inst. 4 : 1 : 9. [5] Inst. 4 : 1 : 8.

ing to those who are tempted to withdraw from the Church because of its impurity, the faults of its members, or because they do not agree with the way it is governed. Christ told the parable of the wheat and the tares "to restrain and moderate the zeal of those who fancy that they are not at liberty to join in a society with any but pure angels."[1] "If we feel disgust at being associated by Baptism and the Lord's Supper with vile men, and regard our connexion with them as a sort of stain upon us, we ought immediately to descend into ourselves and to search without flattery our own evils. Such an examination will make us willing to be washed in the same fountain as the most impure."[2] There always have been, and there always will be, "master builders" in the Church who seem to try to subvert the rule of Christ, but "it would certainly indicate a sad state of the Church if she never had any pastors except those who were deadly enemies of her welfare." We cannot say that the leaders of the Church have in every age been continually blind! And if we have no excuse for separating from the Church when the builders build wrongly, much less will we be excusable when the master builders build well. Moreover, Calvin adds, since it is God who superintends the government of the Church whether it be wise or unwise, "it is unreasonable to expect that the Church must be governed according to our understanding of matters, inasmuch as that which is miraculous surpasses our comprehension."[3]

Therefore all of us, however exalted we are in the world, must divest ourselves of pride and become "obedient children of the Church."[4] The ministry of the Word and Sacraments cannot but have beneficial results if it is received by faith even within a Church and from the hands of the ministry in which we see many faults, for the ordinances of God are too great and powerful to be deprived of their efficacy by the fault of some ungodly men.[5] The fact that amidst "such a conflux of evils" as at Corinth Paul recognised a Church to exist means that "the faults of individuals do

---

[1] Comm. on Matt. 13 : 39, C.O. 45 : 369.
[2] Comm. on Matt. 9 : 12, C.O. 45 : 250; cf. Inst. 4 : 1 : 15, "Paul does not require that we should examine others, or . . . the whole Church, but that each should examine himself."
[3] Comm. on Ps. 118 : 25–6, C.O. 32 : 212.
[4] Comm. on Ps. 48 : 10, C.O. 31 : 471.
[5] Inst. 4 : 1 : 9, 10, 16; C.O. 9 : 26; comm. on John 4 : 2, C.O. 47 : 78.

not prevent a society that has the genuine marks of religion from being recognised as a Church."[1]

2. Membership of the Church involves deliberate separation from the evil of the world

Since the Church is an elect community separated from the world[2] and with a quite distinctive life of its own, it is obvious that in adhering to the Church we must in daily life deliberately to some extent separate ourselves from the fellowship of the ungodly who live apart from the Church, and seek constantly the fellowship and company of those who fear God.[3] "It is befitting that we keep ourselves undefiled from all uncleanliness that we may not pollute the sanctuary of God."[4] Yet we must associate to some extent with the ungodly if we are to remain in this world at all, for the world is filled with them. "We eat the same bread, we breathe the same air," and God means us to try as far as possible to lead them into the way of salvation.[5] Yet while we cannot avoid ordinary intercourse (*commercium*) with the ungodly, we must avoid "participation (*participatio*) in works in which Christians cannot lawfully have fellowship (*communicare*)."[6] We can converse but not commune with them nor involve ourselves in intimacy with them.[7]

Calvin's basic conviction on this matter seems to be that if we have any such intimate fellowship with the ungodly they are much

---

[1] Comm. on 2 Cor. 1 : 2, C.O. 50 : 9. *Notandum semper, ut ecclesiam agnoscat, ubi tanta erat malorum colluvies. Non enim quorundam vitia impediunt quominus ecclesia censeatur quae veras religionis tesseras habet.*

[2] Cf. pp. 202–5.

[3] Serm. on 1 Cor. 10 : 25–30, C.O. 49 : 691. *En somme notons de ce passage, que songneusement les enfans de Dieu se doyvent retirer de toute mauvaise compagnie, de peur d'en tirer quelque mauvaise infection. Et là dessus ils taschent de pratiquer ce qui est contenu au Pseaume 15, c'est à sçavoir d'honorer les gens craignans Dieu et d'aimer leur compagnie, afin que nous y profitions: et quant aux meschans, et ceux qui se mocquent de Dieu, de les avoir en mespris comme des brebis rongneuses qui sont pour infecter tout le troupeau.*

[4] Comm. on 2 Cor. 6 : 7, C.O. 50 : 83.

[5] Ibid.; and on 2 Cor. 6 : 14, C.O. 50 : 81: and serm. on Deut. 7 : 1–4, C.O. 26 : 506; serm. on 2 Sam. 3 : 12–13, p. 65.

[6] Comm. on 2 Cor. 6 : 14 and 17, C.O. 50 : 81 and 83.

[7] Serm. on Deut. 7 : 1–4, C.O. 26 : 506. *Il nous faut donc habiter avec eux. Mais en quelle sorte? Que ce soit avec telle mesure, que nous n'ayons point accointance, ne de privauté avec eux. . . . Nous devons converser avec les meschans. Mais de nous envelopper parmi eux, d'avoir accointance ni privauté: c'est manifestement tenter Dieu.*

more likely to influence us for evil than we are to influence them for good.[1] Our main reason for maintaining such separation from the society of the ungodly is simply that it is dangerous.

We are already infected enough with evil without drawing more infection.[2] Our battle with evil in our weakness is already desperate enough without allying ourselves with those who can only help us to lose. We are already cold and unenthusiastic enough without mixing with those who can only discourage us further.[3] Therefore let us not deceive ourselves by imagining we are stronger than we really are—as if God did not know us better than we know ourselves when He warns us of our weakness![4]

Therefore Calvin advises us as Christ's sheep not to "howl with the wolves."[5] He can be very specific on this subject. We must

[1] Serm. on Deut. 7 : 1–4, C.O. 26 : 506. *Voici Dieu qui nous admonneste de la fragilité qui est en nous, et nous dit que si nous sommes meslez parmi les meschans, qu'ils nous attireront à mal plustost que nous ne les pourrons pas reduire à bien: que donc il nous faut garder de leur compagnie.*

[2] Serm. on 1 Cor. 10 : 25–30, C.O. 49 : 690. *Ainsi donc S. Paul parlant de frequenter parmi les infideles, dit qu'il ne le peut pas defendre simplement, pour dire, Voyla un peché mortel: mais tant y a que par conseil il monstre que c'est une chose dangereuse, et qu'on en doit user sobrement: et qu'il est possible de s'en abstenir, on le doit faire. Et pourquoy? Car quand nous tacherons de attirer l'infection, qui est desia par trop en nous, ce sera un merveilleux làbyrinthe que nostre train.* Calvin often seems to argue that even though there is no law forbidding any particular indulgence or pleasure, it is wrong if it is at all dangerous. We have an instinct within us for stumbling (*une semence de trebuscher*). So weak and perverse is our nature that if we have no occasion to fall we will go out of our way to seek one. Indeed we will hurl ourselves down to destruction on the very ladders God has given us for climbing up to heaven (serm. on Deut. 4 : 19–24, C.O. 26 : 162). It is for this reason that Calvin warns his hearers against such things as the dances and games (*ieux*). *Si les hommes sentent en eux une telle fragilité, il ne faut point qu'ils cerchent les occasions: car si un homme se va ietter au milieu du feu à son escient, ne bataille-il pas manifestement contre Dieu?* (Serm. on Deut. 7 : 22–6, C.O. 26 : 579). Therefore it is no use asking Calvin where such things are forbidden in Holy Scripture. A drunkard could also ask, "Where is wine-drinking forbidden?" Such an approach would justify drunkenness for wine-drinking is not forbidden. The obvious answer is, "You can take what you can hold." But Calvin obviously regards dancing, etc. as a universally dangerous pastime leading men to an excess they cannot avoid, and this is why it is generally wrong in his eyes (serm. on 1 Cor. 10 : 25–30, C.O. 49 : 689).

[3] Serm. on Deut. 20 : 2–9, C.O. 27 : 614. Calvin especially warns his congregation against mixing with those who indulge in blasphemous or unchaste talk or sing dissolute songs (Evil communications corrupt good manners), no matter with how much brilliance and wit and conviviality. We must flee from such like devils (it is not quite clear whether they or we are compared to devils!). Who would bare and present his throat if he saw someone with an open dagger in his hand—or go in search of someone to murder his body ? Why then should we mix with those who in such a way are out to murder our souls? (Serm. on Eph. 4 : 29–30, C.O. 51 : 647; on 1 Cor. 10 : 25–30, C.O. 49 : 690; on Deut. 7 : 22–6, C.O. 26 : 579.)

[4] Serm. on Deut. 7 : 1–6, C.O. 26 : 507.

[5] Comm. on Ps. 12 : 2, C.O. 31 : 127; and on Ps. 17 : 4, C.O. 31 : 161.

repel and keep ourselves aloof from the wild and execrable opinions that prevail in the world.[1] We must "abstain from having any association with or giving any consent or advice or assistance to" any wickedness—for this means having fellowship (*communicare*) with the unclean works of darkness.[2] We must avoid flattering or accommodating ourselves to or giving honour to the persons of any evil men in authority, even if we have to obey them, for not to reprove such is also fellowship with darkness.[3] And, above all, we must avoid plunging ourselves into evil and renouncing God by contracting any marriage-contract with anyone who might despise Him.[4] And in avoiding bad company we must remember the strength and courage that can come to us through the friendship and leadership of those who have already proved themselves in the service of God.[5]

We must seek to ensure that the Church itself is a community cleansed as far as possible from evil. Even though we must not separate ourselves from the Church because of its impurity, and may not have the power to cleanse it, nevertheless "it is our duty to desire her purity."[6] "It is no new thing if we see in our own day the Church of God polluted by profane men. We ought, however, to beseech God quickly to purge His house and not to leave His holy temple exposed to swine and dogs as if it were a dung-pit."[7] Our zeal for the welfare of the Church as the holy habitation of God should stir us up to remove all the abuses which disfigure and defile it.[8] Not only "public care" but also the private efforts of each man in his own sphere of Church life are required if the Church is to be purified.[9] History teaches only too clearly the grave dangers that beset the Church when she "cherishes within her bosom" hypocrisy and wickedness. Nevertheless we must soberly

---

[1] Comm. on Ps. 10 : 14, C.O. 31 : 116–17.

[2] Comm. on Eph. 5 : 11, C.O. 51 : 217.

[3] Comm. on Ps. 15 : 4, C.O. 31 : 145–6.

[4] Serm. on Deut. 7 : 1–4, C.O. 26 : 506–7. *Et sur tout quand on contractera alliance de mariage: n'est-ce pas comme se plonger au mal? Si on voit quelque contemteur de Dieu, si on voit sa fille qui sera semblable, et on s'en ira là accoupler n'est-ce pas comme si on renonçoit pleinement à Dieu?* (p. 507).

[5] Serm. on Deut. 20 : 2–9, C.O. 27 : 615.

[6] Comm. on Ps. 22 : 25, C.O. 31 : 233.

[7] Comm. on Ps. 10 : 16, C.O. 31 : 119.

[8] Comm. on Ps. 118 : 19 f., C.O. 32 : 208.

[9] Comm. on Ps. 26 : 5, C.O. 31 : 267. Cf. comm. on Ps. 15 : 1, C.O. 31 : 143. *Simul tamen iubentur fideles, pro se quisque dare operam, ut a corruptelis purgetur Dei ecclesia.*

acknowledge that God alone can truly cleanse the Church, and He will do so in His own time. "We must bear with the evils which it is not in our power to correct, until all things become ripe and the proper season for purging the Church arrives."[1]

3. Membership of the Church involves witness with the whole Church before the world

Our adherence to the visible Church, and our separation from the world is bound to involve us in an obligation, along with the whole Church, to witness to and to serve all men in the name of Jesus Christ. We are elected and separated within the Church, not merely for the purpose of our own individual sanctification and salvation, but in order that we might be witnesses. "We are called by the Lord on this condition, that everyone should afterwards strive to lead others to the truth, to restore the wandering to the right way, to extend a helping hand to the fallen, to win over those that are without."[2] In Baptism we are pledged to allegiance to Him before men.[3] Therefore our separation from the world should in no way make us proud in our isolation or our privilege, but should make us tireless in toiling to share our faith with others. We should have our arms extended as our Heavenly Father has, towards those outside.[4] The Christian who is indebted to God's mercy is bound to become, like the psalmist, "the loud herald of the grace of God" to all men.[5] We are reconciled to God "in order that each should endeavour to make his brethren partakers of the same benefit."[6] The light of "heavenly doctrine" is given us not

[1] Comm. on Ps. 15 : 1, C.O. 31 : 143. But cf. comm. on Matt. 13 : 24 ff., C.O. 45 : 368, where Calvin says we must not extend this principle of toleration (that what cannot be corrected must be endured) to "wicked errors which infect the purity of the faith."

[2] Comm. on Heb. 10 : 24, C.O. 55 : 132.

[3] Inst. 4 : 15 : 3.

[4] Serm. on Eph. 4 : 15–16, C.O. 51 : 583. *Que donc nous ne soyons point separez d'avec le monde de nostre bon gré: mais que nous ayons comme les bras tendus pour amener tous ceux qui se viendront rendre dociles à l'obeissance de Dieu, à ce que nous puissions avoir une mesme foy ensemble, et que nous mettions peine à cela. Et c'est aussi pourquoy sainct Paul nous declare ici que la foy et obeissance que nous rendons à Dieu, n'est pas pour enfler nostre cœur de fierté, en sorte que nous reiettions les autres, et que chacun se prise et se contente de soy: mais c'est à fin que nous ensuyvions l'exemple de nostre Pere celeste, d'autant qu'il convie à soy ceux qui en estoyent eslongnez.*

[5] Comm. on Ps. 51 : 16, C.O. 31 : 521.

[6] Comm. on Ps. 32 : 8, C.O. 31 : 322.

only that we may judge ourselves and guide ourselves, but also "that we may show it to others."[1]

Such witness should also be the outcome of our desire for the glory of God.[2] To remain careless about bringing our neighbours and unbelievers to Christ is not only to be careless of God's honour and to set limits to His Kingdom but is also to limit the scope and the power of the death of Christ which was for the whole world.[3] Therefore our witness to the Gospel must be borne to all mankind. "A true Christian will not be content with walking by himself in the right way but will try to draw the whole world into the same way."[4]

Our witness is given not simply as isolated individuals but within and through the witnessing fellowship of the Church. The Church is the sphere in and through which the witness of Christ's people to Himself is most potently given. Calvin can speak in exalted terms about the influence which the "examples of the saints" within the Church should have upon us.[5] "The virtues of the saints are so many testimonies to confirm us, that we, relying on them as our guides and associates, ought to go onward to God with more alacrity."[6] To reverence and love and imitate the servants of God is an essential part of the "study of godliness."[7] To see them triumph in the midst of suffering should be a pledge to us of our certainty of victory.[8] In spite of what he says elsewhere about the hiddenness and obscurity of the new divine life in the believer, Calvin can go the length of saying that in the examples of the saints we see the image of God and that in the

---

[1] Comm. on Phil. 2 : 16, C.O. 52 : 35.

[2] Comm. on Ps. 51 : 14–15, C.O. 31 : 520. *Sed huc etiam impellere eos debet pietatis studium et zelus gloriae Dei, ut omnes, quantum in se est, eiusdem gratiae participes faciant.*

[3] Serm. on 1 Tim. 2 : 5–6, C.O. 53 : 161–2. *Notons que tous ceux qui ne tiennent conte d'amener leurs prochains au chemin de salut, ceux qui ne soucient d'amener aussi les povres incredules, et qui les laissent aller à perdition, monstrent bien qu'ils ne portent nul honneur à Dieu, et qu'ils diminuent la puissance de son empire entant qu'en eux est, et qu'ils luy veulent assigner des bornes, afin qu'il ne domine point sur tout le monde: et d'avantage qu'ils obscurcissent en partie la vertu de la mort et passion de nostre Seigneur Iesus Christ, qu'ils amoindrissent la dignité qui luy a esté donnee de Dieu son Pere.*

[4] Serm. on Job 4 : 1–6, C.O. 33 : 181.

[5] Comm. on 2 Cor. 1 : 6, C.O. 50 : 12. *Hic succurrere nobis debent sanctorum exempla, quae nos animosiores reddant.*

[6] Comm. on Heb. 12 : 1, C.O. 55 : 170.

[7] Comm. on Ps. 15 : 4, C.O. 31 : 146. . . . *ad pietatis studium.*

[8] Comm. on Phil. 1 : 14, C.O. 52 : 14. *Hac freti, plus solito audere debemus, iam in persona fratrum pignus victoriae nostrae habentes.*

righteousness and holiness which we see in the servants of God "the brightness of God's Spirit shines forth. It is the will of God that even in this world there should be conspicuous marks and, as it were, visible escutcheons of His glory which may serve to conduct us to Himself. The faithful, therefore, bear His image that by their example we may be stirred up to meditation upon the heavenly life."[1] Not only the examples of the living saints, but the past history of those who have gone before us in the Church ought to stir us with new courage and faith. Calvin quotes Tertullian's dictum that "The blood of the martyrs is the seed of the Church," and adds: "The slaughter of so many martyrs has been attended at least with this advantage that they have been as it were so many seals by which the Gospel has been sealed in our hearts."[2] It is our duty, moreover, not only to profit from this means of grace, but continually to add our own witness and testimony in thanksgiving before the assembly of God's people. "It is highly necessary that everyone should publicly celebrate his experience of the grace of God as an example for others to confide in Him."[3]

4. Though our lives must seal our witness, we cannot avoid misunderstanding and shame

Though Calvin always emphasises that the Church must continually witness to men by proclaiming the Word, he acknowledges the futility of our trying to witness merely by spoken words if at the same time our confession of His name does not come from the heart.[4] If we are to convince men, "we must show in very deed

---

[1] Comm. on Ps. 16 : 3, C.O. 31 : 151. *Sanctos autem qui in terra sunt, diserte exprimit, quia Deus etiam in hoc mundo illustres gloriae suae notas exstare vult, quibus nos ad se deducat. Ac ideo fideles imaginem eius gestant, ut nos suo exemplo incitent ad coelestis vitae meditationem. Eadem causa praeclaros vocat, vel magnificos, quia iustitia ac sanctitate, in quibus relucet spiritus eius claritas, nihil pretiosius esse nobis debet.*

[2] Comm. on Phil. 1 : 7, C.O. 52 : 11.

[3] Comm. on Ps. 26 : 12, C.O. 31 : 270. *Nec vero tantum dicit se privatim fore beneficii memorem, sed publicos etiam conventus testes fore, quia ad exemplum interest, quam quisque expertus est Dei gratiam, palam celebrari.* Cf. comm. on Ps. 115 : 2, C.O. 32 : 183.

[4] Serm. on Deut. 32 : 1–4, C.O. 28 : 661. *Nous sommes ici enseignez, que les principal que nous ayons à faire en toute nostre vie, c'est de magnifier le nom de Dieu, et de prescher ses louanges, non seulement de bouche pour inciter un chacun à le louer d'un accord avec nous, mais de coeur, qu'un chacun s'employe là, et qu'on s'y exerce.*

that we have not spoken superficially (*comme dehors*—the old translation gives "from the teeth outwards!), but that the word which has come out of our mouth retains at the same time its root within our hearts."[1] Moreover, our outward lives must seal our witness by word and heart, "for this is the proof we ought to give of our faith, and of the hope we have of eternal life. If we do nothing but speak, that is a very meagre thing. But when a man conducts himself so that others see that his profession to serve God is made in good earnest, and that he lives out his teaching— that is something convincing and sure."[2] Calvin was also very conscious of the need for the witness of the Church to be borne not only by the ministers of the Word but also by the laymen under every kind of circumstances and in a multitude of varied ways. "A more public confession of faith, no doubt, is demanded from teachers than from persons in private station. Besides, all are not endued with an equal measure of faith, and in proportion as anyone excels in the gifts of the Spirit he ought to go before others by his example. But there is no believer whom the Son of God does not require to be His witness. In what place, at what time, with what degree of frequency, in what manner, and to what extent, we ought to profess our faith, cannot easily be determined by a fixed rule, but we must consider the occasion that not one of us may fail to discharge his duty at the proper time. We must also ask from the Lord the Spirit of wisdom and courage, that under His direction we may know what is proper, and may boldly follow whatever we shall have ascertained that He commands us."[3]

If we are going to be witnesses we must seek to have a good reputation with men. "It were indeed desirable that our integrity should be approved of by men, not so much on our own account as for the edification of our brethren."[4] We should seek to stand high in the esteem of the outside world provided that we seek this reputation for the glory of God and are always prepared to bear shame as well for the sake of our faith. Calvin quotes Augustine with approval: "He that is regardless of fame is cruel, because it is not less necessary before our neighbour than a good conscience

[1] Serm. on Job 4 : 1–6, C.O. 33 : 181.
[2] Serm. on 1 Tim. 6 : 12–14, C.O. 53 : 603.
[3] Comm. on Matt. 10 : 32, C.O. 45 : 291.
[4] Comm. on Ps. 69 : 5–6, C.O. 31 : 639.

is before God."[1] A Christian who is of good reputation and who is known by his fellow men to seek their good can, like Abraham, have a strong influence on the outsider.[2] Moreover, though it is a difficult task, we must not underestimate the influence we can have on the ungodly, for we are apt to conclude too hastily that attempts to reclaim them are hopeless.[3]

Yet here Calvin realistically and frankly recognises the difficulties. It is impossible that all men should speak well of us. After we have done all in our power to win men's approval they may misconstrue and pervert all our words and actions,[4] for there are plenty of dogs going about whose bites and barks we cannot avoid.[5] We must realise that "to be ill-spoken-of for doing well is something which daily befalls the saints."[6] Moreover, the Church in its witness must be content to take its share in the misunderstanding and scorn that were the lot of Christ Himself in bearing His own witness during His earthly life. Men refused to accept His witness, not simply because they hated His doctrine, but also because they could see no manifest glory or divinity in Him. "He had no form or comeliness" (Isa. 53 : 2). Commenting on this text, Calvin says, "This must be understood to relate not merely to the person of Christ, . . . but to His whole Kingdom, which in the eyes of men had no beauty, no comeliness, no splendour."[7] This means that even in its attempt to bear witness to the glory of Christ, the Church must at the same time be content to share in the deformity that marred and obscured the

---

[1] Comm. on 2 Cor. 8 : 21, C.O. 50 : 105. Cf. serm. on Gen. 14 : 20–4, C.O. 23 : 674. *Ce n'est point assez d'avoir nostre conscience pure devant Dieu, mais aussi qu'il nous faut procurer (comme sainct Paul nous en monstre l'exemple) d'avoir bonne estime et reputation envers nos prochains. Pourquoy? Afin qu'ils ne nous condamnent point, quand ils cuideront qu'une chose mauvaise ait esté faite par nos mains: plus tost que nous les incitions à bien faire. Il est vray que nous ne pourrons pas eschapper les morsures et les abaiz de beaucoup de chiens: et quand nous serons sans aucune tache et macule, si ne laisseront-ils pas de detracter et mesdire de nous: car le Fils de Dieu a bien passé par là; tous les Prophetes et Apostres ont esté chargez de fausses calomnies.*

[2] Serm. on Gen. 14 : 13–16, C.O. 23 : 643.

[3] Comm. on Ps. 51 : 15, C.O. 31 : 520.

[4] Comm. on Ps. 69 : 5–6, C.O. 31 : 639. Cf. Calvin's own difficulty in witnessing for the truth in Geneva, e.g. in serm. on 1 Tim. 1 : 8–11, C.O. 53 : 57–8.

[5] Serm. on Gen. 14 : 20–4, C.O. 23 : 674.

[6] Comm. on Ps. 4 : 2, C.O. 31 : 58. If it happens to us in this way we must make sure "that we do not make ourselves odious through our own fault so that the saying should be fulfilled in us 'They hated me without a cause'!" Comm. on Phil. 2 : 14, C.O. 52–34.

[7] C.O. 37 : 256.

glory of Jesus Christ—especially when He hung on the Cross. The beauty of the Church itself is hidden under the Cross.[1] Even though the Church truly has Christ within its life and is truly seeking to show forth the grace and beauty of Christ, those who have not faith are unable to see even in that witness the glory that the Church is seeking to proclaim. We have to *believe* in the Holy Catholic Church because "oftentimes no difference can be observed between the children of God and the profane,"[2] and this is not always the fault of the children of God. Indeed, it may be a condition due to the faithfulness of the children of God. If it is to be conformed to Christ in His death, the Church must be prepared to appear "even contemptible in the eyes of the world under the revolting guise of the Cross," with its glory recognised only by the "faith which comprehends heavenly and invisible things."[3] If the Church in its witness must share thus in the shame and darkness that beset Christ in the Cross, the individual Christian must also accept the same limitation, remembering that He participates here and now more manifestly in the Cross than in the Resurrection.

But this does not mean that to witness to the glory of Christ becomes impossible or our duty in this respect any less urgent. If the Church (and the Christian) is faithful to its witness even when it finds it has little glory to show to the world, there will come times and occasions when its hidden glory will shine forth to bear glorious witness. The dove lying amongst the pots does not always appear as dirty and broken as the vessels that surround it, but "retains its native beauty of colour, and contracts no defilement on its wings. From this we learn that the Church does not always enjoy happy serenity, but it emerges at times from darkness, and recovers its splendour as if it were always undefiled by any evil."[4] This breaking-forth of the glory of the Church is an event that happens, rather than a continuous state, and men are apt to complain that this "splendour of the Church" is not of long duration. Yet, answers Calvin, "under the Cross the Glory of Christ shines forth, so that the name of God remains and there is a people that calls on Him by faith."[5] Even if we remain under

[1] Cf. introd. to comm. on Ps. 87, C.O. 31 : 800.
[2] Inst. 4 : 1 : 2.   [3] Comm. on Isa. 61 : 10, C.O. 37 : 379.
[4] Comm. on Ps. 68 : 13–14, C.O. 31 : 624–5.
[5] Comm. on Isa. 60 : 15, C.O. 37 : 365

the Cross we can always at least seek to "represent Christ" in our lives and "express the form of His example."[1] We can seek to make certain that the virtue of sanctification should overcome the power of sin within us "that our life may testify that we are indeed the members of Christ."[2] "No one" says Calvin, "ought to be reckoned among the disciples of Christ, unless we perceive the glory of God impressed upon him, as by a signet ring, by the likeness of Christ."[3]

5. The Christian must observe religious ordinances, and cultivate the unity of the whole Church in humility and love

Since the Christian life cannot be lived apart from the visible Church, it is an important part of the Christian life to observe carefully the ceremonies and "religious exercises"[4] which are such an important part of the life of the Church. To pay honour vaguely and at random to some supposed deity is not enough. "We must distinctly yield to the true and only living God the worship that is fitting to Him."[5] As in the Old Testament times the Temple was the place where God was met and worshipped, so today God still keeps His people under a certain "external order (*Sub externo aliquo ordine*), the Word, Sacraments, public prayers and other helps replacing the Temple and being to us no less than the Temple was to the Jews.[6] We must see in the "common discipline and order" of the Church a means whereby God allures us to Himself. Nothing but the most reckless pride could make us desert or despise the common services of worship which God has instituted to be helps to the weakness of our faith.[7] Therefore we must frequent the holy assemblies (*sacros conventus*) where the faithful incite one another to the worship of God. "Thus, in order that we may be one in Him, God gathers us together by

[1] Inst. 3 : 6 : 3.
[2] Comm. on Rom. 6 : 12, C.O. 49 : 111.
[3] Comm. on John 17 : 22, C.O. 47 : 388.
[4] Comm. on Ps. 42 : 2, C.O. 31 : 426. *Pietatis exercitia.*
[5] Comm. on Ps. 9 : 12, C.O. 31 : 101.
[6] Comm. on Ps. 27 : 4, C.O. 31 : 274; cf. on Ps. 42 : 2, C.O. 31 : 426.
[7] Comm. on Ps. 26 : 8, C.O. 31 : 268. *Ostendit autem haec contestatio, Davidem, quamlibet alios fide praecelleret, veritum tamen fuisse ne vulgaribus istis rudimentis, quae Deus ecclesiae suae tradiderat, eum privaret tyrranica hostium violentia. Nam se communi disciplina et ordine opus habere videns, de retinenda templi possessione sollicite contendit.*

common sacraments in hope of eternal life and in the united celebration of His name."[1] Private Bible-reading and meditation can never be a substitute for attending the public preaching of the Word,[2] even though we may be forced to listen with docility to a word that comes through a mere feeble man sprung from the dust.[3] Moreover, "we must hold that he who declines to pray in the public meeting of the saints knows not what it is to pray apart in retirement, or at home."[4]

If we set any value on the presence of Christ, we will not only observe the ordinances of the Church, but must also cultivate the unity of the Church in love.[5] It is within the Church that the mutual communication of offices which, as we have seen,[6] is that aspect of the order of nature which is the basis of human society, finds its truest and best expression in the service of one member for another within the body of Christ—this "beautiful order" and "symmetry" of the Church being a true reflexion of the order and symmetry of man's original creation in the image of God.[7] "The perfection of the faithful . . . consists in love."[8] The bond of faith and unity created by the Holy Spirit between Christ and His people is not real unless it expresses itself in love. We can have no access in prayer to God, no union with Christ our Head, no hope of future inheritance, unless we are united in love to all our other brethren.[9] Christ "embraces all His people together that they may cherish one another."[10]

[1] Comm. on Ps. 52 : 10, C.O. 31 : 529.   [2] Inst. 4 : 1 : 5.

[3] Inst. 4 : 3 : 1. This trains us in humility and tests our obedience.

[4] Inst. 3 : 20 : 29. Therefore it is necessary to keep the Sabbath day. It is true that its "external observance" has been abolished (see p. 120 n.). If we could be trusted to meet for worship every day we would not need a Sabbath (Inst. 2 : 8 : 32). But since this is impossible, we need the Sabbath as a politic arrangement to preserve the Church (Ibid., comm. on Exod. 20 : 8, C.O. 24 : 597). *Il est vray que nous ne sommes point astraints au septieme iour. . . . Mais pour monstrer la liberté des Chrestiens le iour a este changé. . . . Mais tant y a que nous devons observer ceste police, d'avoir quelque iour la sepmaine, soit un soit deux: car on laissera tout cela en la liberté des Chrestiens.* Serm. on Deut. 5 : 12–14, C.O. 26 : 294. This liberty means that we need not be so narrow in our observance as the Jews were. But we must employ the day in meditating on the works of God, and not in playing or shutting ourselves in our houses and gorging ourselves where no one can see us (Ibid.).

[5] Comm. on Matt. 18 : 20, C.O. 45 : 517. *Nam quisquis vel sacros conventus negligit, vel se disiungit a fratribus, ac segniter se gerit in colenda unitate, hoc ipso demonstrat se Christi praesentiam pro nihilo ducere.*

[6] See pp. 152–5.   [7] Comm. on Rom. 12 : 6, C.O. 49 : 238.

[8] Comm. on 1 Pet. 1 : 22, C.O. 55 : 228.

[9] Comm. on 1 Pet. 3 : 7, C.O. 55 : 257; Inst. 4 : 1 : 2.

[10] Comm. on John 15 : 12, C.O. 47 : 344.

Therefore we must cultivate brotherly love within the Church. Whether or not we do this is the sure test of whether or not we love God,[1] for "though God is invisible He represents Himself to us in the brethren, and in their persons demands what is due to Himself."[2] Therefore we should dread any dissension that might estrange us from the fellowship, realising that "Whoever cuts himself off from the brethren is alienated from the Kingdom of God."[3] It is particularly within the Church that we must cultivate this unity with our fellow men, for we are bound to those within the household of faith in a closer relationship than any we have with other men.[4] Therefore, if we ought to love and serve those who are still aliens to the flock of Christ, how much more care should we give to those with whom God has already united us![5] Though we must love and care for all men, our first duty in serving God aright is nevertheless, "to endeavour to do good to His holy servants," realising that God, "since our good deeds cannot extend to Him, substitutes the saints in His place towards whom we are to exercise our love."[6]

Such love within the Church should be practical. The hand which we extend to our brother as a sign of our fellowship with him should also be a token of our willingness to lend him practical help.[7] We must also fulfil in love the "office of mutual intercession" one for another,[8] and remember too that the Lord has given us prayer as an exercise of love (*caritatis exercitium*) between us in the Church, and that such intercessory prayer one for another cannot be in vain.[9] Here is Calvin's cure for us when no great

---

[1] Comm. on 1 Pet. 1 : 22, C.O. 55 : 228.
[2] Comm. on Gal. 5 : 14, C.O. 50 : 251.
[3] Comm. on Eph. 4 : 4, C.O. 51 : 191.
[4] Comm. on 1 Pet. 2 : 17, C.O. 55 : 247. *Loquitur enim, de singulari amore, quo domesticos fidei prosequi iubemur: quia magis arcta necessitudine cum illis sumus coniuncti.*
[5] Comm. on Heb. 10 : 25, C.O. 55 : 132. Cf. serm. on 1 Tim. 2 : 1–2, C.O. 53 : 129. *Ce passage nous admoneste de nostre devoir: c'est ascavoir que tous ceux qui portent le nom de Iesus Christ, nous doivent estre recommandez par special, que nous les aimions comme nos freres, que nous soyons conioints et unis avec eux: car autrement nous ne sommes pas dignes que Dieu nous advoue pour ses enfans. Car quand nous deschirons le corps de Iesus Christ, quelle part et portion pretendons nous en cest heritage immortel auquel nous sommes appelez?*
[6] Comm. on Ps. 16 : 3, C.O. 31 : 150.
[7] Comm. on Ps. 119 : 63, C.O. 32 : 242.
[8] Comm. on 2 Cor. 1 : 10, C.O. 50 : 15.
[9] Comm. on Col. 4 : 3, C.O. 52 : 127–8. Calvin in both above passages reminds us that this does not justify praying for the dead.

and pressing personal need drives us to our knees, and we accordingly are tempted to grow slack in our prayer-life: "Let us think how many of our brethren are worn out by varied and heavy afflictions—are weighed down by sore perplexity, or reduced to the lowest distress. If reflexions like these do not rouse us from our lethargy, we must have hearts of stone."[1] Intercession is not, of course, confined to the Church.[2] We are not to pray for believers only, but for all men. "And yet in prayer, as in all other offices of love, our first care is unquestionably due to the saints."[3]

To participate in such offices of love within the Church requires humility, which is the bond of mutual communication, and through which a man recognises that not having enough by himself he must borrow from others.[4] We must have the humility, for instance, not to overlook any assistance that has been appointed for us by God, and follow the example of the Apostle Paul, who, though he surpassed all others in prayer, nevertheless implored his brethren to help him by their intercessions.[5] We must "diligently seek help from the prayers of others."[6] Calvin often speaks of our need for humility if we are to profit from the ministry of the Word within the Church, for those through whom God gives us the Word are certainly always "contemptible mortals,"[7] and frequently "vile and worthless persons"[8] and "inconsiderable men."[9] Yet we must remember that our unity in love with them in the body of Christ means that we should be humble enough to receive what edification it pleases God to give us through them— and indeed we must not be too proud to constantly open our minds to, and be willing to test and receive, whatever new truths are presented to us from whatever source within the Church, for it is the Spirit who gives others the zeal to edify us.[10]

---

[1] Comm. on Eph. 6 : 18, C.O. 51 : 237.
[2] See chapter on Prayer.　　　　[3] Comm. on Eph. 6 : 18, C.O. 51 : 237–8.
[4] Comm. on Rom. 12 : 6, C.O. 49 : 238.
[5] Comm. on 2 Thess. 3 : 1, C.O. 52 : 208; on 2 Cor. 1 : 10, C.O. 50 : 157.
[6] Comm. on Col. 4 : 3, C.O. 52 : 128.
[7] Inst. 4 : 3 : 1.　　　　[8] Comm. on John 9 : 34, C.O. 47 : 231.
[9] Comm. on Luke 2 : 17, C.O. 45 : 79.
[10] Serm. on Job 18 : 1–11, C.O. 34 : 66. *Toutes fois nous sommes ici admonnestez quand on nous presentera quelque doctrine, de discerner ce qui en est: que nous ne reiettions point ce qui nous est incognu: comme nous en verrons qui ne font pas grand cas, si on leur veut monstrer ce qui seroit utile pour leur salut, de reietter tout. Que nous n'ayons point donc cest orgueil-là en nous; car non seulement nous constristerions . . . l'Esprit de Dieu qui habite en eux, et qui leur donne ce zele de nous edifier.*

Thus we can take our place within the unity of the fellowship only if we begin with humility.[1] The psalmist's ambition to be a doorkeeper in the house of the Lord is unfortunately all too rare an ambition, and we see far too many who can never rest till they attain eminence even in the Church.[2] The only consideration that can keep us in true humility is that all men should realise their poverty and miserable condition apart from the grace of God.[3]

Cultivating unity in brotherly love within the Church means also limiting our liberty in face of the demands of love towards our weaker brethren, who might be offended or led astray if we expressed within the Church our full freedom before God.[4] In this connexion Calvin speaks of our "matching" or "yoking in" (*accoupler*) with one another in meekness,[5] of our "tempering ourselves" to the weak (*infirmis attemperare*).[6] We must in no way despise anyone in the Church, for "love must be connected with respect."[7] It is true that we cannot accommodate ourselves to everybody. While we must seek to please the weak we need not be uneasy at offending the obstinate.[8] We must maintain always our "liberty before God in our hearts."[9] But though we may imagine that many things are lawful, "participation is in no case lawful unless it be regulated by the law of love."[10] Liberty must always be subservient to love.[11]

The Church, then, must be the chief concern of all its members. "If we do not prefer the Church to all other objects of our solicitude, we are unworthy of being accounted among her members."[12]

[1] Comm. on Eph. 4 : 2, C.O. 51 : 190.
[2] Comm. on Ps. 84 : 11, C.O. 31 : 784.
[3] Comm. on Eph. 2 : 13–15, C.O. 51 : 402.
[4] Serm. on Gal. 2 : 6–8, C.O. 50 : 377–8. *Si nous voyons que quelqu'un soit retardé de venir à l'Evangile, ou bien qu'on le trouble, d'autant qu'il n'est pas encores bien fortifié, il nous faut abstenir de ce qui nous estoit licite: comme nous avons veu par cidevant qu'il nous faut tousiours regarder ce qui est expedient et propre pour le salut de chacun.* Serm. on 1 Cor. 10 : 25–30, C.O. 49 : 687. *Mais quand ie verray que l'acte que ie fay pourra troubler mes freres, qu'ils pourront tourner cela en mal, ou concevoir quelque suspeçon, que (brief) ils pourront estre mal edifiez de moy . . . il faut que ie me proive de ce qui me seroit licite: et ceste servitude là est licite: car ma conscience demeure neantmoins tousiours en son entier.*
[5] Serm. on Gal. 5 : 11–14, C.O. 51 : 18.
[6] Comm. on 1 Cor. 9 : 22, C.O. 49 : 448; cf. serm. on 1 Cor. 11 : 11–16, C.O. 49 : 742. *Que ceux qui sont grans descendent, pour se conformer avec les petis.*
[7] Comm. on 1 Pet. 3 : 7, C.O. 55 : 256.
[8] Comm. on Matt. 15 : 14, C.O. 45 : 453.
[9] Cf. pp. 308–12.
[10] Comm. on 1 Cor. 8 : 13, C.O. 49 : 435.
[11] Inst. 3 : 19 : 12; comm. on Rom. 14 : 14, C.O. 49 : 264.
[12] Comm. on Ps. 102 : 4, C.O. 32 : 62.

Moreover, like David, we must have a greater concern for the welfare of the Church than for our own individual welfare. We must realise that we are so closely bound up with the body of the Church that no individual member can flourish without the whole body flourishing.[1] In this Jesus Christ is our example, for He sought nothing for Himself, His only concern being for the common good of His own people.[2] Nothing, therefore, must vex us more or give us more anxious concern than to see disputes in the life of the Church or scandals in the conduct of any member.[3] The accounts of civil strife in the life of Israel draw from Calvin the comment that no victory in internal war within the Church is ever worth having when such strife causes weakness within the body. Therefore the peace of the Church must be our first concern.[4] Schism within the Church is a sign that individuals "find it difficult to accommodate themselves to the ways and habits of others," and that each of us would have a Church of his own if he could.[5] But such a splitting-up of the Church sunders it from Christ.[6] The Church can be strong only when united.[7] Calvin can look forward in hope to the possibility that the Papists might return "to that holy concord from which they have apostatised."[8]

[1] Comm. on Ps. 128 : 5, C.O. 32 : 329.
[2] Comm. on Ps. 28 : 9, C.O. 31 : 285–6.
[3] Comm. on 1 Cor. 5 : 2, C.O. 49 : 378–9; on Gal. 5 : 15, C.O. 50 : 252.
[4] Serm. on 2 Sam. 2 : 14 f., p. 42. *Or par cecy nous sommes admonestez que nulle victoire de guerre interieure n'est a desirer . . . D'autant que l'Eglise de Dieu en sera cependant amoindrie . . . il vaudroit beacoup mieux cercher paix et faire tout ce qui nous est possible, a ce que Iesus Christ regne, sans entrer en combat.*
[5] Comm. on Heb. 10 : 25, C.O. 55 : 132.
[6] Comm. on 1 Cor. 1 : 13, C.O. 49 : 316.
[7] Comm. on Ps. 122 : 3, C.O. 32 : 304.
[8] Comm. on Ps. 133 : 1, C.O. 32 : 354.

PART FIVE

THE EXERCISE OF FAITH

Chapter I

The trial and temptation of faith

1. Jesus Christ's conflict with evil foreshadows our own unceasing trial and temptation

THE man of faith continually finds himself in a conflict which exercises his faith, and which demands from him both constant watchfulness and an ever-growing dependence upon the Word of God.

Faith cannot exist except under tension and conflict with evil. "We must be good soldiers, or we cannot be men of faith," says Calvin.[1] "Our faith neither can nor should exist without fighting something."[2] It is true that all human life is hard. Merely by reason of their humanity, all men are involved in a multitude of varied trials, cares, sorrows, fears and griefs,[3] and God's people are "subject in common with all to the miseries of human life."[4] Yet the hardness of the struggle is especially severe for the Christian.[5]

We must prepare ourselves, then, for "a hard warfare."[6] Christ Himself was subject to far more than the common troubles that beset ordinary men. He suffered unusual shame and reproach and a unique degree of enmity from those who hated to see His Kingdom advancing. We must remember that the antagonism that He had to face during His earthly life is a foreshadowing of something that would continually confront and harass the life of the Church and its members in the "gradual development of His Kingdom even until the end of the world."[7] The fact that the

[1] Serm. on 1 Tim. 6 : 12–14, C.O. 53 : 595.
[2] Serm. on 1 Tim. 1 : 5–7, C.O. 53 : 29. *Nostre foy ne peut et ne doit estre sans combat.*
[3] Comm. on Ps. 90 : 10, C.O. 31 : 838.
[4] Comm. on Ps. 121 : 6, C.O. 32 : 301. . . . *humanae vitae miseriis promiscue subiaceant fideles.*
[5] See also pp. 47–8 and 68–9.
[6] Comm. on Ps. 18 : 1, C.O. 31 : 170. *Quod nobis cognitu non parum utile est, ne immunitatem speremus ab omni molestia, ubi sequimur vocantem Deum, sed nos potius ad duram militiam paremus.*
[7] Comm. on Ps. 69 : 5, C.O. 31 : 639; and on Ps. 118 : 25, C.O. 32 : 211–12. *Interea meminerimus, quod in Christi persona impletum fuit, spectare ad continuum regni eius cursum usque ad finem mundi.*

innocents were massacred round Christ's cradle is to Calvin a sign that His whole career was to be a career of conflict with evil forces and that those who take Him as their captain today must not expect peaceful repose in quiet obscurity, but must fight the same deadly and determined enemy.[1] To enlist in His army is "to have the greater part of the world rising in hostility against us, and pursuing us even to death,"[2] and is to have the Devil as "our perpetual enemy."[3] He will heap up difficulties in our way. He will inspire and use malice against us in the hearts of others. He will make our path thorny and our progress slow.[4]

2. God may providentially train and discipline our faith by allowing affliction and a sense of His wrath to come to us.

As Christians we are assailed not only by evil men and evil powers, but we are also especially tempted and tried by God Himself—indeed, the assault upon us by the powers of evil is possible only because God deliberately allows us to become so assailed![5] Our Christian experience, under the guidance of God, is always such as to train us in the faith and to assist the growth of our faith, for we are continually brought into situations in which we can live only by faith. Sometimes we find ourselves subject to a painful kind of temptation, when God seems to cast off all care about us, and to pass over our groanings and miseries as if He did not see them.[6] Sometimes He removes the light of His countenance or allows it to be clouded over. This means that either the "sense of His love" or the "outward signs of His favour" are withdrawn, and the conscience may be struck with terrors,[7] and the Word

---

[1] Serm. on Matt. 2 : 16–22, C.O. 46 : 444.

[2] Comm. on Matt. 5 : 10, C.O. 45 : 164.

[3] Serm. on Matt. 26 : 40–50, C.O. 46 : 849. *Le diable est nostre ennemi perpetuel, si nous sommes membres de nostre Seigneur Iesus Christ.*

[4] Serm. on 1 Tim. 6 : 12–14, C.O. 53 : 595. Even though there is no wickedness perpetrated by men to which Satan does not excite them, nevertheless Satan merely kindles into a fierce furnace a flame that is already there. Therefore men under the power of Satan are inexcusable for their misdeeds. Comm. on John 13 : 2, C.O. 47 : 305–6.

[5] This, Calvin finds, is the meaning of the dialogue between God and Satan in Job. Serm. on Job 1 : 9–12, C.O. 33 : 74.

[6] Comm. on Ps. 22 : 2, C.O. 31 : 221. *Hac tentationis specie . . . ubi Deus quasi abiecta nostri cura ad nostras miserias et gemitus connivet.*

[7] Comm. on Ps. 67 : 2, C.O. 31 : 618.

ceases to have any real flavour for us.¹ Indeed, when David prays
in his psalms and describes his condition in what seems to be
exaggerated language signifying extreme physical distress and
sorrow of heart, he is describing not so much his bodily state as
his condition of mind and soul. When he is under a sense of God's
wrath, he seems to see, "as it were, Hell, open to receive him."
Such experience, Calvin asserts, can be ours if we follow Christ
today. "Nothing should hinder us today, but the stupidity of our
flesh, from experiencing in ourselves what David describes con-
cerning himself."² God can be, as it were, angry with His own
people.³ He treats us more severely than the Devil, who flatters
men to destroy them.⁴

The fact that in the assaults which our faith receives the enemy
is under the control and direction of God Himself, can be not
simply a terror to us but a great comfort and strength, for it
means that our trial is bound to have a blessed issue.⁵ Calvin gives
many different reasons why God allows such persecutions to come
upon us and inflicts such suffering with His own hand. Too much
unmingled happiness would make us intoxicated, indulgent in
excess, so God has, as it were, to save us by putting water in our
wine, sending sorrow when we are over-elated by joy.⁶ Any slack-
ening of discipline over us would cause us to become like wild
rebellious horses,⁷ therefore God has to check our impetuosity
and make us more cautious for the future by constantly using the
whip.⁸ Such discipline must be continuous and prolonged, for if
the rod were not held out to us continually we would constantly
relapse into disobedience.⁹

God never ceases to be a father to us even in His anger. In

¹ Comm. on Ps. 119 : 135, C.O. 32 : 276. *Saepe autem contingit ipsis quoque obnubilari in hac parte Dei faciem, dum genuino verbi sui gustu eos privat.*
² Comm. on Ps. 6 : 6–7, C.O. 31 : 77.
³ Comm. on Ps. 79 : 8, C.O. 31 : 750.
⁴ Serm. on 2 Tim. 3 : 16–17, C.O. 54 : 291. *Ho nous voulons estre gagnez par douceur. . . . Allez-vous en à l'escole du diable, car il vous flattera assez à vostre perdition.*
⁵ Serm. on 1 Tim. 6 : 12–14, C.O. 53 : 598. *Le second est, qu'il ne nous doit point fascher si Dieu nous esprouve, car ce n'est point à l'aventure que nous bataillons, nous ne sommes point en danger de perdre nostre vie sans la recouvrer . . . mais l'issue de nostre gendarmerie est desirable, d'autant que Dieu preside sur nous.*
⁶ Serm. on 2 Sam. 1 : 1–16, p. 2.
⁷ Serm. on Deut. 6 : 10–13, C.O. 26 : 448.
⁸ Comm. on John 5 : 14, C.O. 47 : 109–10; and on Heb. 12 : 4, C.O. 55 : 173.
⁹ Comm. on Ps. 85 : 9, C.O. 45 : 788.

afflicting His people He continually moderates the Cross which He calls on them to bear.[1] He always mingles comfort with sorrow and gives them real experience of His mercy and love even as He punishes them.[2] He never gives men what they deserve in the way of chastisement and in giving them the punishment He does mete out, He always supports those whom He afflicts.[3] He takes care that whatever affliction He sends to us will not be so bitter as to drive us out of His service.[4] He studies our weaknesses and our ability to bear suffering, and never lays on us a burden heavier than we have the experience to bear. It is only as our strength increases that He increases our affliction.[5]

Always, then, it is the true welfare of His people that determines the nature of the affliction which God sends upon them. He adapts His method of discipline to the diversity of our vices, "humbling some by poverty, some by shame, some by diseases, some by domestic distresses, some by hard and painful labours."[6] Commenting on Paul's "thorn in the flesh," Calvin suggests that to be "buffeted (*colaphis caedi*)" by God is a peculiarly severe kind of affliction sent to the proud in which, besides pain and fear, there is a large element of shame.[7] But there are "no certain or uniform rules" by which we can fully understand God's providence in this matter. "He chastises some, while He spares others. He heals the secret ills of some, and passes others by because they have no need of such a cure. He exercises the patience of some, inasmuch as He has given them the spirit of fortitude; and finally He sets forth

---

[1] Comm. on Ps. 74 : 9, C.O. 31 : 695. *Proinde nos quoque si materiam patientiae et consolationis quaerimus, ubi nos Deus castigat, discamus ad istam moderationem, qua nos Deus ad spem invitat, oculos intendere: atque inde statuamus, Deum ita irasci ut non desinat tamen esse pater. Correctio vero quae salutem affert laetitiam continet dolori admistam.* Cf. comm. on John 21 : 18, C.O. 47 : 454. *Sic temperat Dominus crucem, qua vult servos suos experiri.*

[2] Comm. on Ps. 39 : 11, C.O. 31 : 403.

[3] Serm. on Job 34 : 10–15, C.O. 35 : 146–7. *Ainsi donc notons que Dieu ne punit point les pescheurs, et qu'il ne leur fait point sentir sa vengeance en mesure egale, si tost qu'ils l'ont desservi: mais il les supporte, tellement que tous les chastimens que nous recevons en ce monde, ne sont qu'advertissemens que Dieu nous fait, nous donnant encores lieu de repentance.*

[4] Comm. on Ps. 125 : 3, C.O. 32 : 315.

[5] Serm. on Job 2 : 7–10, C.O. 33 : 116. *Dieu donc regarde nostre portee, et selon que nous sommes exercez à endurer les afflictions, il nous les envoye petites ou moyennes: mais quand nous y sommes, comme endurcis, alors il nous peut bien charger d'avantage: car il nous a donné aussi dequoi le porter.* Cf. comm. on John 21 : 18, C.O. 47 : 454.

[6] Comm. on Ps. 119 : 67, C.O. 32 : 244.

[7] Comm. on 2 Cor. 12 : 7, C.O. 50 : 139–40.

others by way of example. But He humbles all in common with the tokens of His anger that by such incitements they may be stirred up to repentance."[1] Certain it is, however, that God encourages us to walk in His ways and to serve Him, not only by changing our minds and hearts, but sometimes also by compelling us through the sheer force of outward circumstances.[2]

3. Our conflict is made harder by our struggle with the flesh and the Devil

The conflict in which the Christian man is involved is the more acute because he not only has to contend with the hostility of external enemies, but also never ceases to find himself confronted from within his own heart by temptations and doubts that arise from the flesh. The whole process of self-denial[3] is indeed simply the constant struggle between the spirit and the flesh which is described by Paul in Romans 7 and Galatians 5.[4] The "flesh" here is for Calvin simply the old human nature whose inclinations remain constantly against the will of God, and which must be constantly restrained and mortified if man would obey the will of God. The "spirit" is the new spiritual nature of the regenerate man.[5] Therefore the Christian constantly feels himself divided between the flesh, which seeks to plunge his life into sin and excess and disorder and which can never be perfectly controlled,

[1] Comm. on Ps. 37 : 25, C.O. 31 : 378; cf. on James 1 : 2, C.O. 55 : 383–4.

[2] Serm. on 2 Sam. 4, p. 85. Here again we have to remember that the children of God are afflicted more than the wicked because God reserves the judgment of the wicked for the last day and treats His people with greater severity in this present life. See p.198. Comm. on 1 Pet. 4 : 17, C.O. 55 : 281–2; and on John 9 : 2, C.O. 47 : 217; Inst. 1 : 5 : 6.

[3] See pp. 50–67.

[4] Cf. comm. on Rom. 7; on Gal. 5 : 17, C.O. 50 : 252–3; and on Col. 3 : 15, C.O. 52 : 123; serm. on Deut. 5 : 12–14, C.O. 26 : 290. *Or tant y a que nous ne pouvons point nous acquitter tellement en renonçant à nos affections, qu'il n'y ait tousiours à redire. Sainct Paul se glorifie bien que le monde luy est crucifié, et qu'il est crucifié au monde: mais cependant il ne laisse pas de dire que sa chair combat contre l'esprit: et qu'il n'y a iamais d'accord: et mesmes il confesse au septieme des Romains qu'il a tousiours senti en soy ceste repugnance, qu'il ne faisoit pas le bien qu'il eust voulu, c'est à dire, il ne l'accomplissoit pas d'une affection si ardente, il n'estoit pas si resolu de cheminer selon Dieu, qu'il n'y eust tousiours des empeschemens pour le retarder.* In comm. on John 21 : 18, C.O. 47 : 455, Calvin traces Peter's unwillingness to face martyrdom to this conflict between flesh and spirit. In serm. on Job 34 : 4–10, C.O. 35 : 132 he links up Job's conflict with himself, and Jacob's wrestling, with Rom. 7, and Gal. 5 : 17.

[5] Comm. on Gal. 5 : 17, C.O. 50 : 252–3.

and his new spiritual desires and powers, which seek to conform the life to the law of God.[1] "The godly in whom the regeneration of God is begun, are so divided that with a special desire of the heart they fervently aspire to God, they covet celestial righteousness and hate sin, but again by the relics of their flesh they are drawn towards the earth."[2] This conflict is felt only by the regenerate man. The natural man does not resist the flesh in this way.[3]

The struggle with the flesh means a constant inward struggle, not only against wrong desires but also against false ideas and unbelief, for unbelief is also an activity of the flesh (or old nature), whose judgment about God and our situation is always opposed to faith. In the experience of the people of God the judgment of faith—that God is always near and victorious—has continually to oppose and wrestle against the weakness and judgment of the flesh. Calvin finds in this conflict the explanation of the many apparently contradictory utterances of the psalmists in the midst of their trials. Even though faith may firmly believe that God loves us, nevertheless at the same time the unbelief of the flesh may give rise to apparently faithless questions as to why God is absent.[4] One verse of a psalm can be a magnificent expression of faith, only to be soon followed by a very contrary expression of natural doubt.[5] The cry "My God, my God, why hast thou forsaken me?" expresses "the contrary affections" which are mingled and interwoven with the prayers of the faithful.[6]

[1] Serm. on Job 34 : 4–10, C.O. 35 : 132; comm. on Rom. 7 : 14–15, C.O. 49 : 128–130.
[2] Comm. on Rom. 7 : 15, C.O. 49 : 130. *Pii contra, in quibus coepta est Dei regeneratio, sic divisi sunt, ut praecipuo cordis desiderio ad Deum suspirent, coelestem iustitiam expetant, peccatum oderint: sed rursum carnis suae reliquiis in terram retrahantur.*
[3] Comm. on Gal. 5 : 17, C.O. 50 : 253. Cf. comm. on Rom. 7 : 15, C.O. 49 : 129. *Notandum est, hoc certamen, de quo loquitur apostolus, non prius exstare in homine quam spiritu Dei fuerit sanctificatus. Nam homo naturae suae relictus totus sine repugnantia in cupiditates fertur.*
[4] Comm. on Ps. 44 : 24, C.O. 31 : 448. *Statuendum quidem est, a Deo nos respici, etiamsi dissimulet: quia tamen haec persuasio fidei est, non carnis, contrarium illum sensum quem ex praesenti rei adspectu concipiunt, familiariter exonerant in sinum Dei.* [5] Comm. on Ps. 69 : 15–19, C.O. 31 : 645.
[6] Comm. on Ps. 22 : 2, C.O. 31 : 220. *Idem quotidie quisque fidelium in se experitur, ut pro carnis sensu, a Deo se reiectum et desertum existimet: fide tamen apprehendat absconditam gratiam. Ita fit ut in eorum precibus contrarii affectus simul permixti sint ac impliciti.* Cf. comm. on Ps. 13 : 2, C.O. 31 : 132. *Davidem non prohibuit a quaerendo Deo carnis infirmitas, sed affectus in speciem contrarios optime coniunxit.*

Our temptation to unbelief arises not only through the weakness of the flesh but also through the insinuations of the Devil, who comes to us in the midst of the combat and makes faithless insinuations, suggesting that God has withdrawn the support of His Spirit[1] and instigating us to despair.[2] "The Devil desires nothing more than . . . to put it in our heads that God has cast us off."[3]

Thus in the midst of great afflictions, Calvin asserts, none of us need any outside agent such as Eliphaz was to Job in order to impress upon us the desperate nature of our position. We each of us carry in our own nature the seed-bed of sufficient vexation to drive us to despair.[4] Against such temptation to despair our faith must stand and refuse to yield.[5] "It becomes us to wrestle against despair, in order that our sorrow, incurable though it may seem, may not shut our mouths and keep us from pouring out our prayers before God."[6]

[1] Comm. on Ps. 55 : 5, C.O. 31 : 536.
[2] Serm. on Job 14 : 13–15, C.O. 33 : 686.
[3] Serm. on Job 2 : 11–13, C.O. 33 : 140.
[4] Serm. on Job 4 : 7–10, C.O. 33 : 190.
[5] Comm. on Ps. 49 : 7, C.O. 31 : 484.
[6] Comm. on Ps. 77 : 3, C.O. 31 : 712. *Atque ita cum desperatione luctari nos decet, ut dolor, licet insanabilis, ianuam tamen votis nostris minime praecludat.* Comm. on Ps. 13 : 2, C.O. 31 : 132. *Sic nobis cum tentationibus luctandum est, ut ipso conflictu fides nobis dictet superanda esse mala quae nos ad desperationem sollicitant.* Cf. comm. on Ps. 42 : 6, C.O. 31 : 429.

Chapter II

The attitude of faith in conflict and suffering

1. Faith "looks to the hand of God" alone in submission and self-denial

UNDER his afflictions and trials, the man of faith takes up an attitude completely different from that of the unbeliever. Whereas affliction can make the faithless and godless more and more obstinate, the same affliction tends to turn the man of faith towards God in true repentance.[1]

It is characteristic of the man of faith that in the midst of all the assaults of evil and the blows administered by providence, he says to God: "Thou art my God." He looks to God alone and puts his trust in God alone.[2] He is forced to do so because our real state of affairs on earth is that "to whatever quarter we turn our eyes we will see everywhere nothing but ground for despair till we come to God." Within ourselves we see simply a "mirror of death" full of rottenness. Around ourselves, in whatever direction our eyes turn, we see corruption and decay. All earthly change is a "prelude to destruction." Stability is to be sought and found in God alone.[3]

Therefore he will look constantly to God alone. Nothing will make him turn his eyes to any other quarter for help and comfort save to God, for if he does he will fall.[4] He will not transfer even to man the smallest portion of confidence which he should place in God alone.[5] In contrast to the unbelievers who "gaze about" looking hither and thither, turning now here for help and now there, all his prayers and desires have one aim and direction.[6]

To look thus to God alone means not only to have renounced all help from the world but also to have become convinced of our

---

[1] Inst. 3 : 8 : 6.
[2] Comm. on Ps. 31 : 14, C.O. 31 : 307–8.
[3] Comm. on Ps. 102 : 25–6, C.O. 32 : 73.
[4] Comm. on Ps. 16 : 8, C.O. 31 : 155; and on Ps. 71 : 16, C.O. 31 : 660.
[5] Comm. on Ps. 118 : 8, C.O. 32 : 204.
[6] Comm. on Ps. 25 : 1, C.O. 31 : 250; on Ps. 71 : 1, C.O. 31 : 654; and on Ps. 73 : 25, C.O. 31 : 688.

own inability to help ourselves.[1] Calvin always emphasises that to have faith in God involves "renouncing ourselves."[2] Therefore under affliction faith will take up an attitude of stern self-denial, for it happens that in the midst of suffering we are most severely tempted to let our feelings run riot and drive us to wrong actions and to give way to despair and blasphemy.[3] Since God through the Cross is seeking to soften our hearts, "we should at least endeavour to grow gentle, and, laying aside all stubbornness, cheerfully bear the yoke which He imposes upon us."[4] Since God through the Cross is seeking to reduce us to nothing," we ought patiently to permit God to mortify us."[5] Calvin frequently warns us that under deep affliction we must, as it were, "pull ourselves together," and continually "hold ourselves in check."[6] He finds in the phrase "poor in spirit," as it occurs in the Beatitudes of Jesus, a description of the right attitude of those who would truly bear suffering according to the will of God.[7]

The Christian man will look to God in faith that his suffering comes from the hand of God and that his situation is entirely under the control of God. Since God orders all things by His counsel, therefore whatever His children suffer they suffer under His good hand and according to His ordinance and command.[8] "Whether poverty, or exile, or imprisonment, or contumely, or disease, or bereavement, or any such evil affects us, we must think

---

[1] Comm. on Ps. 28 : 1, C.O. 31 : 281.

[2] Comm. on Matt. 21 : 32, C.O. 45 : 590. To have faith involves "distrusting our own strength" (comm. on Phil. 1 : 6, C.O. 52 : 9), "self-despair" (serm. on Gen. 15 : 6, C.O. 23 : 699), becoming "destitute of all good" (ibid. p. 700). The Holy Spirit sometimes "sets the assistance of God in opposition to human strength" (comm. on Ps. 20 : 7–8, C.O. 31 : 211).

[3] Comm. on Ps. 143 : 10, C.O. 32 : 404.

[4] Comm. on Ps. 119 : 67, C.O. 32 : 244. *Suo interim exemplo docet propheta, saltem ubi duritiem nostram subigendo ostendit Deus, se velle nos habere discipulos, dandam esse operam ut mitescamus, et deposita ferocia, quod nobis imponit iugum, libenter feramus.*

[5] Comm. on John 12 : 25, C.O. 47 : 288. *Nam si mori nos oportet ut fructum feramus, patienter ferendum est ut Deus nos mortificet.*

[6] Comm. on Ps. 10 : 18, C.O. 31 : 120. *Verum si locum dare cupimus eius auxilio, domandus est fervor noster, sedanda impatientia, mitigandi dolores, usque-dum miseriae nostrae Dei gratiam provocent.* Cf. serm. on Job 1 : 9–12, C.O. 33 : 71. *Il nous faut apprester quand il plaira à Dieu de nous affliger et nous exercer en beaucoup de maux, et de miseres, que toutesfois nous soyons tenus en bride, que nous ayons ceste humilité-là de nous assubiettir à luy, que nous soyons patiens et paisibles pour recevoir toutes ses corrections.*

[7] Cf. comm. on Matt. 5 : 3, C.O. 45 : 161–2.

[8] Inst. 1 : 16 : 3. *Hoc solatio in rebus adversis se leniant fideles nihil se perpeti nisi Dei ordinatione et mandato.*

that none of them happens except by the will of God: moreover, that everything He does is in most perfect order."[1] Calvin approves of the Augustinian view that even the apparently unreasonable calamities that make suffering such a dark mystery to the questioning mind should be thought of as occurring not simply by the permission of God but rather by His will and decree[2]—though sometimes he can speak of certain calamities as happening "by the permission of God."[3]

The lament and warning of Isaiah about those who under affliction will not look to Him that smites them is obviously often in Calvin's mind. He mourns that most men are quite thoughtless and insensible on this subject. They do not differ from the beasts of the field in estimating their affliction "only by the feeling of pain which it produces."[4] But our thoughts under affliction should not dwell only on the extent of the calamities which have happened in their relation to our own comfort and hopes and bodily well-being. We must get beyond all this, and in the time of our affliction we must look to the hand that strikes.[5] "We ought to acknowledge the hand of God which strikes us and not to imagine that our distresses arise from blind impetuosity of fortune."[6] What distinguishes the attitude of the truly faithful under suffering in the Old Testament is that in all their afflictions they related their suffering to God. They discerned that it was He who was afflicting them. Their suffering was to them a sign that the hand

---

[1] Inst. 3 : 8 : 11.

[2] Comm. on Ps. 115 : 3, C.O. 32 : 184. *Ideo apposite et scite Augustinus hoc testimonio probat, non simplici Dei permissu accidere quae videntur nobis absurda, sed nutu etiam et decreto.* Calvin's reasons are cogent: *Nam si facit Deus noster quaecunque vult, cur permitteret fieri quae non vult? Cur diabolum et omnes impios sibi repugnantes non coercet? Si medius fingitur inter actionem et passionem, ut toleret quae fieri non vult: erit igitur otiosus in coelo, ut Epicurei somniant.*

[3] Comm. on 1 Pet. 4 : 19, C.O. 55 : 283. *Reducit tamen in memoriam, nihil nisi Dei permissu nos pati: quod multum ad consolationem valet.* Cf. comm. on Ps. 79 : 5, C.O. 31 : 748–9.

[4] Comm. on Ps. 38 : 3, C.O. 31 : 387. *Atqui David in morbo, sicut in aliis rebus adversis, manum Dei suis oculis proponit ad punienda peccata armatam. Et sane quisquis in mali sui sensu subsistit, nihil a pecudibus differt.*

[5] Comm. on Ps. 6 : 2, C.O. 31 : 73. *Et tamen videmus quantus torpor omnes fere occupet in hac parte, nam quum se miseros esse clamitent, ad manum ferientem vix centesimus quisque respicit.* Cf. comm. on Ps. 38 : 3, C.O. 31 : 387. *Sed quum nos de iudicio admoneant omnia eius flagella, haec vera fidelium prudentia est, manum percutientis respicere, ut propheta Ies. 9 : 13 loquitur.* Comm. on Ps. 79 : 5, C.O. 31 : 749. *Quoties nos flagellis suis ferit Deus, ad manum eius attendere convenit.*

[6] Comm. on John 5 : 14, C.O. 47 : 109.

of God was upon them.[1] If the wicked were persecuting them, their first thought was that it was God who was deliberately giving loose rein to the bridle by which He held the wicked.[2] If the help of friends failed them they did not so much brood over human frailty as over the thought that this human failure was a sign that God had deliberately withdrawn his aid.[3] It is precisely in the experience of such afflictions that we have one of our prime opportunities for seeking the Lord. For since He is the personal agent in all such affliction, to yield submissive obedience under the Cross is a better and surer way of seeking God than the ceremonious prayers, fastings and tears of the hypocrites.[4] "The Lordship of life and death is ascribed to God that every man might better bear his estate as the yoke imposed by Him. . . . If, therefore, at any time the flesh recoils in adversity, let us remember that he who is not free has no right over himself, and perverts law and order if he does not depend on the good pleasure of his Lord."[5]

2. In affliction faith finds tokens both of God's wrath and of His fatherly love

In looking to the hand of God the believer will meditate on the fact that his affliction is in some way connected with the deserved punishment of his past sins.[6] "Whenever we are afflicted, we ought immediately to call to our mind our past life."[7] He will look on his suffering as a token of God's wrath against sin and God's judgment upon it.[8] "Those persons have made little

[1] Comm. on Ps. 74 : 1, C.O. 31 : 691. *Notandum autem est, quod fideles a profanis gentibus vexati, oculos tamen ad Deum attollunt, ac si plagas omnes sola eius manus infligeret.* Cf. comm. on Ps. 79 : 5, C.O. 31 : 749.

[2] Cf. ibid.

[3] Comm. on Ps. 88 : 9, C.O. 31 : 808. *Quod notatu dignum est: quia nisi in memoriam succurrat, ideo nos destitui humanis mediis, quia Deus manum suam subducit, tumultuamur sine fine et modo.*

[4] Comm. on Isa. 9 : 13, C.O. 36 : 204.

[5] Comm. on Rom. 14 : 8, C.O. 49 : 261.

[6] Comm. on John 5 : 14, C.O. 47 : 109. *Docet etiam haec admonitio, quidquid patimur mali peccatis nostris imputandum esse.*   [7] Inst. 3 : 8 : 6.

[8] Serm. on Job 5 : 17–18, C.O. 33 : 260. *Nous avons à retenir . . . que si tost qu'il nous advient quelque mal, l'ire de Dieu nous doit venir devant les yeux, que nous devons cognoistre qu'il ne peut porter le peché: et sur cela faut que nous sentions la rigueur de son iugement.* Cf. serm. on Job 3 : 20–26, C.O. 33 : 168. *Ainsi quand il est question de nous fascher, que nous ne regardions point ni à froid, ni à chaud, ni à povreté, ni à maladies, mais que nous regardions à nos pechez: et mesmes quand Dieu nous affligera . . . que cela nous advise de monter plus haut: ne nous arrestons point au mal corporel, mais cognoissons, Voici les fruicts de nos fautes.*

progress under their afflictions who do not immediately face their
sins squarely so that they can feel that they have deserved the
wrath of God."[1] Indeed affliction is often sent precisely for the
purpose of bringing such thoughts into our minds, and it is in this
respect that unbelieving men who are incapable of so relating
suffering to sin differ from believers in their attitude to affliction.[2]
Calvin therefore undoubtedly teaches that the Christian will accept
whatever suffering comes to him as being in some relation to his
own sin.[3]

When Calvin tells us to look on affliction as a token of the wrath
and judgment of God on our sin, he also at the same time urges
us to seek to discern in the same affliction the token of God's
fatherly love.[4] The aim of affliction is to humble us in order that
God may have mercy upon us. If God casts us down, it is in order
that He may raise us up. Therefore we must not allow our suffering to have merely a negative effect on us.[5] Suffering can thus be
to us a sign that God thinks of us in His fatherly love, for the very

---

[1] Comm. on Ps. 6 : 2, C.O. 31 : 73.

[2] Serm. on Job 3 : 1–10, C.O. 33 : 144. *Or cependant il est vray qu'il y a dequoy
gemir et pleurer, d'autant que quand nous sommes ici, nous sommes en un abysme
de toutes miseres: mais quoy? il nous faut regarder d'où cela procede. Les Payens
n'ont cognu sinon que la condition des hommes estoit miserable: mais il nous faut
regarder pourquoy Dieu nous a assubiettis à tant de maux: c'est à cause du péché.*

[3] But Calvin never teaches that we should as any general rule assert that when
any person suffers, that is due to his or her sins. Calvin's comments on the problem of the man born blind in John 9 are important in this connexion. "It is
undoubtedly true," he asserts, "that all our distresses arise from sin." But, he
points out, often the cause of suffering is concealed and we ought, in judging
cases, to restrain our curiosity that we may neither dishonour God nor be
malicious to our brethren. It is difficult to make any judgment on individual
instances, for sometimes God, in sending affliction has the purpose simply of
training us to obedience or testing our patience. Moreover, God is far more
severe in punishing his Church (which must be conformed to Christ in His
death) at present than the wicked whose punishment is reserved for the judgment day. "They are false interpreters therefore who say that all afflictions,
without any distinction, are sent on account of sins." Comm. on John 9 : 1 ff.,
C.O. 47 : 217–8.

[4] Inst. 3 : 8 : 6. *Ergo in ipsa quoque tribulationem acerbitate, Patris nostri clem-
entiam erga nos ac benignitatem recognoscere convenit: quando ne tum quidem
desinit salutem nostram promovere.* Cf. serm. on Job 5 : 17–18, C.O. 33 : 260.
*Nous avons à retenir ces deux poincts . . . l'un est, que . . . l'ire de Dieu nous doit
venir devant les yeux. . . . Et au reste que cependant aussi nous apprehendions la
bonté de Dieu de ce qu'il ne nous laisse point aller en perdition sans nous retirer à soy.*

[5] Comm. on Ps. 6 : 3, C.O. 31 : 75. *Quia autem hunc finem in poenis sumendis
Deo propositum esse scimus, ut nos humiliet, simul ac ferulis eius subacti sumus,
eius misericordiae aperta est ianua. Adde quod quum proprium sit eius munus
infirmos sanare, iacentes erigere, fulcire debiles, mortuis denique vitam restituere:
haec una ratio ad petendam eius gratiam nobis sufficit, si malis succumbimus.* Cf.
serm. on Luke 1 : 26–30, C.O. 46 : 71.

fact that God is punishing us means that He is planning for us in love, and does not will to leave us alone to perish, and is calling us to repent.[1] The fate most to be dreaded would be if God did not punish us for our sins nor sought to remedy them and bring us to repentance.[2] God exercises His anger towards His people only in such a way as never to be forgetful of His mercy and in such a way that His punishments are to be taken as evidences of His paternal love rather than of His anger.[3] The scourges of God which in themselves are signs of God's wrath can be blessed in Christ and can provide the occasion for us to lay hold of the fatherly love of God.[4] Therefore under affliction we must tremble before God's judgments "as far as is requisite for the mortification of the flesh," but at the same time not miss the consolation they can give us by reminding us of God's watchful providence over the human race.[5]

There is therefore always cause for thankfulness when we suffer affliction. Indeed, when we consider the suffering of men like Job, we are bound to realise that whatever suffering comes our way is but a gentle chastisement, a mild and comforting affliction compared with what might have been.[6] When we consider the massacre of the innocents by wicked Herod, we must also realise that the powers of evil around us are so fierce and determined on our annihilation that our lot would be cruel and terrible indeed did not God continually stretch out His hand to restrain the powers that are against us[7]—and just as Satan cast down on the

---

[1] Serm. on Job 14 : 13–15, C.O. 33 : 684. *Au reste, cependant que nous vivons que ceci nous soit bien resolu, qu'il n'y a rien meilleur pour nous que quand Dieu pense de nous: voire et fust-ce mesmes pour nous punir. Si Dieu pense de nous, afin de nous faire sentir sa grace, voila où consiste toute nostre ioye et nostre gloire, comme il est dit au Pseaume huitieme (v. 5) . . . mais comme i'ai dit, s'il nous chastie de nos pechez, encores nous fait-il grace: car il monstre par cela qu'il ne veut point que nous perissions.*

[2] Comm. on Ps. 81 : 12, C.O. 31 : 764–5.

[3] Comm. on 1 Cor. 11 : 32, C.O. 49 : 495.

[4] Comm. on Rom. 8 : 31, C.O. 49 : 162.

[5] Comm. on Ps. 119 : 52, C.O. 32 : 237. *Si quis obiiciat contrarium esse Dei iudiciis ut consolationem nobis afferant quae debebant terrorem incutere: responsio facilis est, iudiciis Dei terreri fideles quatenus illis ad carnis suae mortificationem expedit: sed quatenus inde agnoscunt Deo curae esse genus humanum, ampla consolationis materia sese offert.*

[6] Serm. on Job 2 : 7–10, C.O. 33 : 118. *Or nos afflictions sont moyennes et douces, si on les accompare à celles dont il est ici parlé. Concluons donc que Dieu se monstre benin et pitoyable envers nous, quand nous sommes chastiez ainsi doucement de sa main.*

[7] Serm. on Matt. 2 : 16–22, C.O. 46 : 446–7.

ground in violence the little epileptic boy whom Jesus was in the process of saving, so the powers of evil are all the more violent in their attacks against the faithful who are in the hand of Christ for eternal redemption.[1] Our very suffering is the necessary accompaniment of such redemption, and since we are in His hand we cannot be overcome or confounded.[2]

3. Under affliction faith lays hold of God's Word

In looking to God and renouncing all other help in the midst of the conflicts and contradictions that face his faith, the Christian is enabled to stand and endure because he lays hold of the Word of God. The Word of God alone is the source from which we derive our patience and become habituated to the endurance of the Cross.[3] The Word of God alone is the place in which we find a true wisdom which contrasts with all the blind wisdom that gives such mistaken direction to the life of this world.[4] No matter how apparently God-forsaken and abandoned we may seem, we can find satisfaction and solid ground for joy by resting on the truth of God's promises.[5] Indeed God is seeking to teach His people, in the midst of the hard struggle that exercises their faith, precisely this lesson, that when all other supports are taken away they should rest upon the "naked Word."[6] Therefore they must turn their minds away from the "present aspect of things," and, inspired by the Word, "stand, as it were upon a watch tower, waiting patiently for the fulfilment of what God has promised."[7]

[1] Serm. on Mark 1 : 23–7, C.O. 46 : 744. *Et cependant aussi notons, que comme ce povre homme a este delivré de Satan avec grans tourmens qu'il a endurez, que le diable l'a ietté par terre, et l'a comme deschiré, encore qu'il ne luy ait peu nuire pour le ruiner du tout, aussi quand Iesus Christ nous tire et delivre, de la tyrranie de Satan, si nous endurons quelque violences qu'il ne nous faut point trouver cela estrange.*

[2] Cf. Inst. 1 : 14 : 18.

[3] Comm. on Ps. 94 : 12. C.O. 32 : 24.

[4] Comm. on Ps. 119 : 24, C.O. 32 : 224–5; and on Ps. 86 : 11, C.O. 31 : 795; serm. on Deut. 6 : 13–15, C.O. 26 : 465.

[5] Comm. on Ps. 56 : 5, C.O. 31 : 548–9; and on Ps. 11 : 1, C.O. 31 : 120; serm. on Luke 1 : 69–72, C.O. 46 : 173.

[6] Comm. on Ps. 56 : 11, C.O. 31 : 552. *Ad hanc meditationem se assuefaciant fideles, ut inter tentationes firmam gloriam retineant, nudo verbo contenti. . . . Vix tamen unquam tres passus conficere licebit, nisi in solum verbum recumbere didicerint.* Cf. on Ps. 51 : 9–11, C.O. 31 : 516.

[7] Comm. on Ps. 87 : 3, C.O. 31 : 801. Cf. serm. on Gal. 2 : 20–1, C.O. 50 : 448. *Voilà donc comme il nous faut vivre par foy . . . que nous prenions ce miroir de la parole de Dieu, pour regarder les choses qui surmontent tout nostre sens, qui sont*

"In place of the reality," says Calvin, "We rest upon the Word."[1]
It is thus the Word that retains us, holds us back, and enables us
to say, "Lord thou art just," in the midst of circumstances that
seem to contradict altogether His righteousness.[2]

4. Faith is aggressive as well as submissive towards evil

While Calvin admits that a large part of our Christian warfare
consists in patiently standing up against the onslaughts of evil
rather than in aggressive action,[3] and while he is always emphasising
the need for abstinence and detachment in the face of the entice-
ments of what is evil,[4] he nevertheless lays it down clearly that it
is not enough merely to abstain from participating in and practising
evil, but that God means us to attack evil in any form in which it
meets us. We must espouse the cause of the innocent when they
are oppressed, and take up the fight for justice.[5] We must show
ourselves the enemies of evil-doers and seek to take action against
them. Otherwise in the sight of God we will be held as accomplices
in those things that we do not actively condemn.[6] Calvin looks on
it as equivalent to renouncing the cause of God and separating
ourselves from Him when out of fear for the displeasure of those
who are involved in evil, we consent to their evil-doing by our
silence and lack of protest. To do this is to uphold the cause of
wickedness.[7] It is our duty also to attack evils and abuses within
the Church. We may have no authority and no power to do such,
yet even in such circumstances it is the duty of those who do not
possess authority to "oppose with their tongue, which they have at
liberty, those vices which they cannot remedy with their hands."[8]

eslongnees de ce monde et qui sont invisibles du tout: et que nous eslevions nos yeux
iusques là: non point selon que nostre raison et prudence nous y pourra guider (car
ce n'est point assez), mais que nous surmontions ce monde, et que nous quittions les
choses presentes, afin de nous entretenir en l'attente des promesses de Dieu.
[1] Comm. on 2 Cor. 5 : 7, C.O. 50 : 63. Loco rei, in verbo acquiescimus.
[2] Serm. on Job 34 : 4–10, C.O. 35 : 139–40.
[3] Comm. on 2 Tim. 2 : 3, C.O. 52 : 361.   [4] See pp. 203–5 and 234–6.
[5] Serm. on Matt. 5 : 11–12, C.O. 46 : 811. Car la malice des hommes est si
grande, qu'il faut entrer souvent en combat pour maintenir les bons et innocens qu'on
afflige: et pour prendre en main les bonnes causes et iustes. . . . Ce n'est point assez
que chacun s'abstiene de malefice et d'outrage, mais il faut que nous procurions le
bien, entant qu'en nous est.
[6] Serm. on Deut. 9 : 20–4, C.O. 26 : 703–4.
[7] Serm. on Job 27 : 5–8, C.O. 34 : 457–9; cf. comm. on Ps. 119 : 158, C.O.
32 : 285–6.
[8] Comm. on Matt. 21 : 12, C.O. 45 : 580.

Our attitude towards the evils and wrongs we see around us must be determined by zeal to maintain the glory and cause of Christ. We must see God's honour at stake when evil is allowed to flourish unchecked. We must realise that God had put the vindication of His righteousness in our hands[1] and it is our business to "maintain God's quarrel," no matter what men may think of us or do to us.[2] A Christian must remember that Christ is the heir of the whole world, and has indeed already sanctified the whole world in His death, and therefore everything should be even now subject to Him.[3] If we are sensitive about the wrongs done to ourselves and inflamed with anger when our own honour is injured, we should be much more concerned and filled with sorrow when God's honour is attacked by evil.[4]

5. Faith can face death, feeling the horror of its curse, and
acknowledging its judgment, but finding in it a means
of blessing to be desired

Calvin has a good deal to say about the way in which a Christian should face and overcome not only suffering but also death itself. Death, if we face it frankly, is always so fearful a fact as to arouse within us naturally implanted feelings of dread and revulsion, for it is a corruption of nature due to the curse of God, and a reversal of the true order which God established before the Fall.[5] "A horror of death is naturally implanted in all of us, for to wish to be dissolved (*dissolvi*) is revolting to nature."[6] Death is thus a witness to the wrath of God, to man's rejection from His presence and

[1] Comm. on Ps. 139 : 22, C.O. 32 : 385. *Quisquis ad scelera connivet, eaque fovet suo silentio, perfidus est causae Dei proditor, qui nobis omnibus iustitiae suae patrocinium commendat.*
[2] Serm. on Gal, 5 : 11–14, C.O. 51 : 14.
[3] Comm. on Matt. 17 : 25, C.O. 45 : 522–3; and serm. on Deut. 6 : 1–4, C.O. 26 : 427. *Notons qu'auiourd'huy nous devons estre incitez beaucoup plus de servir à Dieu, veu qu'il a dedié toute la terre à soy, et qu'il veut que son Nom soit reclamé par tout: car le sang que nostre Seigneur Iesus Christ a espandu, a sanctifié tout le monde qui estoit pour lors comme en pollution. Car nous savons qu'il n'y avoit que ceste terre que Dieu se reservast, et en laquelle il voulust dominer iusques à la venue de son Fils.*
[4] Comm. on Ps. 119 : 139, C.O. 32 : 278; and on Ps. 139 : 22, C.O. 32 : 385.
[5] Serm. on Job 27 : 5–8, C.O. 34 : 467–8; cf. comm. on 1 Cor. 15 : 21, C.O. 49 : 545. *Mors non est a natura sed ab hominis peccato.*
[6] Comm. on John 21 : 18, C.O. 47 : 455. This dissolving is the *dissidium carnis et spiritus.*

his alienation from the Kingdom of God.[1] Calvin asserts that even pagans and unbelievers are constrained to recognise that death is a curse of God pronounced on Adam and all his seed, not only because everyone desires to live, and in death we are, as it were, annihilated, but also because God has left some kind of mark (*quelque marque*) so that men understand this without knowing hardly a word of Christian teaching.[2] Death, then, has a twofold purpose. It is ordained "not only for the dissolution of man, but also in order to make him feel the curse of God."[3]

A Christian shares with all men this natural dread of death, for a Christian is not unnatural. But to face and experience death is not so terrifying for a Christian as for an unbeliever who looks on it apart from Christ and thus sees in it the curse alone.[4] If we are Christians, however, we must dread death, but we must so struggle against the dread of death that it does not impair the open confession of our faith, nor overcome the joy and consolation of our hope.[5] Our piety should overcome and suppress our fear.[6] It is when we turn our eyes to the glory of the life that is to come that our dread of death is vanquished.[7] Death for the Christian does not mean the agony of being torn violently and against his will from his earthly surroundings, as it does for the unbeliever.[8] For the Christian the sword of death, which could otherwise mortally penetrate into the heart, has been blunted, and though it can wound it can only wound without danger, for death is the entrance into life. Death, like sin, may dwell in us, but it cannot reign.[9] When faith quickens the soul of man, death already has it sting extracted and its venom removed, so that it cannot inflict a deadly wound.[10]

[1] Serm. on Cant. Zech. v. 9–12, C.O. 35 : 528.
[2] Ibid.
[3] Serm. on Matt. 26 : 36–9, C.O. 46 : 840. Calvin points out here that in His death our Lord, besides His physical pain, suffered far more than being taken from this world and sundered in body and soul, for death is also an entry into the abyss of Hell and should alienate us from God and take away all hope of salvation. This is truly what death means, and if Christ had not suffered it, it would have been our lot.
[4] Comm. on Heb. 2 : 15, C.O. 55 : 33.
[5] Comm. on Matt. 10 : 32, C.O. 45 : 290; and on 2 Cor. 5 : 8, C.O. 50 : 64.
[6] Inst. 3 : 9 : 5.
[7] Comm. on Phil. 1 : 23, C.O. 52 : 18. *Interea non desinunt fideles mortem horrere: sed quum oculos convertunt ad vitam illam quae mortem sequitur, consolatione ista facile vincunt formidinem.*
[8] Serm. on Job 27 : 5–8, C.O. 34 : 465–6.
[9] Comm. on 1 Cor. 15 : 26, C.O. 49 : 548.
[10] Comm. on John 8 : 51, C.O. 47 : 212.

Death for us is no longer a mortal death. It is only a warning of the
curse of God, for Christ has borne the real curse for us.[1]

Though death has been overcome for us, however, it has still a
great deal to say to us, and we must heed its testimony. It reminds
us that we have but one life that quickly vanishes away instead of
the thousand lives that we sometimes imagine we have.[2] It teaches
us that it is mere vanity to rest at our ease amidst earthly goods
and honour.[3] It can shatter our pride and covetousness as well as
our false sense of security by reminding us that the result of
all our ambition, not simply to swallow up this earth, but to
have God create new worlds for us, can be nothing more than to
possess a piece of ground our own length in which to rot and
consume away to nothing![4] It can remind us continually of what
Christ had to suffer for us, for if we ourselves had not to face
death in some form, the death of Christ would not have its true
effect upon us.[5] It should always remind us of the anger of God
against sin.[6] We must, then, "think continually upon death,[7] for
though we can philosophise admirably on the vanity of life when
we see funerals or walk amongst the tombstones, we soon forget,
and relapse into supine security."[8]

Death has not only a message to bring to the Christian man, it
can actually be a means of blessing and communion with Christ.
It is the completion of the process of our mortification in Christ
which helps to complete our vivification in Christ. To die in faith
is the last act in bearing our Cross with Jesus Christ in faith.
Calvin does not seem to say as clearly as Luther that death is the
fulfilment of our baptism, but he nevertheless emphasises that
"we perish in order to be revived."[9] Death is the way by which
Christ leads us into life in fulfilment of His purpose that we

---

[1] Serm. on Isa. 53 : 11, C.O. 35 : 662 and 663. *La mort ne nous est plus mortelle,
. . . et . . . nous sommes affranchis de la malediction de Dieu. . . . Car la mort a
laquelle nous sommes maintenant suiets, n'est qu'un advertissement de la malediction
de Dieu.*   [2] Comm. on Ps. 90 : 5, C.O. 31 : 836.
[3] Serm. on Job 27 : 5–8, C.O. 34 : 464–5.
[4] Serm. on Job 1 : 20–2, C.O. 33 : 97–8. Calvin goes on to indicate that he
regarded pompous funerals and magnificent tombs as a rebellion against God.
*Et neantmoins on en voit beaucoup qui bataillent contre une telle necessité: ils
feront des sepulchres braves, ils auront des funerailles triomphantes: il semble que
telles gens veulent resister à Dieu.*   [5] Serm. on Isa. 53 : 11, C.O. 35 : 663.
[6] Comm. on Phil. 2 : 27, C.O. 52 : 41. *Hoc primo fidelibus perpetuum est, quod
in morte cuiusvis de ira Dei adversus peccatum commonefiunt.*
[7] Serm. on Job 3 : 11–19, C.O. 33 : 162.
[8] Inst. 3 : 9 : 2. Comm. on Luke 12 : 17, C.O. 45 : 385.   [9] Inst. 3 : 9 : 5.

should be like Himself in death and resurrection, and since this is
so our submission to death is something we have "in common
with Him."[1] "We do not die apart, but along with Christ, that we
may afterwards have life in common with Him."[2] Death is our
"sleep in Christ," which means that we retain in death our *coniunctio cum Christo*.[3]

Death, then, and indeed our whole tendency to corruption,
can be used by the Christian, in faith, almost as a sacrament to
confirm our union with Christ and to further our renewal in
Christ. But it is only by means of faith that death can have this
use. For the unbeliever death can bring no hope and no blessing.[4]
A Christian can, however, learn throughout his life to die well as
well as to live well, and by facing and using death by faith can
profit as much from death as from life.[5] He can make this poison-
ous thing serve him like medicine, since Jesus Christ has swallowed
all the poison that was there.[6] To be able to take up this attitude
to death is to reach the stage at which we are able to "despise
death."[7] Such "contempt of death" means that a man is able to
face death and the other extreme troubles of life, and to use them
by faith to further his ultimate salvation. This is the greatest
miracle that faith can achieve—far greater than if a man could
prolong his life for five generations or recover miraculously from
incurable sickness.[8] Our Lord Himself in His teaching sought to
"incite His disciples to contempt of death."[9] Thus the *horror
mortis* must become the *contemptus mortis*.

---

[1] Comm. on John 12 : 26, C.O. 47 : 290. *Est autem nobis dux itineris ad
obeundam mortem. Mitescit ergo, et quodammodo suavis redditur mortis acerbitas,
dum nobis eius subeundae conditio cum filio Dei communis est.*

[2] Comm. on 2 Tim. 2 : 11, C.O. 52 : 365.

[3] Comm. on 1 Thess. 4 : 14, C.O. 53 : 165.

[4] Serm. on Gal. 2 : 20–21, C.O. 50 : 445–6. *Nous ne pourrions pas estre
renouvellez pour parvenir au royaume de Dieu, sinon que nous mourions. Il nous
faut tousiours tendre à ceste corruption, et cependant n'estre point arrestez à ce que
nous appercevons à veuë d'oeil: car ce n'est qu'un ombrage que de ceste vie terrestre,
ce n'est que fumee qui s'escoule et s'esvanouit: par cela neantmoins nous sommes
renouvellez au dedans. Non pas que cela soit commun à tous, car les incredules
appercevront assez leurs foiblesses, ils sont contraints de sentir les adiournemens de
la mort, surtout quand ils viennent en viellesse, ils cognoissent qu'il ne faut quasi
qu'un souffle pour les mettre bas. Sur cela ils se tempestent, et veulent quasi despiter
Dieu et nature. Quoy qu'il en soit, ils ne sont pas renouvellez, combien qu'ils pouris-
sent.* [5] Serm. on Deut. 31 : 14–17, C.O. 28 : 629–30.

[6] Serm. on Matt. 26 : 36 f., C.O. 46 : 841.

[7] Comm. on Ps. 16 : 10, C.O. 31 : 156.

[8] Comm. on Heb. 11 : 35, C.O. 55 : 167.

[9] Comm. on Matt. 10 : 28; C.O. 45 : 288.

Faith in enabling us to overcome the horror of death begets in us not only a contempt of death but also a "desire of death (*desiderium mortis*)."[1] Thus faith can "compel us eagerly to desire what nature dreads."[2] Calvin can be very emphatic in urging us to long for death.[3] In this matter he can employ very cold logic. To wish to die is not simply something we are permitted to do but something which is our duty. Everything should tend to strive towards the end for which it was created. But the end to which we must aspire is beyond. Therefore we must wish to leave this world, and to do that soon.[4] But this longing for death must be moderated. It must not become an "unbridled passion," for we must submit quietly to the will of God, to "whom we ought to live and die."[5] Moreover, in desiring death we must be impelled by the right desire to leave the present world. We must not wish to depart merely because we hate life and are made unhappy by misfortune or sickness or poverty, but because here we are held in bondage to sin, and have many imperfections and are not yet fully reformed in the image of God.[6]

A Christian, then, will always be "ready to go,"[7] and in spite of the horror that death still holds will face it cheerfully being able "not only to live well, but also to die happily."[8]

---

[1] Comm. on 2 Cor. 5 : 8, C.O. 50 : 64. *Observa hic . . . veram fidem non contemptum modo, sed etiam desiderium mortis gignere. Itaque e converso infidelitatis signum esse, quum mortis horror supra apei gaudium et consolationem in nobis dominatur.*

[2] Inst. 3 : 9 : 5.

[3] Inst. 3 : 9 : 4.

[4] Serm. on Job 3 : 20–26, C.O. 33 : 170.

[5] Comm. on Rom. 7 : 24, C.O. 49 : 135.

[6] Serm. on Job 3 : 20–26, C.O. 33 : 167 and 170.

[7] Serm. on Deut. 31 : 14–17, C.O. 28 : 629.

[8] Inst. 2 : 16 : 14; comm. on 2 Cor. 5 : 1, C.O. 50 : 60–1.

Chapter III
Prayer as the principal exercise of faith

1. Prayer as the exercise of faith and repentance in response to the grace of God

"THE principal exercise which the children of God have," says Calvin, "is to pray; for in this way they give a true proof of their faith."[1] In the chapter on prayer in the *Institutes* he calls prayer the "perpetual exercise of faith."[2] Prayer is the inevitable outcome of the presence of faith in the human heart, for wherever faith exists it cannot be sluggish. It is bound to break out spontaneously and immediately into prayer.[3] By prayer, faith, as it were, "digs up those treasures which the Gospel of our Lord discovers" to its eye.[4] Therefore prayer is nothing else but the expression of a living faith.[5] Prayer is faith uttering the love and desire towards God which is natural to it.[6] The same promises which give rise to faith in the heart are a constant call and challenge to prayer for their realisation, and the same Spirit who creates faith in the heart constrains the believer also to pray.[7] The exercise of prayer is therefore sure evidence of the presence of faith but without prayer faith cannot be genuine.[8] Moreover, the exercise of prayer is given so that faith can be kept alive and active. The constant challenge and call to prayer arouses faith out of sloth and keeps it from going languid and torpid or from lying idle or dead.[9]

[1] Serm. on 1 Tim. 2 : 1–2, C.O. 53 : 125.　　　　[2] Inst. 3 : 20.
[3] Comm. on Matt. 21 : 21, C.O. 45 : 585. *Fidem Dei habere tantundem valet atque certo sibi promittere, et exspectare a Deo quidquid opus fuerit. Sed quia fides, si qua est nobis, erumpit statim in preces, et ad thesauros gratiae Dei, qui verbo ostensi sunt, penetrat, ut illis fruatur, ideo fidei precationem subiungit Christus.* Comm. on Acts 1 : 4, C.O. 48 : 16.　　　　[4] Inst. 3 : 20 : 1–2.
[5] Comm. on Ps. 54 : 6, C.O. 31 : 533. *Docet . . . precatum esse ex vivo fidei sensu.*
[6] Comm. on Ps. 91 : 15, C.O. 32 : 8. *Amor enim ille et desiderium, quae ex fide nascuntur, nos ad eum invocandum adducunt.*
[7] Serm. on 1 Cor. 10 : 12–14, C.O. 49 : 648. Cf. comm. on Ps. 145 : 18, C.O. 32 : 418.　　　　[8] Inst. 3 : 20 : 1.
[9] Inst. 3 : 20 : 3–4. Cf. comm. on Ps. 119 : 58, C.O. 32 : 239. *Sine precibus otiosa torperet fides.* Comm. on Ps. 145 : 18, C.O. 32 : 418.

Calvin admits that pagans and unbelievers may utter prayers for help and deliverance, and such prayers may be heard and answered by God even though they do not spring from faith.[1] But this fact has no important significance for believers. Though the heathen under the constraint of their need call upon God, they do so in a "confused and tumultous manner." There is all the difference in the world between such an approach to God and the approach of the Christian guided and inspired by his faith and knowledge of the fatherly favour and goodness of God.[2] True and genuine prayer is "not the mere idle lifting up of the voice, but the presentation of our petitions from an inward principle of faith."[3] Since prayer is the testimony to our hope that we can obtain from God all that we need, then to pray without faith is to "pray dissemblingly"[4] and is to irritate God by our distrust and insincerity.[5] "Doubtful prayer is nothing else than mere make-belief."[6] Therefore Calvin makes it one of his four conditions and rules of prayer that "we should be animated to pray with the sure hope of succeeding."[7] Elsewhere he says that the first step of prayer is "the firm belief that our prayers are not in vain."[8] Our prayers must "follow the footsteps of faith,"[9] which "goes before to illumine the way, giving us the full persuasion that he is our Father" and opening the gate that we may converse freely with Him.[10] To be able to pray is a miracle. "It is not within the power of man either to convert himself or to pray."[11]

Prayer therefore must be thought of as response to the forgiving grace of God in Jesus Christ. It is an approach to God made

---

[1] Inst. 3 : 20 : 15.

[2] Comm. on Ps. 18 : 7, C.O. 31 : 173. *Deinde appellans Deum suum, se a crassis Dei contemptoribus vel hypocritis discernit, qui necessitate quidem coacti coeleste numen confuse invocant: sed nec familiariter, nec puro corde ad Deum accedunt, de cuius paterna gratia nihil tenent.* Cf. on Ps. 79 : 7, C.O. 31 : 750. *Significat propheta, nisi praecedat Dei cognitio, non posse ipsum invocari.* Serm. on Eph. 1 : 3–4, C.O. 51 : 265.

[3] Comm. on Ps. 140 : 6, C.O. 32 : 388–9. *Haec igitur vera precandi regula est, non futiliter vocem attollere, sed ex fide intus concepta proferre nostras preces.* Calvin also speaks here of *se orare serio, et recondito fidei sensu.* (p. 388.)

[4] Comm. on James 1 : 6, C.O. 55 : 387.

[5] Inst. 3 : 20 : 11.

[6] Comm. on Ps. 140 : 13, C.O. 32 : 390.

[7] Inst. 3 : 20 : 11.

[8] Comm. on Mark 9 : 22, C.O., 45 : 495.

[9] Inst. 3 : 20 : 11.

[10] Comm. on Ps. 18 : 7, C.O. 31 : 173.

[11] Comm. on Jer. 29 : 12, C.O. 38 : 595 (quoting Augustine).

possible only through His initiative in coming near to men in His fatherly forgiving love.[1] Prayer is essentially the activity of the forgiven within the relationship of reconciliation. It is true that we need to pray for pardon. Indeed, according to Calvin, we must not begin to pray without pleading for forgiveness.[2] But we pray for pardon only because we are already sure of His pardon and have already been caught up in His pardoning love.[3] As with faith, so with prayer. We pray only because God presents Himself to us with open arms to receive us as His children.[4] We could not possibly pray without God Himself being there beforehand to "anticipate us with His invitation."[5] Before we turn to Him, He is ready to receive us; before we have our mouth opened, He has His hand stretched out ready to give us all that we need.[6] Moreover, what we say to Him we can say only as the echo of His own gracious Word of encouragement and invitation. In prayer we claim Him as our God because He has pronounced us in His Word to be His people. Our confidence in praying is inspired by the "lovely and soothing" titles with which He invests Himself in His Word and the promises to hear and answer which are always attached to His command that we should pray.[7]

The prayer of faith will thus be the prayer of self-abasement and humility. Though faith gives rise to an approach of childlike confidence to the Heavenly Father, faith is also inseparably linked up with repentance. The attitude of the believing man as he approaches God is bound to be one of fear and trembling,[8] and his prayer is bound to be prefaced with a confession of his guilt not only for the sins of the passing day which he can call to mind, but also of the sinfulness of his very nature.[9] Therefore

---

[1] Comm. on Ps. 143 : 10, C.O. 32 : 405. *Iam quum dicit, quia tu Deus meus, ostendit non aliunde quam ex gratuita adoptione et promissionibus se petere impetrandi fiduciam. Neque enim in arbitrio nostro est facere ut sit Deus noster, donec gratis nos praeveniat.*

[2] Comm. on Ps. 130 : 4, C.O. 32 : 335. *Ut autem orando quis proficiat, eum necesse est a gratuita peccatorum remissione incipere.*

[3] Comm. on Ps. 51 : 9 f., C.O. 31 : 517. *Imo sic habendum est, non posse nos serio precari, ut Deus peccanti ignoscat, nisi iam fide conceperimus, ipsum fore placabilem.* Calvin goes on to point out that in the Lord's Prayer "we . . . begin by addressing God as our Father, and yet afterwards . . . pray for remission of sins." Cf. comm. on Isa. 63 : 16, C.O. 27 : 402. "Believers do not contend (*litigare*) with God."

[4] Serm. on Luke 1 : 45–8, C.O. 46 : 111.
[5] Inst. 3 : 20 : 13.
[6] 10th serm. on Ps. 119, C.O. 32 : 596.
[7] Inst. 3 : 20 : 13.
[8] Inst. 3 : 20 : 11.
[9] Inst. 3 : 20 : 9.

though, being persuaded of the paternal love of God, believers have no hesitation in approaching Him, they do so, "not eleated with supine and presumptuous security," but as "humble and abased suppliants."[1] From an examination of many of the prayers of the Bible Calvin proves that the confidence of the man who prays is based solely on the mercy of God,[2] for God rejects those who imagine that there is any good either in themselves or in the service they render to Him.[3]

2. Prayer and the mediation of Christ

Prayer can be made only in the name of Christ, and through Christ as Mediator. There can be no approach to God with any hope of that filial and familiar intercourse which we know to be the basis of prayer unless the name and the sacrifice of Jesus Christ are made the sole ground of that hope. It is only through the interposition of Christ that the throne of God's dreadful glory and majesty is converted into a throne of grace.[4] We are clean and acceptable in God's sight only if we cleanse ourselves by faith in Jesus Christ and present to God the grace which has been acquired for us by His death and passion.[5] Indeed, if we wish to use the title "Father" when we speak to God in prayer, we can only do so as we have recourse to the death and passion of Christ.[6] "In no other way than through Christ can God be called Father."[7] Moreover we must remember that the promises of the Word which inspire our prayers and invite us to pray are all themselves sealed in the blood of Christ.[8] Only, therefore, by such an approach to God through the mediation of Christ can we have any confidence in our praying.[9] But such an approach is effective in breaking down all the barriers that might otherwise make prayer an impos-

---

[1] Inst. 3 : 20 : 14.   [2] Inst. 3 : 20 : 8–9.
[3] Comm. on Ps. 16 : 2, C.O. 31 : 150. *Summa est, quum ad Deum accedimus, exuendam esse omnem confidentiam. Nam si quid penes nos esse fingimus, quia praecipuam honoris sui partem ei detrahimus, non mirum est si nos repudiet. Si vero nostra obsequia agnoscimus per se nihili esse, nulloque pretio digna haec humilitas quasi suffitus est boni odoris qui illis gratiam conciliet.*
[4] Inst. 3 : 20 : 17.   [5] Serm. on Job 1 : 2–5, C.O. 33 : 46.
[6] Serm. on Deut. 21 : 22–3, C.O. 27 : 700. *Ainsi, quand nous voudrons trouver Dieu propice, que nous le voudrons nommer nostre Pere (comme il faut que nous usions de ce tiltre, si nous le voulons prier en vraye confiance) recourons tousiours à la mort et passion de nostre Seigneur Iesus Christ.*
[7] Comm. on Isa. 53 : 16, C.O. 37 : 402. Cf. Inst. 3 : 20 : 36.
[8] Serm. on Deut. 26 : 16–19, C.O. 28 : 292.   [9] Inst. 3 : 20 : 16.

sible task. "We have the heart of God," says Calvin, "as soon as we have placed before Him the name of His Son."[1]

Calvin frequently speaks of our prayers as being washed in, or sprinkled with, the blood of Christ, or sanctified through the death of Christ.[2] He speaks also of our prayers as having a connexion with the intercession of Christ, and is always ready to notice in the Bible the close connexion between sacrifice and prayer. In Old Testament times, "when the fathers prayed..., their hope of obtaining what they asked for was founded upon sacrifices."[3] God commanded in the Law that "the priest alone should enter the sanctuary bearing the names of the twelve tribes of Israel on his shoulders and as many precious stones on his breast, while the people stand at a distance in the outer court, and thereafter united their prayers with the priest." The sacrifice "had the effect of ratifying and confirming their prayers."[4] As sacrifice made prayer effective in the Old Testament, so the sacrifice of Christ makes His intercession for us at the right hand of God for ever effective.[5] Calvin asserts that "the blood by which He atoned for our sins, the obedience which He rendered, is a continual intercession for us."[6] Indeed, when we think of the intercession of Christ, we are not meant to imagine that Christ is continually on his knees before the Father imploring for His people, but simply that "He appears in the presence of God and that the power of His death has the effect of a perpetual intercession for us."[7]

Since it is the intercession of Christ, then, that makes the atonement efficacious continually before God, we ourselves, in our approach to prayer in the name of Christ, in pleading the sacrifice of Christ, must link up our prayers with the intercession

[1] Comm. on John 16 : 26, C.O. 47 : 371. *Docemur cor Dei nos tenere, simul ac filii nomen illi opposuimus.*

[2] Serm. on Job 42 : 9–17, C.O. 35 : 504. *Il faut que nos prieres soyent arrousees du sang qu'il a espandu pour laver nos macules.* Cf. serm. on Deut. 21 : 22–3, C.O. 27 : 700. Cf. comm. on Ps. 20 : 4 f., C.O. 31 : 209. *Hodie non aliter gratae sunt nostrae orationes Deo, nisi quatenus eas sui sacrifii odore Christus perfundit et sanctificat.* Cf. comm. on Heb. 8 : 3, C.O. 55 : 97.

[3] Comm. on Ps. 20 : 4 f., C.O. 31 : 209.

[4] Inst. 3 : 20 : 18.

[5] Comm. on 1 Tim. 2 : 6, C.O. 52 : 272. *Lege quartum caput ad Hebraeos circa finem, et initium quinti: reperies quod dico, intercessionem, qua propitiatur nobis Deus, in sacrificio fundatam esse.*

[6] Comm. on John 16 : 26, C.O. 47 : 371. *Virtus sacrificii, quo semel Deum nobis placavit, semper vigens et efficax, sanguis quo expiavit peccata nostra, obedientia quam praestitit, continua est pro nobis intercessio.*

[7] Inst. 3 : 20 : 20.

of Christ in the same way as the people in the Old Testament linked up their prayers with those of the priest who bore their sacrifices into the sanctuary. All prayers which are not supported by Christ's intercession are rejected,[1] says Calvin. Not only must our prayers be grounded on His sacrifice, but we must at the same time be assured that it is He who is carrying the word to God for us and causing us to be heard.[2] He presents the prayers of His people continually.[3] Therefore Calvin insists not only that all our mutual intercessions within the Church must have reference to the one intercession of Christ upon which they are all grounded[4] but also that our thanksgivings too can be sanctified only in connexion with the sacrifice and intercession of Christ.[5]

3. Prayer must be controlled, formed and inspired by the Word

In order to be a genuine exercise of faith, prayer must be founded upon the Word of God. The faith that gives rise to prayer is created by the Word and is ever aroused to fresh life and vigour by listening to the promises of the Word. Through the Word, God continually acknowledges us to be His people and presents Himself so that we can lay hold of Him.[6] This means not only that faith can respond "Amen" to such promises, but that the door is thrown wide open for us all to "introduce ourselves into God's favour" without subtle artifice, to seek God and to pray, not as the hypocrites or the ungodly, "who pray under the constraint of present necessity," and "with a mere expectation of a chance issue," but to make a bold approach inspired by the fact that God has anticipated our fears and has given us a clear and cordial

[1] Comm. on Heb. 7 : 26, C.O. 55 : 95.
[2] Serm. on Job 42 : 9–17, C.O. 35 : 507. *Nous serons là receus à pitié: voire, quand nos oraisons seront fondees sur ce sacrifice qu'il a offert, et que nous cognoistrons que c'est à luy de porter la parole pour nous, et de faire que nous soyons exaucez.*
[3] Inst. 3 : 20 : 20.
[4] Inst. 3 : 20 : 9.
[5] Comm. on Ps. 66 : 15, C.O. 31 : 615; Inst. 3 : 20 : 28; comm. on Ps. 118 : 27 f., C.O. 32 : 214.
[6] Serm. on Luke 1 : 18–25, C.O. 46 : 53–4. *Car si tost que Dieu parle, nostre office est de respondre Amen: c'est à dire, d'accepter sans replique ne murmure pour certain et infallible tout ce qu'il prononce: comme il est dit que quand il nous tiendra pour son peuple, nous avons à respondre de nostre costé, Tu sera nostre Dieu. Il faut donc qu'il y ait un accord mutuel entre les promesses que Deu nous offre, et la foy qui s'y range.*

invitation, and has even commanded us to come to Him.[1] Unless God makes such a personal and gracious approach to us through the Word and our confidence in prayer is a response to such a Word, none of us can have any access to the presence of God through prayer, for we must wait till He invites and calls us.[2] "What mortal man otherwise would dare present Himself before God and say, 'Do me an obligement, and let us make a pact together to the effect that you will be my God and I will be numbered among your people'?" Such an approach could be regarded only as "diabolical boldness."[3] Therefore there can be no access to God for any prayer that is not founded upon the Word of God.[4]

It is necessary not only that the Word of God should precede and inspire the approach to prayer but also that in its direction and in all its details our prayer should be governed and restrained by the same Word.[5] We are not at liberty in this matter to follow the suggestions of our own minds, or to form our wishes according to our own fancy. We dare not ask for more than God would freely bestow.[6] To do so would be to tempt God.[7] In the exercise of faith, self-denial and self-control and obedience to the Word of God are always the ruling principles. "As nothing is more at variance with faith than the foolish and irregular desires of the flesh, it follows that those in whom faith reigns do not desire everything without discrimination, but only that which the Lord promises to give."[8] Therefore we cannot pray in faith unless we moderate our desires and confine our prayers to what God has

[1] Comm. on Ps. 27 : 8, C.O. 31 : 275–6. *Dixi nuper fieri non posse ut quisquam fide assurgat ad Deum quaerendum, donec eius invitatione patefactus fuerit aditus. . . . Iam ergo David se hac clave ianuam sibi ad Deum quaerendum fuisse apertam dicit. . . . Ita nihil opus est anxium artificium et longas ambages quaerere, quibus se fideles in Dei gratiam insinuent.* Cf. comm. on Ps. 65 : 2, C.O. 31 : 603.

[2] Comm. on Ps. 71 : 22, C.O. 31 : 663.

[3] Serm. on Deut. 26 : 16–19, C.O. 28 : 289. Cf. comm. on Ps. 80 : 10, C.O. 31 : 756. *Quis enim in nostrum Dei conspectum prosilire audeat, donec praeveniat nos ipse?*

[4] Serm. on Ps. 119 (10th), C.O. 32 : 601.

[5] Comm. on Ps. 35 : 23, C.O. 31 : 356. *Ergo ut rite composita sint vota nostra, fulgeat in cordibus nostris primum necesse est fides providentiae Dei: nec tantum ordine praecedat omnes affectus, sed etiam temperet ac dirigat.*

[6] Comm. on Ps. 91 : 15, C.O. 32 : 8. *Unde iterum patet . . . legitimam precandi rationem fundatam esse in Dei verbo: quia hic nihil proprio arbitrio audendum est.* Cf. comm. on John 15 : 7, C.O. 47 : 341; and on John 17 : 2, C.O. 47 : 376. *Haec perpetua est orandi regula, non plus petere quam quod ultro daturus esset Deus.*

[7] Comm. on Ps. 106 : 14, C.O. 32 : 121–2.

[8] Comm. on Matt. 17 : 19, C.O. 45 : 496.

laid down.[1] For in this respect the rule of prayer follows the rule of faith.[2] The one safe rule, then, is to form our prayers only in the clear light of the Word of God, in compliance with what He has commanded, making our prayers an echo in our hearts of His promises, and not allowing ourselves to seek anything more than He has promised.[3] Calvin frequently warns us to avoid trying to make God subservient to our own humour and caprice or ambition, to our over-hasty or vague and incoherent desires, or foolish headstrong passions.[4] "The sole end and legitimate use of prayer . . . is that we may reap the fruits of God's promises."[5]

Calvin constantly recommends the use of the actual language of Holy Scripture in the prayers we utter to God. It is true that in the Lord's Prayer and elsewhere the main purpose of Scripture is to "guide and restrain our wishes" rather than to dictate words from which we are not at liberty to depart,[6] nevertheless, even of the Lord's Prayer Calvin can say that our Lord "puts words in our lips."[7] He recommends meditation upon the promises of Scripture so "that we may be furnished with words" for prayer.[8] He speaks of the Holy Ghost in the Psalms as "dictating" to us "forms of prayer."[9] Such forms of prayer are "accommodated to our understanding" by the Holy Ghost.[10] In the use by the crowd on Palm Sunday of the prayer "Hosanna" he notes that here we have a prayer originating in the Scripture and used by the Church throughout an uninterrupted succession of ages, and he urges us, not only to cherish in our hearts the same desires as are expressed in the prayer, but to note that in order to stir us up to true ardour in this matter God "dictates to us the words."[11] The very fact that

---

[1] Comm. on Ps. 7 : 7, C.O. 31 : 82. *Nec sane aliter ex fide concipitur oratio, nisi dum in primis respicimus quid Deus praecipiat, ne temere vel fortuito prosiliant animi nostri ad appetendum plus quam licet.*

[2] Comm. on Matt. 21 : 21, C.O. 45 : 585.

[3] Comm. on Ps. 7 : 7, C.O. 31 : 82; and on Ps. 50 : 15, C.O. 31 : 503.

[4] Cf. comm. on Ps. 119 : 38, C.O. 32 : 231; on Ps. 55 : 23, C.O. 31 : 545; on Ps. 7 : 7, C.O. 31 : 82; and on Ps. 109 : 6, C.O. 32 : 149; Inst. 3 : 20 : 44.

[5] Comm. on Ps. 119 : 38, C.O. 32 : 231.

[6] Comm. on Matt. 6 : 9, C.O. 45 : 195.　　　　　　[7] Inst. 3 : 20 : 34.

[8] Comm. on Ps. 85 : 6, C.O. 31 : 787. *Sic enim inter precandum promissiones Dei meditari convenit, quae nobis verba suppeditent.*

[9] Comm. on Ps. 102 : 9, C.O. 32 : 64. *Nam spiritus sanctus hanc precandi formam dictando, testari voluit, Deum talibus contumeliis moveri ut suis succurrat.* Comm. on Ps. 44 : 20, C.O. 31 : 445. *Sciamus autem in his verbis dictari nobis a spiritu sancto precandi formam.*

[10] Comm. on Ps. 13 : 4, C.O. 31 : 133.

[11] Comm. on John 12 : 13, C.O. 47 : 282–3.

such forms of prayer have been inspired and put in the mouths of God's saints should be regarded as implying the promise that the use of them will not be in vain.[1]

When it is founded upon the Word of God in the way that has been described, prayer becomes characterised by true boldness. Calvin insists that we must come with our heads erect to the throne of grace and that a pusillanimous spirit defiles our prayers and profanes the name of God.[2] It is the Word of God which inspires such boldness. The Word is continually encouraging us to expect from God things far greater than all our human imagination or reason can conceive, and to cease measuring the love and power of God by our own thoughts and standards. We must take His great promises seriously and let them encourage us to come to Him with all the greater boldness and do Him the honour of holding Him to what He has declared in His Word, and if He does not fulfil at first our demands, then, like Moses and Abraham, we must refuse to be put off, even when He seems to tell us to go away and let Him alone.[3] "Let us learn that God in His promises is set before us as if He were our willing debtor,"[4] says Calvin. We can go to Him and with full assurance that it is not in vain require Him to behave towards us as He has promised.[5] The very clarity of the promises given in Scripture incite us to so much more boldness.[6] Thus it is that the same Word which inspires humility and fear in those who hear it, and which restrains the desires of the flesh and constrains to absolute submission to the will of God, nevertheless at the same time inspires those who submit to it with a remarkable boldness and confidence in their approach to God. "A bold spirit in prayer," says Calvin, "well accords with fear, reverence and anxiety."[7]

---

[1] Comm. on Ps. 17 : 8, C.O. 31 : 163. *Nam quum haec precandi forma a spiritu sancto dictata sit, promissionem in se continet.*

[2] Serm. on Luke 1 : 73–8, C.O. 46 : 186. *Il faut . . . que nous puissions nous presenter devant luy la teste levée, et que nous l'invoquions en fiance et hardiesse, comme il est dit au 3 ch. des Ephesiens. Car sans cela aussi toutes nos prieres seront souillées et n'y aura que puantise, et nous profanerons mesmes le nom de Dieu.*

[3] Comm. on Ps. 31 : 19, C.O. 31 : 309; 10th serm. on Ps. 119, C.O. 32 : 593; serm. on Deut. 9 : 13–14, C.O. 26 : 686–8.

[4] Comm. on Ps. 119 : 58, C.O. 32 : 240.

[5] Serm. on Deut. 26 : 16–19, C.O. 28 : 292.

[6] Comm. on Rom. 8 : 15, C.O. 49 : 150. *Nam quo apertior est promissio etiam maior precandi libertas.*

[7] Inst. 3 : 20 : 14

4. Prayer must be constantly related to our human need.

Prayer must arise out of human need. "To seek when we feel
the need of God's grace is nothing else but to pray."[1] Prayer is the
genuine cry of the human heart for help in the midst of circumstances that cannot be met by merely human resources. It is true
that prayer must also be inspired by the Spirit of God and must
be a response to the love and grace of Jesus Christ; nevertheless at
the same time it must find its inspiration in our human need,[2]
otherwise it can become the mere performance of a formal devotional exercise. It is true that in all prayer the glory of God, and
not the mere relief of human need, must be the first motive,[3] and
yet it would defraud God of His honour did we not refer every
cause and every situation in which we are involved to Him and
leave Him to determine the issue.[4] All who truly give themselves
to the service of God are made to feel keenly their need of His
help and are brought into such situations that only in prayer can
they find relief and assurance, and only through prayer can they
win the day. God thus exercises His people under a Cross in order
to teach them to come to the knowledge of their need and thus to
pray.[5] "No one can give himself cheerfully to prayer until he has
been softened by the Cross and thoroughly subdued."[6]

We must therefore not be ashamed of making our need the
pretext and inspiration of our prayers. Indeed, David made his
need a chariot by which he ascended upwards to God.[7] We must
realise that the exercise of prayer is "the most effectual solace"
given to us by God for all our miseries, and is to be accepted as
His gift while our troubles continue.[8] It is true that we should
pray under all circumstances, however comfortable and quiet our
situation. Indeed, if we only realised it, our need to depend on the

[1] Comm. on Jer. 29 : 13, C.O. 38 : 595. *Quaerendi autem ratio, ubi opus
habemus Dei gratia, non alia est quam precari.*
[2] Inst. 3 : 20 : 6.
[3] Comm. on Ps. 115 : 1, C.O. 32 : 183. *Imo hic etiam, quum iuvari petimus,
scopus nobis esse debet, ut illustret nomen Dei liberatio quam adepti erimus.* Cf.
comm. on Ps. 118 : 26, C.O. 32 : 213.
[4] Comm. on Ps. 17 : 1, C.O. 31 : 159.
[5] Comm. on Zech. 13 : 9, C.O. 44 : 359. *Ergo eruditio crucis necessaria est,
ut vigeant inter nos seriae precationes.* Cf. comm. on Ps. 39 : 8, C.O. 31 : 401.
[6] Comm. on Ps. 30 : 9, C.O. 31 : 297.
[7] Comm. on Ps. 143 : 6 f., C.O. 32 : 403.
[8] Comm. on Ps. 14 : 7, C.O. 31 : 141.

grace of God under such circumstances is just as desperate as at any other time. But times of affliction are to be regarded as times when we must specially exercise ourselves in prayer.[1] The more adverse and cruel our circumstances, "the more we ought to be roused to eagerness in prayer,"[2] realising that severe affliction is a call and challenge from God to us to pray the more earnestly.[3] "Whenever, therefore, we are assailed by any temptation, let us betake ourselves forthwith to prayer as to a sacred asylum."[4]

We must remember always in our praying that our true need before God is for forgiveness. Though we may have many other urgent needs, "the thing which we must principally and particularly request is that He will have mercy upon us, which is the source of every other blessing."[5] The penitent man of faith before God will implore the cure of his sin and will "beware of imitating foolish patients, who anxious about curing accidental symptoms, neglect the root of the disease."[6] Even in praying for release from the most severe affliction we must do so in "a duly chastened spirit of devotion" without any sinful complaining and with the confession of sin and the hope of forgiveness, not demanding the complete removal of the affliction but willing to be content with its least mitigation.[7]

5. Prayer as the expression of the heart to God

Calvin stresses the fact that prayer is the disburdening of the heart before God.[8] It is a pouring-out of the soul with its complaints into His bosom.[9] God's purpose in sending us affliction is

---

[1] Comm. on Ps. 50 : 15, C.O. 31 : 502.

[2] Comm. on Ps. 17 : 9, C.O. 31 : 163.

[3] Comm. on Ps. 118 : 5, C.O. 32 : 203. *Circumstantia temporis quam exprimit, admonet, quo magis nos premunt res adversae, tunc vere opportunum esse orandi tempus.*

[4] Comm. on Phil. 4 : 6, C.O. 52 : 61.

[5] Comm. on Ps. 119 : 58, C.O. 32 : 239–40.

[6] Inst. 3 : 20 : 9.

[7] Comm. on Ps. 38 : 2, C.O. 31 : 386. Cf. on Ps. 109 : 21, C.O. 32 : 155.

[8] Comm. on Isa. 63 : 16, C.O. 37 : 402. *Nam oratio nihil aliud quam explicatio cordis nostri coram Deo est.* Cf. Inst. 3 : 20 : 3. . . . *dum vota nostra omnia coram eius oculis sistere adeoque totum cor effundere discimus.* Cf. comm. on Ps. 62 : 8, C.O. 31 : 588. *Optimum remedium adhibet David, ut fideles curas suas in Deum exonerando, quodammodo ante euis oculos corda sua effundant.*

[9] Comm. on Ps. 3 : 2, C.O. 31 : 53. *Sed rarae fidei signum fuit, quod tanto metu perculsus, querimoniam suam in Dei sinum deponere ausus est.* Cf. comm. on Ps. 73 : 11, C.O. 31 : 680.

that, instead of allowing hidden sorrow to eat into our hearts, we
should unburden ourselves to Him in prayer and thus exercise our
faith.[1] All prayer, whether it takes the form of thanksgiving or
supplication or confession, is thus an "effusion and manifestation
of internal feeling before Him who is the searcher of the heart."[2]
Through this exercise God seeks to enter deeply into our hearts
and to hold communion with the inward feelings of our mind.[3]
Only when we can disburden our souls thus into the bosom of
God can we prevent detestable thoughts from entering deeply
into our souls.[4] We have all a natural tendency to shut up our
afflictions in our own breasts,[5] to suppress our fears and griefs
with stoical obstinacy,[6] to drink up our own sorrow and keep it to
ourselves,[7] to complain to our fellow men rather than to God, and
to covet retirement.[8] All this is bad for us, and it is the mark which
distinguishes the believing man from the unbeliever that he in-
stinctively casts his burden on the Lord in prayer.[9] It is an
infallible proof, in the midst of distress, that a man has faith when
he refuses sullenly to gnaw the bit or withhold his groaning from
God, but will have fellowship with God over his need.[10] Here is
one answer to the question why we should pray when God already
knows our need before we ask Him. It is true that there is no need
to inform God of what He already knows. It is superfluous to argue
with Him. Nevertheless, when we willingly make God the witness
of all our afflictions by pouring out our hearts before Him, "our
cares are greatly lightened and our confidence of obtaining our
requests increases."[11] Calvin, pointing out the frequent repetition

---

[1] Comm. on Rom. 8 : 26, C.O. 49 : 157. *Non ideo aerumnis eos Deus affligit ut
intus caecum dolorem vorent, sed ut se exonerent precando, atque ita fidem suam
exerceant.*

[2] Inst. 3 : 20 : 29. *Quando vero hunc esse orationis scopum iam prius dictum est,
ut erecti in Deum animi ferantur, tum ad confessionem laudis, tum ad opem implor-
andam: ex eo intelligere licet primas eius partes in mente et animo positas esse: vel
potius orationem ipsam, esse proprie interioris cordis affectum, qui apud Deum,
cordium scrutatorem, effunditur et exponitur.*

[3] Ibid.   [4] Comm. on Ps. 73 : 11, C.O. 31 : 680.

[5] Comm. on Ps. 62 : 8, C.O. 31 : 588.

[6] Comm. on Ps. 143 : 6 f., C.O. 32 : 403.

[7] Comm. on Ps. 89 : 46, C.O. 31 : 828.

[8] Comm. on Ps. 88 : 2, C.O. 31 : 806.   [9] Ibid.

[10] Comm. on Ps. 3 : 5, C.O. 31 : 54–5.

[11] Comm. on Ps. 10 : 13, C.O. 31 : 116. *Nam usus precandi semper notandus
est: ut scilicet Deus omnium nostrorum affectuum testis sit: non quod alioqui ipsum
lateant, sed quia, dum coram ipso effundimus corda nostra tantundem levantur
curae nostrae, et augescit impetrandi fiducia.* Cf. comm. on Ps. 54 : 4, C.O. 31 :
532.

of the same request in prayer in one of the Psalms, can say, "Nor
is this repetition . . . to be thought vain, for hereby the saints, by
little and little, discharge their cares upon God, and this impor-
tunity is a sacrifice of a sweet savour before Him."[1]

In prayer both the posture of the body and the words in which
the prayer is expressed should be a genuine expression of what the
heart either feels or wills to feel.[2] Since in prayer we direct ourselves not to men but to God who sees the heart unerringly,
artificial eloquence or the rhetoric that we might use successfully
to impress our fellow men is entirely out of place. All that matters is
"pure simplicity."[3] It was to emphasise this that Jesus gave us the
advice when we pray to go into our closets and shut the door and
pray secretly. He did not thereby mean to teach that prayer
necessarily was to be a solitary exercise, but that prayer is so much
a matter of the inward secret heart before God alone that we can
only be natural and spontaneous in it when we are conscious that
we have no other witness than God.[4] We should not normally,
however, attempt to communicate this inward feeling of the heart
to God without any outward form of expression. It is fitting,
though not, of course, necessary, that the attitude of the heart
should express itself in definite speech,[5] and that it should be
reflected in a posture of humility,[6] and with the hands and eyes
so directed as to indicate that our desire is that our heart should be
raised to Heaven from whence alone can come our help.[7] The ideal

---

[1] Comm. on Ps. 86 : 6, C.O. 31 : 793.

[2] Comm. on John 17 : 1, C.O. 47 : 375. *Cavendum est ne plus exprimant
caeremoniae quam sit in animo, sed interior affectus oculos, manus, linguam, et
quidquid est impellat.*

[3] Comm. on Ps. 17 : 1, C.O. 31 : 159. *Discamus praeterea, ubi ad Deum accedimus, fucose agendum non esse: quia tota rhetoricae nostrae gratia coram Deo mera
est simplicitas.* Cf. Inst. 3 : 20 : 29.

[4] Comm. on Matt. 6 : 6, C.O. 45 : 193. *Utile quidem est fidelibus, quo liberius
vota sua et gemitus coram Deo effundant, subducere se ab hominum conspectu. . . .
Summa autem est: sive quis solus, sive coram aliis precetur, hunc tamen affectum
induendum esse, quasi abditus in conclave solum Deum haberet testem.* Cf. Inst.
3 : 20 : 29.

[5] Comm. on Ps. 109 : 30, C.O. 32 : 158. *Etsi enim pectus linguam praeire
debet in celebrandis Dei laudibus, frigoris tamen signum est nisi lingua etiam comes
accedat.*

[6] Inst. 3 : 20 : 33; comm. on Ps. 95 : 6, C.O. 32 : 31. *Hoc enim tribus verbis
exprimitur, officio suo non defungi fideles, nisi palam et genu flexione et aliis signis
se in sacrificium offerant.*

[7] Serm. on Gen. 14 : 20–24, C.O. 23 : 677–8. *Voila donc comme par la cere-
monie et le geste exterieur nous monstrons que les prieres nous conioignent à Dieu,
et qu'elles font que nous entrions au ciel par foy, et que Dieu aussi de son costé*

in prayer is that the heart should "move and direct the tongue,"[1] and that the tongue "should not go before the heart,"[2] and that "the body should follow the mind of its own accord."[3] Indeed, the feeling of the heart should be so overpowering that "the tongue spontaneously breaks forth into utterance and our other members into gesture."[4] Nevertheless there are times when the heart is cold and sluggish. At such times both the external exercise of the body and the use of the words and singing by the tongue can come to the aid of the heart,[5] provided that the heart responds to the external ceremony,[6] and the feeling of the mind goes along with the words that are used, so that hypocrisy is avoided.[7]

6. Thanksgiving and prayer

Though Calvin can often treat of thanksgiving as an aspect of prayer, he nevertheless can view it at other times as an important aspect of the Christian life worthy of independent treatment apart from anything we may say about prayer.[8] Thanksgiving is "the chief exercise of godliness" in which we ought to engage during the whole of our life.[9] God's whole purpose in creating us, in adorning the world with such a magnificent variety of beautiful and good things, and in watching over us with such careful providence is that we might be moved continually to render praise back to Him.[10] God is satisfied even with the "bare and simple acknow-

descende vers nous, pour se monstrer prochain. Cf. comm. on Ps. 134 : 2, C.O. 32 : 356; and on Ps. 28 : 2, C.O. 31 : 281; also Inst. 3 : 20 : 5 and 33. Comm. on John 11 : 41, C.O. 47 : 268–9.

[1] Comm. on Ps. 102 : 2, C.O. 32 : 62.

[2] Comm. on Matt. 6 : 7, C.O. 45 : 193.

[3] Comm. on John 11 : 41, C.O. 47 : 268–9.

[4] Inst. 3 : 20 : 33.

[5] Comm. on Acts 9 : 40, C.O. 48 : 220. Inst. 3 : 20 : 31; on Ps. 28 : 2, C.O. 31 : 281; and on Ps. 102 : 2, C.O. 32 : 62. Est hic igitur aliquid reciprocum: quia sicuti cor praeire verba debet ac formare, sic et lingua ipsa cordis torpori opitulatur.

[6] Comm. on Acts 9 : 40, C.O. 48 : 220. Nobis autem quoties in genua procumbimus, videndum est, ut ceremoniae, ne fallax sit ac lusoria, interior cordis submissio respondeat.

[7] Inst. 3 : 20 : 31. Cf. comm. on John 17 : 1, C.O. 47 : 375.

[8] Cf. e.g. comm. on Ps. 50 : 14, C.O. 31 : 501; and on Heb. 13 : 15, C.O. 55 : 192–3.

[9] Comm. on Ps. 50 : 23, C.O. 31 : 507. Nam quum praecipuum sit pietatis officium, in quo nos tota vita exerceri vult Deus.

[10] Comm. on Ps. 146 : 1, C.O. 32 : 421. In hunc finem alit et sustinet suos Deus in mundo, ut toto vitae cursu se in ipso laudando exerceant. Comm. on Ps. 7 : 18, C.O. 31 : 87; and on Ps. 104 : 31, C.O. 32 : 96.

ledgement" from man that he owed every good thing to God.[1] To omit such thanksgiving is to rob God of the honour due to His name.[2] Where all other attempts to recompense God will fail, the gratitude of the heart is acceptable as a "singular recompense" for His love.[3]

Calvin almost invariably refers to thanksgiving in Biblical terms as a "sacrifice of praise."[4] In the Old Testament ritual, when the people brought sacrifices to the altar, God was seeking, not primarily the sacrifices themselves, but the grateful hearts of which the gifts were meant to be a sign.[5] Under the New Covenant in Christ, since the propitiatory aspect of the sacrificial ritual has been fulfilled and abolished, mere thanksgiving offered as a sacrifice pleases God in a way that nothing else can do.[6] Without thanksgiving, nothing can please God. He accepts all service only as it is an expression of grateful thanks for His mercy. Therefore thanksgiving sanctifies the rest of life and the rest of our service to God.[7] But since it is Christ alone who offered to God the perfect sacrifice of thanksgiving we must remember that all our attempts to offer this sacrifice will be polluted if they are not sanctified by the intervention of His priesthood.[8]

Thanksgiving sanctifies not only the rest of life but also the whole activity of prayer. We can pray aright only if our hearts are pervaded by a true sense of gratitude to God, since prayer must arise from a feeling of love.[9] Otherwise the heart will not unburden itself with true spontaneity before God.[10] Moreover, by making the

[1] Comm. on Ps. 116 : 13, C.O. 32 : 198. *Summa huc tendit, non esse magnopere laborandum fidelibus quomodo se liberent, quia Deus satisfactiones non quaerit quibus eos scit carere, sed nuda et simplici gratitudine contentus est: nam haec iusta solutio est, fateri omnia illi nos debere.*

[2] Comm. on Ps. 109 : 30, C.O. 32 : 158.

[3] Comm. on Ps. 104 : 31, C.O. 32 : 96. *Haec gratitudo unicae compensationis loco est apud Deum, ubi debita eum laude prosequimur.*

[4] Cf. comm. on Ps. 50 : 23, C.O. 31 : 507; and on Ps. 7 : 18, C.O. 31 : 87; Inst. 3 : 20 : 28.

[5] Comm. on Jonah 2 : 8–9, C.O. 43 : 245; and on Hosea 14 : 3, C.O. 42 : 501.

[6] Comm. on Heb. 13 : 15, C.O. 55 : 192–3; and on Hosea 14 : 3, C.O. 42 : 501.

[7] Comm. on Heb. 13 : 16, C.O. 55 : 194. *Summa haec est, si Deo sacrificare libeat, ipsum esse invocandum, et cum gratiarum actione praedicandam esse eius bonitatem, deinde fratribus nostris benefaciendum esse.*

[8] Inst. 3 : 20 : 28; comm. on Heb. 13 : 15, C.O. 55 : 193.

[9] Inst. 3 : 20 : 28.

[10] Comm. on Ps. 18 : 4, C.O. 31 : 172. *Et certe nisi qui gratiae Dei memoria se eriget, nunquam libere precabitur.*

will of God the "grand sum of our desires," gratitude will sanctify the requests we make so that these are in line with what is His will.[1] Only when our feelings are regulated and our desires restrained by thanksgiving can we avoid the fretful and morose murmuring against God, and the impatience with His slowness in answering or His refusal to grant selfish wishes, which mars the prayer-life of so many.[2] But thanksgiving is not merely a restraining influence in the life of prayer. It invigorates our faith and stirs us up to new fervour in prayer, to give place in our minds to the acknowledgment of God's goodness and to remember what He has done for us in the past.[3] Through such thankful remembrance David encourages himself to good hope for the future emergencies, "and by this means opens the gate of prayer."[4]

7. The Holy Spirit and prayer

Even though prayer must be a genuine expression of the heart in its felt need and in its gratitude, it should not be dictated or inspired by merely the natural impulse of the heart.[5] No man can pray aright through the spontaneous impulse of his own feeling.[6] Such prayer apart from the Spirit of God is nothing more than mere heathen babble and a mockery of God.[7] Indeed, to allow our own natural impulses to direct our prayers is to seek to make God the agent of our wicked concupiscence, rather than to approach Him as our judge.[8] It is dangerous, therefore, to open our

[1] Comm. on Phil. 4 : 6, C.O. 52 : 61.
[2] Inst. 3 : 20 : 28. *Nam quia multos impellit morositas, taedium, impatientia, doloris acerbitas, et metus ut orando obmurmurent, iubet ita temperari affectus, ut fideles, antequam adepti sint quod cupiunt, hilariter nihilominus benedicant Deo.* Comm. on 1 Thess. 5 : 17, C.O. 52 : 175. *Atqui desideria nostra sic fraenari convenit, ut contenti eo, quod datur, gratiarum actionem semper misceamus votis.* Cf. comm. on Phil. 4 : 6, C.O. 52 : 61; and on Ps. 18 : 4, C.O. 31 : 172.
[3] Comm. on Ps. 85 : 2, C.O. 32 : 785. *Diximus autem alibi, nulla re nos melius animari ad precandum, quam ubi recordamur superiores Dei gratias.* Comm. on Ps. 7 : 11, C.O. 31 : 84.
[4] Comm. on Ps. 9 : 2, C.O. 31 : 96; Inst. 3 : 20 : 3.
[5] In comm. on Jer. 29 : 12, C.O. 38 : 595, Calvin quotes Augustine: *Sequitur ergo nos non proprio carnis impulsu orare, sed quum spiritus sanctus corda nos dirigit, et quodammodo orat in nobis.* In comm. on Rom. 12 : 19, C.O. 49 : 247, we are warned against praying *ex privato affectu* rather than *ex puro spiritus zelo.*
[6] Comm. on Rom. 8 : 26, C.O. 49 : 157. *Nemo sancta et pia vota sponte conciperet.*
[7] Ibid.
[8] Comm. on Rom. 12 : 19, C.O. 49 : 247.

lips before God "unless the Spirit instruct us how to pray aright."[1] The ability to engage in true prayer is therefore the gift of the Spirit.[2] God must be allowed the initiative within the heart in the inspiration of prayer. "We cannot pray to God unless He anticipates us by His own Spirit."[3] Even our very prayers for the Spirit of God to come into our hearts can arise only because we already have the first-fruits of the Spirit within us. We should pray, therefore, for the *increase* of the Spirit,[4] rather than for the coming of the Spirit.

The Spirit, then, helps us in the framing both of the mind and of the heart, making both "intent upon God" and regulating our requests and our affections.[5] The Spirit of adoption is the author of that filial approach in boldness and confident hope of succeeding in our requests which is the distinguishing mark of true prayer.[6] It is the Spirit, too, who inspires our prayers with the ardour and earnestness which are also important characteristics of Christian prayer. It is the Spirit who moves our hearts with such fervency that they can "pierce into the very heaven."[7] Yet "while the inspiration of the Spirit is effectual to the formation of prayer, it by no means impedes or retards our own efforts," and we have to discipline ourselves to wait on the Spirit in prayer. Moreover, however great or small our spiritual fervour may be, it is of the utmost importance that in prayer the mind and understanding should be continually employed.[8]

8. Intercession

Our prayer must not be self-centred. It must arise not only because we feel our own need as a burden which we must lay upon

---

[1] Inst. 3 : 20 : 34.

[2] Comm. on Rom. 8 : 26, C.O. 49 : 157. *Deo exauditas, colligit tamen Paulus in ipso precandi studio iam lucere coelestis gratiae praesentiam. . . . Quare bene precandi modum a spiritu dictari necesse est.*

[3] Comm. on Jer. 29 : 12, C.O. 38 : 595.

[4] Comm. on Acts 1 : 14, C.O. 48 : 16.

[5] Inst. 3 : 20 : 5.

[6] Comm. on Rom. 8 : 15. C.O. 49 : 148; Inst. 3 : 20 : 1 and 37. *Petere ab ipso meminerimus, ut correcta nostra timiditate. Spiritum illum magnanimitatis ducem ad audacter orandum praeficiat.*

[7] Comm. on Rom. 8 : 26, C.O. 49 : 157. *Deinde corda nostra sic officiat (spiritus) ut suo ardore in coelum usque penetrent.*

[8] Inst. 3 : 20 : 5; comm. on 1 Cor. 14 : 15, C.O. 49 : 522. . . . *quod praecipuum est, requirit (in precationibus), ne mens sit otiosa.*

God but also because we are so bound up in love with our fellow-men that we feel their need as acutely as our own.[1] In this matter we must guard against the danger of becoming engrossed in our own personal sorrows which are intended by God "to admonish us to direct our concern to the whole body of the Church."[2] We are to feel so much one with the Church in our common fate, afflictions, wrongs, rejoicings, and destiny that our prayers arising out of our personal sorrows, like those of David in the Psalms, will inevitably pass into intercession for the Church in all its afflictions.[3] Therefore our prayers are bound always to seek to express themselves in intercession for all mankind, but especially for the whole Church, not only in this generation, but in generations yet unborn.[4]

To make intercession for men is the most powerful and practical way in which we can express our love for them. "The greatest help we can give to those in need is to pray God that He will not reject them altogether."[5] It is an outstanding sign of God's goodness to us that in saving us He not only allows us to further our own salvation by prayer, but also gives us the privilege of helping others by this ministry of intercession, and indeed "the higher honour of committing to God the glory of the Kingdom of Christ, which is more precious than the salvation of the whole world."[6] Thus to every Christian Christ commits the welfare of the Church by committing to him the vital task of interceding for the Church and Kingdom. It is the presence in the midst of the Church in every age of those who come before God to make intercession that continually saves the Church in each generation

---

[1] Serm. on 1 Tim. 2 : 1–2, C.O. 53 : 125. *Il s'ensuit donc que nous devons prattiquer ce moyen-ci en priant Dieu: et ne faut pas qu'un chacun soit addonné à sa personne, ni à ses amis particuliers: mais que nous estendions nostre charité et solicitude envers tous, et grans et petis, et ceux qui nous sont privez, et ceux qui nous sont incognus. . . . Il faut commencer par eux avec lesquels nous sommes conioints en foy. . . . Mais . . . il faut aussi que nous ayons pitié et compassion des povres incredules, qui cheminent encores en erreur et ignorance.* (Here are at least the seeds of Foreign Mission enterprise!)

[2] Comm. on Ps. 14 : 7, C.O. 31 : 142.

[3] Comm. on Ps. 25 : 22, C.O. 31 : 262. *Hoc vero ad fidei confirmationem non parum valuit, quod David nihil se a toto fidelium corpore separatum habere cogitans, quas patiebatur iniurias, sibi cum omnibus piis duxit esse communes, sed illa etiam tenenda ratio, ut dum sua quisque mala deplorat, simul etiam curas suas et vota extendat ad totam ecclesiam.*

[4] Comm. on Ps. 90 : 16, C.O. 31 : 841.

[5] Serm. on Job 2 : 11–13, C.O. 33 : 137.

[6] Comm. on Ps. 51 : 20, C.O. 31 : 523.

from perishing through the coldness and indifference of the rest of its members.[1]

In exercising the ministry of intercession for our brethren in their need, we must feel ourselves identified with and personally involved in the need of those we pray for. We must "keep them company" in our spirits, mourning with them and humbling ourselves before God with them.[2] We must lay aside all our selfish personal considerations and "clothe ourselves with a public character."[3] It is as members of the body of Christ, sharing in the intercession and priesthood of the Head, that we are inspired with love to make our intercessions.[4] Our intercession for the Church is an echo of the continued intercession of Christ. It is our expression of our unity with one another in the body of the Church and with our great High Priest and Head. Calvin notes the picture given in Psalm 20 of the people praying that David's prayers might be heard, and he sees in it an analogy (*anagoge*) of the relation between Christ's priestly intercession and the prayers of the Church. "Since Christ, our King, being an everlasting priest, never ceases to make intercession to God, the whole body of the Church should unite in prayer with Him, and further we can have no hope of being heard except He go before us and conduct us to God."[5] But it must be asserted that our intercession within the Church is not something which we add in order to perfect or supplement the prevailing intercession of Jesus Christ. It is rather an echo within our hearts of His intercession in which we participate by the Spirit who prays within us. It is only thus that we are enabled to enter the sufferings of others in love. By sharing in the one Spirit and by allowing the prayers which the Spirit inspires to

---

[1] Serm. on Deut. 9 : 13–14, C.O. 26 : 682–3. *C'est une chose desirable qu'il y ait gens entre nous qui intercedent envers Dieu, et qui le supplient: car nous voyons la froidure qui est en la plus part. Quelquefois en un peuple, en une fort grande multitude on ne trouvera point ou trente ou dix personnes qui ayent un droit zele pour prier Dieu. . . . Or que seroit-ce si ceux-la n'estoyent à la bresche?* . . . *Et ainsi apprenons que souventesfois Dieu nous espargne, d'autant qu'il y en a que nous ne cognoissons point, mesmes qui intercedent pour nous. . . . Helas! si i'estoye seul, et si tout le monde estoit semblable à moy: que seroit ce? Nous pourrions perir . . . mais . . . nostre Seigneur ne nous veut point laisser perir, quand il ordonne gens qui viennent ainsi au devant de luy.*

[2] Serm. on Job 12 : 11–13, C.O. 33 : 137.

[3] Comm. on Ps. 79 : 6, C.O. 31 : 749–50. *Tenendum est . . . non posse in hunc modum precari nisi qui publicam personam induerint, et omisso sui respectu, curam susceperint totius ecclesiae.*

[4] Inst. 3 : 20 : 19.

[5] Comm. on Ps. 20 : 2, C.O. 31 : 208.

D.C.L.—20

find their true echo in our hearts we find ourselves praying "each
for the whole body, in common, as it were, under the person of all
men."[1] Indeed the very privilege of calling God "our Father" in
prayer is given to us only as we are bound together in brotherly
love within the Church.[2]

9. God as the hearer and answerer of prayer

God cannot do otherwise than answer the prayers which arise
out of our human need in His service and which He Himself inspires according to the Word. On the psalmist's invocation, "O
thou that hearest prayer," Calvin comments, "The title here given
to God conveys a highly important truth. Our prayers will never
be in vain. For in rejecting them God would, in a way, deny His
own nature. Nor does David say that hearing prayer is something
God does only on occasion but that it is an abiding part of His
glory, so that He can as soon deny Himself as become deaf to our
petition. If we could only impress it upon our hearts that it is
something peculiar to God and inseparable from Him to hear
prayer, our faith in prayer would never be shaken."[3] For us to be
able to pray means not only that we have open access to God but
also that His hand is always stretched out to assist His people.[4]
The Old Testament examples of Elijah and Joshua defeating the
enemies of the Lord and changing the order of nature by prayer
are not utterly unique and exceptional instances, but are, rather,
vivid illustrations of a privilege that is open to us who have access
in prayer to Jesus Christ.[5]

Holy Scripture gives us authority to speak as if by prayer we
can in some way prevail upon God to do things He would not have
done unless we had prayed. When the psalmist asserts that God
will "gratify the desires of all those that fear Him,"[6] it is difficult
to say how seriously we ought to take such an expression. "Who is
man that God should show complaisance to his will? . . . Yet he

---

[1] Comm. on Acts 1 : 14, C.O. 48 : 17. *Christus singulos pro toto corpore, et in
commune, quasi sub omnium persona orare iubet: Pater noster, da nobis etc. Unde
haec linguarum unitas nisi ab uno spiritu?*
[2] Cf. ibid. and comm. on Isa. 63 : 16, C.O. 37 : 402.
[3] Comm. on Ps. 65 : 3, C.O. 31 : 603.
[4] Inst. 3 : 20 : 3.
[5] Serm. on Deut. 9 : 13–14, C.O. 26 : 682.
[6] Ps. 145 : 19; cf. serm. on Deut. 9 : 13–14, C.O. 26 : 680–1.

voluntarily subjects Himself to these conditions so that He can comply with our desires."[1] "Faith will succeed in obtaining anything from the Lord," says Calvin, "because He values it so much that He is always ready to gratify our desires as far as is good for us."[2] The Parable of the Importunate Widow teaches men that "they ought importunately to harass God the Father till at length they wrest from Him what He would otherwise appear unwilling to give."[3] God "wills to be, as it were, wearied out by prayers," and will give way if men persist in the exercise of prayer.[4] Calvin makes much of the fact that God is spoken of as saying to Moses, "Let me alone, that I may destroy them and blot out their name from under heaven."[5] Here it seems to be indicated that God is hindered by Moses' prayer from giving free expression to His anger. Moses seems to be able by prayer to set bounds to God's liberty. Out of His goodness He "brings Himself so much under obligation (s'oblige) to our prayers and supplications that they are like obstacles to His wrath, that where at times He would cause everything to perish, yet if we will come and humiliate ourselves before Him it is as if He were changed."[6]

Yet to say such things is simply to use analogies suitable to our crudity and weakness. God does not vary in purpose. He is not subject to changes in passions and attitudes. He does not go back on what He has previously decided. In using such language, then, He is humiliating Himself to speak in our way. He wants us to understand that "He has made a pact with us that when we shall require it He will accomplish all that we ask so that we can always feel that He has willed to accord to our will and desire."[7] We must not therefore imagine that by our prayers "we gain a victory over God and bend Him slowly and reluctantly to compassion."[8]

If our prayers are thus to prevail with God they must be according to His will. "The first thing requisite in prayer is consent to

---

[1] Comm. on Ps. 145 : 19, C.O. 32 : 419. *Quid enim est homo, ut eius voluntati se morigerum praebeat Deus . . . ? atqui ad hanc legem ultro se demittit ut nostris desideriis obtemperet.*

[2] Comm. on Matt. 15 : 28, C.O. 45 : 460. *Fides quidvis impetret a Domino, quia tanti eam aestimat, ut semper paratus sit votis nostris quoad expedit morem gerere.*

[3] Comm. on Luke 18 : 1–8, C.O. 45 : 416.   [4] Ibid.

[5] Deut. 9 : 14.

[6] Serm. on Deut. 9 : 13–14, C.O. 26 : 680–1.

[7] Serm. on Deut. 9 : 13–14, C.O. 26 : 680–1.

[8] Comm. on Luke 18 : 1–8, C.O. 45 : 416.

the will of the Lord, whom our desires in no way hold in bonds."[1]
In this matter of prayer God is the one who takes the initiative by
His Word. He is always there before us, calling us to Himself, and
our prayers are simply a summing-up of His promises.[2] Therefore
there is nothing more blasphemous than for us to try to give the
naturally corrupt and unruly desires of our hearts loose rein in
prayer.[3] In this, as in every aspect of the Christian life, the flesh
must be subdued, and the desires of the heart must be moderated
and inspired by the Spirit, for then our desires become the work
of His Spirit and He will not reject them.[4] It is if we are satisfied
with the enjoyment of God alone that He literally bestows upon us
all that we shall desire.[5] He is always ready to direct the hearts of
His people into prayers that are according to His will.[6] There is,
nevertheless, room in prayer for tension between the human will
and the will of God. There can be "a kind of indirect disagreement"
with the will of God which is free from guilt and regarded as
blameless. Calvin gives, as an example of this, our prayers that the
Church may be flourishing and peaceful when, indeed, it pleases
God to make it quite otherwise.[7]

In praying for those things that we know are God's will for us
and for this world, we must be careful not to specify too closely
the means God should use in answering our prayers and the exact
manner and time in which His answer should come. It is often
when we try to prescribe the way in which the Kingdom of God
should advance that we fall into error in our praying. For though

---

[1] Comm. on Rom. 8 : 27, C.O. 49 : 158. *Primas tenere partes in oratione consensum cum voluntate Domini: quem nostra ipsorum desideria minime alligatum tenent.*

[2] Serm. on Deut. 26 : 16–19, C.O. 28 : 291.

[3] Comm. on Ps. 145 : 19, C.O. 32 : 419.

[4] Comm. on Rom. 8 : 27, C.O. 49 : 158. *Vota nostra, quorum pse moderator est, minime frustratum iri.*

[5] Comm. on Ps. 37 : 4, C.O. 31 : 368.

[6] Comm. on Ps. 10 : 17, C.O. 31 : 119.

[7] Comm. on Luke 22 : 39, C.O. 45 : 722. . . . *esse tamen quandam obliquae dissensionis speciem, quae culpa caret, nec in peccatum imputatur.* In Inst. 3 : 20 : 15 Calvin notes that in Holy Scripture there are cases where the prayers of men were not in perfect accord with God's will, and yet God complied to them (Judges 9 : 20; 16 : 28). This is exceptional and cannot be made a general rule for believers—yet it demonstrates the mercy of God. Other cases, where e.g. Abraham, Samuel, Jeremiah (Gen. 18 : 23; 1 Sam. 15 : 11; Jer. 33 : 16) uttered with true faith rejected prayers "without any instruction from the Word of God," are more difficult. God regulates events so that even such prayers are not in vain, but we must not imitate such prayers.

God always answers our prayers for salvation and for deliverance in real need, He does not always answer in the way that we seek His answer.[1] Sometimes, indeed, God does not grant even what we ask, for we do not always pray aright in this respect, but nevertheless in hearing even such prayer He finds a way to help us, and thus we obtain from Him an answer more than we would have had had He fully granted our original request.[2] It is therefore often out of love for us that He crosses our wrong desires by His refusals to answer our prayers or gives us a different answer than we had expected. In thus refusing us the answer, He is indeed truly hearing and answering our prayers, for it is only to the wicked and perverse that God sometimes yields in His wrath the exact answer their flesh seeks—and to their own damnation.[3]

God may make us wait until he answers our prayers, or at least till we realise that He has heard and is answering. "The actual facts do not all at once make it evident that He is sympathetic to our prayers."[4] Yet even though the answer may be long delayed God will never allow the faith of His servants to faint or fail, nor does He allow them to desist from praying. He thus "holds them to Himself until it actually appears that their hope has been neither vain nor ineffectual."[5] Therefore, even if God seems to be inexorable towards us, we must not imagine that He will act contrary to His real character or that He is fickle in His purpose.[6] We must believe if we are to receive.[7] If our prayers are according to His Word, His Word cannot but effect its own fulfilment.[8]

10. The need for discipline and perseverance in prayer

For a Christian to pray as he ought requires hard effort and discipline, and a firm resolve not to be discouraged by the many difficulties men experience in trying to pray. We will not pray unless we make ourselves pray, in spite of our feelings. If we were left to our own inclination in this matter our prayer-life would die

[1] Comm. on 2 Cor. 12 : 8, C.O. 50 : 140–1.
[2] Comm. on Heb. 5 : 7, C.O. 55 : 63.
[3] Comm. on Ps. 78 : 26, C.O. 31 : 731.
[4] Comm. on Luke 18 : 1–8, C.O. 45 : 416.
[5] Comm. on Ps. 10 : 17, C.O. 31 : 119.
[6] Comm. on Ps. 25 : 6, C.O. 31 : 253.
[7] Comm. on Ps. 6 : 9–11, C.O. 31 : 78.
[8] Serm. on Luke 1 : 36–8, C.O. 46 : 95.

out.[1] Even affliction, which should drive us to our knees and stimulate us in prayer, can have the contrary effect and can stupefy us and render us prayerless unless we "stir up our minds to pray."[2] We will be constantly tempted to look on our prayers as fruitless.[3] Even in the act of praying we will have to confess this feeling of the flesh and the doubts that arise in our minds.[4] Even in the series of unrelievedly hopeless lamentations and murmurings of the 88th Psalm Calvin finds a true example of a prayer of faith and an illustration of what Paul means in Rom. 8 : 26, for the psalmist could not have prayed in this way had he not believed.[5] We must believe that such feelings do not in any way render our petitions inefficacious, for if we confess them they are forgiven and do not defile our prayers.[6]

Since all this is so, we must make all the more strenuous efforts in the midst of our perplexity and heaviness of heart to break through such obstacles in our approach to God.[7] Under these circumstances it is good that, as in public worship, we observe particular and fixed hours for our secret devotions. Making such rules can save our prayer-life from dying out.[8] We must pray even though we feel no inspiration whatever to do so. We must not make it an excuse for our sloth that we are waiting for the Holy Spirit to inspire us—"as if we were to leave the office of prayer to the Holy Spirit!"[9] Even if the Word of God should be silent—a distressing experience!—we must not be discouraged from engaging in prayer.[10] Nor must we be discouraged by distracting thoughts gradually stealing our attention in the midst of prayer—especially when we are in trouble. We need not expect that when we turn to prayer our faith will always "immediately penetrate to heaven," for faith can lose its liveliness and yet still remain living faith.[11] We must learn to persevere, even though there are no clear signs that God is immediately taking us back into His favour.[12] Even

[1] Comm. on Ps. 55 : 18, C.O. 31 : 542.
[2] Comm. on Ps. 130 : 1–2, C.O. 32 : 333; and on Ps. 106 : 58, C.O. 32 : 135.
[3] Comm. on Ps. 145 : 18, C.O. 32 : 419.
[4] Comm. on Ps. 38 : 22–3, C.O. 31 : 395.
[5] Comm. on Ps. 88 : 15–19, C.O. 31 : 810.
[6] Comm. on Ps. 44 : 24, C.O. 31 : 448.
[7] Comm. on Ps. 61 : 1–3, C.O. 31 : 581.
[8] Comm. on Ps. 55 : 17–18, C.O. 31 : 542.   [9] Inst. 3 : 20 : 5.
[10] Comm. on Ps. 77 : 8–9, C.O. 31 : 714.
[11] Comm. on Ps. 89 : 47–8, C.O. 31 : 829.
[12] Comm. on Ps. 85 : 6, C.O. 31 : 787.

though we are disappointed in our expectations in our prayers we can at least carry on making known to God our perplexities about our very prayers—unburdening even this burden into His bosom.[1] We must remember that we have never any excuse for refusing to pray. We may by unfortunate circumstances be deprived of the use of the Sacraments or of the privileges of public worship, but the privilege can never be taken from us of communicating thus with Heaven by the way which has been opened up for ever by the blood of Christ.[2] Even when paralysed by our sense of guilt we will find forms of prayer in Holy Scripture which can give boldness and hope to those in the most desperate of such conditions.[3] We must not allow any feeling that God has rejected us hinder us from having recourse to prayer.[4]

In the midst of our prayers we must struggle with wandering thoughts. "In this matter we must labour the more earnestly the more difficult we experience it to be."[5] Calvin recognises the value of our Lord's own example in removing Himself from all the interruptions that could easily have destroyed the ardour of His prayers.[6] He makes helpful practical suggestions in His frequent exhortations to meditation as an incentive to prayer, and as a means of helping us to persevere in prayer. He notes how in the Psalms the "continuity of prayer is broken" and the prayers are often punctuated by meditations on various aspects of God's nature.[7] David "intermingles his prayers with meditations for the comfort of his own soul."[8] Such meditation can "re-animate our languid minds with new vigour."[9] "As one must frequently lay on fuel to preserve a fire, so the exercise of prayer requires the aid of such helps."[10]

[1] Comm. on Ps. 22 : 3, C.O. 31 : 222.
[2] Comm. on Ps. 61 : 1–3, C.O. 31 : 581.
[3] Comm. on Ps. 80 : 6, C.O. 31 : 756.
[4] Comm. on Ps. 44 : 3, C.O. 31 : 437.
[5] Inst. 3 : 20 : 5.
[6] Comm. on Matt. 14 : 23, C.O. 45 : 441.
[7] Inst. 3 : 20 : 13.
[8] Comm. on Ps. 57 : 4, C.O. 31 : 556; and on Ps. 7 : 11, C.O. 31 : 84.
[9] Inst. 3 : 20 : 13. Cf. comm. on Ps. 7 : 10, C.O. 31 : 84.
[10] Comm. on Ps. 25 : 8, C.O. 31 : 254.

PART SIX

THE EFFECT AND FRUIT
OF FAITH

Chapter I

Assurance, boldness and stability

1. The place of assurance of forgiveness in the Christian life

THE Christian life can be lived only if we have assured consciences and are certain that God is propitious to us and that our lives are accepted by Him.[1] Calvin often dwells on the necessity of our being first assured, if we are to be wholehearted in our response to Jesus Christ. It is only when we have lost all anxiety on our own account that we can be wholehearted in sacrificing ourselves for the service of God. Men follow Christ most readily when they cease to have to care for themselves and realise that Christ "takes care of those who neglect themselves to follow Him."[2] Only the assurance that we are in the hands of the Good Shepherd, and that love and self-sacrifice bring their own reward, can prevent men from reacting with revenge when others offend them.[3] Only the assurance that God will provide for all our needs if we deprive ourselves of financial security can make us truly open-handed in our Christian liberality. "What makes us more close-handed than we ought to be is that we look too carefully and too far forward in contemplation of the dangers that may occur, that we are excessively cautious and careful—that we calculate too narrowly what we will require during our whole life—or, in short, how much we lose when the smallest portion is taken away. The man that depends upon the blessing of the Lord has his mind set free from these trammels and has at the same time his hands opened for beneficience."[4]

Moreover, no matter how good an action may be in itself, it is

---

[1] Serm. on Luke 1 : 73–8, C.O. 46 : 185. *Les fideles s'addonneront à craindre Dieu quand ils seront asseurez. Car de fait, cependent que nous sommes en trouble, et agitez assavoir si Dieu nous sera propice ou non, et si nos services luy seront agreables ou non, cependant donc que nous serons en tel bransle, il faut que nous soyons esgardez quant et quant et que nous quittions le service de Dieu.*
[2] Comm. on John 6 : 2, C.O. 47 : 131.
[3] Serm. on Job 42 : 5–17, C.O. 35 : 507–8.
[4] Comm. on 2 Cor. 8 : 2, C.O. 50 : 96.

spoilt if it is done with an uncertain or doubting conscience. "Every work, however excellent and glorious it be, if it is not grounded upon a right conscience, is counted for sin. . . . Wavering and doubtfulness corrupt all our actions."[1] Tranquillity of mind and conscience alone can be the basis of the true worship of God.[2] Without it the whole of faith and religion falls to the ground.[3] Those who "fluctuate in uncertainty between hope and fear" can never sincerely and honestly obey God, however anxiously they may labour to do so.[4]

But such assurance can come to us only by the constant exercise of faith in the forgiveness of sins. Every Christian man must admit that even in its highest reaches his Christian life is hopelessly spoiled and distorted by sin.[5] Even his best works, which may be inspired and carried out under the inspiration of the Spirit of God, apparently with the whole consent of all his heart, are nevertheless impure in the sight of God and could be totally rejected by Him. No Christian can love the Lord with *all* his mind and heart and soul and strength.[6] Even our best prayers need to be pardoned.[7] At our best we are unprofitable servants.[8] We need therefore constantly to lay hold by faith of the comfort and assurance that the continual pardon of God can give us.[9] "Those are grossly mis-

[1] Comm. on Rom. 14 : 23, C.O. 49 : 268–9; cf. comm. on 1 Cor. 8 : 7, C.O. 49 : 433. *Sicut enim operum bonitas ex timore Dei et conscientiae rectitudine manat.*

[2] Comm. on Luke 1 : 74, C.O. 45   49. *Significat enim, non posse nisi tranquillis animis rite Deum coli.*

[3] Comm. on Heb. 4 : 16, C.O. 55 : 55. *Concidit ac perit tota religio quum eripitur haec certitudo conscientiis.* Cf. serm. on Luke 2 : 50–2, C.O. 46 : 482. *La foy donc est perdue, quand elle n'est point enclose en bonne conscience.*

[4] Comm. on Luke 1 : 74, C.O. 45 : 49. In this context Calvin emphasises the necessity of cheerfulness in carrying out the service of God. Cf. comm. on Ps. 130 : 4, C.O. 32 : 335; and on Luke 1 : 74, C.O. 45 : 49.

[5] Comm. on Matt. 6 : 24, C.O. 45 : 208.

[6] Serm. on Job 10 : 16–17, C.O. 33 : 499. Serm. on Luke 1 : 5–10, C.O. 46 : 20–1. *Et mesme qu'on prenne les meilleures œuvres des fideles, si est-ce qu'on ne trouvera pas encore qu'il y ait une telle pureté qu'il est requis, car iamais n'aiment Dieu de tout leur cœur, et de toutes leurs pensees et affections, d'autant qu'ils ne se peuvent despouiller de beaucoup d'infirmitez. Il est vray qu'ils tendront à Dieu d'un desir rond et entier: mais quoy qu'il en soit, il y a tousiours à redire, tellement que tout ce que nous pourrons faire, ie di mesmes par la vertu de l'Esprit de Dieu, tout cela sera comme entaché de quelque macule, et Dieu n'en accepteroit rien, quand il le voudroit iuger à la rigueur.* Cf. comm. on Ps. 32 : 1, C.O. 31 : 315; and on Rom. 7 : 18, C.O. 49 : 132; serm. on 1 Cor. 10 : 3–6, C.O. 49 : 606.

[7] Comm. on Ps. 89 : 47, C.O. 31 : 830.

[8] Serm. on Isa. 53 : 11, C.O. 35 : 666.

[9] Comm. on Rom. 4 : 6, C.O. 49 : 72. *Praeterea hinc gratuitae iustitiae perpetua in totam vitam duratio colligi potest.*

taken," says Calvin, "who conceive that the pardon of sin is necessary only to the beginning of righteousness. As believers are every day involved in many faults, it will profit them nothing that they have once entered the way of righteousness, unless the same grace which brought them into it accompany them to the last step of their life."[1] The conflict with despair fought under such a sense of the sinfulness of our being and our works is not won merely through one battle. It is a war that continues all our days and in which we need a continual recourse to the repeated promises of forgiveness in the Word of God.[2]

2. Evidence of good works as a help to assurance

There is a state of assured "integrity of conscience"[3] which we can be helped to attain by the signs of divine favour towards us that are manifested in our own good works. Our assurance must first be "founded, built up, and established" on the mercy of God alone. But it can be "further established" when we review ourselves before God and find evidence of God's dwelling and reigning within us in the works he has enabled us to do.[4] Purity of life can be to us a true evidence and proof of election,[5] for the righteousness which God gives us does not always remain buried in our hearts and our newness of life is testified by good works.[6] But all such evidence is "an inferior aid, a prop to our faith, not a foundation on which it rests.[7]

Calvin finds this "consciousness of purity before the Lord,"[8] which arises from the evidence of God's regenerating work in the heart, referred to in the Psalms where, in the midst of persecution and danger, the psalmists find their own good conscience to be a great comfort and strength.[9] This confidence (*fiducia*) or consciousness of integrity (*conscientia probitatis or integritatis*) is the basis of their ability to pray to God, and of all their assurance in

[1] Comm. on Ps. 32 : 1, C.O. 31 : 317.
[2] Ibid., p. 316.
[3] Inst. 3 : 14 : 18–19. *Conscientiae innocentia.*
[4] Inst. 3 : 14 : 18.
[5] Comm. on Pet. 1 : 10, C.P. 55 : 450.
[6] Comm. on 1 John 3 : 7, C.O. 55 : 334.
[7] Comm. on 1 John 3 : 19, C.O. 55 : 341–2; Inst. 3 : 14 : 19.
[8] Inst. 3 : 20 : 10.
[9] Comm. on Ps. 58 : 2, C.O. 31 : 559; on Ps. 55 : 1–4, C.O. 31 : 536; and on Ps. 5 : 10–11, C.O. 31 : 71.

their prayers that God will vindicate their cause in judgment between them and their enemies.[1]

When he examines his own works, however, the Christian must find comfort in the fact that God continually justifies not only the persons of believers but also their works.[2] "Even our works are reckoned as righteous before God."[3] The same gratuitous imputation of righteousness which covers over the evil that resides in our persons also covers over the evil that is always inherent in our works.[4] God does not examine our works according to the "severe rule of the Law."[5] His attitude to our works is rather like that of the father who is pleased to watch and accept what his little child tries to do even though it be of no practical value.[6] "He looks not so much on our works as upon His grace in our works,"[7] and in accepting them as righteous he acknowledges and receives the gifts which proceed from His own grace.[8] Not only does God accept our works as righteous, He actually rewards us for them as if they were worthy of such reward, though such reward proceeds not from our merit but from His own undeserved grace.[9] If, in

---

[1] Comm. on Ps. 7 : 5–6, C.O. 31 : 81; on Ps. 54 : 2–3, C.O. 31 : 532; on Ps. 71 : 4, C.O. 31 : 655; and on Ps. 17 : 1–2, C.O. 31 : 158–9. As to the question "How can David boast of his own integrity before God, when in other places he deprecates God entering into judgment with him?" Calvin finds the answer "easy." (Comm. on Ps. 7 : 8–9, C.O. 31 : 83.) When David boasts of his integrity he is not thinking of his whole life but merely comparing himself with his enemies in the matter on hand. (Ibid. and Inst. 3 : 20 : 10; 3 : 14 : 18.) It is the justice of their cause rather than their persons that they are pleading and boasting of (comm. on Ps. 25 : 21, C.O. 31 : 262). Moreover they think of themselves in the light of the free grace and electing love of God who in spite of their sins declared them to be among His children (comm. on Ps. 139 : 23, C.O. 32 : 386; Inst. 3 : 20 : 10).

[2] Comm. on Gen. 7 : 1, C.O. 23 : 129. *Ita non modo fideles amat, sed eorum quoque opera. Notandum tamen est, quia semper aliquid vitii haeret in operibus, non posse probari nisi cum indulgentia.*

[3] Serm. on Deut. 6 : 20–25, C.O. 26 : 493–4.

[4] Comm. on Gen. 15 : 6, C.O. 23 : 214. *Caeterum ut bona eorum opera Deo placeant, ea quoque ipsa iustificari gratuita imputatione oportet.*

[5] Comm. on Rom. 6 : 14, C.O. 49 : 112.

[6] Serm. on Job 10 : 16–17, C.O. 33 : 499. *Si est-ce que toutes les bonnes œuvres . . . tant s'en faut qu'il y ait dignite ou merite . . . qu'il n'y ait qu'infection. Voire, mais Dieu les reçoit. Ouy, comme un père recevra ce qui procede de son enfant, encores qu'il ne vaille rien.*

[7] Comm. on Heb. 6 : 10, C.O. 55 : 74.

[8] Ibid. and comm. on Gen. 7 : 1, C.O. 23 : 129.

[9] Comm. on Ps. 18 : 21, C.O. 23 : 129. *Respondeo, mercedis nomine non ostendit quid Deus nobis debeat, ideoque perperam et falso meritum vel operum dignitatem ex eo colligi, sic enim Deus iustus iudex cuique retribuit secundum sua opera, ut tamen omnes sibi teneat obnoxios, nemini vero sit ipse adstrictus. Ratio est non ea solum quam Augustinus reddit, nullam eum iustitiam in nobis invenire cui praemium reddat, nisi quam gratis donavit: sed etiam quia operum nostrorum*

offering God such imperfect works, believers sincerely desire to serve God, then, in spite of their sins and self-dissatisfaction, they are reckoned as keeping the commandments of God and are not looked on by Him as unbelievers or hypocrites who seek to serve two masters.[1] If, however, we comfort ourselves in this undeserved liberty to walk and work before God with such boldness, we must, at the same time, groan within ourselves at the compromise in which we are involved, and must continually detest ourselves, taking care to yield to God, as much as is in us, the undivided and pure devotion of our hearts.[2]

3. Assurance means boldness and joy before God and the dangers of life

Calvin teaches that the Christian should be bold and joyful in his assurance before God. Faith which begins with reliance on the promises of God should develop, in two further stages, into confidence (*fiducia*) and boldness (*audacia*). Confidence is the possession of a peaceful and good heart and mind. Boldness is the power to "banish fear and to come with firmness and boldness into the presence of God."[3] This development is less in some men than in others, but it must, in some measure, take place in all. Faith must inevitably produce these "effects and fruits."[4] "Faith cannot be without a settled peace of mind from whence proceeds the bold confidence of rejoicing."[5] But boldness must be carefully distinquished from pride, for it is the boldness of one who is at the same time humble enough to receive without question whatever God speaks.[6] It must also be distinguished from the foolish

maculis ignoscens, iniustitiam imputat quod iure respuere posset. In this discussion Calvin in the citations given in the two previous notes also acknowledges his debt to Augustine.

[1] Comm. on John 15 : 10, C.O. 47 : 343. *Censentur itaque fideles servare Christi praecepta, quum huc suum studium applicant, etiamsi longe a meta distent: quia soluti sunt ab illo rigore legis: Maledictus omnis qui non impleverit omnia etc.* Comm. on Matt. 6 : 24, C.O. 45 : 208; serm. on Job 9 : 29–35, C.O. 33 : 456–7.

[2] Serm. on Job 34 : 4–10, C.O. 35 : 135; serm. on Deut. 26 : 16–19, C.O. 28 : 285.

[3] Comm. on Eph. 3 : 12, C.O. 51 : 183–4. Cf. serm. on Deut. 26 : 16–19, C.O. 28 : 289–90. *Par la foy que nous avons en Iesus Christ, la confiance nous est donnee avec audace ou hardiesse de venir à Dieu.*

[4] Ibid.

[5] Comm. on Heb. 3 : 6, C.O. 55 : 38. Here Calvin says that the *duo perpetui fidei effectus* are *fiducia et gloriatio* referring also to Rom. 5 and Eph. 3.

[6] Serm. on Deut. 26 : 16–19, C.O. 28 : 289–90.

religious presumption that makes men careless and prayerless, for it stirs men up to pray and to seek help from God.[1] The "nature of evangelical peace" is "widely different from a stupefied conscience, from false confidence, from proud boasting, from ignorance of our own wretchedness. It is a peaceful calmness (*serena tranquillitas*) which leads us to seek the face of God as something we desire and love rather than to dread it."[2]

This assurance and boldness before God will tend to express itself also in fearlessness before earthly danger. Even the daily life of the ordinary man is full of such dangers that if they were faced frankly we would be appalled by fear and life would be miserable indeed,[3] for fear and worry destroy happiness.[4] But "we obtain, by knowing the love of God towards us, a peaceful calmness beyond the reach of fear."[5] In the midst of all persecution and danger, we can be upheld by "the testimony of a good conscience."[6] Calvin insists that the Christian can overcome fear and worry. Faith and prayer, he asserts, can give us the "peaceful and undisturbed state of a well-regulated mind."[7] The light of divine providence can enable us to overcome, not only the extreme fear and anxiety which once oppressed us, but also "all care."[8]

4. Christian assurance is always accompanied by fear and trembling

Freedom from fear and worry in no way means insensibility to the fears and worries of life. Christian assurance is the assurance of one who in the midst of his fears and cares is enabled so to cast them upon God that though he still feels them acutely he is now in no way dominated or controlled by them.[9] When the psalmist

---

[1] Serm. on 1 Cor. 10 : 12–14, C.O. 49 : 647–8.

[2] Comm. on Eph. 2 : 18, C.O. 51 : 174.

[3] Inst. 1 : 17 : 10; comm. on John 7 : 30, C.O. 47 : 176.

[4] Comm. on Ps. 16 : 9, C.O. 31 : 155–6. *Scimus praecipuum beatae vitae caput esse εὐθυμίαν, sicuti nihil infelicius est quam inter varias curas et pavores aestuare.*

[5] Comm. on 1 John 1, 4 : 18, C.O. 55 : 358.

[6] Comm. on Ps. 69 : 4–5, C.O. 31 : 638.

[7] Comm. on Ps. 3 : 6–7, C.O. 31 : 56. *Quantum bonum ex fide et precibus adeptus fuerit, David commemorat, nempe pacem et tranquillum animi bene compositi statum.*

[8] Inst. 1 : 17 : 11. *At ubi lux illa divinae providentiae semel homini pio affulsit: iam non extrema modo, qua ante premebatur, anxietate et formidine, sed omni cura relevatur ac solvitur.*

[9] Comm. on 1 Pet. 5 : 7, C.O. 55 : 288–9.

declares, "What time I am afraid I will trust in thee," says Calvin, "he makes no pretension to that lofty heroism which confidently despises all danger," but admits his fear at the same time as he confesses his confidence in God.[1] The dangers of life are such that for a man to claim in literal truth that he had no fear at all in his heart would be more an indication of insensibility than of virtue.[2] Only an unbeliever, wrapping himself up in "carnal security" and sleeping the sleep of death, can claim himself thus devoid of fear.[3] When the men of the Bible claimed that they were not afraid, they meant that "fear is not so expelled that it no longer assails our minds, but *is* so expelled that it no longer torments us nor impedes that peace which we obtain by faith."[4] Calvin points out that when, in the 23rd Psalm, David said "I will fear no evil," he cannot have meant that he would be devoid of all fear; "*For thy staff and crook comfort me. . . .* What need would he have had of that consolation if he had not been disquieted and agitated with fear?"[5]

The "fearlessness" of the Christian man, then, simply means constant victory in the struggle against anxiety and distrust in various degrees. Since we have always to struggle with the flesh, we never get beyond the need to resist the fears that arise within our hearts,[6] or beyond the need continually to listen to the Word of God when it commands us not to fear.[7] In this conflict, then, we are never free from fear, but can always rise above fear to such

---

[1] Comm. on Ps. 56 : 3–4, C.O. 31 : 548.

[2] Comm. on Ps. 27 : 3, C.O. 31 : 272. *Porro se pronuntians securum fore, non prorsus a metu se exinit: (quod magis stupori tribuendum esset, quam virtuti) sed opponit fidei clypeum, ne obiectis terroribus cor suum succumbat.*

[3] Comm. on Ps. 23 : 4, C.O. 31 : 240.

[4] Comm. on 1 John 4 : 18, C.O. 55 : 358. *Ergo non ita pellitur timor, quin animos nostros sollicitet: sed ita pellitur, ut non turbet, neque impediat pacem nostram quam fide obtinemus.*

[5] Comm. on Ps. 23 : 4, C.O. 31 : 240.

[6] Comm. on Ps. 27 : 1, C.O. 31 : 271. *Discamus ergo tanti facere Dei virtutem ad nos servandos, ut ad profligandos omnes metus praevaleat: non quod in hac carnis infirmitate a pavore semper intactae sint fidelium mentes, sed quia statim recepto vigore ex alta fiduciae arce pericula omnia despicimus.* Cf. comm. on John 7 : 30, C.O. 47 : 176; and on Ps. 46 : 2–3, C.O. 31 : 461.

[7] Serm. on Deut. 7 : 19–24, C.O. 26 : 561. *Et là dessus il adiouste: Tu ne craindras point: comme s'il disoit: Il est vray que vostre nature sera tousiours timide; mais tant y a qu'il ne vous faut point craindre, il vous faut resister à une telle crainte.* (Calvin in this sermon reminds us that the very presence of such fear in the heart is sinful: *Tousiours ceste crainte est à condamner. Car regardons la source: si nous avions une foy parfaite en nostre Dieu, elle seroit pour abolir toute crainte,* p. 561.)

an extent that we can speak of fear and trembling as being ban-
ished from our hearts.[1] Yet it is an extremely hard conflict. There
is "nothing more difficult" than for men either to attain or preserve peace of mind when they are so constantly agitated in heart
by their sense of misery and subject to so many dangers.[2]

Here, again, we must beware lest our boldness should degenerate into pride and presumption. God's promises are such that
if we add faith to them we are bound to be made bold. Indeed, if
we tremble, it is a sign that we do not know Him.[3] Yet, on the
other hand, believers must "guard against that stupidity which
shakes off all anxiety and fills their minds with pride and extin-
guishes the desire to pray." The middle course between two
faulty extremes Calvin finds "very beautifully expressed" by Paul
in the text "Work out your own salvation with fear and trembling;
for God is at work in you" (Phil. 2 : 12).[4]

5. Faith shares in the stability of the Word and the Heavenly Kingdom

Calvin refers to the stability or magnanimity[5] which faith in the
Word gives to the believing man in face of the changes and adver-
sities of life, that are bound to bring despondency and ruin to the
faithless. "The world turns round as it were upon a wheel, by
which it comes to pass that those who were raised to the very top
are precipitated to the bottom in a moment. But the Kingdom of
Judah and the Kingdom of Christ of which it is a type are ex-
cepted. But let us remember that those only can depend on this
stability who betake themselves to the bosom of God by an assured
faith."[6]

Faith may become disconcerted and alarmed in the midst of the
instability of the present state of the world, but it is never shaken,
for the confidence which men place in God enables them to rise
above all care.[7] Calvin finds that Holy Scripture "sets Heaven in

[1] Comm. on John 12 : 14, C.O. 47 : 285; cf. comm. on 1 John 4 : 18, C.O. 55 : 358.
[2] Comm. on Ps. 37 : 3, C.O. 31 : 366.
[3] Serm. on Deut. 20 : 2–9, C.O. 27 : 609.
[4] Comm. on Matt. 26 : 33, C.O. 45 : 715.
[5] Comm. on Ps. 112 : 7, C.O. 32 : 175. *Magnanimitas. . . . recta stabilitas . . .* ; comm. on Rom. 8 : 31, C.O. 49 : 162. *. . . magnitudo animi.*
[6] Comm. on Ps. 21 : 7–8, C.O. 31 : 216.
[7] Comm. on Ps. 112 : 7, C.O. 32 : 175.

opposition to this earth."[1] In contrast to the confusion and turmoil of this present world faith can see and penetrate the heavenly realm which cannot be seen by sense or reason but where Christ is glorified and God reigns over all things in perfect order.[2] By faith, then (and also by means of the Word and Sacraments), our souls are enabled to rise up beyond this world to make contact with the invisible and transcendental realm into which Christ has been exalted,[3] in which we are to seek Him spiritually, not with carnal sense, and through contact with which Christ is present with us.[4] Faith is indeed the lifting up of the heart above the world and Heaven itself to Christ alone who is above all things.[5]

It is through its ability thus to "rise above the world" that faith can always conquer unbelief and the temptation to despair. The faith that has risen above the world finds adequate strength in the Word of God to keep itself supported firm.[6] "If faith reach to Heaven," says Calvin, "it will be an easy matter to emerge from despair."[7] This is true no matter now profound the depths of adversity in which we have been plunged. In such circumstances, faith can not only sustain us, but lift us to God.[8] By faith itself we are enabled to "withdraw from the present aspect of things lest the miseries by which we are surrounded should shake our faith."[9]

It is because faith is founded on the unchangeable Word of God that its possession imparts stability. Since the truth of God's Word is "settled in Heaven" and therefore independent of the changing conditions and disorders of earth, the Word enables the believer to share in its own stability which far transcends that of this present world.[10] It is for this reason that Calvin can speak of

---

[1] Comm. on Ps. 119 : 89, C.O. 32 : 253.
[2] Comm. on Ps. 11 : 4, C.O. 31 : 123–4; on Ps. 13 : 2, C.O. 31 : 132; and on John 14 : 9, C.O. 47 : 330–1.   [3] Cf. pp. 21–3.
[4] Cf. e.g. comm. on John 14 : 19, C.O. 47 : 330–1; and on John 6 : 63, C.O. 47 : 160.
[5] Comm. on 1 Pet. 1 : 8, C.O. 55 : 214.
[6] Comm. on Ps. 119 : 90, C.O. 32 : 254.
[7] Comm. on Ps. 119 : 87, C.O. 32 : 252.
[8] Comm. on Ps. 69 : 4, C.O. 31 : 638.
[9] Comm. on 1 John 3 : 2, C.O. 55 : 330; cf. on Ps. 87 : 3, C.O. 31 : 801; and on John 20 : 29, C.O. 47 : 445.
[10] Comm. on Ps. 119 : 89, C.O. 32 : 253. *Quia periculum erat ne suspensae haererent piorum animae si veritatem proponeret in mundo, ubi variae sunt agitationes, eam in coelis locans, domicilium attribuit nullis mutationibus obnoxius. . . . Nam Petro interprete, 1 Petr. 1, 24 significat salutis certitudinem in verbo esse quaerendam: ideoque perperam facere qui in mundo subsidunt: quia verbi Dei firmitas mundi naturam longe transcendit.*

the faith which relies on the Word as rising "above the whole world" so as to fix its anchor in Heaven[1] and of the light of the Word and Spirit as enabling our minds to emerge out of the midst of the darkness above the world.[2]

6. Assurance depends on maintaining liberty of conscience before God in face of human scrupulosity

The assurance which we have through faith will express itself in liberty of conscience. We dare not do anything against our conscience. Even if a thing is not evil in itself, we cannot allow ourselves to do it or think it if it be in opposition to conscience.[3] "God would have us try or attempt nothing but what we know is agreeable to Him. Whatever, therefore, is done with a doubting conscience is in consequence of doubts of that kind faulty in the sight of God. And this is what He says (Rom. 14 : 23), 'Whatever does not proceed from faith is sin.' Hence the truth of the common saying that 'Those build for Hell who build against their conscience.' "[4] To take a step in opposition to conscience is to be "on the high road to ruin."[5] To violate conscience even in an apparently insignificant matter is to destroy our faith, for so closely is faith bound up with conscience that Calvin can say that faith is of itself goodness of conscience.[6]

But this means that a Christian will refuse to allow his conscience to be brought into bondage to anything other than the Word of God. A good conscience, according to Calvin, is integrity of heart before God, conscience being that which "stands between God and man, not suffering man to suppress than which he knows in himself."[7] By our conscience, then, we are not bound to our fellow man in any direct manner, but strictly speaking only to

---

[1] Comm. on John 20 : 29, C.O. 47 : 445.
[2] Comm. on Heb. 11 : 1, C.O. 55 : 144.
[3] Comm. on 1 Cor. 8 : 11, C.O. 49 : 435. *Scopus enim, quo tendere nos tota vita convenit, est Domini voluntas. Hoc ergo unum est quod omnes actiones nostras vitiat, dum in eam impingimus: id fit non externo solum opere, sed etiam cogitatione animi, dum nobis quidquam permittimus repugnante conscientia, etiamsi id per se malum non sit.*
[4] Comm. on 1 Cor. 8 : 7, C.O. 49 : 433.
[5] Comm. on 1 Cor. 8 : 11, C.O. 49 : 435.
[6] Comm. on Phil. 1 : 23, C.O. 52 : 18. *O bona conscientia, quantum polles ac vales! Bonae autem conscientiae fundamentum est fides: imo ipsa est conscientiae bonitas.*
[7] Comm. on 1 Tim. 1 : 5, C.O. 52 : 253–4; Inst. 3 : 19 : 15.

God.[1] Yet we are tempted constantly to allow this direct relationship between our conscience and God to become distorted by other factors and thus to allow our conscience to be brought into bondage.

The problem of maintaining liberty of conscience presents itself in an acute form when we are dealing with the use of things which are neither good nor bad in themselves and about which God has left us an entirely free choice either to use and enjoy, or to deny ourselves, "things which God has put in our own power, but in the use of which we ought to observe moderation." Calvin calls such things "indifferent" or "external" or "intermediate."[2] To guard our consciences against coming into bondage to men or to our own selves by developing scruples about such outward things is, for Calvin, a most important aspect of our struggle for Christian liberty.[3]

He is very emphatic about the dangers of such scrupulosity. Under certain circumstances, he suggests it might even be right to allow others to do us injustice without protest, but under no circumstances dare we ever allow others to bind our consciences. To allow this would be to lose the light that is in us, and is to offer insult, to Christ the author of freedom.[4] Calvin admits that

---

[1] Calvin points out that Scripture at times speaks as if by our conscience we were directly bound to our fellow men, e.g. in Rom. 13 : 5, 1 Tim. 1 : 5, Acts 24 : 16. But he insists that in those instances Scripture is speaking loosely, rather than strictly indicating that "the fruits of a good conscience go forth and reach even to men." Properly speaking, conscience refers to God only. Inst. 3 : 19 : 16. Cf. comm. on 1 Cor. 10 : 29, C.O. 49 : 470.

[2] Inst. 3 : 19 : 7, 8, 16. Serm. on Gal. 2 : 6–8, C.O. 50 : 377–8. Comm. on 1 Cor. 8 : 1, C.O. 49 : 428. *Res medias voco, quae nec bonae sunt per se, nec malae, sed indifferentes: quas Deus potestati nostrae subiecit. Sed in usu debemus modum servare, ut discrimen sit inter libertatem et licentiam.* Cf. serm. on 1 Cor. 10 : 19–24, C.O. 49 : 680. *Il nous faut user sobrement de nostre liberte en toutes choses qui sont moyennes, et esquelles (comme on dit) il n'y a ne bien ne mal.*

[3] Serm. on Gal. 5 : 1–3, C.O. 50 : 658–9. *Voila donc comme nous sommes affranchis, c'est en cognoissant que Dieu nous reçoit à merci au nom de nostre Seigneur Iesus Christ. . . . Il y a pour le second, que nous ne soyons point agitez de costé et d'autre pour faire scrupule de tout ce que les hommes auront inventé en leur teste: mais qu'il nous suffise de cheminer selon la parole de Dieu, sçachans au reste que nos consciences sont libres.* Cf. Inst. 3 : 19 : 7, where Calvin makes "freedom of conscience touching the use of indifferent things" the third part of Christian liberty, the first part being freedom of conscience from the terrors of the Law, the second part being the free and unconstrained obedience of conscience to obey the Law from the heart.

[4] Comm. on Gal. 5 : 1, C.O. 50 : 243. *Nam si onus humeris nostris iniquum imponant homines, sustineri potest: conscientias si redigere velint in servitutem, fortiter et usque ad mortem resistendum. Spoliabimur enim inaestimabili beneficio, si licebit hominibus conscientias nostras ligare. Et simul Christo libertatis autori fiet iniuria.* Cf. Inst. 3 : 19 : 14.

discussion on this matter may seem trivial, for it descends to trivialities such as the eating of flesh and the free use of days and clothes, and suchlike things, but he points out that it is precisely through such trivialities that an abyss is opened up into which a man can fall to his ruin. "When a man begins to doubt whether it is lawful for him to use linen for sheets, shirts, napkins and handkerchiefs, he will not long be secure as to hemp, and will at last have doubts as to tow; for he will revolve in his mind whether he cannot sup without napkins, or dispense with handkerchiefs. Should he deem a daintier food unlawful he will afterwards feel uneasy about using loaf-bread and common eatables, because he will think that his body might possibly be supported on a still meaner food. If he hesitates as to a more genial wine, he will scarcely drink the worst with a good conscience; at last he will not dare to touch water if more than unusually sweet and pure. In fine, he will come to this, that he will deem it criminal to trample on a straw lying in his way."[1]

Judging from the frequent occurrence of similar passages in his sermons and other writings, the danger of falling into such extreme scrupulosity over trivial matters was a real and common one in Calvin's time, partly owing to the attitude of mind encouraged by the teaching and customs of the Roman Church.[2] Calvin reminds his hearers that a man can be brought into such bondage of conscience, not only by other men, but also by following his own uncontrolled imagination and imposing on himself moral burdens that have no relation to the Word of God,[3] and by bringing to the interpretation of Scripture an attitude that is slavishly literal and legalistic.[4] Calvin clearly saw two grave dangers which might

---

[1] Inst. 3 : 19 : 7.

[2] Cf. e.g. serm. on Gal. 5 : 11–14, C.O. 51 : 17. *Nous voyons comme les poures ignorans qui sont detenus en superstitions sont tousiours en doute et en scrupule. . . . Chacun dira selon que son cerveau le porte, il me semble que telle chose seroit bonne, voilà que ma devotion me dit: il sera bon de faire encore ceci et cela. Or quand ils sont entres en un tel labyrinthe, en la fin ils douteront de se peigner, ils feront scrupule de manger d'un tel doigt, et ceci et cela: brief il n'y a ne fin ne mesure.* Also serm. on Job 1 : 2–5, C.O. 33 : 41; and serm. on 1 Cor. 10 : 19–24, C.O. 49 : 680, where Calvin refers again to the fear of stepping on straws as being due to the fear of stepping on anything that might be in the shape of a cross.

[3] Serm. on 1 Cor. 10 : 19–24, C.O. 49 : 680; on Gal. 5 : 11–14, C.O. 51 : 17.

[4] Comm. on Luke 3 : 10, C.O. 45 : 120. *Atqui non trepidationem modo iniiciunt conscientiis, sed eas desperatione obruunt, quicunque legem imponunt, ne quisquam proprium aliquid possideat. . . . Si fas non est duas habere tunicas, idem de patinis, salinis, indusiis, totaque supellectile erit dicendum.*

ensue when a man reached such an extreme state of bondage to scruples as he describes. He came under the danger either of losing himself in despair, or of throwing aside all restraint in reaction to his bondage, and of plunging into a licence to which there are no bounds.[1]

It is true that, as we have seen already,[2] there are occasions when we must refuse to express our liberty of conscience in outward behaviour, lest we offend others within the Church. Yet even when we are subjecting the outward expression of our liberty of conscience to the law of charity, our consciences can at the same time remain free before God and unbound by our outward behaviour.[3] It is our brother's conscience that is bound, and not our own, when we abstain for his sake from things which produce offence. Calvin notes that Paul "always carefully takes heed not to diminish liberty . . . in any degree."[4] Our own liberty remains unimpaired when we accommodate ourselves to our neighbours.[5] There is no need, therefore, to imagine that, in order to be preserved, our freedom to do what we like in things indifferent must be constantly expressed, and that therefore we must continually in public be asserting it by indulging in behaviour which runs counter to accepted custom within the fellowship of the Church. Our liberty can remain unimpaired before God even though we never use it. It "consists as much in abstaining as in using.'[6]

Yet there are occasions when our liberty should be clearly asserted before men. We are to accommodate ourselves to the weak, but not to the Pharisees, who want to bring all men under bondage to their self-appointed austerity. If it is the Pharisees that are offended we must obey the injunction of our Lord: "Let them

---

[1] Serm. on Job 1 : 2–5, C.O. 33 : 41. *Et puis quand ils ont fait de tels scrupules, pour dire, nous pechons, quelque chose que nous sachions faire: et à la parfin, bien, il faut donc nous desborder du tout.* Inst. 3 : 19 : 7. *Hinc alios desperatione in confusam voraginem abripi necesse est: alios contempto Deo et abiecto eius timore, viam sibi ruina facere quam expeditam non habeant.*

[2] Cf. p. 247.

[3] Inst. 3 : 19 : 16. *Sed utcunque fratris respectu necessaria illi sit abstinentia, ut a Deo praescribitur, non tamen conscientiae libertatem retinere desinit. Videmus ut lex ista externum opus ligans, conscientiam solutam relinquat.*

[4] Comm. on 1 Cor. 10 : 29, C.O. 49 : 470.

[5] Comm. on 1 Cor. 10 : 23, C.O. 49 : 468. *Agnosces libertatem nihilominus manere illibatam, dum proximis te accommodas.*

[6] Inst. 3 : 19 : 10.

alone: they be blind leaders of the blind."[1] There are times when charity must be subservient to purity of faith, and when we must beware of offending God for the sake of our neighbour.[2]

In the realms of conscience, a man must always and can always remain in his freedom before God—no matter how he may be bound at the same time in outward behaviour in apparent compromise to this freedom. "The soul of a pious man looks exclusively to the tribunal of God, has no regard for man, is satisfied with the blessing of liberty secured for it by Christ, and is bound to no individuals, and to no circumstances of time and place."[3]

[1] Inst. 3 : 19 : 11 and 12. Cf. serm. on Gal. 2 : 6–8, C.O. 50 : 377–8. *Mais si nous voyons que sous ombre qu'une chose ne sera bonne ne mauvaise on y vueille mesler quelque saincteté, et qu'il y ait quant et quant obligation pour astreindre les ames et les asservir, là nous avons à resister iusques au bout.*

[2] Inst. 3 : 19 : 13.

[3] Comm. 1 Cor. 10 : 29, C.O. 49 : 470.

Chapter II

Satisfaction and hope

I. The Christian life is joyful in the midst of contrary feelings

CALVIN affirms that the life of the Christian even in this present world is a happy and satisfying life.[1] All believers receive this fruit of their faith, that, being satisfied with Christ alone, in whom they are fully and completely happy and blessed, their consciences are calm and cheerful.[2] The comfort and happiness that God gives to those who willingly give up all for Christ are to be preferred to all the riches of the world, and more than compensates for anything that has been given up. Moreover, they also have the knowledge that their chief reward awaits them in Heaven.[3] "Man is made happy by self-denial,"[4] says Calvin, and this happiness is not a momentary, fleeting feeling but an assured state that no change of fortune can take away.[5]

But the Christian lives in the flesh as well as in the Spirit. He is no log of wood, and therefore, as we have already seen,[6] he keenly feels sorrow, fear and danger, and he is sensitive to the persecutions that come to him because of his faith.[7] How he can be happy in this world is, therefore, a mystery which passes human understanding.[8] "It is a paradox strongly at variance with the feelings of the flesh, that God supplies His people in this world with

---

[1] Comm. on Ps. 128 : 2, C.O. 32 : 327. *Meminerimus autem, prophetam non de ultima felicitate loqui . . . sed promittere etiam in hac peregrinatione vel terreno hospito fidelibus felicem vitam quatenus patitur mundi conditio: quemadmodum dicit Paulus, pietati utrumque promitti, ut scilicet Deus toto vitae curriculo nostri curam gerat* (1 Tim. 4 : 8) *donec ad aeternam gloriam tandem nos perducat.*

[2] Comm. on John 8 : 56, C.O. 47 : 215.

[3] Comm. on Matt. 19 : 29, C.O. 45 : 546.

[4] Comm. on Heb. 4 : 10, C.O. 55 : 48.

[5] Comm. on Ps. 13 : 6, C.O. 31 : 134.

[6] See pp. 191–2.

[7] Comm. on 1 Pet. 1 : 6, C.O. 55 : 212.

[8] Comm. on Isa. 33 : 20, C.O. 36 : 575. *Ergo non promittitur eiusmodi tranquillitas quae carnis nostrae sensibus apprehendi possit: sed ad intimos animi sensus veniendum spiritu Dei reformatos, ut pace illa fruamur, quae nullo humano ingenio apprehendi potest.*

everything that is necessary to a happy and joyful life."[1] The Word
of God promises hope to those who are in despair, wealth to those
who are in poverty, strength to those who are in weakness—and,
therefore, happiness to those who at the same time are in misery.[2]
Therefore believers in their Christian experience are "conscious of
two very different states of mind. On the one hand, they are
afflicted and distressed with various fears and anxieties; on the
other hand, God inspires them with secret joy."[3] Calvin indicates
that in the midst of these "contrary feelings" joy is the dominant
feeling which constantly displaces and overcomes sorrow, though
it never puts an end to it, since it does not divest us of our humanity.[4] At any rate, our "spiritual joy" is always enough to com-
pensate for the bitterness of our cross, and to give rise to thanksgiving.[5]

2. Our main source of Christian happiness is found above and beyond this world

Calvin recognises that "happiness is connected with the state
of mind of that man who enjoys it."[6] It will evade those who imagine that it is to be found in ease, honours or worldly wealth. The
servants of God therefore find contentment in moderating their
expectations of what this life should offer them, and in practising
contentment with what they have in God alone.[7] "In this way we
will find our lot always pleasant and agreeable, for he who has
God as his portion is destitute of nothing which makes a happy
life."[8] God blesses with happiness those who are willing to obey
Him and commit themselves to His care in the belief that all things

[1] Comm. on 1 Tim. 4 : 9, C.O. 52 : 300.
[2] Comm. on Phil. 4 : 7, C.O. 52 : 62.
[3] Comm. on Ps. 94 : 19, C.O. 32 : 27. *Nam fideles duplicem in animis suis affectum gerunt, quia ab una parte anguntur, distrahuntur etiam in varios metus et curas: sed Deus arcanam illis laetitiam inspirat.*
[4] Comm. on 1 Pet. 1 : 6, C.O. 55 : 212. *Tristitiam ergo ex malis sentiunt: sed quae ita lenitur fide, ut gaudere propterea non desinant. Ita non impedit tristitia ipsorum gaudium, sed potius locum illi cedit. Rursus gaudium tametsi tristitiam superat, eam tamen non abolet: quia nos humanitate non spoliat.*
[5] Inst. 3 : 8 : 11.
[6] Comm. on Ps. 49 : 7 f., C.O. 31 : 484–5.
[7] Comm. on Ps. 128 : 2, C.O. 32 : 327; and comm. on Ps. 125 : 3, C.O. 32 : 314–5. Serm. on Eph. 1 : 13–14, C.O. 51 : 306–7. *Il nous faut donc resoudre de tousiours gemir et souspirer, et cependant nous esiouir.*
[8] Comm. on Ps. 16 : 6, C.O. 31 : 154. *Sic fiet ut nobis semper iucunda sit ac suavis nostra conditio: quia nulla beatae vitae parte destituitur qui Deum possidet.*

work together for good to those that love God.[1] "God gladdens His people so that the small portion of good that they enjoy is more highly valued by them and far sweeter than if, out of Christ, they had enjoyed an unlimited abundance of good things."[2]

There are several aspects of the faith in which the Christian man should especially find real happiness. Happiness is a gift of the grace of God which itself is not known otherwise than through the Word and in the inward earnest of the Spirit."[3] The Word is the continual and never-changing source of our earthly happiness since it assures us that even in this life God will be our Father.[4] This should be enough to bring us abundant joy whatever our circumstances otherwise. Calvin lays great stress on the comfort it brings to be assured thus of God's protection in this life. "Although we collect together all the circumstances which seem to contribute to a happy life, surely nothing will be found more desirable than to be kept hidden under the guardianship of God."[5] But the basis even of this joy, as Calvin admits, must be a good conscience, the assurance that our sins are fogiven, and thus the knowledge that in the service of God we do not labour in vain or without hope of recompense.[6] Moreover, a Christian has a sense of the living presence of God Himself with him and looking down on him, in possession of which he can find true satisfaction.[7] "It would not be enough for God to take care of us and provide for us unless on the other hand He irradiated us with the light of His serene countenance and made us taste of His goodness."[8] True

---

[1] Comm. on Ps. 119 : 45, C.O. 32 : 234. *Si quis simpliciter Deo obtemperet, hanc ei mercedem rependi, ut quieto et securo animo iter faciat.*

[2] Comm. on Matt. 19 : 29, C.O. 45 : 546. Cf. serm. on Deut. 7 : 11–15. *Quand il ne leur donneroit qu'un morceau de pain ils ont une ioye interieure, qu'il pourront mieux remercier Dieu, que ne feront point les meschans qui se rongent la dedans, qu'encores qu'ils taschent de s'assoupir, afin de n'avoir aucun remords de conscience.*

[3] Comm. on Phil. 4 : 7, C.O. 52 : 62. *Sola Dei gratia, quae ipsa non cognoscitur nisi per verbum et interiorem arrham spiritus.*

[4] Comm. on 1 Tim. 4 : 8, C.O. 52 : 300.

[5] Comm. on Ps. 128 : 1, C.O. 32 : 326. Cf. comm. on Ps. 5 : 12, C.O. 31 : 72. *Porro docet hic locus, non aliunde quam ex Dei praesidio nasci verum gaudium.*

[6] Comm. on Ps. 19 : 8, C.O. 31 : 200–1. *Nulla alia est nisi bonae conscientiae solida laetitia: qua tunc demum fruimur, ubi certo sumus persuasi vitam nostram Deo placere. . . . Hinc etiam piis Dei cultoribus inaestimabile guadium oritur, quod sciunt non temere nec frustra se fatigari.*

[7] Comm. on Ps. 16 : 5, C.O. 31 : 153.

[8] Comm. on Ps. 21 : 7, C.O. 31 : 215–6. *Neque enim sufficeret, Deum curam nostri gerere, nobisque prospicere, nisi vicissim nobis sereno suo vultu irradians, bonitatis suae gustum praeberet.*

happiness consists in dwelling "as it were under His eyes,"[1] and in finding in His presence a source of full and overflowing abundance of joy.[2]

But all this present experience is not sufficient for the Christian unless he has also learnt to "seek his happiness out of the world" so that by the consolation of hope the bitterness of the Cross might be mitigated.[3] "The happiness which is promised to us in Christ does not consist in external advantages such as leading a joyful and tranquil life . . . but properly belongs to the heavenly life."[4] Calvin frequently reminds us that in the midst of our afflictions only the certainty of the blessed and joyful end that awaits us can alleviate our present bitterness.[5] Moreover, the glory and fullness of the life to come surpasses by far the shortness of our experience of misery here, even were that itself life-long.[6] The discipline through which God puts His people in this life is at times so severe and causes them such pain that a Christian would be of all men most miserable did he not mix and season his grief with the joy of anticipating deliverance and hoping in the resurrection.[7] In learning how to live a happy life, the disciples of Christ must, therefore, "learn the philosophy of placing their happiness beyond the world and above the affections of the flesh," thus sweetening even the bitterness of the Cross by hope.[8] We have to find our happiness in dying as well as in living,[9] for it is the children of this world who are more happy on earth than in Heaven.[10]

[1] Ibid.
[2] Comm. on Ps. 9 : 3, C.O. 31 : 97.
[3] Comm. on Rom. 12 : 12, C.O. 49 : 242. *Extra mundum suam felicitatem quaerere didicerit.*
[4] Inst. 3 : 2 : 15.
[5] Comm. on 1 Tim. 4 : 10, C.O. 52 : 300; and on Ps. 94 : 12–13, C.O. 32 : 24.
[6] Serm. on Acts 1 : 4–5, C.O. 48 : 603–4.
[7] Comm. on 1 Cor. 15 : 19, C.O. 49 : 544–5; on 1 Pet. 4 : 17, C.O. 55 : 282. Comm. on Ps. 14 : 7, C.O. 31 : 142. *Quamvis autem sancti populi laetitiam David in tempus liberationis differat, consolatio tamen haec non modo ad temperandum dolorem nostrum valere debet, sed etiam laetitia condiendum.*
[8] Comm. on Matt. 5 : 2, C.O. 45 : 161. *Ita Christi discipulos philosophari convenit, ut suam felicitatem extra mundum et supra carnis affectum constituant.*
[9] Comm. on Phil. 1 : 21, C.O. 52 : 17.
[10] Comm. on Ps. 119 : 69, C.O. 32 : 245.

3. Our present foretaste of happiness makes us aspire after its fullness in the life to come

When Calvin speaks of our present happiness as being a "taste (*gustus*)" of God's goodness,[1] he means that it is in reality a small foretaste of the experience of God's presence which will be ours in the life to come. Even now in the midst of their sufferings, God bestows upon His people blessings that are a foretaste of the felicity that will be theirs in eternal glory.[2] Through faith, and through the presence of the Holy Spirit in our hearts, we have here and now a participation in the blessed life to come, and thus we experience the first fruits, "a few drops," of that eternal gladness which is laid up for us in Heaven.[3] This foretaste should both satisfy us and at the same time lead us to aspire after the real fullness of such experience, which can be ours only in the future life. Thus both present happiness and future hope are elements in our Christian experience.[4] Our present satisfaction is directly related to the glory of the life to come. When David said, "I will behold thy face in righteousness: I shall be satisfied when I awake with thy likeness," this did not mean that he expected to have no joy till he attained the after-life. Though the vision and satisfaction of which he speaks cannot be complete for believers until the second coming of Christ, nevertheless there are rays of the knowledge of His love which even now penetrate our heart and through the Holy Spirit give us great joy.[5]

4. Our Christian life and warfare are maintained by hope

This earnest or foretaste of eternal life is given to us now to help us to maintain, by means of hope, our Christian warfare in the

[1] Comm. on Ps. 21 : 7, C.O. 31 : 215.
[2] Comm. on Ps. 73 : 24, C.O. 31 : 687. *Consilio deinde adiungitur gloria, quae, meo iudicio, ad aeternam vitam restringi non debet, sicuti faciunt quidam: sed totum felicitatis nostrae cursum complectitur, a principio quod nunc cernitur in terra: usque ad finem, quem speramus in coelo.*
[3] Comm. on John 16 : 21, C.O. 47 : 367.
[4] Serm. on 1 Cor. 11 : 2 and 3, C.O. 49 : 720. *Nous en iouissons en partie, en partie nous esperons encores. Nous iouissons du tesmoignage qu'il nous donne de la remission de nos pechez: nous iouissons du privilege que nous pouvons venir à Dieu, estans asseurez qu'il nous a adoptez, semblablement qu'il nous gouverne par son sainct Esprit, mortifie toutes nos meschantes cupiditez, qui autrement regneroyent du tout en nous: mais nous esperons la vie eternelle, nous esperons ceste delivrance par laquelle Dieu nous monstrera que ce n'est point en vain que nous avons creu en son Fils unique, et luy avons fait hommage comme à nostre chef.*
[5] Comm. on Ps. 17 : 15, C.O. 31 : 168.

midst of all the difficulties we have to face.[1] If we weigh the signs
of God's favour against the signs of His anger we will always find
that His anger is but for a moment, while His favour endures to
the end and continues beyond it.[2] But we must also look beyond
this life in faith to the blessed resurrection and "view from a distance the divine grace even though it is still hidden,"[3] for "the
day has not yet shone which will reveal the treasures that lie
hidden in hope."[4]

Therefore it requires hard and sustained effort to begin to
hope and to grow in the exercise of hope.[5] Yet it is no more difficult to live by hope than by faith. For Calvin, "hope is nothing
else but constancy of faith."[6] He uses exactly the same language in
speaking of hope as he does in speaking of faith, so that the two
words become in many contexts interchangeable. Hope as well as
faith finds its foundation and inspiration through its inseparable
connexion with the Word of God.[7] Hope as well as faith has the
power to raise the hearts of men upwards above this world so that
even though their earthly surroundings be comparable to a grave
they can at the same time "dwell in Heaven by hope."[8] Hope as
well as faith can exist only in constant tension with unbelief and
fear and the temptation to despair.[9] Hope as well as faith is maintained by patience,[10] and is intent on the good things which are in
the future though absent.[11] It is possible that the main distinction
between these inseparable gifts, faith and hope, is that faith is the
most suitable word to use when speaking of our relation to those
realities which are regarded as invisible rather than as future, and
hope is the more suitable word to use when speaking of our relation to those realities which are to be regarded as future rather

[1] Comm. on Eph. 1 : 14, C.O. 51 : 154.
[2] Comm. on Ps. 30 : 5–6, C.O. 31 : 295.
[3] Comm. on Ps. 63 : 5–6, C.O. 31 : 596.
[4] Comm. on Phil. 1 : 6, C.O. 52 : 10.
[5] Comm. on Ps. 61 : 4–5, C.O. 31 : 548.
[6] Comm. on Heb. 3 : 6, C.O. 55 : 38. *Nam spei vocabulum, pro fide accipio:
et profecto spes alioqui nihil aliud est quam fidei constantia.*
[7] Comm. on Ps. 119 : 123, C.O. 32 : 269.
[8] Comm. on Ps. 9 : 18, C.O. 31 : 106. *Descendunt quidem et fideles in sepulcrum,
sed non illo violento impulsu, qui eos sine spe exitus demergat, quin potius in sepulcro
reconditi, spe tamen in coelo habitant.*
[9] Comm. on Ps. 63 : 4, C.O. 31 : 548.
[10] Comm. on Rom. 8 : 24–5, C.O. 49 : 156. *Iam spes non nisi per patientiam
sustinetur.*
[11] Ibid. *Proprium spei est, futuris et absentibus bonis intentam esse.*

than as invisible. Hope alleviates present sorrow by reaching into the distant future and promising itself what at present there is no appearance of obtaining.[1]

Calvin is not ashamed to speak frequently about the hope of reward as a worthy incentive to Christian living. "Surely we know well enough, as the Scripture shows us, that it is not lost labour to serve God, for He has promised us a plentiful reward, and we shall not be disappointed in our expectation."[2] The promises of reward given in Holy Scripture are a concession to our weakness. "The eye of our mind being too dim to be attracted by the mere beauty of goodness, our most merciful Father has been pleased, in His great indulgence, to allure us to love and long after it by the hope of reward."[3] That we should be rewarded for our good works is also a gracious outcome of the fact that God justifies not only the person but also the works of a believer. God, out of His grace, not only accepts our services but also bestows on them a reward. This reward, then, "is so far from being inconsistent with the righteousness of faith that it may be viewed as an appendage to it."[4] Any such reward is given not because our works in any way deserve it, but simply because God is gracious enough, not only to accept our persons and works, but even to reward our service.[5] Though God cannot be put into debt by us,[6] nevertheless He is so gracious that He is willing to become our debtor so that He can reward our works.[7]

Both our present experience of contentment and happiness, and our future hope, play a large part in determining the quality of our Christian life. The contentment and happiness which we at present enjoy give us a moral stability that can prevent us from straying

---

[1] Comm. on Ps. 42 : 6, C.O. 31 : 429. *Spem suam . . . in longum tempus extendit. Atque ut emergat ex praesenti moerore, sibi promittit quod non apparet.*
[2] Serm. on Job 4 : 7–11, C.O. 33 : 187.
[3] Inst. 2 : 8 : 4.
[4] Comm. on 1 Tim. 6 : 19, C.O. 52 : 334.
[5] Serm. on Job 4 : 7–11, C.O. 33 : 187–8. *Or ici quand ie parle du loyer, ie ne traite point si le loyer nous est deu ou non: car nous ne sommes pas sur ceste matiere. Quand nous aurons fait tout ce qui est possible, Dieu ne nous sera point redevable, mais quand il nous promet loyer, i'entens qu'il est gratuit, que cela n'est pas que nous l'ayons merité . . . mais c'est d'autant que comme il nous a receus en sa grace, il veut aussi advouer nos œuvres, ouy, lesquelles il fait par son sainct Esprit . . . cela est pour nous donner tant meilleur courage de le servir, regardans à ses promesses.* Cf. comm. on Ps. 62 : 12–13, C.O. 31 : 593.
[6] Ibid.
[7] Comm. on Luke 17 : 7–9, C.O. 45 : 415.

into sin or being drawn away from God by the allurement of evil.[1]
They enlarge the heart so that it can move freely to keep God's
Law without being contracted by its own narrowness.[2] To have
hope in our hearts when we are wronged and afflicted can make us
meek instead of vengeful and can train us to equanimity and
patience.[3] Hope prevents us, in contrast to other men, from being
"driven by restlessness into mischievous practices."[4] The hope of
reward, too, must be allowed to have its due place in our motive
for Christian service.[5] Calvin asserts that just as the hope of resurrection is an essential part of the Christian faith, without belief in
which the whole structure of our piety would fall to the ground, so
the hope of reward must be an integral part of our Christian
ethics apart from which there can be no solid motive for good
living.[6] He holds out the hope of a great reward to men as an incentive to generosity in Christian giving. "If a heathen poet could
say, 'What riches you give away, those alone shall you always
have,' how much more ought that consideration to have influence
among us who are not dependent on the gratitude of men, but
have God to look to, who makes Himself a debtor in the place of
the poor man, to restore to us one day, with large interest, whatever we give away."[7] Indeed, he can preach to the commercially-
minded men of his day that their best investment a man can make
is in the service of God who is more reliable and gives greater
interest and enables us to make a greater profit than elsewhere.[8]

---

[1] Serm. on Deut. 5 : 19, C.O. 26 : 356. *La vraye richesse . . . est la benediction
de Dieu. Il nous faut donc boire de ceste fontaine, et en estre rassasiez, si nous
voulons nous abstenir de tous larrecins.* Cf. comm. on Ps. 116 : 1, C.O. 32 : 192–3.
[2] Comm. on Ps. 119 : 32, C.O. 32 : 227–8.
[3] Comm. on Ps. 37 : 10–11, C.O. 31 : 371.
[4] Comm. on Ps. 26 : 3, C.O. 31 : 265.
[5] Cf. also pp. 34–40
[6] Comm. on 1 Cor. 15 : 58, C.O. 49 : 565. *Ex adverso autem significat sublata
spe resurrectionis, quasi evulso fundamento, ruere totum pietatio aedificium. Certe
spe praemii remota et exstincta non frigescet tantum, sed concidet currendi alacritas.*
[7] Comm. on 1 Cor. 16 : 2, C.O. 49 : 567.
[8] Serm. on Gal. 6 : 9–11, C.O. 51 : 101. *Celuy qui a argent en bourse, voyant
un profit s'offrir, espandra et de costé et d'autre, car il presuppose que rien ne sera
perdu, et que la somme principale reviendra à luy: et puis il s'augmentera d'autant
par le profit qui luy en reviendra. . . . Voilà Dieu qui parle ainsi quant au mot de
profit. Il adiouste aussi bien la promesse qu'il n'y a ni usure ni gain si grand comme
le profit qu'il nous faut esperer de luy.* Yet here, again, Calvin counsels care lest we
imagine that in this matter we can start bargaining with God (serm. on Job
4 : 7–11, C.O. 33 : 187) or give way to proud self-confidence (comm. on Ps.
62 : 12–13, C.O. 31 : 593).

Chapter III

Progress towards perfection

1. Christian perfection means a wholehearted response to the grace of God

THERE is a standard of perfection towards which a Christian must constantly strive in this life and against which he must constantly measure his progress, no matter how far short of true attainment his efforts may seem to come.[1] Calvin is very careful to define the nature of this Christian perfection. He constantly criticises the view of the "subtle doctors" of the Roman Church. They taught that in commanding men to "be perfect" our Lord could not possibly be commanding something impossible of human attainment, and they claimed, therefore, that their monks could attain to an angelic state in this life in which the perfection set forth in the Sermon on the Mount was really achieved. They taught also that for the laity the command to be perfect was not really a command, but simply "advice" which enables them to live on a lower plane of morality with a good conscience.[2] Equally does Calvin condemn the views of the "enthusiasts," who taught that through union with Christ our inward corruption could be completely destroyed and angelic perfection attained to in this life.[3] Only men "blinded" by "devilish pride" and lacking entirely in the fear of God could entertain such doctrines.[4]

Calvin describes in various terms the perfection at which we

[1] Cf. e.g. comm. on Phil. 3 : 16, C.O. 52 : 53–4. Comm. on 2 Tim. 1 : 6, C.O. 52 : 349. *Sedulo itaque nos contra eniti decet, ut quidquid inchoatum est boni in nobis, expoliamus: ut quod tepet, accendamus.*

[2] Serm. on Deut. 22 : 1–4, C.O. 28 : 14. Comm. on Matt. 5 : 44, C.O. 45 : 188–9.

[3] Comm. on Ps. 89 : 31, C.O. 31 : 822. *Ostendit porro hic locus, dum cooptantur homines a Deo, non protinus exuere carnem suam cum vitiis: sicuti somniant fanatici homines, simulac inserimur in corpus Christi debere aboleri quidquid est in nobis corruptelae. Utinam quidem possemus repente mutare ingenium, ut vigeret in nobis ista, quam requirunt, angelica perfectio!*

[4] Serm. on Eph. 1 : 4–6, C.O. 51 : 273; cf. serm. on Gal. 5 : 14–18, C.O. 51 : 31. *Comme nous voyons des chiens mastins ausquelles il n'y a nulle crainte de Dieu ni religion, lesquels toutesfois preschent que les fideles doivent estre parfaits. Or c'est un blaspheme diabolique et qui nous doit estre en execration.*

have to aim. The perfection of God consists in His "free and pure kindness" in overcoming the malice and ingratitude of men. Our aim must be, therefore, to respond fittingly in our own humble sphere to this perfect grace in which God has presented Himself to us.[1] It is obvious that for Calvin Christian perfection is perfection of faith, for God can ask no more of us than to add faith to His promises and to make them the foundation of our life and salvation.[2] This perfection will express itself in wholehearted self-denial, in conforming ourselves to the will of God when it goes against the judgment of our own mind and the desires of our own heart, and in bearing the yoke of affliction without rebellion when it pleases God to send us troubles of various kinds.[3] Calvin notes that Job is called in some translations of Scripture a "perfect man." But he prefers to use the words "rondeur" or "integrité" to describe Job's "perfection," since what the Scripture really means by "perfection" is the dedication of the whole heart and mind to God with one single aim, without any doubleness or hypocrisy or holding back in any part.[4] To approve ourselves to God means to conform our whole life to God, not in one or two particulars, but without making any reserve whatever the cost. Our lives should wholly correspond to the Word of God.[5]

2. Though such perfection is unattainable in this life, we must strive towards it

Though it must be striven after, such perfection is never to be attained in this life.[6] When we are forgiven and regenerated we do not lay aside the old nature with its constantly sinful concupiscence. The failure of Job with all his patience to submit to God's will without being able to control his passions, and the half-victory of Jacob, lamed because of his infirmity in the very hour of his victory, are for Calvin typical of the failure of the best of

---

[1] Comm. on Matt. 5 : 48, C.O. 45 : 190. Cf. comm. on Ps. 33 : 19, C.O. 31 : 333. *Fideles duobus insignit titulis, quibus tota vitae nostrae perfectio continetur, primum enim est, ut Deum reverenter colamus, deinde ut intenti simus in eius gratiam.*

[2] Serm. on Luke 1 : 45–8, C.O. 46 : 111.

[3] Serm. on Gal. 5 : 22–6, C.O. 51 : 52. *La vraye perfection des enfans de Dieu consiste à s'aneantir.* Cf. serm. on Deut. 8 : 10–14, C.O. 26 : 613.

[4] Serm. on Job 1 : 1, C.O. 33 : 27–8.

[5] Serm. on Deut. 5 : 28–33, C.O. 26 : 416.

[6] Serm. on Luke 2 : 50–2, C.O. 46 : 479.

God's saints in living the Christian life.[1] The fact that Jesus washed the feet of His disciples is a sign that because of the mere fact that we are involved in the life of this present sinful world we are bound to be involved constantly in its sin and therefore "Christ always finds in us something to cleanse."[2] We are never truly wholehearted in our response to Jesus Christ. The Holy Spirit is never able to occupy the whole of us. His work is to subdue instead of transform the unruly flesh.[3] We never therefore possess the Holy Spirit in a perfect relationship to ourselves. This means, therefore, that we are kept humble and constantly aware of our need to call upon God.[4] It means, too, that we are kept in a state of requiring to make constant progress. "So long as there is daily progress there cannot be perfection."[5] It means, too, that "the more eminently anyone excels in holiness, the farther he feels from perfect righteousness, and the more clearly he perceives that he can trust in nothing but the mercy of God alone."[6] The Christian man, therefore, can live only by being continually justified by faith.[7] The more he attains towards the goal of perfection the more he will acknowledge his own weakness. The perfect Christian man is he who, conscious of his sin and misery, had learned to live by grace.[8]

Though it is a device of the Devil to fill our minds with a confident belief in the attainability of perfection, we are, nevertheless,

---

[1] Serm. on Job 34 : 4–10, C.O. 35 : 132. Cf. comm. on Ps. 62 : 2, C.O. 31 : 585.

[2] Comm. on John 13 : 9, C.O. 47 : 308. *Ergo pedes metaphorice vocantur omnes affectus et curae, quibus mundum contingimus. Nam si omnes nostri partes occuparet spiritus, nihil cum mundi sordibus nobis amplius esset: nunc vero qua parte sumus carnales humi reptando, vel saltem pedes in lutum figendo, tantundem immundi sumus.*

[3] Comm. on John 13 : 9, C.O. 47 : 308.

[4] Serm. on Acts 1 : 4–5, C.O. 48 : 601. *Vray est que nous n'en (i.e. du S. Esprit) aurons pas en perfection, d'autant qu'il nous est besoin d'estre tenus en humilité. Et si nous en avions en perfection, que seroit-ce? Nous n'aurions plus soin d'invoquer Dieu, et ne penserions point avoir besoin de luy.*

[5] Comm. on Eph. 5 : 27, C.O. 51 : 224–5. Cf. serm. on Job 15 : 11–16, C.O. 33 : 721. *Cependant que nous vivons au monde, cognoissons que nous sommes seulement au chemin.*

[6] Comm. on Ps. 32 : 1, C.O. 31 : 317.

[7] Comm. on Gen. 15 : 6, C.O. 23 : 213. *Fide iustificari sanctos quandiu in mundo vivunt.*

[8] Serm. on Eph. 1 : 4–6, C.O. 51 : 273. *Car la perfection des fideles et des enfans de Dieu, c'est de cognoistre combien ils sont encores debiles, non seulement pour prier Dieu qu'il corrige tous leurs defauts, mais qu'il les supporte par sa bonté infinie, et qu'il ne les appelle point à conte en rigueur extreme.* Cf. serm. on Deut. 7 : 11–15, C.O. 26 : 534

"not to labour feebly or coldly in urging perfection" or in striving towards it.[1] Progress towards perfection should be our constant aim.[2] Indeed, says Calvin, "the highest perfection of the godly in this life is an earnest desire to make progress."[3] Since the goal of the Christian life is to attain to the perfect manhood of Christ, the course of the Christian life should be like the period of youth, a course of steady growth in vigour and wisdom, "marked by a constant desire and progress towards those attainments which they shall ultimately reach."[4] "We must learn, then, to be always growing as long as we live in this world," regarding ourselves in humility as little children,[5] and always conscious of our weakness, realising that we will always remain apprentices and novices requiring constant instruction.[6] Even if we feel satisfied with what we already have, we must realise that God is always waiting for us to enlarge our capacity for receiving His blessing, to open our mouth wider that He may fill it with much more than we already have. "Our own narrowness is what hinders God from pouring upon us an abundance of His blessings," for God "accommodates His liberality to the measure of our expectations."[7]

The Christian life, then, is no "settled state."[8] It is true that our complete justification can take place at one moment of time so that there and then we are accounted as wholly righteous before God, but our sanctification is a process that is more and more completed throughout the whole course of our lives to be perfected only through death.[9] It is true that on receiving the Gospel we enter the Kingdom of God, but "Is it sufficient to have entered?" asks Calvin, and answers, "Not at all, unless we recognise that our life is a road on which we must continue to march

---

[1] Inst. 4 : 1 : 20.
[2] Serm. on Gal. 5 : 14–18, C.O. 51 : 26–7. *Or il est vray qu'il faut tendre à ceste perfection et y aspirer tousiours. Mais quoy qu'il en soit, ne laissons pas de cercher Dieu, combien que nous ne puissions pas parvenir à luy, et qu'il y ait beaucoup d'empeschemens.*
[3] Comm. on Eph. 3 : 16, C.O. 51 : 186. *Summa itaque piorum in hac vita perfectio est proficiendi studium.*
[4] Comm. on Eph. 4 : 14, C.O. 51 : 200–1.
[5] Serm. on Luke 1 : 1–4, C.O. 46 : 11.
[6] Serm. on Ps. 119, C.O. 32 : 595; and serm. on Eph. 4 : 15–16, C.O. 51 : 584.
[7] Comm. on Ps. 65 : 4–5, C.O. 31 : 606.
[8] Serm. on Acts 1 : 1–4, C.O. 48 : 591. *Dieu ne nous appelle pas à soy pour nous tenir en un estat, mais qu'il nous poussera tousiours iusques à ce qu'il nous ait amenez à perfection.*
[9] Comm. on John 17 : 17, C.O. 47 : 385.

until we come to our Lord Jesus Christ. Thus the Kingdom of God must increase in us more and more."[1]

3. There is a state of achieved victory over sin and whole-hearted surrender which by the grace of God may be called "perfection"

If we seek to make progress we will find that we can attain here and now a decisive victory over sin, the flesh, and the Devil. The power to "bruise Satan" under heel given to Eve and fulfilled in Christ's victory on the Cross, is imparted already to the Church,[2] and though our full victory over evil, as exemplified in the triumph of Christ, our Head, will be perfectly enjoyed by us only after death, nevertheless it is now "partially obtained."[3] Though Satan is indeed still the "prince of this world"[4] in respect to his dominion over unbelievers, and, to some extent, the material realm, God does not allow him to have dominion over the souls of believers.[5] Though in the hearts of the faithful the "flesh lusts against the Spirit," nevertheless the Spirit of God always overcomes and subdues the flesh if we do not prevent Him.[6] The believer may be "tied to the flesh"[7] and may be vexed by the felt power of indwelling sin, nevertheless he can always allow himself to be ruled by the Spirit of God in such a way that he always has the upper hand of sin,[8] and can have confident joy in facing temptations.[9] Sin is

---

[1] Serm. on Acts 1 : 1–4, C.O. 48 : 590.

[2] Comm. on Gen. 3 : 15, C.O. 23 : 71. *Quibus verbis significat Satanae conterendi virtutem diffundi in homines fideles, atque ita communem totius ecclesiae benedictionem esse: verum simul admonet inchoari tantum in hoc mundo.*

[3] Inst. 1 : 14 : 18. *In capite quidem nostro semper ad plenum exstitit haec victoria . . . in nobis autem qui membra eius sumus, ex parte nunc apparet.*

[4] Comm. on Gen. 3 : 15, C.O. 23 : 71. *Filios hominum captivos saeculis omnibus duxit Satan pro sua libidine, et hodie luctuosum illum triumphum continuat: ideo et princeps mundi vocatur.* Comm. on Rom. 16 : 20, C.O. 49 : 288. *Victus quidem est semel a Christo, sed non ita quin bellum assidue renovet.*

[5] Inst. 1 : 14 : 18.

[6] Comm. on John 15 : 4, C.O. 47 : 340. *Spiritum suum promittit semper fore in nobis efficacem, si modo per nos non steterit.*

[7] Comm. on Rom. 8 : 5, C.O. 49 : 141. *Illigati carni suae.*

[8] Ibid., and on Rom. 6 : 14, C.O. 49 : 113. *Utcunque enim peccati aculeis vexemur, non potest tamen nos subigere, quia spiritu Dei superiores reddimur.* Cf. serm. on Gal. 5 : 14–18, C.O. 51 : 24.

[9] Serm. on Eph. 1 : 13–14, C.O. 51 : 307. *Quand le S. Esprit domine en nos cœurs, nous avons de quoy nous glorifier au milieu de toutes nos tentations, comme il est au 8 chapitre des Romans.*

therefore "deprived of kingly power" in the heart of the Christian.[1] Our confidence in seeking to live the Christian life is based on the fact that though sin continues to dwell within us, it does not reign within us, and God will always so work in those who trust Him as to be the ruling force in all their affections and desires.[2] If we wrestle through the power of God in the terrible conflict with passion and trouble we will not be overwhelmed.[3]

Calvin at times speaks as if this achievement of victory over sin can become a settled and stable state. Commenting on 1 John 3 : 9 he points out that a Christian is free from sin in so far as he is regenerated, and that though no one is yet completely regenerated nevertheless "he who is born of God can lead a holy life, because the Spirit of God restrains the lusting of sin." Then he asserts that the government of the Spirit can be so effectual that our hearts are given an "inflexible disposition" (*affectus*) to follow His guidance. "The power of the Spirit is so effectual that it necessarily retains us in continual obedience to righteousness." For Scripture teaches that "the will is so formed that it cannot be otherwise than right."[4] There can be a wholehearted surrender to God and "a real harmony (*un accord et comme une melodie*)" between us and God, when we seek to give the grace of God the chief place in our life,[5] and when the chief desire of our heart is that God should control us by His Spirit. In this case we may be said to serve God with true *rondeur de cœur*, for He does not impute to us the weaknesses that still remain in us.[6] To be thus wholehearted is to be on the way to attaining the goal of purity and holiness, and is to have perfection attributed to us.[7] To this extent we can achieve "perfection."

[1] Comm. on John 13 : 9, C.O. 47 : 308. *Primo dicit fideles totos esse mundos, non quod omni ex parte puri sint, ut nulla in illis macula amplius haereat, sed quoniam praecipua sui parte mundati sunt: dum scilicet ablatum est regnum peccato.* Cf. on Rom. 6 : 10, C.O. 49 : 109; and on Gal. 5 : 16, C.O. 50 : 252.

[2] Serm. on Deut. 5 : 21, C.O. 26 : 383. *Combien que nous ayons eu la victoire par la grace de Dieu, et que le peché n'ait point regné en nous: si est-ce qu'il y habite tousiours, et qu'il y a quelque ordure et macule.*

[3] Comm. on Ps. 31 : 9, C.O. 31 : 306.

[4] Comm. on 1 John 3 : 9, C.O. 55 : 336.

[5] Serm. on Deut. 1 : 34–40, C.O. 25 : 694.

[6] Serm. on Deut. 26 : 16–19, C.O. 28 : 284.

[7] Inst. 4 : 1 : 17.

4. Yet we continually fail, and progress is slow

Yet our progress towards final perfection and full regeneration is slow and our experience in the process of making progress is often disappointing. "Even though we have experienced the victory by the grace of God, and sin has not reigned within us, yet it still dwells within us always, and there are stains and spots on our life. We must groan, then, and we must groan in such a way that it drives us on to do our duty . . . and we must not become discouraged. Even though each day we see a million faults within us yet we must always seek to get beyond."[1] Even after progress and victory, there will come times when we will find ourselves completely swept off our feet and unable to stand or control ourselves and will be forced to cast ourselves in desperation on the help and mercy of God.[2] Our progress is progress made always limping instead of running.[3] Even though we fight and conquer the enemy we receive blows that blind and stagger us and we come out of the fight sorely wounded.[4] This is a battle in which we at times feel feeble and languid and enveloped in darkness and unable to fight with courage.[5] Our very battle with our own selves leaves us weak and exhausted instead of strong and exhilarated.[6] All this makes steadfastness in Christian progress the result only of heroic determination.

5. Christian growth is primarily growth in faith

Since Christian perfection is the perfection of faith, Christian growth is primarily growth in faith. Since faith responds to the preaching of the Gospel, as preaching continues through the

[1] Serm. on Deut. 5 : 21, C.O. 26 : 383.
[2] Serm. on Job 3 : 11–19, C.O. 33 : 154; cf. comm. on Ps. 34 : 4–5, C.O. 31 : 337.
[3] Serm. on Matt. 5 : 11–12, C.O. 46 : 821. *D'avantage, cognoissons que quand encores nous tendrons au bien, ce sera tousiours en clochant, au lieu de courir: il y aura beaucoup d'imperfections et de povretez.* Serm. on Job 1 : 1, C.O. 33 : 28. *Car ceux qui suivent le droit chemin, encores vont ils en clochant, ils sont tousiours debiles, qu'ils trainent les iambes et les ailes.*
[4] Serm. on Job 3 : 1–10, C.O. 33 : 142; comm. on Ps. 121 : 3, C.O. 32 : 300. *Etsi autem fideles contingit saepe nutare, imo labascere: quia tamen sua virtute eos Deus recti stare dicuntur.* Serm. on Job 9 : 29–35, C.O. 33 : 458.
[5] Comm. on Ps. 17 : 15, C.O. 31 : 168.
[6] Serm. on Gen. 15 : 4–6, C.O. 23 : 687.

whole course of our life, so we ought to continue growing in faith."[1] Faith is always mixed with unbelief. Even the faith of Abraham had this patent infirmity.[2] Indeed, viewed as it is in itself, our faith is so weak and insignificant that it finds acceptance with God only by being reckoned as perfect. Nevertheless, in the struggle against unbelief faith can be nourished and increased and unbelief diminished. "As our faith is never perfect it follows that we are partly unbelievers; but God forgives us and exercises such forbearance towards us as to reckon us believers on account of a small proportion of faith. It is our duty in the meantime carefully to shake off the remains of infidelity which adhere to us, to strive against them, to pray to God to correct them."[3]

6. Faith grows in stability and clarity as it increasingly apprehends the exaltation of Christ

In its imperfect state faith suffers from a "twofold weakness" (*duplex debilitas*): it suffers from both ignorance (*ignorantia*) and instability (*dubitatio*), and it requires to be both illuminated and established.[4] The two operations of the Spirit in faith are to "illuminate the mind and confirm the soul," till faith becomes no longer mere knowledge (*notitia*) but a firm and steady conviction which admits of no opposing doubt.[5] The process of confirmation is simply the growth of faith (*fides*) into *fiducia* and *audacia*.[6] Calvin can speak of a stage in the progress of faith that is "no ordinary attainment" in which we learn to "lean with our whole heart on God" knowing with true humility that we ourselves are destitute of all strength.[7]

In the process of being confirmed faith grows in clarity.[8] Growth

---

[1] Comm. on Heb. 3 : 15, C.O. 55 : 43.

[2] Serm. on Gen. 15 : 4–6, C.O. 23 : 68; serm. on Matt. 2 : 23, C.O. 46 : 462.

[3] Comm. on Mark 9 : 24, C.O. 45 : 495. *Nam quum nusquam perfecta exstet fides, sequitur ex parte esse incredulos: sic tamen pro sua indulgentia nobis ignoscit Deus, ut ab exiguo fidei modulo nos fideles aestimet. Nostrum interea est sedulo excutere infidelitatis reliquias, quae in nobis haerent, ut cum illis luctemur, ac petere a Domino ut eas corrigat.*

[4] Comm. on Rom. 4 : 19, C.O. 49 : 83.

[5] Comm. on Eph. 1 : 13, C.O. 51 : 153; cf. comm. on Rom. 4 : 19, C.O. 49 : 83.

[6] Cf. pp. 303–4.

[7] Comm. on Ps. 84 : 5–6, C.O. 31 : 781–2.

[8] Serm. on Eph. 4 : 11–14, C.O. 51 : 567. *Et ainsi, il faut que iournellement nous soyons confermez de plus en plus, que la clairté de nostre foy s'augmente, comme nous voyons le iour aller tousiours en croissant iusques au Midi.*

in faith is accompanied by growth in knowledge.[1] Faith in its very feeble beginnings, when Christ is born within us, can indeed be little more than an "implicit seed of piety" (*implicitum pietatis semen*), rather than the clear knowledge of the truth (*liquida veri cognitio*)—a "confused feeling of piety involving much superstition," like some "hidden root" which will produce fruit ultimately. Such was the case with the disciples of Jesus before the Resurrection in their doubt, hesitation, and sinful grief; and though it was "almost no faith," it nevertheless inspired them with zeal, and it was enough to prevent them from deserting Jesus.[2] It was only after the Resurrection that their knowledge became more clear, and they passed from the stage of little children to a more adult state of faith. Calvin applies to this incipient development of faith the reference in Paul's prayer for the Galatians that Christ might be "formed within" them as an advance on Christ being no more than born within them.[3] But no matter what stage we have reached in the Christian life, there is always much darkness and many clouds of ignorance which obscure the brightness of the Gospel. No matter how much enlightenment we have received we need to pray as the psalmists did for further light.[4]

Faith grows in knowledge by moving from the Cross to the Resurrection. We must beware in case our faith should stop short at the knowledge of the humanity and death of Christ. Faith must begin in this way, for Christ descended and was humbled in order that we might begin with this knowledge of Him as He was on earth, "born in a stable and hanging on a cross." But after His humiliation Christ was exalted to His own and the Father's glory. So also our faith must "rise to the glory of His resurrection and proceed onward till it comes at length to His eternal life and power in which His divine majesty is gloriously displayed." This was the triumph and completion of Thomas's faith when he cried out, "My Lord and my God!"[5] A faith that is truly growing, then, will "leave the sepulchre" and "ascend to the heavenly glory of

---

[1] Comm. on 1 Pet. 1 : 14, C.O. 55 : 222. *Itaque quantum quisque progressus est in vitae novitate, tantum profecit in Dei notitia.*

[2] Comm. on Matt. 17 : 22, C.O. 45 : 498; and on John 20 : 3, C.O. 47 : 428. Calvin distinguishes this from the *fides implicita* of the Roman Church.

[3] Comm. on John 20 : 3, C.O. 47 : 428. Cf. comm. on Gal. 4 : 19, C.O. 50 : 235.

[4] Comm. on Ps. 86 : 11, C.O. 31 : 795; and on John 8 : 32, C.O. 47 : 202.

[5] Comm. on John 20 : 28, C.O. 47 : 444.

Christ."[1] But indeed, even in this movement of faith towards the Resurrection, we must not imagine that we can leave the Cross behind. "Let us learn that when the death of Christ is mentioned, we ought always to take in view at once the whole of the three days, that His death and burial may lead us to a blessed triumph and to a new life."[2]

Calvin lays particular stress on the need of attaining not simply new knowledge, but greater clarity and conviction in our understanding of the things we already know, for believers are "in some measure ignorant of what they know."[3] This process is no doubt simply the unfolding of what is already "implicit" in their faith. Growth in faith enables the faithful "more clearly and fully" to "hold their present views."[4]

7. Growth of faith is accompanied by a deepening experience of Christ and a progressive transformation of life

As our faith grows, our capacity to receive God's gifts and blessings increases, for the straitened faith of most of us is like a narrow mouth which partakes with difficulty of "only a few small drops" of the abundant supply which is available for those who will open their mouth wide.[5] This means that as our faith is increased more and more, we are able more and more to inherit the glorious liberty of the children of God.[6] As our faith grows, moreover, we are able to receive "fresh additions of the Spirit of God," which are given "according to the measure of faith,"[7] and thus we

[1] Comm. on John 20 : 3, C.O. 47 : 428.
[2] Comm. on Matt. 17 : 22, C.O. 45 : 499. Cf. on pp. 78–9 and 220. Calvin can distinguish between the knowledge that comes after faith, which is the *Verum cognitio Dei et arcanae eius sapientiae* and the knowledge that preceded faith and prepares for it which is *operum suorum notitia*. Comm. on John 10 : 38, C.O. 47 : 254.
[3] Comm. on John 8 : 32, C.O. 47 : 202. *Fideles . . . quodammodo id quod sciunt ignorant.*
[4] Comm. on Eph. 1 : 17, C.O. 51 : 155. *Opus simul habebant incrementis, ut ampliore spiritu donati magisque ac magis illuminati, certius et penitius tenerent quod iam tenebant.*
[5] Comm. on Ps. 81 : 11, C.O. 31 : 763–4.
[6] Comm. on John 8 : 32, C.O. 47 : 203. *Hoc notandum est, libertatem suos habere gradus pro fidei suae modo.*
[7] Comm. on John 7 : 38, C.O. 47 : 181–2. *Et sane quum quisque pro fidei suae mensura donorum spiritus compos fiat, non potest in hac vita solida eorum plenitudo constare. Verum sic fideles in fide proficiendo subinde ad nova spiritus incrementa adspirant, ut primitiae quibus imbuti sunt illis ad vitae perpetuitatem sufficient.* Cf. serm. on Acts 2 : 1–4, C.O. 48 : 633.

make progress towards "fullness of life."[1] Indeed, Calvin can say that in proportion as our faith is more or less, not only is the Spirit more or less within us, but Jesus Christ Himself grows or diminishes within us, showing Himself great or small within us as our faith is strong or weak.[2] Though Calvin insists that, whatever our progress has been, our union with Christ is always, in a sense, perfect (in that it can never be broken, and in that it justifies us perfectly), nevertheless, with the increase of faith and participation in the ordinances of Christ, this union is increased more and more[3] "until we are fully united to Jesus Christ."[4]

The growth of faith is thus accompanied by deepening experience. Christ admits us to a "greater familiarity with Himself."[5] The disciples had some faith in the promise of Christ that they would be able to cast out devils, but it was obviously not full faith, for later they came back expressing their astonishment at what had happened through the power of Christ. "This is frequently the case with believers, that they receive from the Word only a slight perception (*gustum*) of the divine power, and are afterwards carried away in admiration by actual experience."[6] The growth of faith must also be accompanied by a growing measure of sanctification. "The true stages in the growth of Christians are when they make progress in knowledge and understanding, and afterwards in love."[7] As our faith grows, it is accompanied by increasing communion with the death of Christ and thus a deepening experience of the work of God in crucifying the flesh.[8] Repentance, says Calvin, "is never perfect at the start, but after God planes us, He

---

[1] Comm. on John 10 : 10, C.O. 47 : 241. *Et certe prout quisque in fide progreditur, eo propius ad vitae plenitudinem accedit, quia in eo crescit spiritus, qui vita est.*

[2] Serm. on Matt. 2 : 23, C.O. 46 : 462. *Car voyla mesmes comme nostre Seigneur Iesus Christ croist auiourd'huy en nous. Il est vray qu'en soy il ne peut augmenter ni diminuer aussi: mais quant à nous, il est certain que selon la mesure de nostre foy, il est petit ou grand.*

[3] Serm. on Acts 2 : 1–4, C.O. 48 : 633. *Nous ne laisserons pas aussi d'estre unis à luy en toute perfection, voire entant que besoin sera. Et voyla pourquoy i'appelle cela perfection: combien que cependant il nous avance de mesure en mesure. Car quoy qu'il en soit, nous ne laisserons pas d'estre conioints à luy.*

[4] Serm. on Acts 1 : 1–4, C.O. 48 : 190.

[5] Comm. on John 8 : 32, C.O. 47 : 202.

[6] Comm. on Luke 10 : 17, C.O. 45 : 315.

[7] Comm. on Phil. 1 : 9, C.O. 52 : 12.

[8] Comm. on Rom. 6 : 7, C.O. 49 : 108. *Hoc enim opus Dei* (i.e. crucifying the flesh) *non primo, quo in nobis inchoatur, die, simul etiam perficitur: sed paulatim augescit, ac quotidianis incrementis paulatim ad finem perducitur.*

also needs to polish us."[1] This is part of the continual "cleansing from all unrighteousness" which is progressively carried on from day to day in the process of sanctification.[2]

To make progress in faith means, therefore, a progressive transformation in our way of living. To make progress in faith and in the knowledge of God means at the same time making progress in conformity to His image, for when faith looks on and meditates on the glory of God revealed in the Gospel it is no dead contemplation but one that transforms us into the image of God. These are the main lessons Calvin draws from the 2 Cor. 3 : 18. "We all with open face beholding as in a glass the glory of the Lord, are changed into the same image from glory to glory, even as by the Spirit of the Lord."[3] This text is often in Calvin's mind when he speaks about Christian growth. He quotes it to justify the place he gives to knowledge in his teaching about the Christian life, "for the true knowledge of God is a living and not a dead thing, and it will manifest itself and bear fruit in our whole way of living," and if this has not happened to us we prove ourselves mere mockers of God in our claim to know Him.[4] He quotes it to remind us that the future glory is promised to none but those in whom the image of God already shines and who are being transformed into it by continued advance of glory.[5] He quotes it to remind us that if this process has already begun within us, even in a feeble and hidden way—of increasing knowledge and contemplation bringing us into increasing conformity to God—then it is bound to go on all our life with increasing force and fullness, for it promises ultimately the entire restoration into the image of God not only of our own beings but also of the whole Creation.[6]

[1] Serm. on Job 42 : 1–5, C.O. 35 : 477.
[2] Comm. on 1 John 1 : 9, C.O. 55 : 307.
[3] Comm. in loc. C.O. 50 : 47.
[4] Serm. on Titus 1 : 15–16, C.O. 54 : 493–4.
[5] Comm. on Matt. 13 : 43, C.O. 45 : 371.
[6] Serm. on 1 Tim. 1 : 5–7 C.O. 53 : 35–6; comm. on Luke 17 : 20, C.O. 45 : 425.

Chapter IV

Perseverance to the end

1. The trial of faith is long and severe

THE trial of faith in this life is long and severe. We are allowed no rest from fearful spiritual and moral conflict, for our whole life is one unceasing battle with Satan.[1] In this battle "Christ will have no discharged soldiers except those who have conquered death itself."[2] Even if there are times of momentary relief after some one victory, we are soon called upon again to face fresh battles.[3]

Therefore it is useless to begin the Christian life unless we have the resolve and the power to persevere. Calvin faces those who ask plausibly, "What can we wish more after having found Christ?" with the fact that "If He is possessed by faith, we must persevere in it, so that He may be our perpetual possession," for the one condition for the enjoyment of Christ is to preserve by faith the blessing we enjoy by faith.[4] If in a moment of good impulse and resolution we put our trust and hope in the promise of God, it is nothing, unless we continue.[5] Time and again after a zealous start in the Christian life our holy zeal will prove to be mixed up with selfish ambition and other unworthy desires which are hard to purge.[6] Therefore we must continue to submit to God's chastisement from which we are apt to be slow in obtaining benefit.[7] The Christian is he who devotes himself to the practice of living rightly and justly in one constant and continual course.[8] Closer fellowship with Christ is a reward that Christ bestows upon perseverance.[9]

[1] Serm. on Deut. 20 : 2–9, C.O. 27 : 613.
[2] Comm. on Heb. 12 : 4, C.O. 55 : 173.
[3] Comm. on Ps. 42 : 5–6, C.O. 31 : 428–9.
[4] Comm. on Heb. 3 : 14, C.O. 55 : 43.
[5] Serm. on Job 14 : 13–15, C.O. 33 : 691.
[6] Comm on Matt. 20 : 20, C.O. 45 : 552.
[7] Comm. on John 5 : 14, C.O. 47 : 110.
[8] Comm. on Ps. 106 : 3, C.O. 32 : 116.
[9] Comm. on John 8 : 32, C.O. 47 : 202. *Hoc autem praemio dignatur Christus suorum constantiam, quod se illis magis familiarem reddit.*

2. Perseverance requires much patience and virtue

It requires much patience and virtue to persevere. The Psalmist whose eyes failed while he waited upon God is held out by Calvin to show us an example of the "perseverance combined with severe and arduous effort" with which we should seek the fulfilment of God's promises.[1] Such steadfastness is the more difficult owing to the fact that such a large element in the Christian life is that of suffering. Christian steadfastness is the power to hold on not in the midst of spectacular victory but more often in the midst of weakness and contempt from men.[2] "The chief virtue of the faithful, therefore, is a patient endurance of the Cross and mortification by which they calmly submit themselves to God."[3] Christian patience involves us, moreover, in the constant exercise of humility—a humility which does not despise the feeble beginnings of faith and the gradual and small steps by which it is increased.[4]

3. Our faith is bound to persevere since God is bound to see us through

In the face of all the difficulties in maintaining constantly our Christian faith and life we would have no rest of mind if we were not certain that God Himself takes the responsibility not only of "preventing" us with His grace but also of sustaining us with His help all our life, and of confirming us in our perseverance.[5] "It is not enough to be able to rely on God's help only for today. I must also be fully persuaded that He will help me tomorrow, and right on to the end,"[6] says Calvin. Faith is not, then, a mere "wavering

---

[1] Comm. on Ps. 119 : 123, C.O. 32 : 269.

[2] Serm. on Matt. 2 : 16–22, C.O. 46 : 452. *Et ainsi advisons . . . que neantmoins iamais nous ne nous lassions au milieu du chemin: et si nous sommes foibles, que nous prions Dieu qu'il nous donne vertu, non point pour nous escarmoucher, ni pour concevoir des opinions, et avoir la main levee quand nostre cerveau sera bouillant: mais que ce soit pour cheminer en infirmite, c'est à dire, que nous soyons comme foulez au monde, que nous soyons gens perdus et desesperez, que nous continuyons en cela: et que la vertu de Dieu se demonstre d'autant plus que nous ne serons rien de nostre costé: et que nous n'attenterons aussi rien à la volee, mais que nous souffrirons qu'il nous gouverne iusqu' à la fin.*   [3] Comm. on Ps. 119 : 166, C.O. 32 : 290.

[4] Comm. on Luke 7 : 29, C.O. 45 : 306.

[5] Comm. on Ps. 68 : 29, C.O. 31 : 633.

[6] Serm. on Deut. 20 : 2–9, C.O. 27 : 603; Cf. serm. on Deut. 4 : 39–43, C.O. 26 : 224 and serm. on 1 Tim. 6 : 12–14, C.O. 53 : 599. *Et ainsi c'est Dieu qui nous met en train il nous dispose à courir, il nous monstre le chemin. A-il fait cela?*

persuasion."¹ There is a felt and steady settledness about true faith that gives its possessors the assured confidence that it will persevere throughout the whole of life.² What God has begun He is bound to complete.³

Yet our faith perseveres in this way not because some new strength of character has been worked up within our psychological make-up by the grace of God, nor because some new-found and unshakable strength has been imparted to our human will but only because God never goes back on His call to us and never disappoints us in His promise that we shall persevere to the end. We remain weak and fickle creatures even after we have come to faith, but God remains faithful. "Our salvation is certain because it is *in the hand* of God; for our faith is weak and we are prone to waver."⁴ Since it is in God's care our ultimate salvation is never in danger even though we ourselves may be continually exposed to overwhelming dangers, and may undergo the most varied fortunes.⁵ His promises, assuring us unfailing help, are not for one day but "for ever."⁶

4. Regeneration is an incorruptible seed of life

Calvin finds further assurance about the "inflexible perseverance" of the elect in the thought that the "seed communicated when God regenerates the elect, since it is incorruptible, retains its virtue perpetually."⁷ He admits that the good seed of the new life can be concealed and crushed and stifled till it appears as if its possessor had cast off all fear of God (as in the case of David when he sinned with Bathsheba) or all faith (as in the case of Thomas' doubt after the crucifixion). Nevertheless, though all religion seem extinct, some latent spark of the new life always remains "like a live coal hid under the ashes." Faith may be choked but it is never wholly extinguished.[1] We must not follow those who teach that if the elect fall into mortal sin they may lose the Spirit altogether.[2] "God restrains His elect by a secret bridle that they may not fall into destruction."[3] It is most important that in the face of our failures in the Christian life we should comfort and encourage ourselves by remembering all this. "It is right for the saints when they have fallen into sin and have thus done what they could to repudiate the grace of God to feel anxiety; but it is their duty to hold fast the truth that grace is the incorruptible seed of God which can never perish where it has once been bestowed."[4]

If we believe thus in God's faithfulness we are bound to reflect in our own attitude to God the same steadfastness as we find in

---

[1] Comm. on John 20 : 28, C.O. 47 : 443–4; comm. on 1 John 3 : 9, C.O. 55 : 336–7.

[2] Comm. on Ps. 51 : 12, C.O. 31 : 519. Discussing Heb. 6 : 4, Calvin distinguishes two kinds of *falling away*—"one particular and the other general". The elect often offend God in some particular thing. They become overtaken in faults and ensnared by Satan but not to the extent of despising God with rooted malice. (Cf. comm. on Heb. 6 : 4, C.O. 55 : 70; and serm. on Gal. 6 : 1–2, C.O. 51 : 59) David fell "through the weakness of his flesh" but at the same time never deserted the service of God. (Comm. on Ps. 18 : 22, C.O. 31 : 181) But there is another kind of falling away, not of the elect, but of those who have been enlightened, of those who have had some taste of the grace of God, some sparks of light, some perception of His goodness and have come to "temporary faith". In such a falling away there is an entire renunciation of the grace of God, an element of virulent rage and deliberate malice, in which there is both blindness and yet enough light to know that they are spitting upon the face of God which is shining on them. (Cf. comm. on Heb. 6 : 4 ff., C.O. 55 : 70 ff. and on Matt. 12 : 31, C.O. 45 : 340–2) Calvin insists that such a falling off cannot take place in those who have been truly regenerated. (C.O. 45 : 341–2) (Nor can it take place in those who have had no enlightenment at all). Nevertheless the thought of such a fall should keep the elect in fear and humility (C.O. 55 : 77).

[3] Comm. on John 20 : 28, C.O. 47 : 444. *Statuendum tamen est, Deum occulto fraeno electos suos retinere ne exitialiter cadant, et miraculo fovere semper in eorum cordibus qualescunque fidei scintillas, quas novo spiritus sui afflatu suo postea tempore accendat.*

[4] Comm. on Ps. 51 : 12, C.O. 31 : 519. Cf. serm. on Job 1 : 6–8, C.O. 33 : 65–6. *Et voila aussi comme Sainct Paul en parle au huitieme des Romains (v 10). Car apres avoir monstré que les fideles sont invincibles, quand l'Esprit de Dieu leur est un tesmoignage de vie, il dit que combien . . . qu'ils n'en ayent qu'une petite goutte, si est-ce que c'est une semence de vie pour les asseurer que Dieu accomplira ce qu'il a commencé . . . que iusques à la fin il leur sera Pere.*

Him. We must "keep pace with God in the steadfastness of our faith." This is not in man's power but it can be accomplished by the grace of God and we must strive towards it.[1] It is precisely because God will continue from day to day to perfect what He has begun in us that we too must continue to the end without falling away from His obedience.[2] To persevere in the grace of God in this matter requires on our part "striving and vigilance."[3]

5. Our confidence in our perseverance must be accompanied by effort, and fear and trembling

We must not, then, in any way presume upon the grace of God but we must live in constant fear and trembling. If God relaxed His restraining care over us even for a moment then no matter how far we may have progressed in sanctification, our hearts would immediately break out in insolent contempt of God.[4] We are always prone to receive lies, to chase after frivolities and to abhor the truth.[5] Even for the believing man nothing is so evanescent as faith[6] and "nothing flows away so easily as love."[7] Even the Christian must remember that he is man, and that man is like a shadow, frail and inconstant, with nothing stable in him that can be laid hold of, looking one day as if he had the courage of a lion, only to prove the next day that he is fainthearted as a woman.[8] "Were God to withdraw His grace, the soul would be nothing more than a puff of wind, even as the body is dust, and there would doubtless be found in the whole man nothing but mere vanity."[9] Even the slightest fall on our part should be a sign to us that we would soon fall to destruction were we not continually upheld by the hand of God.[10] Peter's denial of Jesus is for Calvin a sign of

[1] Comm. on 2 Cor. 1 : 21, C.O. 50 : 24.
[2] Serm. on Luke 1 : 73–8, C.O. 46 : 187.
[3] Comm. on Heb. 12 : 15, C.O. 55 : 179. *Denique contentione et vigilantia opus est, si velimus perseverare in Dei gratia.*
[4] Comm. on Ps. 19 : 13, C.O. 31 : 206.
[5] Serm. on Luke 1 : 69–72, C.O. 46 : 174.　　　　　　　[6] Ibid. p. 175.
[7] Comm. on Heb. 13 : 1, C.O. 55 : 186. *Nihil facilius diffluit quam caritas.*
[8] Serm. on Job 3 : 1–10, C.O. 33 : 141. Cf. serm. on Matt. 26 : 40–50, C.O. 46 : 851. *Ceux qui se peuvent nommer spirituels, c'est à dire qui ont un zele ardent de servir à Dieu, qui sont tout accoustumez de recourir à luy, qui sont exercez en prieres et oraisons, encores sont si debiles, qu'il ne faut qu'une seule minute de temps pour les ruiner, sinon qu'ils invoquent Dieu.*
[9] Comm. on Ps. 103 : 15, C.O. 32 : 81.
[10] Comm. on Ps. 37 : 24, C.O. 31 : 378.

what could have happened to Peter or to any other man hundreds
or thousands of times over unless God had continually spared him
further testing.[1] Therefore, the Christian man living under the
hand of God experiences a life that is marked on the one hand by
humble trembling and fear of falling, and on the other hand by an
assured confidence that we cannot fall and that we shall lack
nothing.[2] The confidence of the godly man in contrast to the undisturbed confidence of the ungodly, is the confidence of one who
knows that his life "hangs only by a thread and is encompassed by
1000 deaths."[3] The Christian is firm only in the midst of infirmity,
and is most firm because of his very infirmity.[4]

[1] Serm. on Matt. 26 : 67–27 : 11, C.O. 46 : 876–7. *Contemplons donc en la
personne de Pierre, qu'il faut bien que Dieu nous fortifie à une chacune minute de
temps. . . . Si sainct Pierre eust este tenté cent fois en un iour, il eust renoncé Iesus
Christ cent fois, et mille avec. Voyla ou il en eust este, sinon que Dieu eust eu pitie
de luy: mais il l'a espargné, et ne l'a point voulu esprouver d'avantage.*
[2] Serm. on Job 1 : 9–12, C.O. 33 : 80.
[3] Comm. on Ps. 10 : 6, C.O. 31 : 113.
[4] Comm. on Rom. 4 : 19, C.O. 49 : 83.

BIBLIOGRAPHY

INDEX

Bibliography

Calvin

In addition to the editions mentioned in the List of Abbreviations on
p. 2, I have used the Calvin Translation Society's English translation
of Calvin's works (Edinburgh 1843 ff.). All references to his sermons
on 2 Samuel are to *J. Calvin: 550 bisher ungedruckte Predigten*, ed.
H. Rückert, Neukirchen 1936.

Other Works

BRUNNER, P. *Vom Glauben bei Calvin.* Tübingen 1925.

ENGELLAND, H. *Gott und Mensch bei Calvin.* Munich 1934.

GÖHLER, A. *Calvins Lehre von der Heiligung.* Berlin 1931.

HAUCK, W. *Calvin und die Rechtfertigung.* Gütersloh 1938.
—— *Die Erwählten.* Gütersloh 1950.

JANSEN, J. F. *Calvin's Doctrine of the Work of Christ.* London 1956.

KOLFHAUS, W. *Christusgemeinschaft nach Johannes Calvin,* 1939.
—— *Vom Christlichen Leben nach Johannes Calvin,* 1949.

MÜLHAUPT, E. *Die Predigt Calvins.* Berlin 1931.

NIESEL, W. *Calvins Lehre vom Abendmahl.* Munich 1930.
—— *Die Theologie Calvins.* Munich 1938.

PARKER, T. H. L. *The Oracles of God.* London 1947.
—— *The Doctrine of the Knowledge of God.* Edinburgh 1953.

QUISTORP, H. *Calvin's Doctrine of the Last Things.* London 1955.

TORRANCE, T. F. *Calvin's Doctrine of Man.* London 1949.
—— *Royal Priesthood.* Edinburgh 1955.
—— *Kingdom and Church.* Edinburgh 1956.

WALLACE, R. S. *Calvin's Doctrine of the Word and Sacrament.* Edinburgh 1953.

WENDEL, F. *Calvin, sources et evolution de sa pensée religieuse.* Paris
1950.

Index

Adoption, consequences of, 131 f., 232.
ambition, 178.
angels, and law, 113.
anxiety, 183 f., 191.
Ascension, Christ's, inaugurates His reign, 83; focus of Christian life, 87; pattern of final glory, 45 f.
assurance, 181, 223 f., 299–306; found within Church, 200 ff.; effect of, 200 f.; founded on election, 214; need of, 300.
Atonement, language about, 4 f.; sacrificial aspect, 5; obedience and, 7; Spirit and, 7–8; applied to individual, 212 f.

Baptism, 19, 65, 204 f., 208, 210, 213 n., 232, 237, 268.
beasts, examples to men, 146.
boldness, in Christian living, 303 f.; in approach to God, 35, 279, 287; and wisdom, 185.
burial with Christ, 85.
business, the Christian and, 188.

Calling, keeping within bounds of, 154, 181.
cheerfulness, 300 n.
children, see PARENTS.
Christ, second Adam, 108, 111 n., 131, 134; heir of world, 131 f., 266; human nature of, 6, 9–10, 15 n., 16, 63; obedience of, 6 f.; new order in, 109, 146; as Pattern, 14, 41 f., 45, 62 f., 70, 120, 170, 181, 241 ff., 248, 269, 295; as Priest, 6, 9, 274 ff., 289; as Prophet, 9 n.; Royal Priesthood

of, 8 f.; sanctified by Spirit, 196; second coming of, 83 f., 111; self-sanctification of, 6 f.; separation of, 202; as victim, 6; 267; victory of, 8. See also CHRIST AND THE CHURCH; CONFORMITY TO CHRIST; DEATH OF CHRIST.
—— and the Church, 162; Head and members, 12, 45 f., 52 f., 82 f., 195 f., 200, 202 n., 203, 251 f., 289; Fullness of, 73 f., 74 n. *See also* CONFORMITY TO CHRIST.
Christian life, full of affliction, 68 ff., 81, 251; inseparable from Church, 195–209; conflict in, 327; contraditions in, 257, 313 f.; its glory hidden, 82 f., 84 f., 238, 241 ff.; a continuous dying, 44 f.; truly natural, 144, 191 f., 267; joyful, 303 f., 313 ff.; ordered, 108, 114 (*and see* ORDER); centred beyond, 88 f., 91, 100, 126; constantly developing, 322 f.; relates to God and man, 114 ff.
Church, sanctified in Christ, 12 ff.; sphere of sanctification and separation, 195–205, 236; sphere of Word, 207; sphere of Cross-bearing, 68 f.; sphere of assurance, 200 f., sphere of witness, 238 f.; its glory hidden, 241 f.; image of God within, 152; symmetry of, 122 n., 197; cleansing of, 236–7, 265; always impure, 232 f.; elect people, 201; salvation within, 196; visible and invisible, 232; as school, 195; loyalty to, 232–48; discipline, 185 ff., 236.
Commandments, interpretation of, 119 n., 120 n.